HUNTERS

an encyclopedia of
nature's predators
in the wild

HUNTERS

an encyclopedia of nature's predators in the wild

MICHAEL BRIGHT • JEN GREEN •
ROBIN KERROD • RHONDA KLEVANSKY •
BARBARA TAYLOR

LORENZ BOOKS

This edition is published by Lorenz Books

Lorenz Books is an imprint of Anness Publishing Ltd
Hermes House, 88–89 Blackfriars Road, London SE1 8HA
tel. 020 7401 2077; fax 020 7633 9499
www.lorenzbooks.com; info@anness.com

© Anness Publishing Ltd 2002, 2004

UK agent: The Manning Partnership Ltd, 6 The Old Dairy, Melcombe Road, Bath BA2 3LR;
tel. 01225 478444; fax 01225 478440; sales@manning-partnership.co.uk

UK distributor: Grantham Book Services Ltd, Isaac Newton Way, Alma Park Industrial Estate, Grantham, Lincs NG31 9SD;
tel. 01476 541080; fax 01476 541061; orders@gbs.tbs-ltd.co.uk

North American agent/distributor: National Book Network, 4501 Forbes Boulevard, Suite 200, Lanham, MD 20706;
tel. 301 459 3366; fax 301 429 5746; www.nbnbooks.com

Australian agent/distributor: Pan Macmillan Australia, Level 18, St Martins Tower, 31 Market St, Sydney, NSW 2000;
tel. 1300 135 113; fax 1300 135 103; customer.service@macmillan.com.au

New Zealand agent/distributor: David Bateman Ltd, 30 Tarndale Grove, Off Bush Road, Albany, Auckland;
tel. (09) 415 7664; fax (09) 415 8892

Publisher: Joanna Lorenz
Managing Editor: Linda Fraser
Editor: Sarah Uttridge
Production Controller: Ben Worley
Jacket Design: Adelle Morris
Designers: Vivienne Gordon, Caroline Reeves, Ann Samuel, Simon Wilder
Illustrators: Julian Baker, Peter Bull, Vanessa Card, Stuart Carter, Sarah Smith, David Webb, Rita Wuthrich

Previously published as *Hunters of the Wild*

1 3 5 7 9 10 8 6 4 2

Contents

Introduction   8

Birds of Prey 174

Bears and Pandas 228

Big Cats 282

Introduction

Animals that hunt and eat other animals are known as "predators", and the animals that are eaten are known as "prey". There is an escalating struggle between them. As predators gain the upper hand in catching prey, the prey comes up with its own tricks to get away. Any predators or prey that fail to keep up with the race fall by the wayside. This is evolution in action – survival of the fittest . . and the cleverest.

Most predators invest time and energy in tracking down, running down and bolting down their prey, although there are sneaky meat-eaters, such as gulls and frigate birds, that turn to piracy to steal another predator's hard-won meal, or predators, such as vultures, that resort to scavenging the leftovers of prey captured by other predators.

Many birds of prey specialize in plucking live fish from the water. They have long talons and rough scales on their feet to help them grip their prey.

Although predators kill for a living, they are not "nasty" animals. Even herbivores consume other living things – plants. The difference is that herbivores are surrounded by their food while predators actively look for prey that is mobile – usually herbivores. Many predators are not exclusively meat-eaters, but will resort to plant eating when times are hard. Polar bears prefer blubber but will eat berries and even seaweed in the summer when it is difficult to hunt seals. Foxes will take fallen apples in the autumn.

Predators do not always hunt for the same kind of prey. During a severe winter in Europe not so long ago, northern lynx consumed large numbers of rabbits, weakening an already declining population. The following summer they switched their prey preference to voles and mice, and continued to feast on these until the rabbit population recovered. In some parts of the world, several predators co-exist in the same living area and share the same prey animals. In East Africa,

Zebras are herbivores and spend many hours during the day grazing. They drink fresh water daily, although they can go for long periods without water.

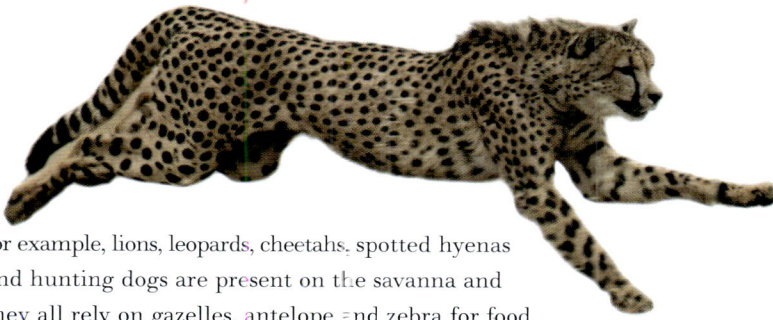

The cheetah is the fastest land animal, but it builds up so much heat in its body it must stop chasing after about 30 seconds or its brain would overheat.

for example, lions, leopards, cheetahs. spotted hyenas and hunting dogs are present on the savanna and they all rely on gazelles, antelope and zebra for food. They avoid serious competition by hunting in different ways, at different times of the day or night, in separate parts of the habitat.

Lions are unusual amongst cats in hunting co-operatively. They hunt on the plains, driving prey into an ambush set by other members of the pride. Leopards are solitary, night hunters, and they restrict themselves to wooded areas where the lions are less likely to go. Cheetahs and wild dogs hunt during the day, when the other predators are resting out of the sun. Wild dogs. like lions, hunt co-operatively in a group. Like running a relay race, they take it in turns to wear their prey down. The cheetah is a sprinter and hunts mainly alone. It has a flexible spine for a greater stride and non-retractable claws that act like the spikes on running shoes.

Many predators are equipped with special "weapons". Birds of prey have formidable talons, the most powerful being those of South America's harpy eagle. It hunts in the tropical rainforests where it flies through the canopy in search of food. It can snatch an unsuspecting monkey from a branch of a tree and with its talons can crush the monkey's skull in an instant.

Tigers have sharp teeth and strong jaws that can give a lethal bite. They use their long, curved canine teeth for killing prey that they have caught.

The tiger uses a combination of claws and teeth to despatch its prey. It has powerful muscles in its rear legs that help it leap onto a deer or wild pig. The claws on its front paws can swipe the prey's legs from under it or fasten on to its back to bring it down. Large canine teeth either pierce the throat and/or help throttle the prey.

Sharks have powerful jaws, and each species is recognized by the shape of its teeth. The fast-swimming mako shark grabs its prey with awl-like grasping teeth that prevent wriggling fish, such as mackerel, or slippery squid from escaping. The great white shark has triangular, serrated teeth in the top jaw and slightly more pointed teeth in the lower jaw. They work much like a knife and fork. The lower teeth impale the prey, such as a seal, to prevent it escaping while the upper teeth slice it up.

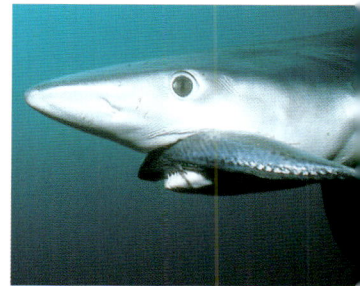

Sharp eyesight, quick reactions and an ability to speed through the water all help the blue shark to chase and catch its chosen target.

Spiders have neither claws nor teeth, but poison glands leading to powerful, stabbing jaws. Some race after their prey, others produce silk to trap their victims. One spider throws a net, and another simply spits.

9

Prey animals use special coloration and camouflage to make them as inconspicuous as possible, so predators must have heightened senses in order to find any food. In fact, prey detection and location is probably the most difficult part of a predator's life and many species have highly sophisticated prey-detection systems that have evolved over millions of years.

Birds of prey are animals that rely mainly on sight, like us, although their eyes are supersensitive and they can see parts of the light spectrum that are denied to us. The kestrel, for example, can spot a mouse from a mile above the ground and see ultraviolet light reflected from the urine trails of voles in the grass.

The owl is silent as it swoops down on its prey. Owls have dense, soft feathers covering their wings and legs which silence the flow of air as it passes through them.

The grey wolf has 50 times more cells in its nose than we have and is sensitive to smells 1,000 times greater than we are. It can sniff out a moose and her calf from more than 2.5km/1½ miles away. Likewise hunting sharks can pick up a faint odour trail and track it over a mile back to its source, the equivalent of detecting one drop of blood in a large swimming pool.

Owls have incredible hearing. The barn owl's face is a sound-collecting disc (parabolic reflector) with which it can detect the faintest sounds. It can home in on the almost indistinct rustle of a mouse in the grass on a pitch-black night with remarkable accuracy. It aligns its talons with the prey as it zigzags across the ground.

Wolves howl before and after a hunt to gather the pack together. They also howl at their neighbours to tell them to keep out of their territory.

Dolphins "see" with sound. They produce very high-frequency sounds that focus into a beam ahead of them and then listen for the echoes. In experiments, a dolphin recognized an object the size of a tangerine from 320m/350yds away, and worked out whether it was hollow or solid, living or dead. Its echo-location system was working at such a high level if it produced any more energy it would have been turned into heat rather than sound. It is thought that dolphins can turn this into a weapon and disable prey with sound.

Snakes gain a heat picture, much like an infrared camera, of their prey, such as a mouse or rat, but the target must be within 15cm/6in of the snake's snout before it can see it. Long-distance tracking is by detection of odours with its forked tongue.

The rattlesnake "sees" with heat and tastes the air with its tongue. It has heat-sensitive pits below the eyes that can detect a rise in temperature as small as 0.005°C/0.009°F.

Crocodiles are the ultimate ambushers. They lie quite still in the water like logs and then leap out suddenly, pulling the prey down and drowning it.

The most remarkable sensory systems must be those of the active hunting sharks. Over the course of 400 million years of evolution they have become the ultimate predators. In addition to a keen sense of smell, the shark has an entire arsenal of prey detectors. From over a mile away, a hunting bull shark — one of the most dangerous sharks to people — can pick up low-frequency sounds. At 400m/¼ mile it can detect blood or body fluids in the water. At about 91m/100yds, a line of sensors along each side of the shark's body and over its head can "feel" the presence of something moving in the water — a kind of "touch at a distance" known as the lateral line system. At 23m/75ft, but depending on the water clarity, a shark's eyes can begin to see movements. They are ten times more sensitive than our own, and a special dark-adapt system enables the shark to swim rapidly to the surface from the inky depths and not be blinded. When approaching close to prey, a shark protects its eyes with a shield so it cannot see where it is going. At this point a remarkable seventh sense clicks in. Sensors in jelly-filled pits in its snout can pick up minute electrical currents associated with its victim's muscles. They can detect electrical fields that would be the equivalent of a flashlight battery creating a field between two electrodes 1,610km/1,000 miles apart. It is an extraordinarily sensitive system and is shared with the duck-billed platypus.

The bump on a dolphin's forehead contains its "melon", a fat-filled organ that focuses its high-frequency sounds into a tight beam.

Having located prey, predators must assess whether to give chase or pounce. Plant-eaters, such as springbok and Thomson's gazelles, have a way of telling predators not to bother. They "stot", with a stiff-legged gait high into the air. It shows they are fit and healthy and quite capable of outrunning a lion or leopard. Predators are also not averse to a bit of trickery too. They sometimes mimic harmless species in order to approach closer to their prey. North America's zone-tailed hawk, for example, soars with vultures. Small mammals are not afraid of vultures, so the hawk will suddenly drop out of the group and swoop down on its prey by surprise.

A lion is not interested in what is going on above and below it, so its eyes have a visual field that is sensitive to a strip along the horizon — just where its prey will be.

Spiders

They may have been Little Miss Muffet's
nightmare but spiders are some of Nature's
most sophisticated invertebrate predators.
There are sprinters, jumpers and
net-throwers, and those that spin the most
elaborate webs, and there are spiders
that work together to bring down prey
far bigger than themselves. But it's
the way they crawl that gives people
goose bumps. Half of all women and
10 per cent of men have arachnophobia —
a fear of spiders.

Introducing Spiders

Spiders are some of the most feared and least understood creatures in the animal world. These hairy hunters are famous for spinning webs and giving a poisonous bite. There are around 35,000 known species (kinds) of spider, with probably another 35,000 waiting to be discovered. Only about 30 species, however, are dangerous to people. Spiders are very useful to humans, because they eat insect pests and keep their numbers down. Spiders live nearly everywhere, from forests, deserts and grasslands to caves, ships and in our homes. Some spin webs to catch their prey, while others leap out from a hiding place or stalk their meals like tigers. There are even spiders that fish for their supper and one that lives in an air bubble underwater.

The front part of a spider is a joined head and chest called the cephalothorax. The body is covered by hard skin called an exoskeleton. The shield-like plate on the top of the cephalothorax is called the carapace.

Spiders use palps for holding food and as feelers.

The chelicerae (jaws) are used to bite and crush prey. Each ends in a fang that injects poison.

A spider's eight hollow legs are joined to the cephalothorax.

◄ **WHAT IS A SPIDER?**
Spiders are often confused with insects, but they belong to a completely different group. A spider has eight legs, but an insect has six. Its body has two parts while an insect's has three. Many insects have wings and antennae, but spiders do not.

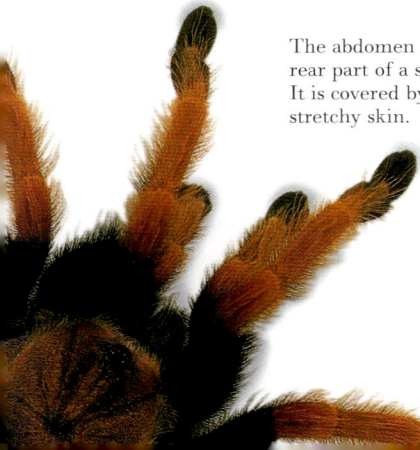

The abdomen is the rear part of a spider. It is covered by soft, stretchy skin.

Silk is spun by organs called spinnerets at the back of the abdomen.

WEB WEAVERS ▷

About half of all spiders spin webs. They know how to do this by instinct from birth, without being taught. Many spiders build a new web each night. They build webs to catch prey. Spiders have a good sense of touch and can quickly tell if anything is caught in the web.

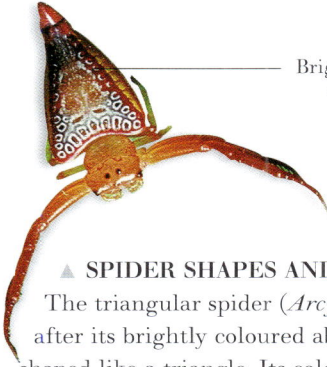

Bright colours help to conceal this spider among flowers.

▲ SPIDER SHAPES AND COLOURS

The triangular spider (*Arcys*) is named after its brightly coloured abdomen, which is shaped like a triangle. Its colour and shape help it to hide in wait for prey on leaves and flowers. Other spiders use bright colours to warn their enemies that they taste nasty.

Arachne's Tale

A Greek legend tells of Arachne, a girl who was very skilled at weaving. The goddess Athene challenged her to a contest, which Arachne won. The goddess became so cross Arachne killed herself. Athene was sorry and turned the girl into a spider so she could spin forever. The Latin name for spiders is arachnids, named after Arachne.

◀ MALES AND FEMALES

Female spiders are usually bigger than the males and not so colourful, although this female *Nephila* spider is boldly marked. The male at the top of the picture is only one-fifth of her size.

Did you know?
All spiders are carnivores (meat-eaters) and many are cannibals.

15

Shapes and Sizes

Can you believe that there are spiders as big as frisbees or dinner plates? The world's biggest spider, the goliath tarantula of South America, is this big. Yet the smallest spider is only the size of a full stop. Apart from size, spiders also vary a great deal in their appearance. Many are an inconspicuous dull brown or grey while others are striking yellows, reds and oranges. Some spiders have short, wide bodies, while others are long, thin and skinny. There are round spiders, flat spiders and spiders with spines, warts and horns. A few spiders even look like ants, wasps or bird droppings!

▲ **FLOWER SPIDERS**

Using its shape and colour to hide on a flower, the flower spider (*Misumena vatia*) waits to ambush a visiting insect. This spider is one of a large family of crab spiders, so named because most of them have a similar shape to crabs.

Red-legged widow (*Latrodectus bishopi*)

Widow spiders often have bold black and red colouring.

Round, shiny abdomen.

Bristles on the back legs give the name comb-footed spider.

▲ **SPINY SPIDERS**

Some spiders have flat abdomens with sharp spines sticking out. This kite spider (*Gasteracantha*) has spines that look like horns. No one knows what these strange spines are for, but they may make it difficult for predators to hold or swallow the spider.

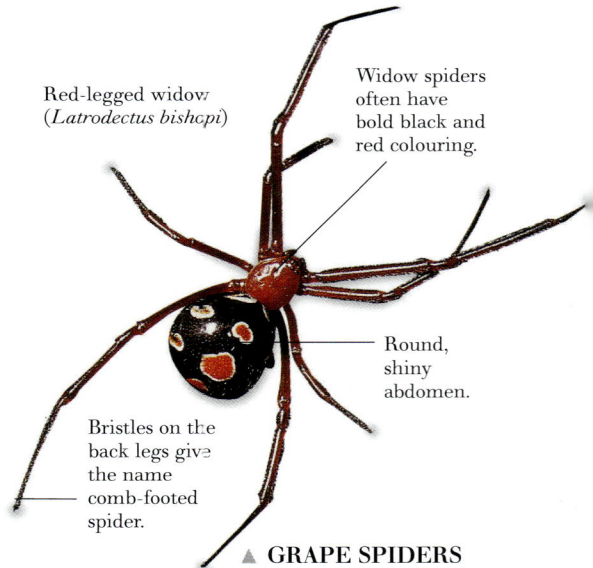

▲ **GRAPE SPIDERS**

Several kinds of widow spiders live in areas where grapes are grown. The females tend to have round abdomens, like a grape. Some of the most poisonous spiders belong to this group.

BIG, HAIRY SPIDERS ▶

The biggest, hairiest and scariest-looking spiders are tarantulas, or bird-eating spiders. All spiders are hairy, but tarantulas are a great deal hairier than most. Tarantulas and their relatives are called mygalomorphs and are relatively primitive spiders.

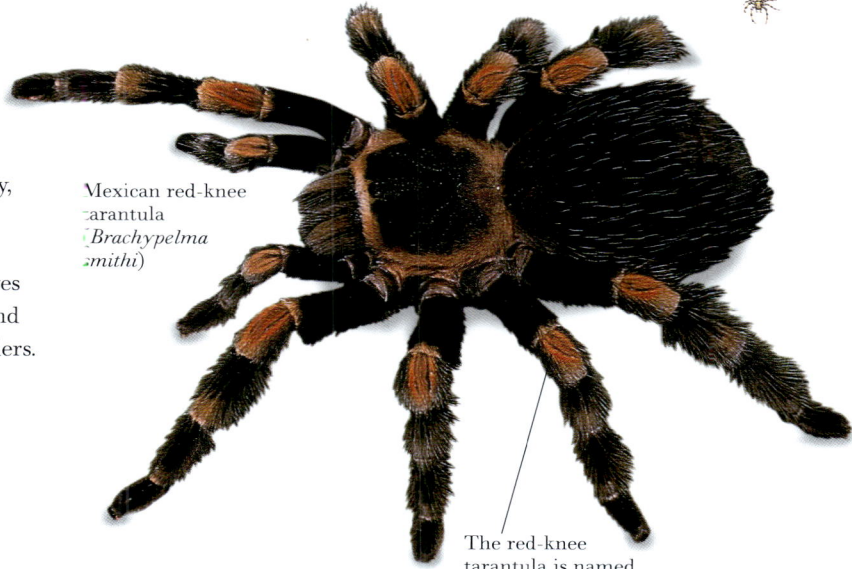

Mexican red-knee tarantula (*Brachypelma smithi*)

The red-knee tarantula is named after the orange or red markings on its legs.

Australian wolf spider

Two large front eyes give good vision.

Did you know? Giant orb-weavers are said to taste like raw potato and lettuce.

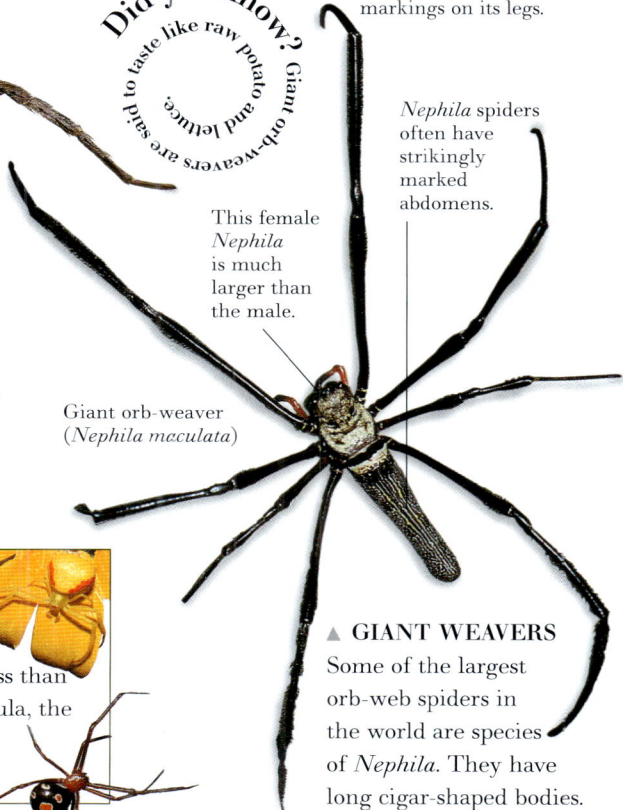

Nephila spiders often have strikingly marked abdomens.

This female *Nephila* is much larger than the male.

Giant orb-weaver (*Nephila maculata*)

▲ WOLF SPIDERS

A skilled daytime hunter, this wolf spider (*Lycosa*) is brown or grey in colour. The dull colours help to hide the spider as it hunts along the ground. It has long back legs to chase after its prey.

SPIDER SIZES

The spiders on this page are shown at their real sizes. Most spiders are tiny, with bodies less than 20mm/¾in long. The goliath tarantula, the largest, is 90mm/3½in long. *Patu digua*, the smallest, is 0.37mm/¹⁄₁₀₀in.

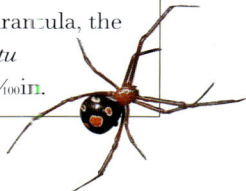

▲ GIANT WEAVERS

Some of the largest orb-web spiders in the world are species of *Nephila*. They have long cigar-shaped bodies.

Giant salmon pink bird-eater (*Lassiodora parahybana*)

Focus on

The biggest, hairiest spiders are often called tarantulas, or bird-eating spiders. The large spiders we call tarantulas are all members of the family Theraphosidae. (The true tarantula, however, is a big wolf spider from southern Europe.) There are about 800 different species of tarantula living in warm or hot places all over the world. Many live in burrows, while some are tree-dwellers. Although they look scary, most tarantulas are shy, timid creatures and are harmless to people. A few can give a very painful bite, but their poison is not deadly to humans.

WHICH NAME?

Known as tarantulas or bird-eating spiders in America and Europe, they are called baboon spiders in Africa. In Central America, they are sometimes called horse spiders – their bite was falsely believed to make a horse's hoof fall off.

Violet-black tarantula (*Pamphobeteus*)

Velvety, black carapace.

Abdomen covered in long brown hairs.

LIFE CYCLES

This red-knee tarantula (*Brachypelma smithi*) is shown guarding her eggs. Female tarantulas can live for more than 20 years and lay eggs at regular intervals when they become adults. After mating they may wait several months before laying their eggs.

FLOOR WALKERS

Violet-black tarantulas live on the floor of the Amazon rainforest. These spiders are active, impressive hunters. They do not build webs or burrows, but live out in the open.

Tarantulas

TARANTULA BODIES

Essentially a tarantula's body has the same parts and works in the same way as other spiders. Its eyesight is poor and it detects prey and danger with the many sensitive hairs that cover its body. Unlike other spiders, a tarantula can flick prickly hairs off its abdomen if it is attacked. On the ends of its legs are brushes of hairs that help it to climb on smooth surfaces. These hairs let some tarantulas walk on water.

Tiger rump doppelganger (*Cyclosternum fasciata*)

The back pair of legs is used to flick hairs off the abdomen at an enemy.

Many tarantulas use their strong legs to dig out burrows.

Tarantulas have eight tiny eyes, closely grouped together.

FEARSOME FANGS

Tarantulas have large, hollow fangs that pump out venom as the spider bites. Most spiders bite with a sideways, pinching movement. Tarantulas bite straight down with great force, like a pickaxe.

FEEDING TIME

Tarantulas usually feed on insects. This *Avicularia metallica* is eating a katydid, an insect like a grasshopper. Large tarantulas are able to take much larger prey, such as birds and snakes. They are slow eaters and may drag prey back to their burrows to feed.

Arizonan blond tarantula (*Aphonopelma chalcodes*)

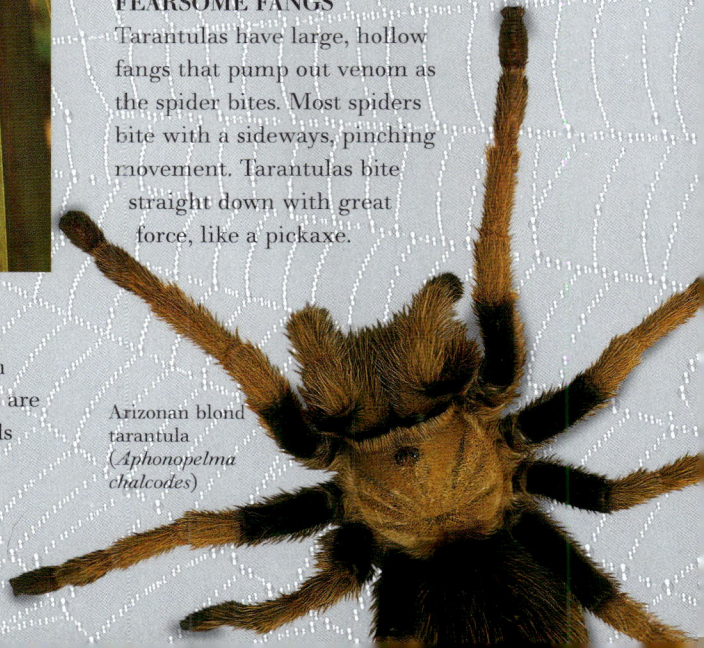

How Spiders Work

From the outside, a spider's body is very different from ours. It has a hard outer skeleton, called an exoskeleton, and legs that have many joints. It has eyes and a mouth, but no ears, nose or tongue. Instead, it relies on a variety of hairs and bristles to touch, taste and hear things and it smells things with microscopic pores on its feet. Inside, a spider has many features common to other animals, such as blood, nerves, a brain and a digestive system. It also has special glands for spinning silk and for making and storing poison.

▲ **SPIDER SKIN**
A spider's exoskeleton protects its body like a suit of armour. It is made of a stiff material called chitin. A waxy layer helps to make it waterproof. The exoskeleton cannot stretch as the spider grows, so must be shed from time to time. The old skin of a huntsman spider (*Isopeda*) is shown here.

Male spiders use taste hairs to pick up scent trails left by females.

◀ **HAIRY SIGNALS**
The sensitive hairs covering a spider send signals to the brain alerting it to food and enemies. Tasting hairs are spread all over the spider's body. On the palps and legs, special hairs (called trichobothria), set in cup-like sockets, pick up movements in the air.

▲ **LEG SENSES**
A green orb-weaver (*Araniella cucurbitina*) pounces on a fly. Spiders use special slits on their bodies to detect when an insect is trapped in their webs. These slits (called lyriform organs) pick up vibrations caused by a struggling insect. Nerve endings in the slits send signals to the spider's brain.

SPIDER POISON ▶

A spider is a delicate creature compared to the prey it catches. By using poison, a spider can kill its prey before the prey has a chance to harm its attacker. Spiders have two poison sacs, one for each fang. Bands of muscle around the sacs squeeze the poison down tubes in the fangs and out of a small opening in the end.

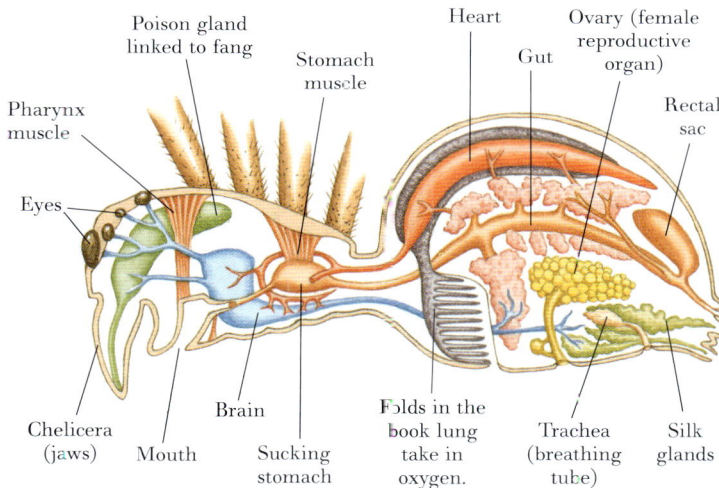

Poison gland linked to fang

Heart

Ovary (female reproductive organ)

Stomach muscle

Gut

Rectal sac

Pharynx muscle

Eyes

Chelicera (jaws)

Mouth

Brain

Sucking stomach

Folds in the book lung take in oxygen.

Trachea (breathing tube)

Silk glands

◀ INSIDE A SPIDER

The front part of a spider, the cephalothorax, contains the brain, poison glands, stomach and muscles. The abdomen contains the heart, lungs, breathing tubes, gut, waste disposal system, silk glands and reproductive organs. A spider's stomach works like a pump, stretching wide to pull in food that has been mashed to a soupy pulp. The heart pumps blue blood around the body.

Raiko and the Earth Spider

People have regarded spiders as dangerous, magical animals for thousands of years. This Japanese print from the 1830s shows the legendary warrior Yorimitsu (also known as Raiko) and his followers slaying the fearsome Earth Spider.

On the Move

Have you ever seen a spider scuttle swiftly away? Spiders sometimes move quickly, but cannot keep going for long. Their breathing system is not very efficient, so they soon run out of puff.

Spiders can walk, run, jump, climb and hang upside down. Each spider's leg has seven sections. The legs are powered by sets of muscles and blood pressure. At the end of each leg are two or three sharp claws for gripping surfaces.

Spiders that spin webs have a special claw to help them hold on to their webs. Hunting spiders have dense tufts of hair between the claws for gripping smooth surfaces and for holding prey.

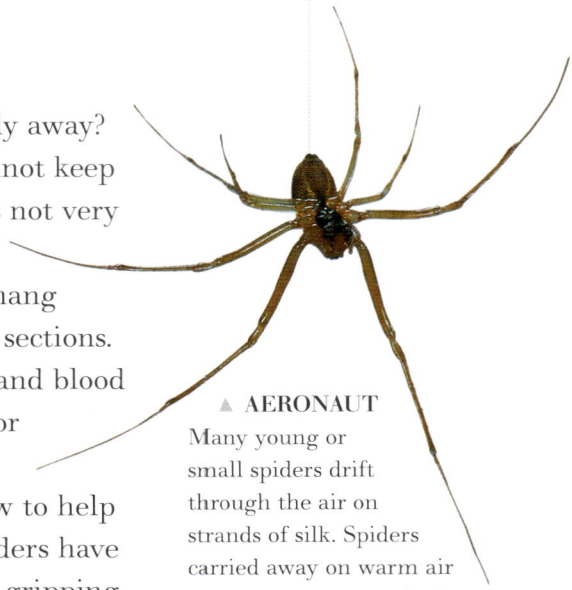

▲ **AERONAUT**
Many young or small spiders drift through the air on strands of silk. Spiders carried away on warm air currents use this method to find new places to live.

▲**WATER WALKER**
The fishing spider (*Dolmedes fimbriatus*) is also called the raft or swamp spider. It floats on the surface skin of water. Its long legs spread its weight over the surface so it does not sink. Little dips form in the stretchy skin of the water around each leg tip.

▲ **SAFETY LINE**
This garden spider (*Araneus*) is climbing up a silk dragline. Spiders drop down these lines if they are disturbed. They pay out the line as they go, moving very quickly. As they fall, spiders pull in their legs, making them harder to see.

▲ **SPIDER LEGS**

Muscles in the legs of this trapdoor spider (*Aname*) bend the joints rather like we bend our knees. To stretch out the legs, however, the spider has to pump blood into them. If a spider is hurt and blood leaks out, it cannot escape from enemies.

▲ **CHAMPION JUMPERS**

Jumping spiders are champions of the long jump. They secure themselves with a safety line before they leap. Some species can leap more than 40 times the length of their own bodies.

▼ **CLAWED FEET**

Two toothed claws on the ends of a spider's feet enable it to grip surfaces as it walks. Web-building spiders have a third, middle claw that hooks over the silk lines of the web and holds the silk against barbed hairs. This allows the spider to grip the smooth, dry silk of its web without falling or slipping.

Scopulate pad

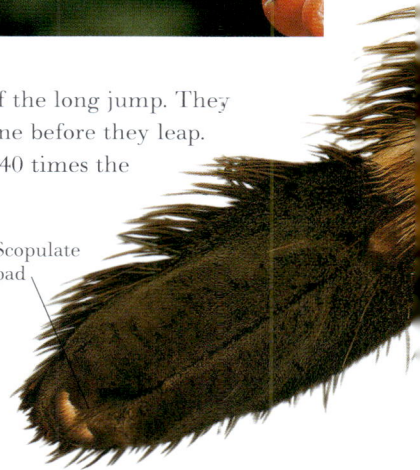

▲ **HAIRY FEET**

Many hunting spiders have dense tufts of short hairs (called scopulae) between the claws. The end of each hair is split into many tiny hairs, a little like a brush. These hairs pull up some of the moisture that coats most surfaces, gluing the spider's leg down. Spiders with these feet can climb up smooth surfaces, such as glass.

Toothed claw

Middle hook

Barbed hair

23

Spider Eyes

Spiders have poor eyesight and rely mainly on scents and vibrations to give them information about their surroundings. Even spiders with good eyesight, such as the jumping spiders, can see only up to 30cm/ 12in away. Most spiders have eight eyes arranged in two or three rows. The eyes are pearly or dark and are usually protected by several bristles. Spider eyes are called ocelli and are of two types. Main eyes produce a focused image and help in pouncing on prey. Secondary eyes have light-sensitive cells to pick up movement from a distance.

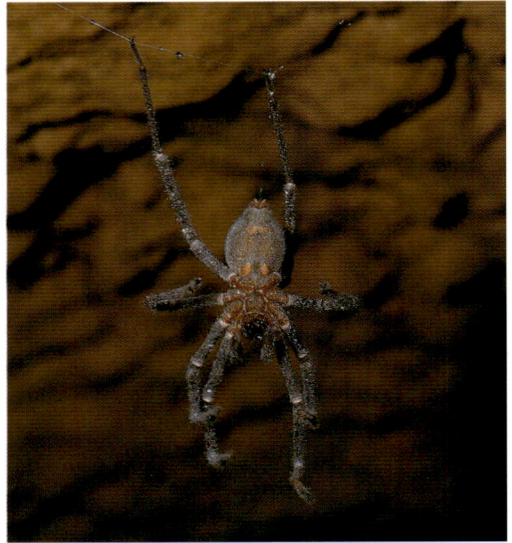

▲ **NO EYES**

This cave spider (*Spelungula cavernicola*) has no need for eyes, because there is no light in the cave for the spider to see. Like many animals that live in the dark, it relies on other senses. It especially uses many sensitive hairs to find its way around, catch its prey and avoid enemies.

◄ **BIG EYES**

A spider's main eyes are always the middle pair of eyes in the front row. In most spiders, the main eyes are small, but this jumping spider has very well-developed main eyes, as this enlarged picture shows. They work rather like a telephoto lens on a camera. Inside, the large lens focuses light on to four layers of sensitive cells. The main eyes see clearly over a small area a short distance away and let the spider stalk and pounce when it gets close to its prey.

Did you know? A jumping spider's two big eyes together are bigger than its brain.

▲ SHORT SIGHT

Spiders that spend much of their time under stones or in burrows usually have small eyes. This trapdoor spider (*Arame*) has eight tiny eyes in a close group. Spiders that catch their prey in webs also have very poor eyesight. These spiders rely much more on their sense of touch than their eyesight. They use their legs to test objects around them.

▲ HUNTSMAN SPIDER

The giant huntsman (*Holconia immanis*) is an agile, night-time hunter. Most hunting spiders have fairly large front eyes to help them find and pounce on prey. Secondary eyes help the hunters see in three dimensions over a wider area. They detect changes in light and dark.

A large-eyed wolf spider (family Lycosidae).

The small eyes of an orb-weaver (family Araneidae).

A six-eyed woodlouse spider (family Dysderidae).

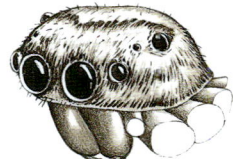

A jumping spider (family Salticidae).

▲ EYES FOR HUNTING

The spiders with the best eyesight are active daylight hunters, such as this jumping spider. A jumping spider's eight eyes are usually arranged in three rows with four in the front, two in the middle and two at the back. Lynx spiders and wolf spiders also have good eyesight.

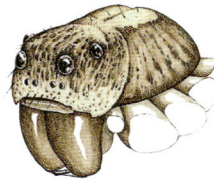

▲ ALL KINDS OF EYES

The position and arrangement of a spider's eyes can be useful in telling which family it belongs to and how it catches food. A small number of spiders have only six eyes or fewer. Many male money spiders have eyes on top of little lobes or turrets sticking up from the head.

SPIDERS

Spinning Silk

All spiders make silk. They pull the silk out of spinnerets on their abdomens, usually with their legs. The silk is a syrupy liquid when it first comes out, but pulling makes it harden. The more silk is pulled, the stronger it becomes. Some spider silk is stronger than steel wire of the same thickness. As well as being very strong, silk is incredibly thin, has more stretch than rubber and is stickier than sticky tape. Spiders make up to six different types of silk in different glands in the abdomen. Each type of silk is used for a different purpose, from making webs to wrapping prey. Female spiders produce a special silk to wrap up eggs.

An *Agroeca* spider hangs its cocoon from a grass stem. It will plaster the cocoon with mud to form a hard protective coating.

▲ EGG PARCELS
Female spiders have an extra silk gland for making egg cases called cocoons. These protect the developing eggs.

The Industrious Spider
Spiders have been admired for their tireless spinning for centuries. This picture was painted by the Italian artist Veronese in the 1500s. He wanted to depict the virtues of the great city of Venice, whose wealth was based on trade. To represent hard work and industry he painted this figure of a woman holding up a spider in its web.

▲ A SILKEN RETREAT
Many spiders build silk shelters or nests. The tube-web spider (*Segestria florentina*) occupies a hole in the bark of a tree. Its tube-shaped retreat has a number of trip lines radiating out like the spokes of a wheel. If an insect trips over a line, the spider rushes out to grab a meal.

26

▲ STICKY SILK

Silk oozes out through a spider's spinnerets. Two or more kinds of silk can be spun at the same time. Orb-web spiders produce gummy silk to make their webs sticky.

SPINNERETS ▶

A spider's spinnerets have many fine tubes on the end. The smaller tubes, or spools, produce finer silk for wrapping prey. Larger tubes, called spigots, produce coarser strands for webs.

Spinnerets vary in size and number.

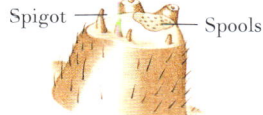

Spigot — Spools

Close up of a spinneret.

▲ COMBING OUT SILK

This lace-weaver (*Amaurobius*) is using its back legs to comb out a special silk. It has an extra spinning organ (the cribellum) in front of its spinnerets that produces loops of very fine silk.

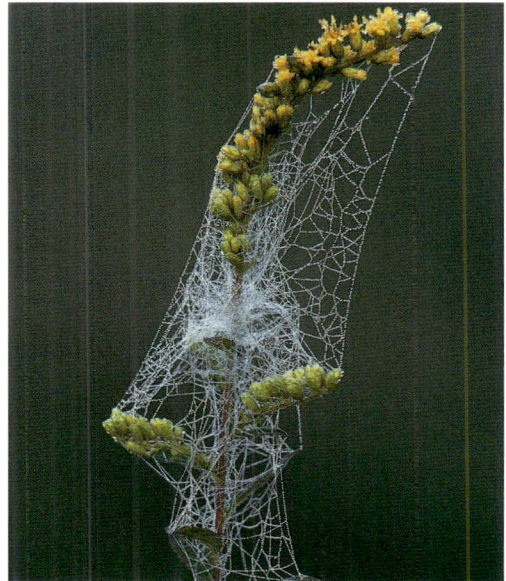

▲ FOOD PARCEL

A garden spider (*Araneus*) stops a grasshopper from escaping by wrapping it in silk. The prey is also paralysed by the spider's poisonous bite. Most spiders make silk for wrapping prey.

▲ VELCRO SILK

The lacy webs made by cribellate spiders contain tiny loops, like Velcro, that catch on the hairs and bristles of insect prey. Combined in bands with normal silk, the fluffy-looking cribellate silk stops insect prey from escaping.

Focus on

The orb-shaped (circular) web of an average garden spider (*Araneus*) is about 25cm/10in across and uses 20–60m/65–200ft of silk. To build its web, the spider first attaches a line across a gap to form a bridge-line. The whole web will hang from this line. Suspended from the line, the spider makes a Y-shaped frame. From the hub (centre) of the Y, the spider spins a series of spoke-like threads. The spider then returns to the hub to spin a circular strengthening zone. From this zone, a temporary dry spiral of threads is laid out towards the edge of the web to hold the spokes in place. Starting from the outside, the spider now uses sticky silk to lay the final spiral. When the web is finished, the spider settles down to wait for a meal.

STICKY BEADS

As a spider spins the sticky spiral of its orb web it pulls the gummy coating into a series of beads, like a necklace. The dry spiral of silk is eaten as it is replaced. This spiral is no longer needed and the spider can recycle the nutrients it contains.

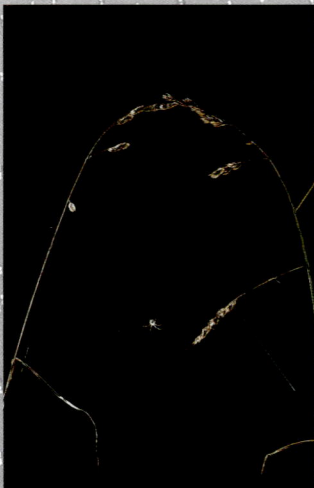

1 This garden spider is starting to spin a web. It has made a bridge-line from which it hangs down to pull the thread into a Y shape. The middle of the Y will be the centre of the web.

2 The spider then makes a framework, which looks like the spokes of a bicycle wheel. The spokes are called radii. From the centre, the spider now spins a dry spiral to hold the radii in place.

Spinning a Web

Spinning an orb web takes less than an hour. The spider either settles head downwards on the hub of the web, or hides in a retreat and keeps in touch through a signal thread held by the front legs.

3 Starting from the outside, the spider spins a sticky spiral. It does not go around in the same direction, but turns several times. A free zone between the sticky and dry spirals is left at the centre.

4 The completed web traps prey for long enough to give the spider time to work out its position. It feels how stretched the threads are in different parts of its web, then zooms in for the kill.

Orb-web Spiders

The typical wheel-shaped orb web is spun by about 3,000 species of spider mostly in the family Araneidae. Some members of the Uloboridae also spin orb-shaped webs, using fluffy cribellar silk. Every orb-web spider will spin about 100 webs in its lifetime and has large silk glands. The orb web is a very clever way of trapping flying prey, using the least amount of silk possible. This is important because spiders use up a lot of valuable body-building protein to spin silk. An orb web is almost invisible, yet it is very strong and elastic.

Australian orb-weaver (*Araneus*)

▲ **ORB-WEAVER**
Like most orb-web spiders, this spider's abdomen is taken up by large silk glands. One gland makes the gummy silk to make its web sticky.

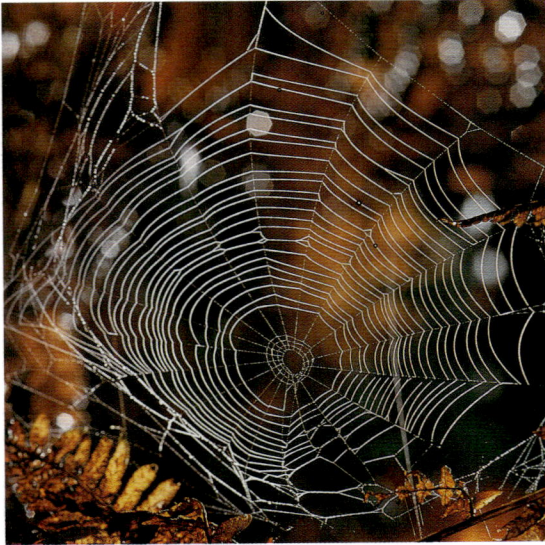

▲ **WEBS IN THE DEW**
Sticky beads on an orb web make it shimmer in the morning dew. The sticky spiral threads capture flying and jumping insects and stop them from escaping.

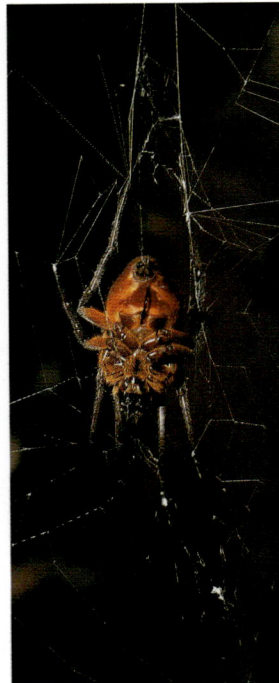

◄ **SPINNING THE WEB**
An orb-web spider may spin a new web every night, as fresh webs are the most efficient traps. The silk from old webs is usually eaten. The size of the web depends on the size of the spider — young spiders and smaller species spin smaller webs.

DECORATED WEBS ▶

Some orb-weavers decorate their webs with stabilimenta (zigzags of silk). Young spiders tend to spin disc shapes, while adults build long lines

No one is sure what they are for – some may be camouflage, but others are very obvious and may warn birds not to fly into the web

▲ WAITING FOR A MEAL

As soon as a spider feels the vibrations made by prey struggling to escape, it moves in for the kill. It keeps its body clear of the sticky spirals, moving along the dry lines.

Did you know? One teaspoon of silk would be enough to make a million webs.

Madagascan orb-weaver (*Nephila inaurata*)

◀ GIANT NETS

Large, tropical *Nephila* spiders use tough yellow silk to build huge orb webs, some up to 2m/6½ft across. These giant nets are incredibly strong and can catch small birds as prey.

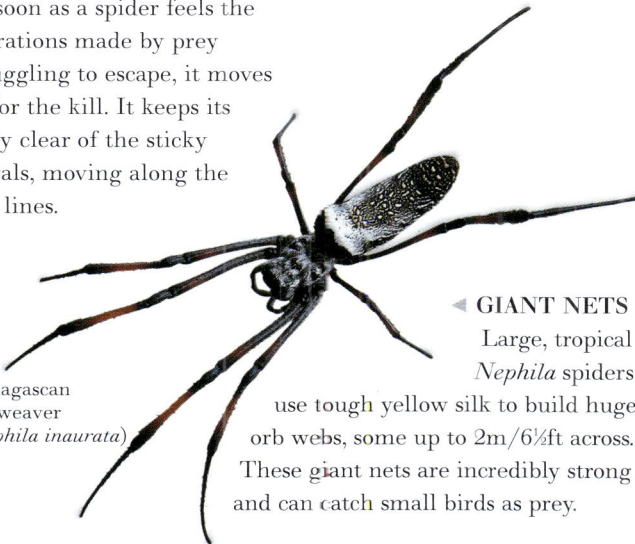

The Spider and the King
In 1306, the king of Scotland, Robert the Bruce, was resting in a barn after defeat by the English. He watched a spider trying to spin its web. Six times the spider failed, but on the seventh attempt it succeeded. Inspired by this to fight on, Robert the Bruce finally defeated the English at Bannockburn in 1314.

Hammocks, Sheets and Scaffolds

Spiders build webs in many shapes and sizes apart from a typical orb web. Webs that look like sheets or hammocks are not sticky, but rely on a maze of criss-crossing threads to trap the prey. These are more suitable for trapping insects that walk or hop, rather than those that fly. Most sheet-web spiders keep adding to their webs long after they are built. Scaffold webs have many dry, tangled threads, too, but they also have threads coated with sticky gum. Social spiders build huge communal webs that the spiders may hunt over in packs or alone.

▲ **HAMMOCK WEB**
A typical hammock web is supported by a maze of threads above and below the web. The silk is not sticky, but prey is tripped up by the threads to fall into the hammock below. The spider hangs upside down on the underside of the hammock waiting to grab prey from below and drag it through the web.

Did you know? One communal spider's web can contain up to 20,000 spiders.

◄ **TARANTULA WEB**
Large sheet webs are made by many tarantulas, trapdoor spiders and funnel-web spiders. This pink-toed tarantula (*Avicularia avicularia*) is sitting over the entrance of its tubular web. It mostly catches tree frogs and insects.

LADEN WITH DEW ▶

The hammock webs of money spiders (family Linyphiidae) show up well in the early morning dew. These webs are so named because the central sheet of the web sags like a hammock when it is laden with dew. Most hammock webs are only a few centimetres across, but some can be as big as dinner plates. There may be 50 or more hammock webs on just one gorse bush.

SHEET WEB ▶

The grass funnel-weaver (*Agelena labyrinthica*) builds a horizontal sheet web with a funnel-shaped shelter in one corner. The spider sits at the entrance to the funnel with its feet on the sheet waiting for an insect to get tangled in the maze of silk threads. The cobwebs made by house spiders (*Tegenaria*) in the corners of rooms are like this.

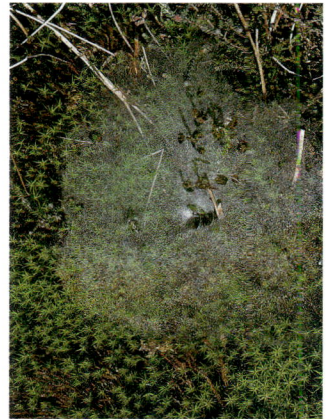

▲ **SPIDER CITIES**

Hundreds of dome-weavers (*Cyrtophora citricola*) build their webs together in what looks like a spider city. These huge webs almost cover trees. In the centre is a domed sheet like a trampoline. Although the spiders live closely together, each one defends its own web and may attack neighbours that come too close. Young spiders build their webs inside the framework of their mother's web.

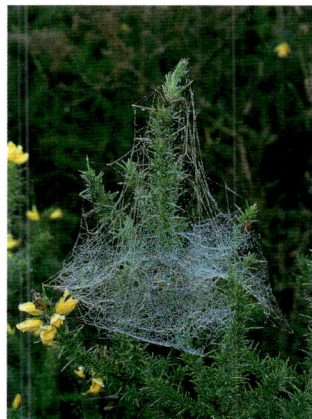

◀ **SCAFFOLD WEB**

Comb-footed spiders (family Theridiidae) build three-dimensional trellises called scaffold webs. This scaffold is slung over a tall plant, but there are many different kinds. Many have a thimble-shaped retreat in which the spider eats its meal. Some threads are sticky, making it difficult for insects to escape.

33

Sticky Traps

A few spiders do not just build a web and wait for a meal to arrive. They go fishing for their food instead. The net-casting, or ogre-faced, spider throws a strong, stretchy net over its prey. It is also named the gladiator spider after the gladiators of ancient Rome. The bolas, or angling, spider is a very unusual orb-web spider that does not spin a web. It traps insects by swinging a thin line of silk with a sticky globule on the end, like a fishing hook on the end of a line. Spitting spiders are even more cunning. They fire poisonous glue to pin their prey to the ground.

Spider-Man
The bite of a radioactive spider gave the comic-book character Spider-Man his special powers. He is very strong, with a keen sense that warns of danger, and he can cling to almost any surface. Web shooters on his wrists spray out sticky webs, which harden in the air. Spider-Man uses his unique powers to catch criminals.

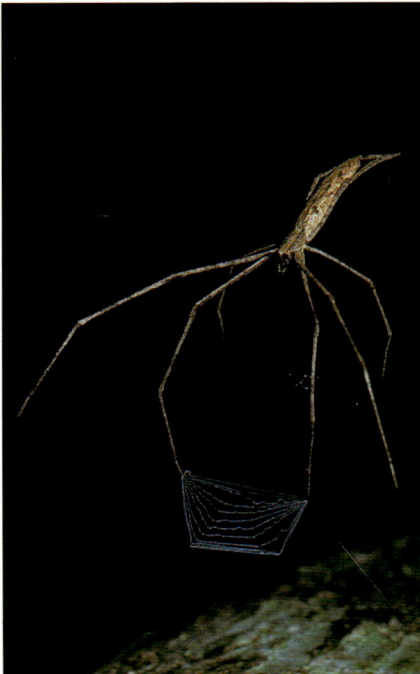

◀ **THE NET-CASTING SPIDER**

At night, the stick-like net-casting spider (*Dinopis*) hangs from a twig holding a very stretchy, sticky silk net. As insects crawl or fly past, the tiny net is stretched wide to trap them. The spider has huge eyes to help it to see at night, hence the name ogre-faced spider. It makes a new net each evening, eating the old one even if it is unused.

The net-casting spider hangs upside down, holding its elastic net in its front four legs. The legs are kept drawn in close to the body while the spider waits.

When an insect, such as an ant, scurries past, the spider opens the net and quickly drops down. It scoops up its meal, then springs back up.

As a moth approaches, the bolas spider whirls the sticky droplet on the end of its fishing line.

A moth is stuck fast to the sticky drop and is trapped. The spider pulls in the line and starts to feed.

◀ FISHING FOR FOOD

This female bolas spider (*Mastophora*) is making a large egg case. Bolas spiders catch moths by using sticky balls on the end of silk lines. The spiders are named after the bolas (a strong cord connecting three balls) used by South American cowboys to trip up cattle. The spider produces a scent just like that made by female moths to draw male moths to its fishing line.

SPITTING SPIDER ▶

This female spitting spider (*Scytodes*) is carrying a ball of eggs in her jaws. Spitting spiders produce glue, as well as poison, inside the poison glands in the front half of the body. When the spider is very close to its prey, it squirts out two lines of gummy poison from its fangs to pin down the victim. It then gives its prey a poisonous bite before tearing it free of the glue and eating its meal.

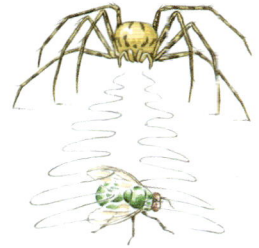

The spitting spider's fangs move from side to side as it squirts out its sticky poison. This imprisons the victim under two zigzag strands of quick-setting glue.

◀ SIMPLE NETS

The daddy-longlegs spider (*Pholcus*) spins a flimsy scaffold web that is almost invisible. When an insect, or another spider, gets tangled up in its web, the daddy-longlegs throws strands of fresh silk over its prey. It can do this from a distance because of its long legs. Once the victim is helpless, the spider moves in for the feast.

35

Catching Food

Only about half of all spiders spin webs to catch prey. Of the other half, some hide and surprise their victims with a sneak attack — crab spiders do this very well. Others, such as trapdoor spiders, set traps as well as ambushing prey. Many spiders, such as jumping spiders, are agile, fast-moving hunters that stalk their prey. Spiders are not usually very fussy about what they eat. Insects, such as grasshoppers, beetles, ants and bees are their main food, but some eat fish, while bigger spiders may catch mice and birds. Many spiders eat other spiders.

▲ **SILK TRAPS**
Orb webs are designed to catch insects up to about the size of the spiders that made them. This orb-web spider is eating a crane fly. The prey has been bitten and wrapped in silk, then cut free from the web and carried away to be eaten. Some insects, such as moths, manage to escape from webs. Smaller spiders tend to free large insects from their webs before they do too much damage.

The empty shell of a partly eaten fly.

Dead flies wrapped in silk are left hanging for eating later.

◄ **DAISY WEB**
In the centre of this ox-eye daisy sits a green orb-web spider (*Araniella cucurbitina*). It has built its web over the middle of the daisy. Small flies, attracted to the innocent-looking flower, are trapped in the web. They end up as food for the spider, who kills them, then crushes them to a pulp before sucking up a meal.

WATER HUNTER ▶

This fishing spider (*Dolomedes*) has caught a blue damselfly. It lives in swamps and pools where it sits on the leaves of water plants. It spreads its legs on the water's surface to detect ripples from insects that fall into the water, then rushes out to grab them. Fish swimming in the water below are also caught by this hunting spider. The spider may even dabble its legs in the water to attract small fish toward its waiting fangs.

◀ HAIRY HUNTER

Tarantulas are also called bird-eating spiders and they really do eat birds, although this one has caught a mouse. They also eat lizards, frogs and even small poisonous snakes. But most of the time, tarantulas feed on insects. They hunt at night, finding their prey by scent or by picking up vibrations with their sensitive hairs. After a quick sprint and a bite from powerful jaws, the spider can tuck into its meal. It may take as long as a day to suck the body of a snake dry.

ATHLETIC HUNTER ▶

Lynx spiders hunt their prey on plants. They sometimes jump from leaf to leaf after their prey, but at other times they sit and wait. The green lynx spider (*Peucetia*) is an athletic hunter with long spiny legs that enable it to leap easily from stem to stem. It often eats other spiders and is even a cannibal, eating members of its own species. This one has caught a termite.

Focus on Hunting

With bright, shiny colours like a peacock, large curious eyes like a cat and the agility to jump like a monkey, little jumping spiders are one of the most extraordinary spider families. Belonging to the family Salticidae, there are about 4,000 different kinds, many of which live in warmer parts of the world. Most jumping spiders are always on the prowl, darting jerkily along, peering all around for a possible meal. They can see in colour and form clear images of their prey. They stalk their prey rather like a cat stalks a mouse, crouching before the final pounce. Jumping spiders will turn their tiny heads to peer closely at a human face looking at them.

SIGN LANGUAGE

A male jumping spider's front legs are longer and thicker than a female's. He uses them in courtship dances, waving them about like sign language.

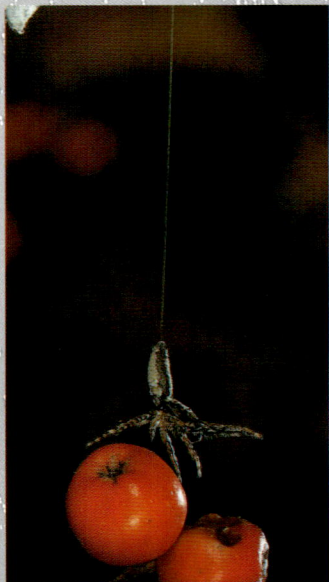

PREPARING TO LEAP

Before it jumps, the spider fixes itself firmly to a surface with a silk safety line. Then it leaps on to its target, pushing off with the four back legs. The Australian flying spider (*Satis volans*) also has wing-like flaps so it can glide during leaps.

STURDY LEGS

This female heavy jumper (*Hyllus giganteus*) is feeding on a leaf-hopper. A jumping spider's legs do not seem to be specially adapted for jumping. Their small size (less than 15mm/⅗in long) and light weight probably help them to make amazing leaps.

Jumping Spiders

THE BIG LEAP

A jumping spider's strong front legs are often raised before a jump, stretched forwards in the air, and used to hold the prey when the spider lands. Scopulae (hairy tufts) on the feet help jumping spiders grip smooth and vertical surfaces. They can even leap away from a vertical surface to seize a flying insect.

JUMPING CANNIBALS

Jumping spiders will feed on their own relatives. This female two-striped jumping spider (*Telamonia dimidiata*) is feeding on another species of jumping spider. Some unusual *Portia* jumping spiders vibrate the webs of orb-weaving spiders, like an insect struggling to escape. When the orb-weaver comes out to investigate, the *Portia* spider pounces.

Hidden Traps

Some spiders do not go hunting for food. They prefer to lurk inside underground burrows or tubes of silk and wait for a meal to come by. Silk threads around the entrance to the burrow trip up passing insects and other small creatures. Inside the burrow, the spider feels the tug on its trip lines, giving it time to rush out and pounce on the prey before it can escape. Patient, lie-in-wait spiders include trapdoor spiders, which have special spines on their fangs to rake away the soil as they dig. The burrows also shelter spiders from the weather and help them to avoid enemies.

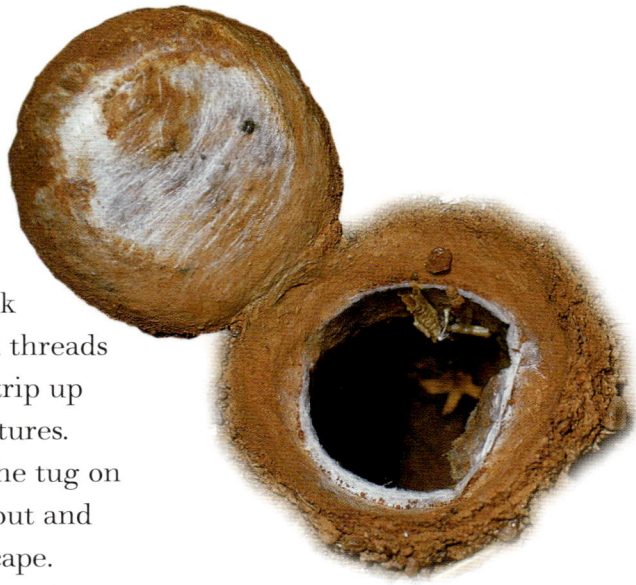

▲ A SILKEN TUBE

This purse-web spider (*Atypus affinis*) is shown outside its burrow. It usually lives inside a tubular purse of densely woven silk. The tube is about 45cm/18in long and the thickness of a finger. Part of it sticks up above the ground or from a tree trunk, and is well camouflaged with debris.

▲ SILK DOORS

The lid of a trapdoor spider's burrow is made of silk and soil, with a silk hinge along one side. The door usually fits tightly into the burrow opening and may be camouflaged with sticks, leaves and moss. Where flooding occurs, walls or turrets are built around the entrance to keep out the water.

The spider waits for an insect to land on its tube-like web.

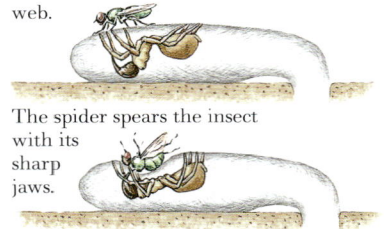

The spider spears the insect with its sharp jaws.

▲ INSIDE A PURSE-WEB

Inside its silken purse the spider waits for any insect to walk over the tube. It spears the insect through the tube with its sharp jaws and drags the prey inside.

▲ FUNNEL-WEB SPIDERS

The Sydney funnel-web (*Atrax robustus*) is one of the deadliest spiders in the world. It lives in an underground burrow lined with silk. From the mouth of the burrow is a funnel that can be up to 1m/39in across. Trip wires leading from the funnel warn the spider that prey is coming. The spider can dig its own burrow with its fangs, but prefers to use existing holes and cracks. Funnel-web spiders eat mainly beetles, large insects, snails and small animals.

▲ TRIP WIRES

The giant trapdoor spider (*Liphistius*) may place silken trip lines around the entrance to its burrow to detect the movements of a passing meal. If it does not have trip lines, the spider relies on detecting the vibrations of prey through the ground. If it senses a meal is nearby, the spider rushes out of its burrow to grab the prey in its jaws.

Did you know?
Trapdoor spiders may live for up to 20 years in their burrows.

Spider looking out for passing prey.

Silk door

Open sock

Centipede enters spider's burrow.

False bottom of closed sock hides spider.

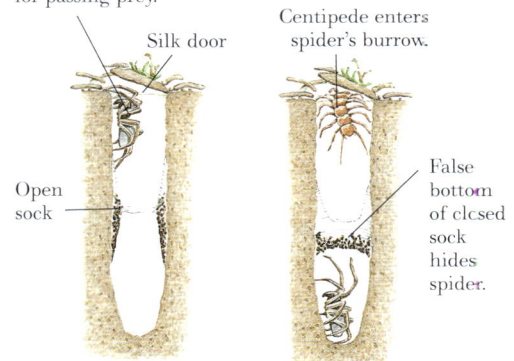

▲ ODD SPIDER OUT

Some unusual wolf spiders live in underground burrows. This tiger-wolf spider (*Lycosa aspersa*) has dug out the soil with its fangs and lined the walls of its burrow with silk. To camouflage the entrance it has built a wall of twigs and litter.

▲ ALL KINDS OF TRAPS

Trapdoor spiders' burrows range from simple tubes to elaborate lairs with hidden doors and escape tunnels. The burrow of *Anidiops villosus* has a collapsible sock. The spider pulls it down to form a false bottom, hiding it from predators.

Spider Venom

Nearly all spiders use poison to kill or paralyse their prey and for defence. (Only spiders in the family Uloboridae have no poison glands.) Spider poison is called venom. It is injected into prey through fangs. There are two main kinds of venom that can have serious effects. Most dangerous spiders, such as widow spiders (*Lactrodectus*), produce nerve poison to paralyse victims quickly. The other kind of venom works more slowly, destroying tissues and causing ulcers and gangrene. It is made by the recluse spiders (*Loxosceles*). Spider venom is intended to kill insects and small prey – only about 30 spider species are dangerous to people.

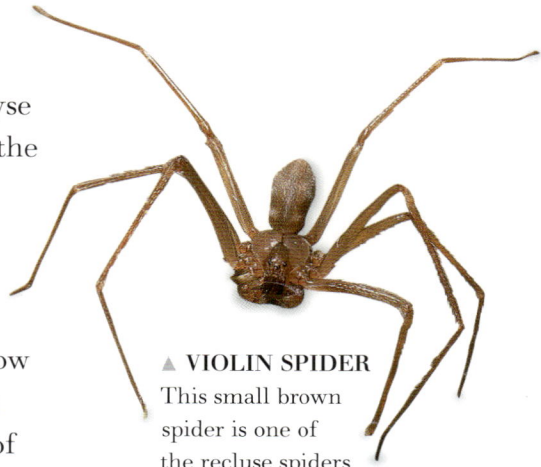

▲ **VIOLIN SPIDER**
This small brown spider is one of the recluse spiders (*Loxosceles*). It lives in people's homes and may crawl into clothes and bedding. Bites from recluse spiders in America have caused ulcers, especially near the wound, and even death in humans.

▲ **WANDERING SPIDER**
The Brazilian wandering spider (*Phoneutria fera*) is a large hunting spider that produces one of the most toxic of all spider venoms. If disturbed, it raises its front legs to expose its threatening jaws. It has the largest venom glands of any spider (up to 10mm/⅖in long), which hold enough venom to kill 225 mice. People have died from this spider's bite.

The Spider Dance
In the Middle Ages people from Taranto in southern Italy called the large wolf spider Lycosa narbonensis *the tarantula. They believed the venom of this spider's bite could only be flushed from the body by doing the tarantella, a lively dance. However, Lycosa's bite is not serious. An epidemic of spider bites at the time was probably caused by the malmignatte spider* (Latrodectus tredecimguttatus).

THE QUICK KILL

Crab spiders do not spin webs so they need to kill their prey quickly. They usually inject their venom into the main nerve cords in the neck where the poison will get to work most rapidly. They are able to kill insects much larger than themselves, such as bees.

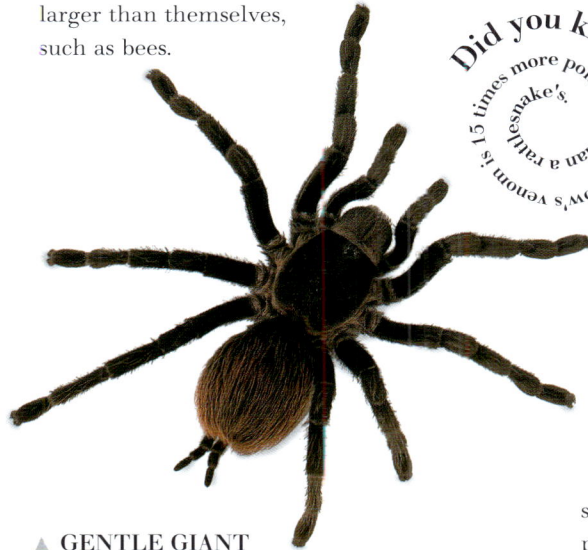

WIDOW SPIDER ▶

The Australian red-back spider (*Latrodectus hasselti*) is one of the deadliest widow spiders. Widow spiders are named after the female's habit of eating the male after mating. Only female widow spiders are dangerous to people – the much smaller male's fangs are too tiny to penetrate human skin.

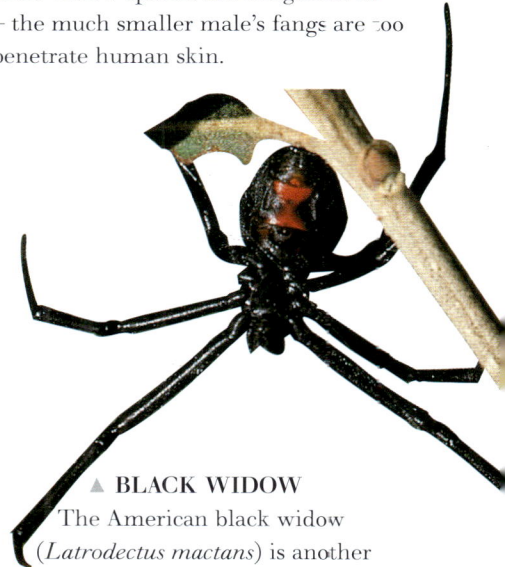

Did you know?
A black widow's venom is 15 times more poisonous than a rattlesnake's.

▲ GENTLE GIANT

Tarantulas look very dangerous and have huge fangs, but at worst their bite is no more painful than a wasp sting. They have small venom glands and are unlikely to bite unless handled roughly. They use venom to digest their prey.

▲ BLACK WIDOW

The American black widow (*Latrodectus mactans*) is another spider with venom powerful enough to kill a person (although medicines can now prevent this happening). These shy spiders hide away if disturbed, but like to live near people. Of the main ingredients in their venom, one knocks out insects and another paralyses mammals and birds by destroying their nervous systems.

Fangs and Feeding

A spider's sharp, pointed fangs are part of its jaws. Each fang is like a curved, hollow needle. It is joined to a basal segment, which joins on to the spider's body just in front of the mouth. The fangs may be used for digging burrows and carrying eggs, but are mainly used for injecting venom and for defence. Venom passes through a tiny hole near the end of each fang. Although the fangs are not very long, the venom they deliver makes them into powerful weapons. Once prey is caught, a spider uses its jaws, palps and digestive juices to mash up its prey into a soggy, soupy lump. This is because a spider's mouth is too small for solid food. Then the spider sucks up the liquid food into its stomach. Its abdomen swells as the food is swallowed, so a spider looks fatter after a meal.

FROG SOUP ▶

Spiders sometimes have to turn quite large items of food into pulp before they can suck up a meal. This rusty wandering spider (*Cupiennius getazi*) is turning a tree frog over and over to mash it up in its jaws. It finds the frogs by using the slit organs on its feet to detect the mating calls they make.

▲ **A SOGGY MEAL**

This garden spider (*Araneus diadematus*) has turned its prey into a soupy meal. The basal segments of the jaws often have jagged edges to help the spider tear and mash up its prey. Smaller jaws, called maxillae, on either side of the mouth are also used to turn prey into a liquid pulp.

Did you know? A Sydney funnel-web's fangs are strong enough to pierce bone.

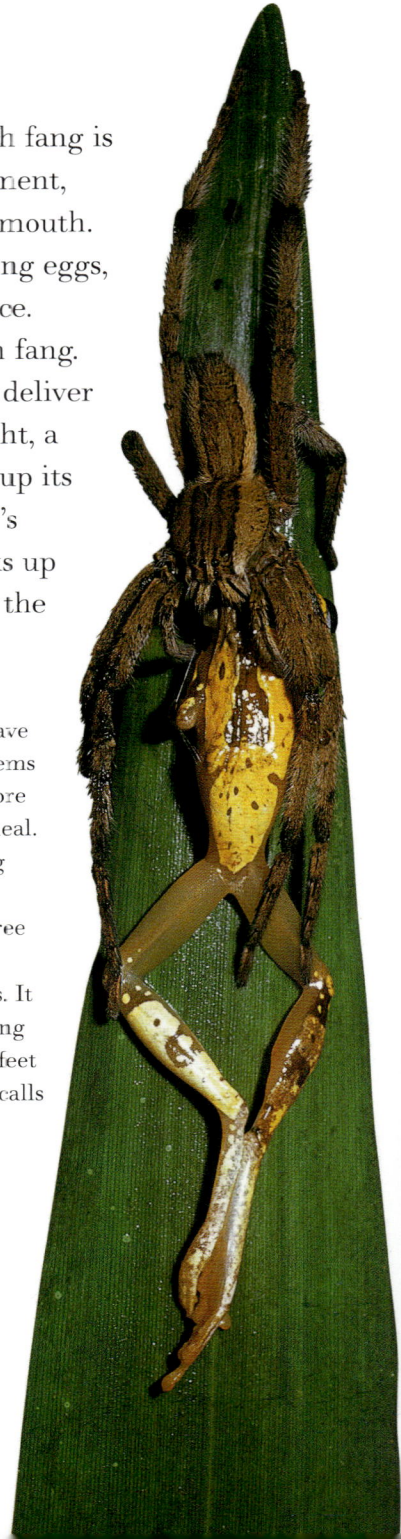

DAGGER FANGS ▶

This tarantula's dagger-like fangs have pierced through the skin of a baby field mouse to inject venom into its body. The venom glands of tarantulas and trapdoor spiders are all inside the basal segments of the jaws. They do not extend into the head as in most other spiders. Tarantula venom can kill a small animal and causes burning and swelling in a person.

HOW FANGS WORK ▶

In most spiders, the fangs face each other and close together like pincers or pliers. In mygalomorph spiders (tarantulas and trapdoor spiders), however, the fangs stab downwards like two daggers. The spider has to raise its front end to strike forwards and down on to its prey. Prey needs to be on a firm surface, such as the ground, for these jaws to work.

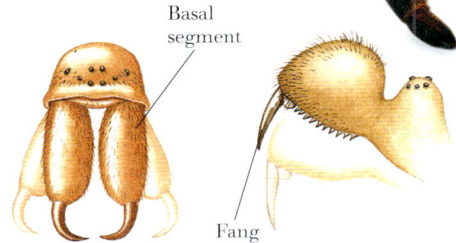

Basal segment

Fang

Pincer fangs swing together. They work well on webs and leaves.

Dagger fangs impale prey on the ground with a downward action.

▲ FANGS FOR DEFENCE

An Australian trapdoor spider (*Aname*) tries to make itself look as frightening as possible if it is threatened. It tilts back its body and raises its front legs so that its long, poisonous fangs are easy to see. It adopts this aggressive pose to warn an enemy to leave it alone.

▲ PINCER FANGS

The lobed argiope spider (*Argiope lobata*) has fangs that work like pincers. It catches large insects in its orb web and wraps them in silk before biting them. As in most spiders, the venom glands go well back inside the head.

45

Defence

Spiders are small, with soft bodies that make a tasty meal for many predators. To avoid their enemies, such as other spiders, hunting wasps, lizards and frogs, many spiders hide away. Trapdoor spiders hide in well-concealed burrows. Other spiders hide themselves by being beautifully camouflaged to blend in with their surroundings. In complete contrast, some spiders copy the bright colours of dangerous insects, such as wasps. This tricks enemies into leaving the spider alone. Spiders will even pretend to be dead, since predators prefer to eat live prey.

▼ **THREATENING DISPLAY**
The golden wheel spider (*Carparachne aureoflava*) lives on the sand dunes of the Namib Desert, southern Africa. Its gold colour blends in well with its surroundings. If caught out in the open, however, the spider rears up to make itself look large and more frightening to enemies.

By raising its abdomen high into the air, the spider makes itself appear larger.

The spider raises its legs high up and waves them about to look more aggressive.

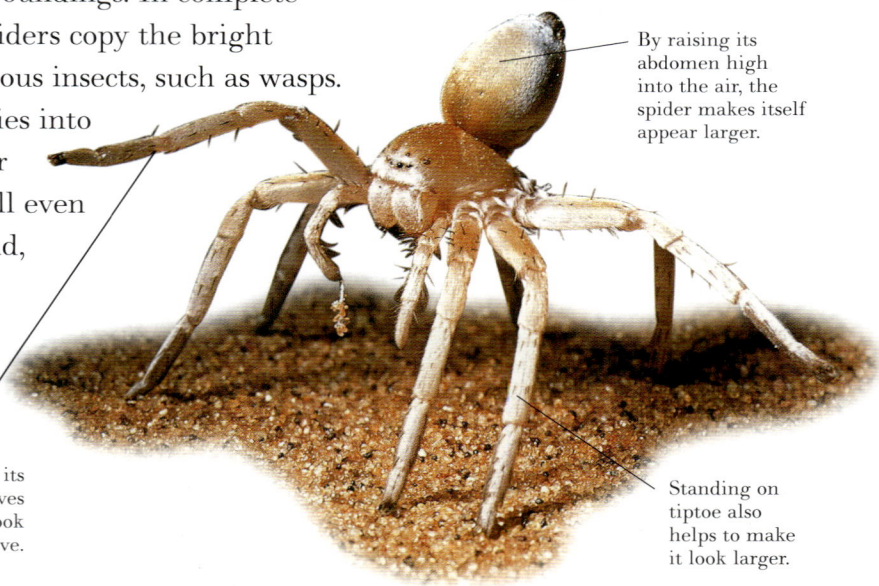

Standing on tiptoe also helps to make it look larger.

ESCAPE WHEEL ▶
If the golden wheel spider's threatening display does not deter an enemy, it has another, remarkable way of escaping. The spider throws itself sideways, pulls in its legs and rolls itself into a ball. It then cartwheels rapidly away down the dunes.

HUNTING WASP ▶

This hunting wasp has just paralysed a spider with its sting. Most wasps that hunt spiders are solitary pompilid wasps. A wasp will attack spiders as large or larger than itself. First it stings the spider to paralyse it. Then it drags the spider off to a burrow, lays an egg on its body and buries the spider alive. When the egg hatches out, the wasp grub feeds on the spider meat. The spider provides a living larder (pantry) for the grub as it grows.

▲ SPIDER ENEMIES

A hungry lizard crunches up a tasty spider meal. Many animals eat spiders, including frogs, toads, mice, shrews, monkeys, bandicoots and possums. Birds are not usually a threat, because most spiders are active at night when few birds are about. The most common enemies of spiders, however, are probably the smaller animals without backbones. These include other spiders, hunting wasps, assassin bugs, scorpions and centipedes.

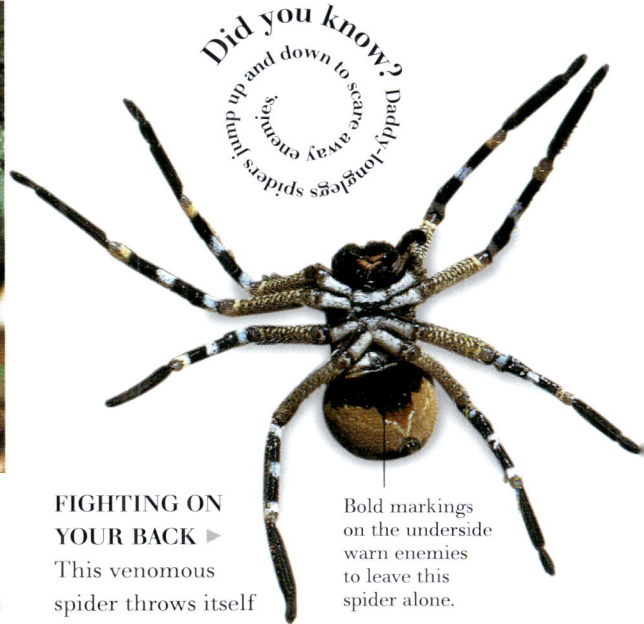

Did you know? Daddy-long-legs spiders jump up and down to scare away enemies.

FIGHTING ON YOUR BACK ▶

This venomous spider throws itself on its back to display its warning colours when it is attacked. Colours such as yellow, orange, red and black are warning signals, saying "I am poisonous, leave me alone". Other active defence tactics include showing off the fangs and squirting liquid or venom at an attacker.

Bold markings on the underside warn enemies to leave this spider alone.

Colour and Camouflage

Is it a leaf, a twig or a piece of bark? Is it a bird dropping? No, it is a spider! Many spiders have bodies that are coloured and shaped just like objects in their surroundings. They are so well camouflaged that they are very hard to see, especially when they keep still. This allows the spider to sit out in the open where it can more easily catch food, yet remain invisible to its enemies and prey. A few spiders, such as crab spiders and some jumping spiders, can even change colour to match different backgrounds. It takes some time for the spider to do this, however. Brightly coloured spiders often taste nasty. These eye-catching colours warn enemies to leave them alone.

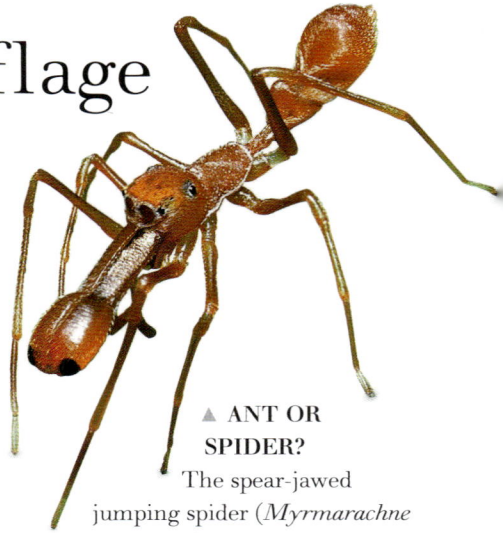

▲ **ANT OR SPIDER?**
The spear-jawed jumping spider (*Myrmarachne plataleoides*) looks just like an insect called a weaver ant. You can tell it is a spider because it has eight legs not six. It even waves its front legs like antennae to make the disguise more realistic. Spiders mimic ants because predators avoid ants' nasty stings.

▲ **SAND SPIDER**
When spiders are the same colour or pattern as their background they can be hard to spot. The wolf spider *Arctosa perita* lives on sand or gravel. Its speckled colouring breaks up the outline of its body so it is hard to see. Until it moves, the spider is almost invisible.

▲ **LOOKING LIKE A FLOWER**
With their colours matching all or part of a flower, many crab spiders lurk on the surface of plants waiting to catch insects. This is the seven-spined crab spider (*Epicadus heterogaster*). The fleshy lobes on its abdomen imitate the host plant's white, orchid-like flowers.

▲ LEAF LOOK-ALIKE

Spiders like this *Augusta glyphica* have lumpy or wrinkled abdomens. With their legs drawn up, they look just like a piece of dead leaf.

▲ BIRD DROPPING

Looking like a bird dropping is a very useful disguise for many spiders. Enemies are not likely to eat droppings and some insects are attracted to feed on the salts they contain. A few spiders even release a scent similar to bird droppings.

Did you know? A South American wolf spider can change colour in 30 minutes.

▲ TWIGGY DISGUISE

Spiders that look like twigs have to sit in a certain way to be well hidden. This *Poltys* spider sits with its front four legs held over its face and rear four pressed tightly against its abdomen. It looks like the jagged end of a broken twig when it keeps still.

LICHEN SPIDER ▶

The lichen huntsman (*Pandercetes gracilis*) from the rainforests of Australia and New Guinea spends all day pressed to the bark of a tree. The spider's mottled colours match the colours of the lichens on the tree. Short hairs also give the colours a matt finish. All along its legs and the sides of its body, fringes of hair stop the spider casting a shadow.

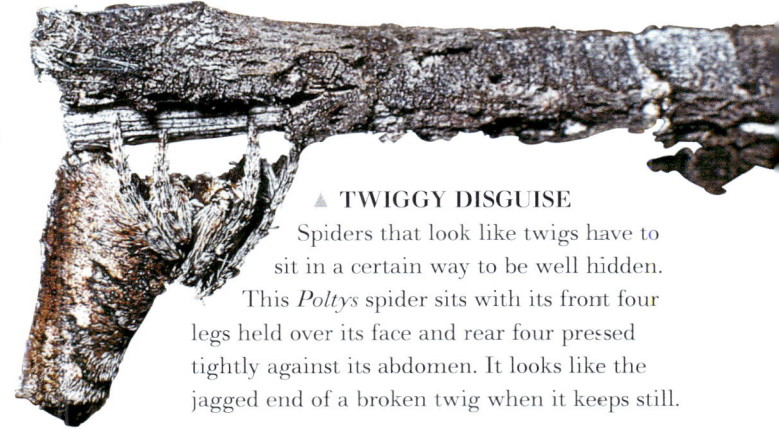

Focus on

With broad, flat bodies and sideways scuttling movements like crabs, the members of the family Thomisidae are called crab spiders. There are about 3,000 species living all over the world. Crab spiders do not usually build webs. They often lie in wait for their prey on flowers, leaves, tree trunks or on the ground. Most are small (less than 20mm/¾in long) and rely on stealth and strong venom to catch prey. Males are often half the size of the females and their colours can be quite different.

BODY PARTS
Crab spiders are usually not very hairy, and many, like this heather spider (*Thomisus onustus*), are brightly coloured. They often have wart-like lumps and bumps on their bodies, especially the females. The front pairs of legs are adapted for grasping prey.

COLOUR CHANGE
Female flower spiders (*Misumena vatia*) can change colour. A yellow pigment is moved from the intestines (gut) to the outer layer of the body to turn yellow and back again to turn white. It takes up to two days for the spider to complete the change.

BIG EATERS
Crab spiders can kill larger prey than themselves. This gold leaf crab spider (*Synema globosum*) has caught a honeybee. Its venom is powerful, quickly paralysing the bee. This avoids a long struggle, which might damage the spider and draw the attention of enemies.

Crab Spiders

SIX-SPOT CRAB SPIDER

The unusual six-spot crab spider (*Platythomisus sexmaculatus*) has very striking markings. These might be warning colours, but very little is known about this spider. No one has ever seen a male six-spot crab spider. The female, shown here, is about 15mm/⅝in long in real life.

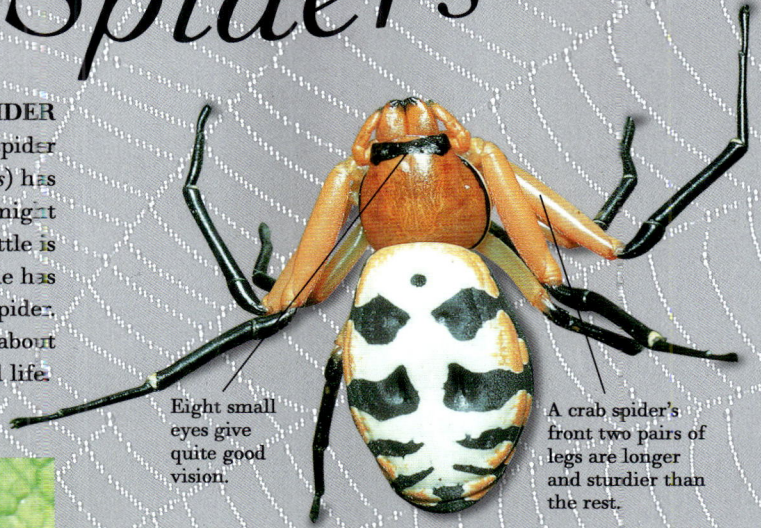

Eight small eyes give quite good vision.

A crab spider's front two pairs of legs are longer and sturdier than the rest.

THE AMBUSH

This flower spider (*Misumena vatia*) has sat on a daisy for several days. It hardly moved as it waited to ambush an insect, such as a bee. The two rear pairs of legs anchored the spider firmly on to the flower. The two front pairs of legs, armed with bristles, grabbed the bee like pincers.

FEEDING TIME

This common crab spider (*Xysticus cristatus*) is eating a dance fly. Crab spiders do not store prey like many other spiders. They can deal with only one meal at a time. Insects can pass close by a feeding crab spider unnoticed. A crab spider's jaws have no teeth and cannot mash up its prey. Instead, fangs inject digestive juices that break down the prey's insides. The spider sucks up its liquid meal, leaving a dry, empty husk behind.

Males and Females

Most spiders spend much of their life alone, only coming together to mate. Females often look different from males. The female is usually larger because she needs to carry a lot of eggs inside her body. She also has extra glands to make a silk covering for her eggs. The female may even guard the eggs and young spiderlings after they hatch. She is also usually a drab colour to help hide her and her young from enemies. The male, on the other hand, takes no part in looking after his family after mating. He is usually smaller and sometimes more colourful. Males often have longer legs to help search for a mate.

▲ SPERM WEB
This male garden spider (*Araneus diadematus*) is filling his palps with sperm before searching for a mate. He has made a small web and squirted some sperm on to it. He sucks up the sperm into the swollen tip of each palp.

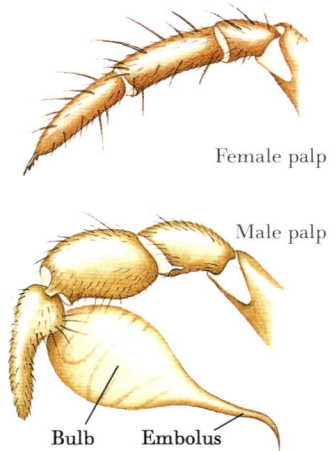

▲ MALE MEALS?
The much larger female black widow spider (*Latrodectus mactans*) sometimes eats the smaller, brown male after mating. Other female spiders occasionally do this, too. The most dangerous time for many males, however, is before mating. If the female is not ready to mate or does not recognize the male's signals, she may eat the male before he has a chance to mate.

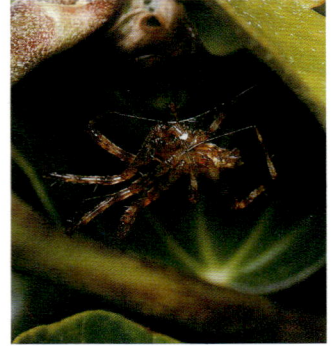

Female palp

Male palp

Bulb   Embolus

▲ DIFFERENT PALPS
Males have larger palps than females. The embolus on the tip of a male's palp is used to suck up sperm into the bulb. It pumps sperm out into the female's body during mating.

◀ **EGG CARRIER**

This female *Sosippus mimus* is spinning a silk cocoon to protect her eggs. The number of eggs laid by a female spider usually depends on her size. Some tiny spiders, such as *Atrophonysia intertidalis*, lay only one egg, while large *Nephila* spiders lay 1,000 or more. A spider's abdomen has a fairly thin covering, so it can stretch a great deal when a female has many eggs developing inside.

SPOT THE DIFFERENCE ▶

This male and female ladybird (ladybug) spider (*Eresus niger*) show very clearly the differences between some male and female spiders. Their difference in size varies a great deal, but adult females can be over three times the size of males. The female is camouflaged in a velvety blue-black skin, while the male looks like a brightly coloured ladybird (ladybug). He will run across open ground in search of a mate in spring. She usually hides away under stones.

Female ladybird (ladybug) spider (maximum body length up to 35mm/1⅜in)

Male ladybird (ladybug) spider (maximum body length up to 10mm/⅖in)

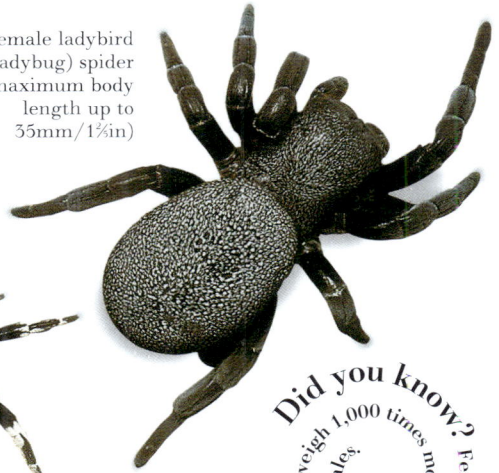

Did you know? Female *Nephila* spiders can weigh 1,000 times more than the males.

LITTLE AND LARGE ▶

A tiny male giant orb-weaver (*Nephila maculata*) mates with a huge female. They look so different it is hard to believe that they are the same species. The very small size of the male helps him to avoid being eaten by the female, since he is smaller than her usual prey. The female has two openings on her underside to receive sperm from the male's palps.

Focus on

Female spiders attract males by giving off a special scent called a pheromone. Each species has a different pheromone, to help the males find the right mate. Once he has found a female, the male has to give off the right signals so that the female realizes he is not a meal. Courtship signals include special dances, drumming, buzzing, or plucking the female's web in a particular way. Some males distract the females with a gift of food, while others tie up the females with strands of silk before mating.

NOISY COURTSHIP

The male buzzing spider (*Anyphaena accentuata*) beats his abdomen against a leaf to attract a mate. The sound is loud enough for people to hear. He often buzzes on the roof of the female's oak-leaf nest. Other male hunting spiders make courtship sounds by rubbing one part of their bodies against another.

The male presents a gift to the female.

MATING SUCCESS

The male grass funnel-weaver (*Agelena labyrinthica*) is almost as large as the female and can be quite aggressive. He taps his palps on her funnel web to announce his arrival. If the female is ready to mate, she draws in her legs and collapses as if she is paralysed.

BEARING GIFTS

A male nursery-web spider (*Pisaura mirabilis*) presents an insect gift to the female. He has neatly gift-wrapped his present in a dense covering of very shiny white silk. Once the female has accepted his gift and is feeding, the male can mate with her in safety.

Courtship

COURTSHIP DANCES

Spiders that can see well at a distance often dance together before mating. This wolf spider (*Lycosa*) waves his palps like semaphore flags to a female in the distance. Male spiders also strike special poses and use their long, stout front legs to make signalling more effective.

A RISKY BUSINESS

Male garden spiders (*Araneus*) often have great difficulty courting a female. They are usually much smaller and lighter than the female and have to persuade her to move on to a special mating thread. The male joins the mating thread to the edge of the female's web. He tweaks the silk strands of her web to lure the female towards him.

COURTSHIP PROBLEMS

This male green orb-weaver (*Araniella cucurbitina*) has lost four legs in the courtship process. When the female attacked him, he swung down a silken dragline. He will climb back up again when it is safe.

JUMPING SPIDERS

This pair of jumping spiders (*Salticus*) are ready to mate. Male jumping spiders impress females by twirling and waltzing, waving their legs, palps and abdomens. Females often attract more than one male and they have to compete to mate with her. The female reaches out and touches the male when she is ready to mate.

Spider Eggs

Female spiders usually lay their eggs a week or two after mating, although some spiders wait several months. Not all the eggs are laid at once and many spiders lay several batches, usually at night when it is safer. The female may lay from one to over 1,000 eggs per batch. Most spiders lay their eggs on a circle of silk together with some of the male's stored sperm. It is not until now that the eggs are fertilized. The outer layer of the eggs gradually hardens and the female spins a cocoon around them for extra protection.

Ananse the Spider Man
A hero of many folk tales in West Africa and the Caribbean is Ananse. He is both a spider and a man. When things are going well he is a man, but in times of danger he becomes a spider. Ananse likes to trick the other animals and get the better of those who are much bigger than himself. He may be greedy and selfish, but he is also funny. He is a hero because he brought the gift of telling stories to people.

◀ **IN DISGUISE**
To hide their eggs from hungry predators, spiders may camouflage the cocoons with plant material, insect bodies, mud or sand. This scorpion spider (*Arachnura*) hangs her brown egg cases from her web like a string of debris, then poses as a dead leaf beneath them. Other spiders hide egg cases under stones or bark, or fix leaves together like a purse.

▲ **SPINNING THE COCOON**
A *Nephila edulis* spins her egg cocoon. She uses special strong, loopy silk that traps a lot of air and helps to stop the eggs drying out. Her eggs are covered with a sticky coating to fix them to the silk. The final protective blanket of yellow silk will turn green, camouflaging the cocoon.

◀ FLIMSY EGG CASE

The daddy-longlegs spider (*Pholcus*) uses hardly any silk for her egg case. Just a few strands hold the eggs loosely together. Producing a large egg case uses up a lot of energy, and females with large egg cases often have shrunken bodies. The daddy-longlegs carries the eggs around in her jaws. She is unable to feed until the eggs hatch.

SILK NEST ▶

The woodlouse spider (*Dysdera crocota*) lays her eggs in a silken cell under the ground. She also lives in this shelter, where she is safer from enemies. At night, the woodlouse spider emerges from its silken house to look for woodlice, which it kills with its enormous fangs.

◀ CAREFUL MOTHER

A green lynx spider (*Peucetia*) protects her egg case on a cactus. She fixes the case with silk lines, like a tent's guy ropes, and drives off any enemies. If necessary, she cuts the silk lines and lets the egg case swing in mid-air, balancing on top like a trapeze artist. If she has to move her eggs to a safer place, she drags the case behind her with silk threads.

GUARD DUTY ▶

Many female spiders carry their eggs around with them. This rusty wandering spider (*Cupiennius getazi*) carries her egg sac attached to her spinnerets. Spiders that do this often moisten the eggs in water and sunbathe to warm them and so speed up their development.

Did you know? A female garden spider can lay over 1,000 eggs in under 10 minutes.

57

Spiderlings

Most spider eggs hatch within a few days or weeks of being laid. The spiderlings (baby spiders) do not usually have any hairs, spines, claws or colour when they first hatch. They feed on the egg yolk stored in their bodies and grow fast. They cast off their first skin in a process called moulting (molting). Spiderlings have to moult several times as they grow into adults. After the first moult, young spiders look like tiny versions of their parents. Most baby spiders look after themselves from the moment of hatching, but some mothers guard and feed their young until they leave the nest. Male spiders do not look after their young at all.

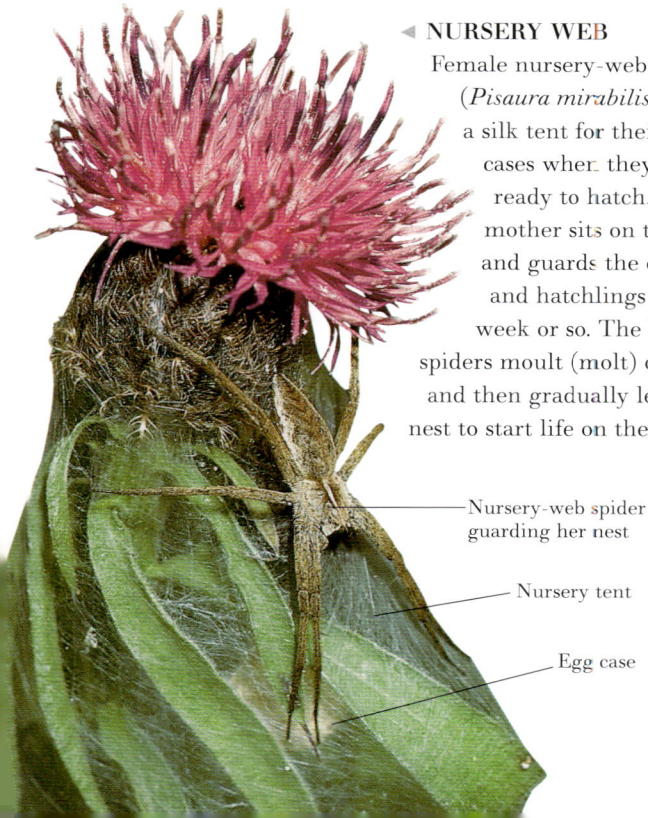

▲ **HATCHING OUT**
These spiderlings are emerging from their egg case. Spiderlings may stay inside the case for some time after hatching. Some spiders have an egg tooth to help them break out of the egg, but mother spiders may also help their young to hatch. Spiderlings from very different species look similar.

◀ **NURSERY WEB**
Female nursery-web spiders (*Pisaura mirabilis*) build a silk tent for their egg cases when they are ready to hatch. The mother sits on the tent and guards the eggs and hatchlings for a week or so. The baby spiders moult (molt) once and then gradually leave the nest to start life on their own.

Nursery-web spider guarding her nest

Nursery tent

Egg case

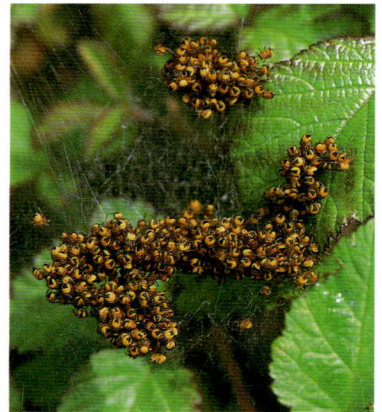

▲ **A SPIDER BALL**
Garden spiderlings (*Araneus*) stay together for several days after hatching. They form small gold and black balls that break apart if danger threatens, but re-form when danger has passed.

◄ BABY BODIES

A female crab spider watches over her young as they hatch out. Spider eggs contain a lot of yolk, which provides a good supply of energy for the baby spiders. They are well developed when they hatch out, with the same body shape and number of legs as adults. Baby spiders cannot produce silk or venom until their first moult (molt).

Spiderlings cling to special hairs on their mother's back for about a week.

BABY CARRIER ►

Pardosa wolf spiders carry their egg cases joined to their spinnerets. When the eggs are ready to hatch, the mother tears open the case and the babies climb on to her back. If the spiderlings fall off, they can find their way back by following silk lines the mother trails behind her.

Spotted wolf spider (*Pardosa amentata*)

Silk threads are called gossamer.

Did you know? Many young spiders often feed on their own mother's body.

▲ FOOD FROM MUM

The mothercare spider (*Theridion sisyphium*) feeds her young on food brought up from her stomach. The rich soup is made of digested insects and cells lining her gut. The babies shake her legs to beg for food. They grow faster than babies that feed themselves.

▲ BALLOON FLIGHT

Many spiderlings take to the air to find new places to live or to avoid being eaten by their brothers and sisters. On a warm day with light winds, they float through the air on strands of silk drawn out from their spinnerets. This is called ballooning.

59

Moulting

Spiders do not grow gradually, like we do. Instead they grow in a series of steps. At each step, the spider grows a new outer skin, or exoskeleton, under the old one and moults (molts) the old one. Lost or damaged legs and other body parts can be replaced during a moult. Small spiders moult in a few hours, but larger spiders may need several days. A young spider moults about five to ten times as it grows into an adult. A few spiders continue to moult throughout their adult lives.

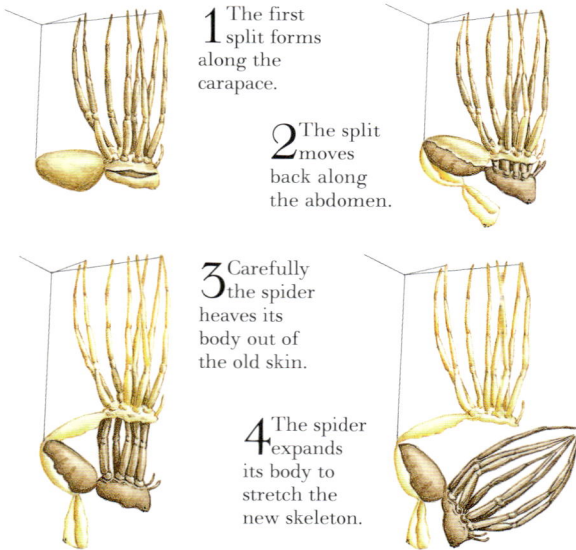

▲ **COLOUR CHANGE**
Adult spiders that have just moulted (molted) are quite pale for a while and do not show their true colours for a day or so. The fangs of this newly moulted tarantula have no colour as yet.

1 The first split forms along the carapace.

2 The split moves back along the abdomen.

3 Carefully the spider heaves its body out of the old skin.

4 The spider expands its body to stretch the new skeleton.

▲ **STAGES IN MOULTING**
The main stages in the moulting (molting) process of a spider are shown above. It is dangerous. Legs can get broken and spiders are vulnerable to enemies as they moult since they cannot defend themselves or run away.

▲ **THE OLD SKIN**
This is the old exoskeleton of a fishing spider (*Dolomedes*). The piece at the top is the lid of the carapace. The holes are where the legs fitted inside the skin.

HOW MANY MOULTS? ▶

This young red and white spider (*Enoplognatha ovata*) is in the middle of moulting (molting). It is hiding under a leaf out of sight of enemies. A larger adult spider seems to have come to investigate. It is not until the final moult that a spider takes on its adult colours. Most spiders stop moulting when they become adults. Smaller species need fewer moults to reach adult size. Males also go through fewer moults than females because they are smaller when fully grown.

◀ **MOULTING PROCESS**

A tarantula pulls itself free of its old skin. Before a spider moults (molts), it stops feeding and rests for a while. During this time, a new wrinkled exoskeleton forms underneath the old one and part of the old skin is absorbed back into the body to be recycled. The spider then pumps blood into the front of its body, making it swell and split the old skin, which is now very thin.

Did you know? Spiders can grow new palps, fangs and spinnerets when they moult.

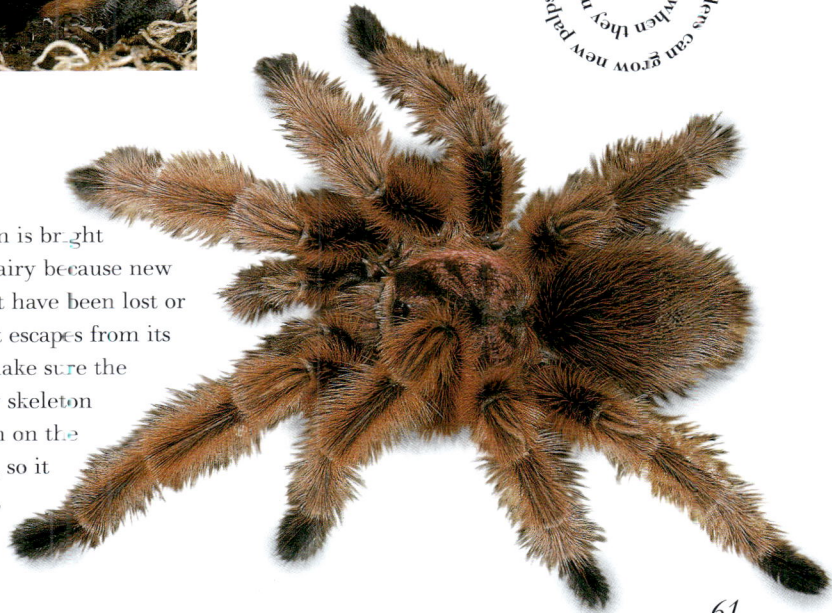

A NEW SKIN ▶

This Chilean rose tarantula (*Grammostola cala*) moulted (molted) recently. Its new skin is bright and colourful. It looks very hairy because new hairs have replaced those that have been lost or damaged. When a spider first escapes from its old skin, it flexes its legs to make sure the joints stay supple. As the new skeleton dries out, it hardens. The skin on the abdomen stays fairly stretchy, so it can expand as the spider eats, or fill with eggs in females.

61

Spiders Everywhere

From mountain tops, caves and deserts to forests, marshes and grasslands, there are few places on Earth without spiders. Even remote islands are inhabited by spiders, perhaps blown there on the wind or carried on floating logs. Many spiders are quite at home in our houses and some travel the world on cargo ships. Many spiders live on sewage works, where there are plenty of flies for them to feed on. Spiders are not very common in watery places, however, since they cannot breathe underwater. There are also no spiders in Antarctica, although they do manage to live on the edge of the Arctic. To survive the winter in cool places, spiders may stay as eggs, hide away under grass, rocks or bark or make nests together. Some even have a type of antifreeze to stop their bodies freezing up.

▲ **HEDGEROW WEBS**
One of the most common spiders on bushes and hedges in Europe and Asia is the hammock web (*Linyphia triangularis*). One hedge may contain thousands of webs with their haphazard threads.

Did you know? Some spiders live in the web of another species and steal its food

◀ **SPIDER IN THE SINK**
The spiders that people sometimes find in the sink or the bath are usually male house spiders (*Tegenaria*) that have fallen in while searching for a mate. They cannot climb back up the smooth sides because they do not have gripping tufts of hair on their feet like hunting spiders.

▲ CAVE SPIDER

The cave orb-weaver (*Meta menardi*) usually builds its web in very dark places, often suspended from the roof. It is found in caves, mines, hollow trees, railway (railroad) tunnels, drains, wells and in outbuildings in Europe, Asia and North America.

▲ DESERT SPIDER

The main problem for desert spiders, such as this white lady (*Leucorhestris arenicola*), is lack of water. It hides away from the intense heat in a burrow beneath the sand and, in times of drought, may go into suspended animation. Desert spiders live in different places to avoid competition for food.

◄ SEASHORE SPIDER

This beach wolf spider (*Arctosa littoralis*) is well camouflaged on the sand. It lives in a very hostile place. Waves pound on the beach and shift the sand, there is little fresh water and the sun quickly dries everything out. There is little food, although insects gather on seaweed, rocks and plants growing along the edge of the shore.

RAINFOREST SPIDER ▶

The greatest variety of spiders is to be found in the rainforests of the tropics. Here the climate is warm all year round and plenty of food is always available. This forest huntsman (*Pandercetes plumipes*) is well camouflaged against a tree trunk covered in lichen. To hide, it presses its body close against the tree. It lives in Malaysia where it is found in gardens as well as the rainforest.

Focus on

No spiders live in the open sea, but several hunt in and around fresh water. If they sense danger, they dive down underwater by holding on to plants. Only one spider, the water spider (*Argyroneta aquatica*), spends its whole life underwater. It lives in ponds, lakes and slow-moving streams in Europe and Asia. It still needs to breathe oxygen from the air, so it lives in a bubble of air called a diving bell. It does not need a regular supply of food because its body works very slowly. It catches prey by sticking its legs out of the diving bell to pick up vibrations in the water.

FOOD FROM THE WATER

This fishing spider (*Dolomedes fimbriatus*) has caught a colourful reed-frog. Fishing spiders also eat tadpoles, small fish and insects that have fallen into the water. Their venom paralyses their prey very quickly, so it has little chance of escape.

FISHING FOR FOOD

Fishing spiders sit on floating leaves or twigs with their front legs resting on the surface of the water. Hairs on their legs detect ripples. The spider can work out the position of prey from the direction and distance between the ripples. Ripples from twigs or leaves falling into the water often confuse the spider.

Water Spiders

DINING TABLE

Neither water spiders nor fishing spiders can eat in the water, because it would dilute their digestive chemicals. Water spiders feed inside their diving bells, while fishing spiders have their meals on the bank or an object floating in the water. This fishing spider is eating a stickleback on a mossy bank. The tail of the fish is caught in the sticky tentacles of a sundew plant.

1 To make a diving bell, the water spider spins a web fixed to an underwater plant. Then it swims to the surface to trap a bubble of air, which it carries down to the web.

2 The spider releases the bubble, which floats up to be trapped inside the roof of the web. To fill the diving bell with air takes up to six trips to and from the surface.

3 Once the bell is finished, the spider eats, mates and lays its eggs inside. This male spider is visiting a female. She will leave her bell only to collect more air or catch food.

Snakes

Doctors adopted the image of the snake as
their symbol. A staff entwined with a single
snake, the Aesculapian snake of southern
Europe, was carried by the Greek god of
healing. The snake itself was allowed
to roam in Greek and Roman hospital-
temples, where it kept down vermin.
Thus the snake was an ancient
symbol of goodness and health,
unlike its association today
with evil and loathing.

Long, thin, bendy body with no legs

Tough scales protect the body and stop it drying out

Snake Life

Snakes are a kind of reptile related to lizards, crocodiles and turtles. Altogether, there are about 2,700 different kinds of snake, but only 300 or so are able to kill people. In Europe or North America, you are more likely to be struck by lightning than to be bitten by a poisonous snake. All snakes have long bodies covered with waterproof scales. They are flesh-eaters and swallow their prey whole. Snakes have always had a special place in myths and legends, being used as symbols of both good and evil.

◄ **A SNAKE'S TAIL**
The tail of a snake is the part behind a small opening called the cloaca, where the body wastes pass out. The snake narrows slightly where the tail begins.

Tail, the part of the body that tapers off to a point

Grass snake
(Natrix natrix)

◄ **SNAKE HEADS**
Most snakes have a definite head and neck. But in some snakes, one end of the body looks very much like the other end!

◄ FORKED TONGUES

Snakes and some lizards have forked tongues. A snake flicks its tongue to taste and smell the air. This gives the snake a picture of what is around it. A snake does this every few seconds if it is hunting or if there is any danger nearby.

Rattlesnake
(Crotalus)

Colombian rainbow boa
(Epicrates cenchria maurus)

▲ SCALY ARMOUR

A covering of tough, dry scales grows out of a snake's skin. The scales usually hide the skin. After a big meal, the scaly skin stretches so that the skin becomes visible between the scales. A snake's scales protect its body while allowing it to stretch, coil and bend. The scales may be either rough or smooth.

Red-tailed boa
(Boa constrictor)

Did you know? Snakes never feel slimy to the touch.

Did you know? A boa squeezes its prey to death in its coils.

Medusa

An ancient Greek myth tells of Medusa, a monster with snakes for hair. Anyone who looked at her was turned to stone. Perseus managed to avoid this fate by using his polished shield to look only at the monster's reflection. He cut off Medusa's head and carried it home, dripping with blood. As each drop touched the earth, it turned into a snake.

Eye has no eyelid

Forked tongue

Shapes and Sizes

Can you imagine a snake as tall as a three-storey house? The reticulated python is this big. The biggest snakes' bodies measure nearly 1m/39in round. Other snakes are as thin as a pencil and small enough to fit into the palm of your hand. Snakes also have different shapes to suit their environments. Sea snakes, for example, have flat bodies and tails like oars to help them push against the water and move forward.

▼ THICK AND THIN

Vipers mostly have thick bodies with much thinner, short tails. The bags of poison on either side of a viper's head take up a lot of space, so the head is quite large.

Rhinoceros viper
(Bitis nasicornis)

◄ LONG AND THIN

A tree snake's long, thin shape helps it slide along leaves and branches. Even its head is long, pointed and very light so that it does not weigh the snake down.

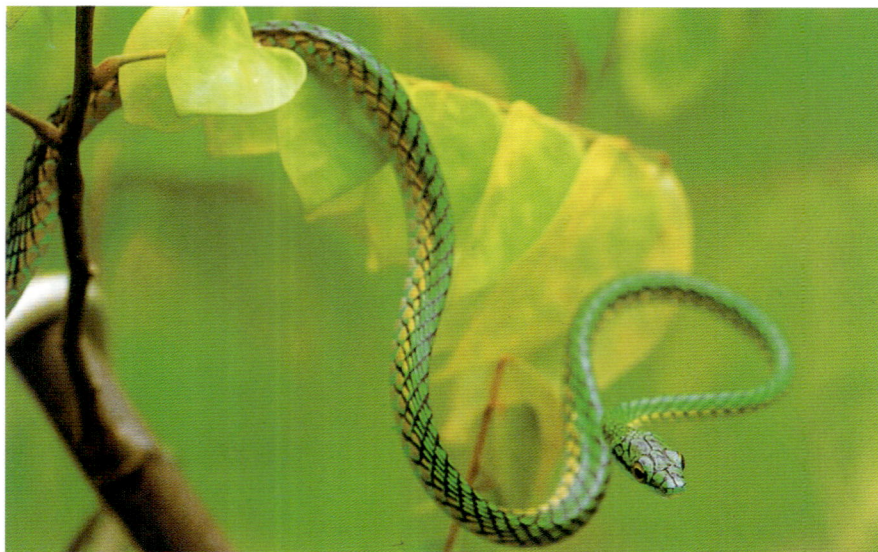

▶ BEING BIG

This picture shows the head of a red-tailed boa at its actual size. The head measures about 15cm/6in. The red-tailed boa usually grows to an overall length of about 3.5m/11½ft. The longest snake in the world is the reticulated python, which can grow up to 10m/33ft. Other giant snakes include the anaconda, other boas and the pythons.

Did you know? *The blind snake, Leptotyphlops bilineata, is the shortest snake in the world at only 10.8cm/4¼in long.*

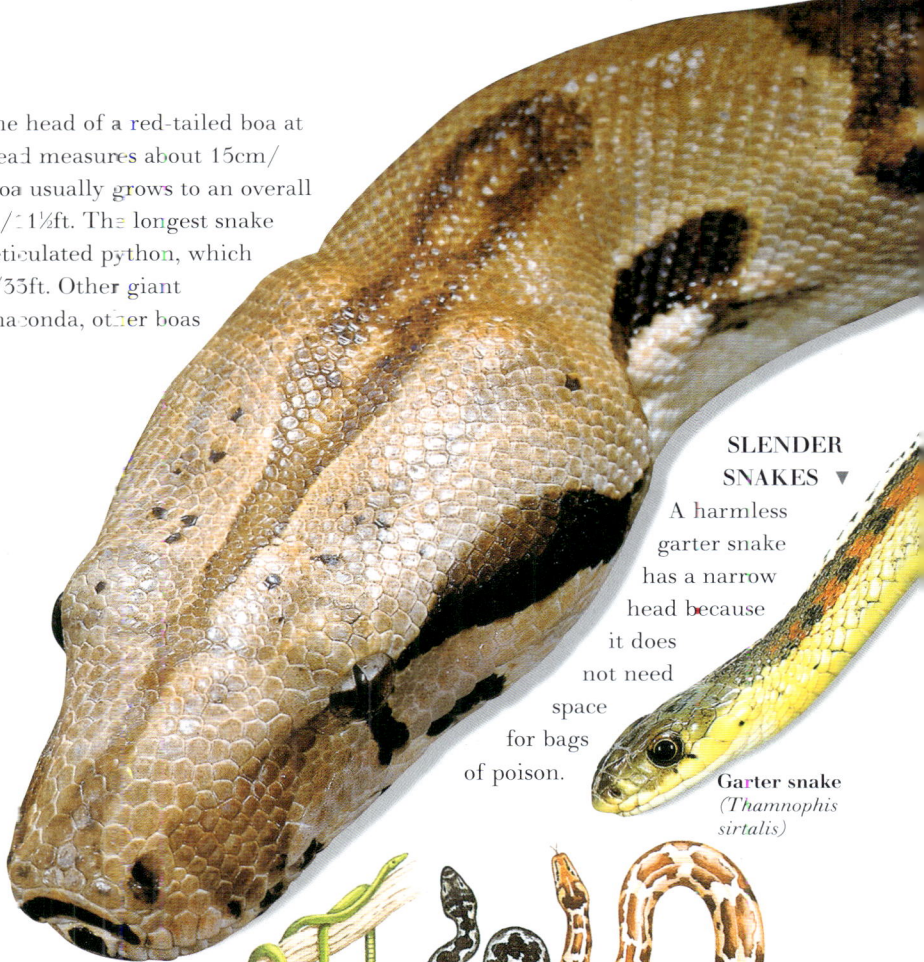

SLENDER SNAKES ▼

A harmless garter snake has a narrow head because it does not need space for bags of poison.

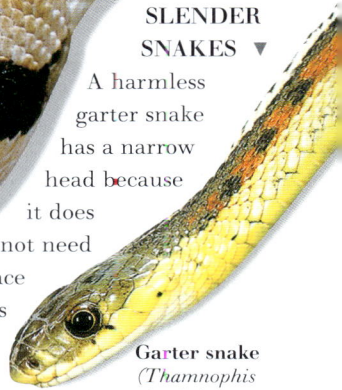

Garter snake
(Thamnophis sirtalis)

Red-tailed boa

Tree snake's long, thin body and pointed head

Burrowing snake's small, thin body

Viper's short, thick body

Python's large, round body

▲ SMALLEST SNAKE

The world's smallest snakes are the blind snakes and the thread snakes. They are less than 40cm/16in long.

▲ SNAKE SHAPES

Snakes have four general body shapes and lengths.

Egg-eating snake
(*Dasypeltis fasciata*)

◄ **STRETCHY STOMACH**
The throat and gut of the egg-eating snake are so elastic that its thin body can stretch enough to swallow a whole egg. Muscles in the throat and first part of the gut help force food down into the stomach.

How Snakes Work

A snake has a stretched-out inside to match its long, thin outside. The backbone extends along the whole body with hundreds of ribs joined to it. There is not much room for organs such as the heart, lungs, kidneys and liver, so these organs are thin shapes to fit inside the snake's body. Many snakes have only one lung. The stomach and gut are stretchy so that they can hold large meals. When a snake swallows big prey, it pushes the opening of the windpipe up from the floor of the mouth in order to keep breathing. Snakes are cold-blooded, which means that their body temperature is the same as their surroundings.

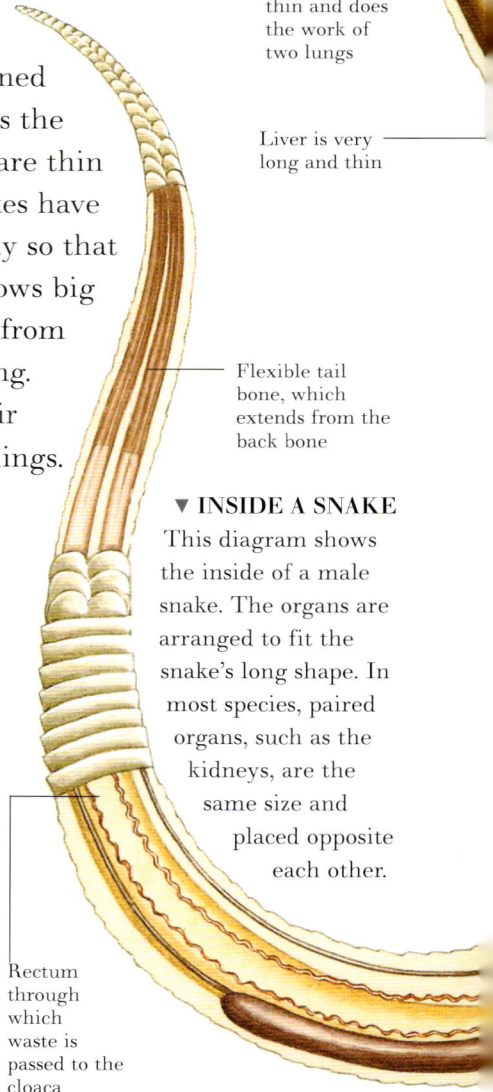

Right lung is very long and thin and does the work of two lungs

Liver is very long and thin

Flexible tail bone, which extends from the back bone

▼ **INSIDE A SNAKE**
This diagram shows the inside of a male snake. The organs are arranged to fit the snake's long shape. In most species, paired organs, such as the kidneys, are the same size and placed opposite each other.

▲ **COLD-BLOODED CREATURE**
Like all snakes, the banded rattlesnake is cold-blooded.

Rectum through which waste is passed to the cloaca

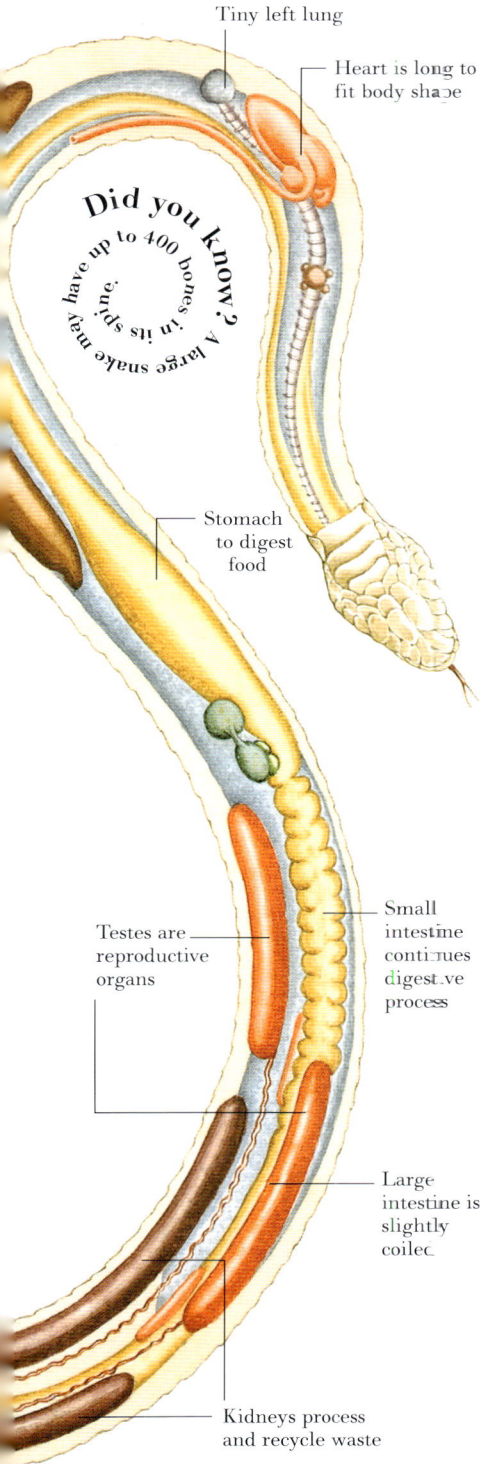

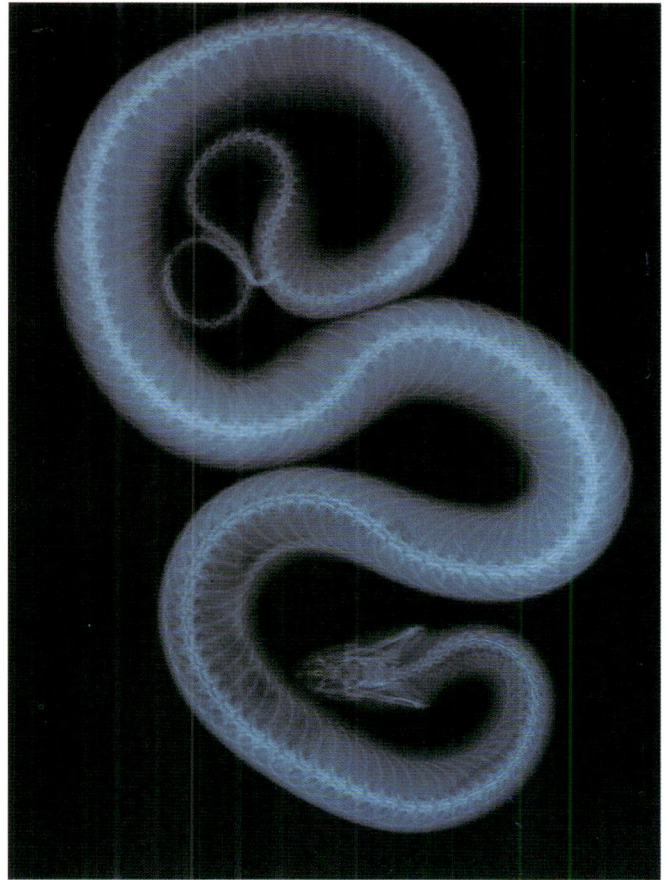

Tiny left lung

Heart is long to
fit body shape

Stomach
to digest
food

Testes are
reproductive
organs

Small
intestine
continues
digestive
process

Large
intestine is
slightly
coiled

Kidneys process
and recycle waste

▲ **SNAKE BONES**

This X-ray of a grass snake shows the delicate bones that
make up its skeleton. There are no arm, leg, shoulder or hip
bones. The snake's ribs do not extend into the tail.

◄ **SKELETON**

A snake's skeleton
is made up of a
skull and a
backbone with
ribs arching out
from it. The free
ends of the ribs
are linked
by muscles.

73

A Scaly Skin

▼ HORNED SNAKE
As its name suggests, the European nose-horned viper has a strange horn on its nose. The horn is made up of small scales that lie over a bony or fleshy lump sticking out at the end of the nose.

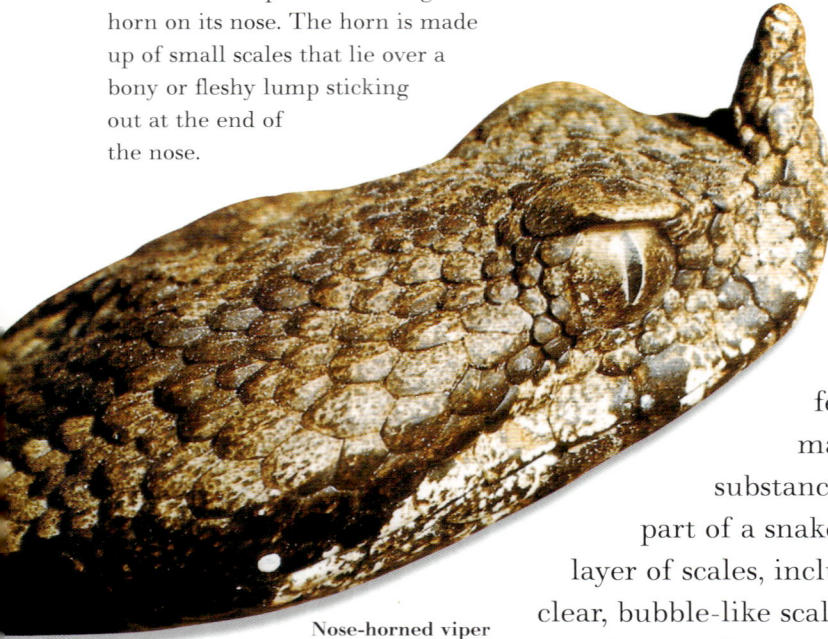

A snake's scales are extra-thick pieces of skin. Like a suit of armour, the scales protect the snake from knocks and scrapes as it moves. They also allow the skin to stretch when the snake moves or feeds. Scales are usually made of a horny substance, called keratin. Every part of a snake's body is covered by a layer of scales, including the eyes. The clear, bubble-like scale that protects each eye is called a brille or spectacle.

Nose-horned viper
(Vipera ammodytes)

▼ SCUTES
Most snakes have a row of broad scales, called scutes, underneath their bodies. The scutes go across a snake's body from side to side, and end where the tail starts. Scutes help snakes to grip the ground.

Corn snake's scutes

▼ WARNING RATTLE
The rattlesnake has a number of hollow tail-tips that make a buzzing sound when shaken. The snake uses this sound to warn enemies. When it sheds its skin, a section at the end of the tail is left, adding another piece to the rattle.

Rattlesnake's rattle

▶ SKIN SCALES

The scales of a snake grow out of the top layer of
the skin, called the epidermis. There are different kinds
of scales. Keeled scales may help snakes to grip surfaces, or
break up a snake's outline for camouflage. Smooth scales
make it easier for the snake to squeeze through tight spaces.

Corn snake's
scales

*Look closely at the
rough scales of the
puff adder (left) and
you will see a raised
ridge, or keel,
sticking up in the
middle of each one.*

*The wart snake
(right) uses its scales
to grip its food. Its
rough scales help the
snake to keep a firm
hold on slippery fish
until it can swallow
them. The snake's
scales do not overlap.*

*The green scales and
stretched blue skin
(left) belong to a
boa. These smooth
scales help the boa to
slide over leafy
branches. Burrowing
snakes have smooth
scales so that they
can slip through soil.*

Eternal Youth

*A poem written in the Middle East about
3,700 years ago tells a story about why
snakes can shed their skins. The hero of
the poem is Gilgamesh (shown here
holding a captured lion).
He finds a
magic plant
that will make a
person young
again. While he
is washing at a
pool, a snake
eats the plant.
Since then,
snakes have
been able to
shed their skins
and become
young again.
But people have
never found the
plant – which
is why they
always grow
old and die.*

Focus on New Skin

About six times a year, an adult snake wriggles out of its old, tight skin to reveal a new, shiny skin underneath. Snakes shed their worn-out skin and scales in one piece. This process is called moulting (molting) or sloughing. Snakes moult only when a new layer of skin and scales has grown underneath the old skin.

2 The paper-thin layer of outer skin and scales first starts to peel away around the mouth. The snake rubs its jaws and chin against rocks or rough bark, and crawls through plants. This helps to push off the loose layer of skin.

Did you know? A baby snake may shed its skin when it is only a few days old.

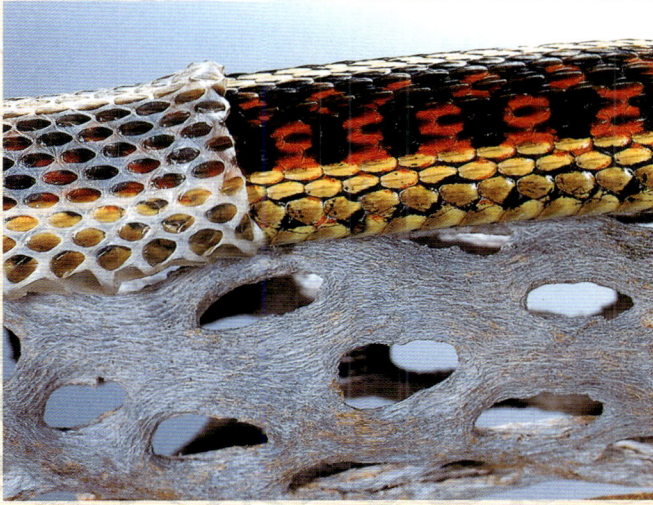

3 The outer layer of skin gradually peels back from the head over the rest of the body. The snake slides out of its old skin, which comes off inside-out. It is rather like taking hold of a long sock at the top and peeling it down over your leg and foot!

Did you know? Female snakes often shed their skin just before giving birth.

4 A snake usually takes several hours to shed its whole skin. The old skin is moist and supple soon after shedding, but gradually dries out to become crinkly and rather brittle. The shed skin is a copy of the snake's scale pattern. It is very delicate, and if you hold it up to the light, it is almost see-through.

5 A shed skin is longer than the snake itself. This is because the skin stretches as the snake wriggles free.

Snakes on the Move

For animals without legs, snakes move around very well. They can glide over or under the ground, climb trees and swim through water. A few snakes can even parachute through the air. Snakes are not speedy – most move at about 3kph/1¾mph. Their bendy backbones give them a wavy movement. They push themselves along using muscles joined to their ribs. The scales on their skin also grip surfaces to help with movement.

Did you know? A person can walk faster than a snake can move.

corn snake
(Elaphe guttata)

▶ S-SHAPED MOVER

Most snakes move in an S-shaped path, pushing the side curves of their bodies backwards against the surface they are travelling on or through. The muscular waves of the snake's body hit surrounding objects and the whole body is pushed forward from there.

▲ SWIMMING SNAKE

The banded sea snake's stripes stand out as it glides through the water. Snakes swim using S-shaped movements. A sea snake's tail is flattened from side to side to give it extra power, like the oar on a row boat.

▼ CONCERTINA SNAKE

The green whip snake moves with an action rather like a concertina. The concertina is played by squeezing it in and out.

► **SIDEWINDING**

The way snakes that live on loose sand move along is called sidewinding. The snake anchors its head and tail in the sand and throws the middle part of its body sideways.

Did you know? The fastest land snake is the black mamba, moving at up to 11kph/6¾ mph.

▼ **HOW SNAKES MOVE**

Most land snakes move in four different ways, depending on the type of terrain they are crossing and the type of snake.

1 S-shaped movement: the snake wriggles from side to side.

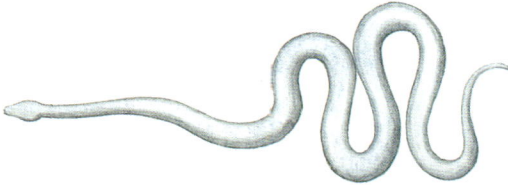

2 Concertina movement: the snake pulls one half of its body along first, then the other half.

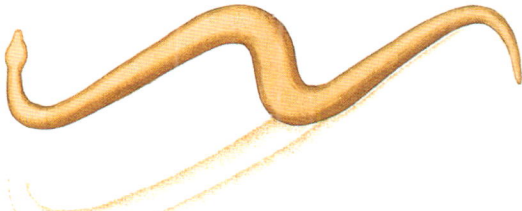

3 Sidewinding movement: the snake throws the middle part of its body forward, keeping the head and tail on the ground.

4 Caterpillar movement: the snake uses its belly scutes to pull itself along in a straight line.

▲ EYESIGHT
Snakes have no eyelids to cover their eyes. The snakes with the best eyesight are tree snakes, such as this green mamba, and day hunters.

Snake Senses

To find prey and avoid enemies, snakes rely more on their senses of smell, taste and touch than on sight and hearing. Snakes have no ears, but they do have one earbone joined at the jaw. The lower jaw picks up sound vibrations travelling through the ground. As well as ordinary senses, snakes also have some special ones. They are one of the few animals that taste and smell with their tongues.

▲ NIGHT HUNTER
The horned viper's eyes open wide at night (*above*). During the day, its pupils close to narrow slits (*below*).

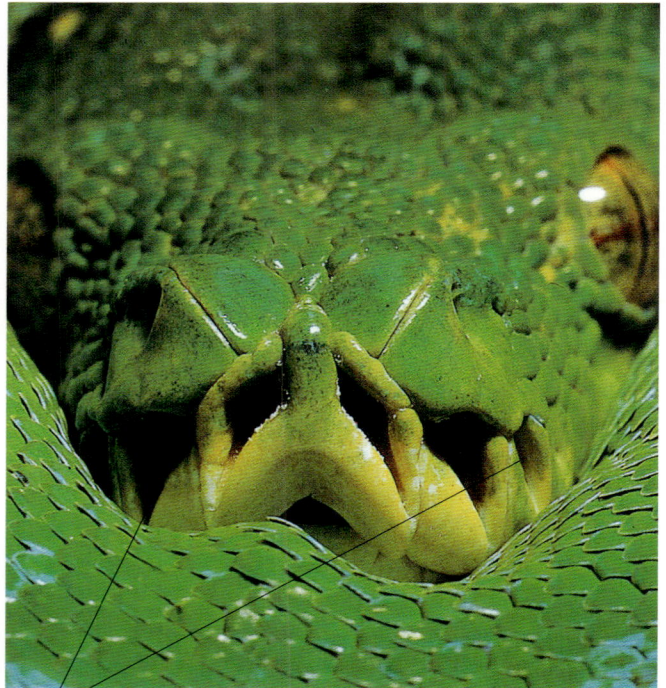

Heat pits

▲ SENSING HEAT
The green tree python senses heat given off by its prey through pits on the sides of its face.

◄ **THE FORKED TONGUE**

When a snake investigates its surroundings, it flicks its tongue to taste the air. The forked tongue picks up tiny chemical particles of scent.

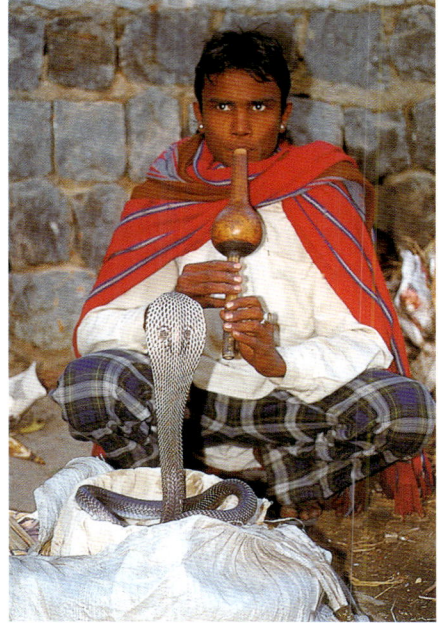

▲ **HEARING**

As it has no ears, the cobra cannot hear the music played by the snake charmer. It follows the movements of the pipe, which resemble a snake, and rises up as it prepares to defend itself.

► **JACOBSON'S ORGAN**

As a snake draws its tongue back into its mouth, it presses the forked tip into the two openings of the Jacobson's organ. This organ is in the roof of the mouth and it analyses tastes and smells.

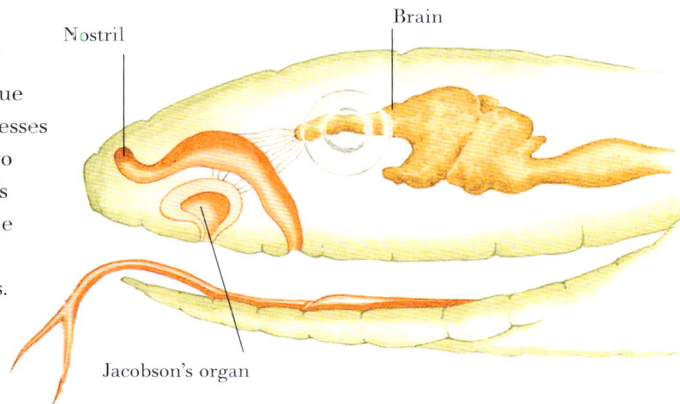

Nostril

Brain

Jacobson's organ

81

Food and Hunting

Snakes eat different foods and hunt in different ways depending on their size, their species and where they live. Some snakes eat a wide variety of food, while others have a more specialized diet. A snake has to make the most of each meal because it moves fairly slowly and does not get the chance to catch prey very often. A snake's body works at a slow rate, so it can go for several months without eating.

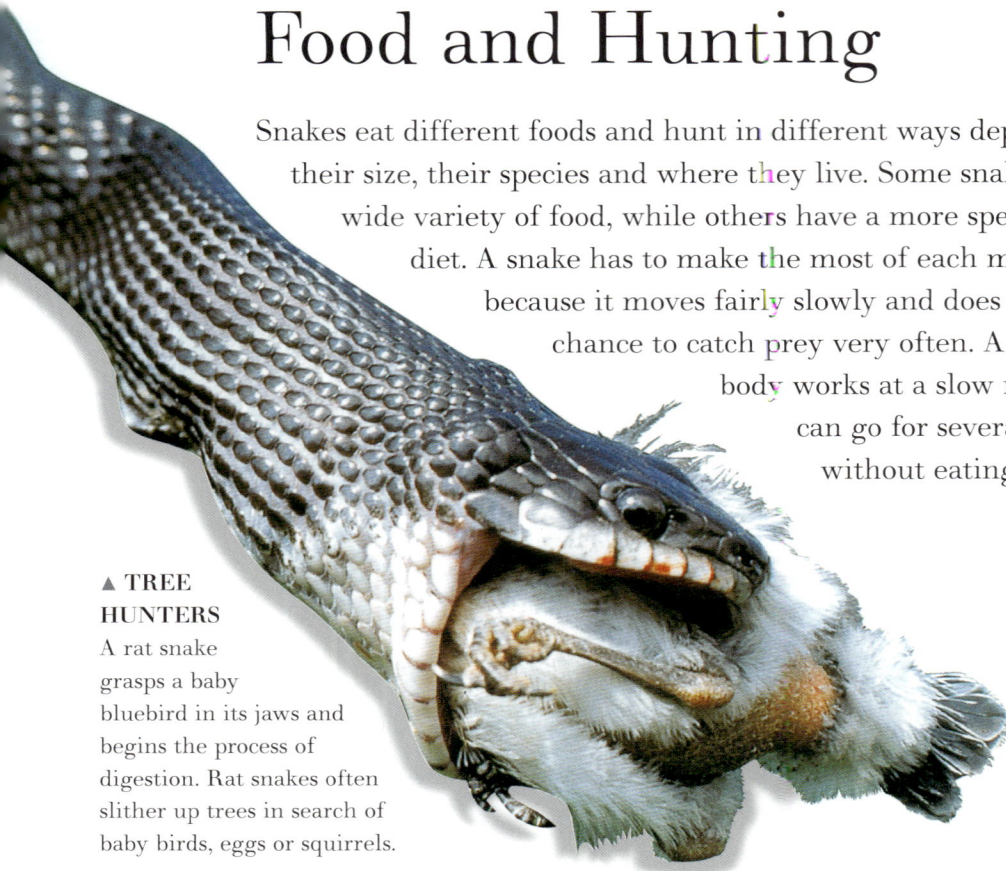

▲ TREE HUNTERS
A rat snake grasps a baby bluebird in its jaws and begins the process of digestion. Rat snakes often slither up trees in search of baby birds, eggs or squirrels.

Rat snake
(Elaphe)

▼ TRICKY LURE
The Australasian death adder's colourful tail tip looks like a worm. The adder wriggles the "worm" to lure lizards, birds and small mammals to come within its range.

▲ FISHY FOOD
The tentacled snake lives on fish. It probably hides among plants in the water and grabs fish as they swim past.

◄ EGG-EATERS

The African egg-eater snake checks an egg with its tongue to make sure it is fresh. Then it swallows the egg whole. It uses the pointed ends of the bones in its backbone to crack the eggshell. It eats the egg and coughs up the crushed shell.

► SURPRISE ATTACK

Lunch for this gaboon viper is a mouse. The gaboon viper hides among dry leaves on the forest floor. Its colouring and markings make it very difficult to spot. It waits for a small animal to pass by, then grabs hold of its prey in a surprise attack. Many other snakes that hunt by day also ambush their prey.

Did you know? Sometimes a snake coughs up its prey – alive!

Smooth snake
(Coronella austriaca)

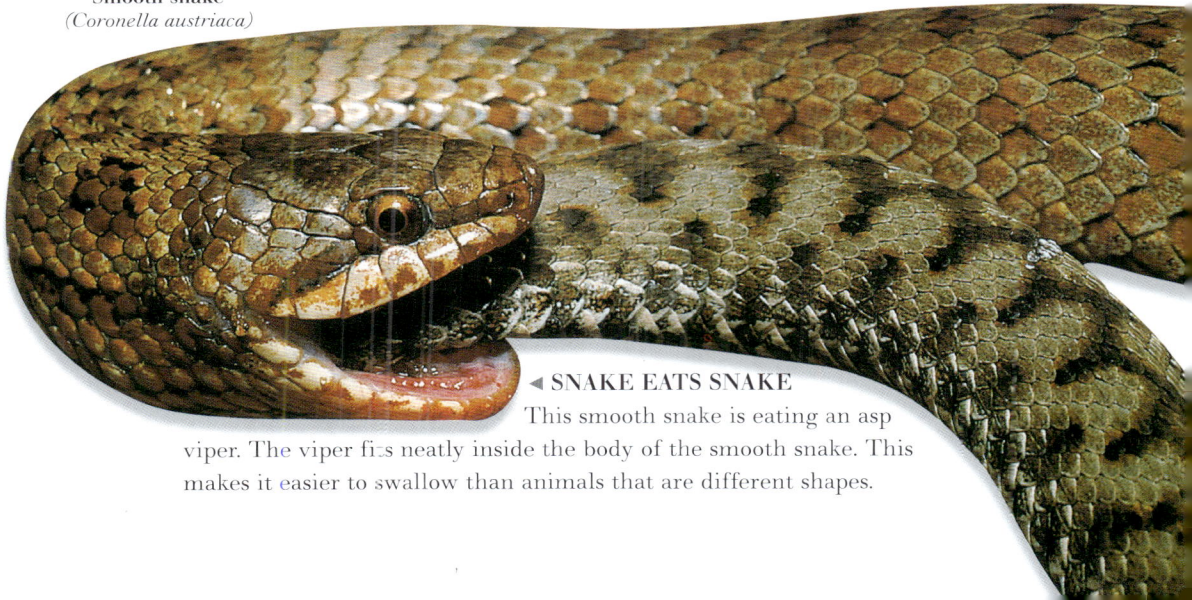

◄ SNAKE EATS SNAKE

This smooth snake is eating an asp viper. The viper fits neatly inside the body of the smooth snake. This makes it easier to swallow than animals that are different shapes.

Teeth and Jaws

Most snakes have short, sharp teeth that are good for gripping and holding prey, but not for chewing it into smaller pieces. The teeth are not very strong and often get broken, so they are continually being replaced. Poisonous snakes also have some larger teeth called fangs. When the snake bites, poison flows down the fangs to paralyse the prey and break down its body. All snakes swallow their prey head-first and whole.

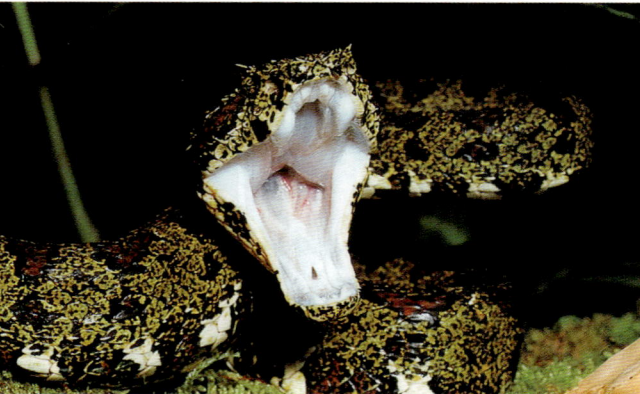

▼ **BACK FANGS**

A few poisonous snakes have fangs at the back of their mouths. This African boomslang is digging its fangs hard into a chameleon's flesh to get enough poison inside.

▲ **OPEN WIDE**

An eyelash viper opens its mouth as wide as possible to scare an enemy. Its fangs are folded back against the roof of the mouth. When it attacks, the fangs swing forwards.

Viper skull

Movable fangs

▲ **FOLDING FANGS**

Vipers and elapid snakes have fangs at the front of the mouth. A viper's long fangs can fold back. When it strikes, the fangs swing forward to stick out in front of the mouth.

84

Upper jaw

Hinge

Lower jaw

Teeth

Python skull

▲ STRETCHY JAWS

When a snake eats, a hinge at the back of the lower jaw lets the jaw swing wide, like a gate. The lower jaw is in two halves connected by a stretchy ligament, so the jaw can stretch sideways, and the two sides of the jaw can move separately. One side holds the prey, while the other side slides forward to get a new grip.

▲ SIMPLE TEETH

A python is not a poisonous snake, so it does not have fangs. The teeth curve backwards to help the python keep hold of its prey. A snake's teeth are attached to the inner edges of the jawbones rather than on top of them.

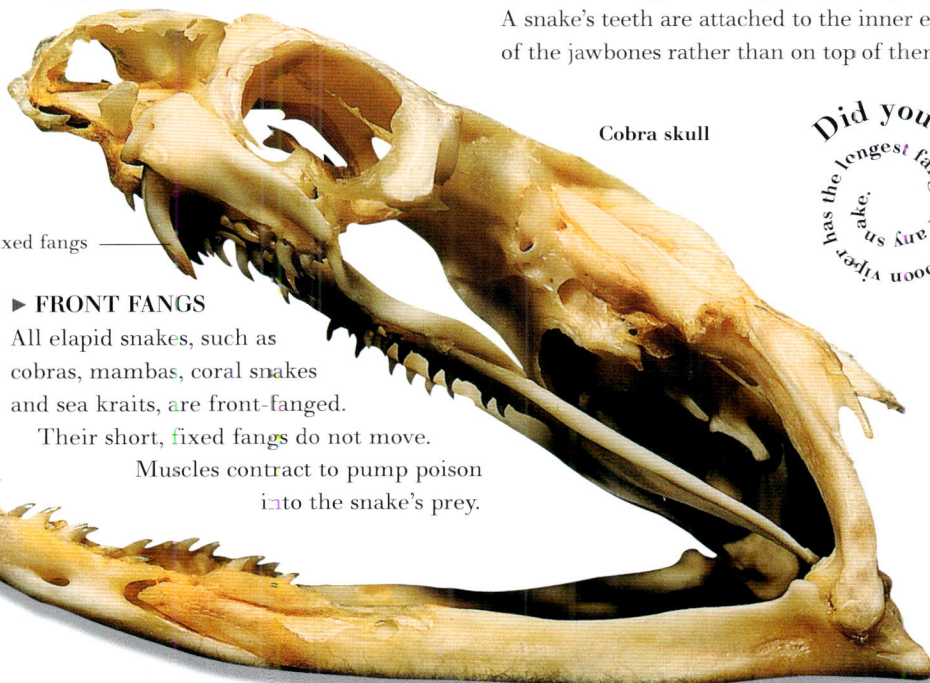

Cobra skull

Did you know? The gaboon viper has the longest fangs of any snake.

Fixed fangs

▶ FRONT FANGS

All elapid snakes, such as cobras, mambas, coral snakes and sea kraits, are front-fanged. Their short, fixed fangs do not move. Muscles contract to pump poison into the snake's prey.

Stranglers and Poisoners

Most snakes kill their prey before eating it. Snakes kill by using poison or by squeezing their prey to death. Snakes that squeeze, called constrictors, stop their prey from breathing. Victims die from suffocation or shock. To swallow living or dead prey, a snake opens its jaws wide. Lots of slimy saliva helps the meal to slide down. After eating, a snake yawns widely to put its jaws back into place. Digestion can take several days, or even weeks.

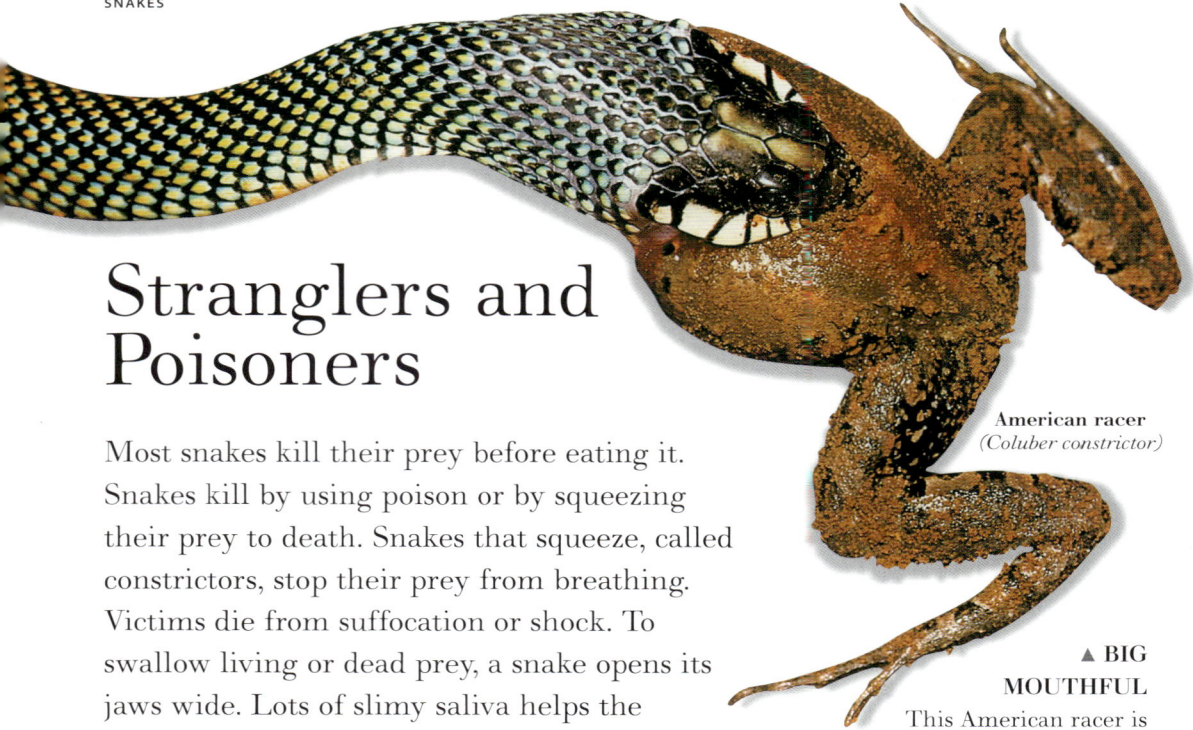

American racer
(Coluber constrictor)

▲ BIG MOUTHFUL
This American racer is trying to swallow a living frog. The frog has puffed up its body with air to make it more difficult for the snake to swallow.

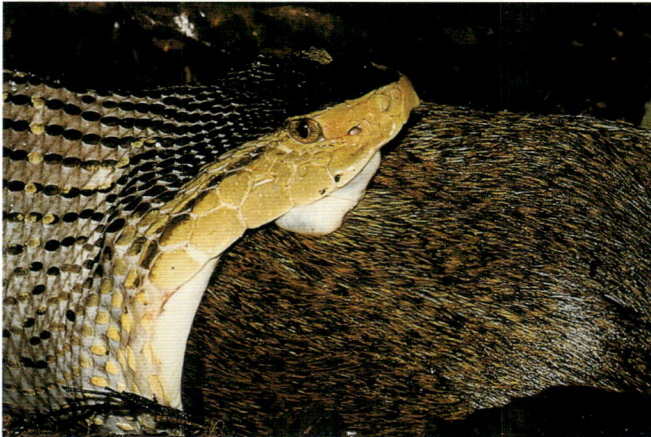

▲ AT FULL STRETCH
This fer-de-lance snake is at full stretch to swallow its huge meal. It is a large pit viper that kills with poison.

▲ SWALLOWING A MEAL
The copperhead, a poisonous snake from North America, holds on to a dead mouse.

Spotted python
(Liasis maculosus)

▲ KILLING TIME

A crocodile is slowly squeezed to death by a
rock python. The time it takes for a
constricting snake to kill its prey depends
on the size of the prey and how strong it is.

Did you know? King cobras sometimes kill Indian elephants by biting them on the trunk.

► COILED KILLER

The spotted python
sinks its teeth into its
victim. It throws coils
around the victim's body,
and tightens its grip until
the animal cannot breathe.

▼ BREATHING TUBE

An African python shows its breathing
tube. As the snake eats, the windpipe
moves to the front of the mouth so
that air can get to and from the lungs.

▲ HEAD-FIRST

A whiptail wallaby's legs disappear inside a carpet python's body.
Snakes usually try to swallow their prey head-first so that
legs, wings or scales fold back. This helps the victim to
slide into the snake's stomach more easily.

1 Rat snakes feed on rats, mice, voles, lizards birds and eggs. Many of them hunt at night. They are good climbers and can even go up trees with smooth bark and no branches. Rat snakes find their prey by following a scent trail or waiting to ambush an animal.

Focus on Lunch

This rat snake is using its strong coils to kill a vole. Rodents, such as voles and rats, are a rat snake's favourite food. With the vole held tightly in its teeth, the snake coils around its body. It squeezes hard to stop the vole breathing. When the vole is dead, the rat snake swallows its meal head-first.

2 When the rat snake is near enough to its prey, it strikes quickly. Its sharp teeth sink into the victim's body to stop it running or flying away. The snake then loops its coils around the victim as fast as possible, before the animal can bite or scratch to defend itself.

3 Each time the vole breathes out, the rat snake squeezes harder around its rib cage to stop the vole breathing in again. Breathing becomes more difficult and soon the victim dies from suffocation.

4 Once the victim is dead, the rat snake loosens its coils and begins the process of swallowing. It unhinges its jaws and "walks" its mouth over its meal. The loose lower jaw stretches sideways to fit around the shape of the dead prey.

5 The rat snake swallows its meal head-first. As the vole moves down the snake's throat, its legs fold back against the sides of its body. The way the fur lies makes the vole easier to swallow. The snake's skin stretches as the meal moves down its body.

6 As the vole moves further down inside the snake's body, the skin stretches more. The ribs move apart at the front to make space for the vole's body. The snake pushes its windpipe to the front of its mouth, so that it can use it like a snorkel for breathing. It may take only one or two gulps for a snake to swallow a small animal whole.

Poisonous Snakes

Only about 700 species of snake are poisonous. Snake poison, called venom, is useful for snakes because it allows them to kill without having to fight a long battle against their prey. Some snake venom works on the prey's body, softening it and making it easier to digest. There are two main kinds of venom. One type attacks the blood and muscles. The other attacks the nervous system, stopping the heart and lungs from working.

Spitting cobra
(Hemachatus haemachatus)

▲ POISONOUS BITE

A copperhead gets ready to strike. Poisonous snakes use their sharp fangs to inject a lethal cocktail of chemicals into their prey. The death of victims often occurs in seconds or minutes, depending on the size of prey and where it was bitten.

▼ WARNING COLOURS

The colourful stripes of coral snakes warn predators that they are very poisonous. There are more than 50 species of coral snake, all with similar patterns, but predators remember the basic pattern and avoid all coral snakes.

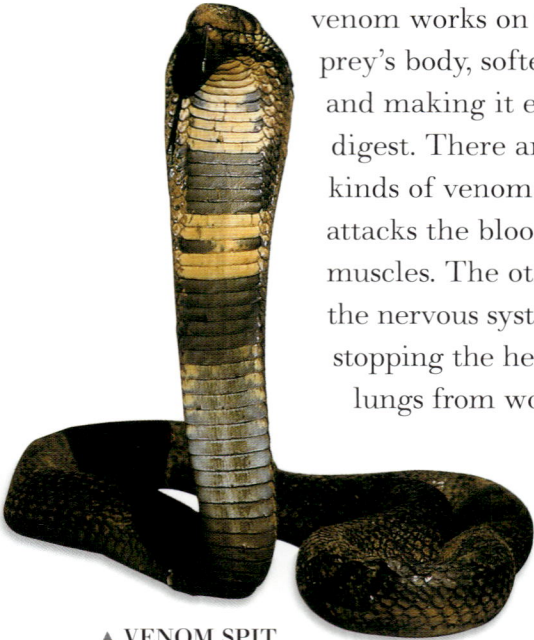

▲ VENOM SPIT

Spitting cobras have an opening in their fangs to squirt venom into an enemy's face. They aim at the eyes, and the venom can cause blindness.

Coral snake
(Micruroides euryxanthus)

Did you know? The most poisonous snake in the world is the black-headed sea snake.

▲ **FANGS FORWARD**

The copperhead is a viper, so its fangs swing down from the roof of the mouth, ready to stab its prey. The muscles around the venom glands squeeze poison through the fangs.

Copperhead
(*Aghistrodon contortrix*)

Bible Snake

At the beginning of the Bible, a snake is the cause of problems in the Garden of Eden. God told Adam and Eve never to eat fruit from the tree of knowledge of good and evil. However, the snake persuaded Eve to eat the fruit. It told Eve that the fruit would make her as clever as God. Eve gave some fruit to Adam too. As a punishment, Adam and Eve had to leave the Garden of Eden and lose the gift of eternal life.

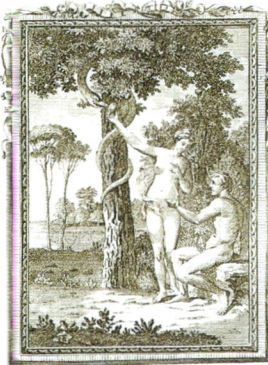

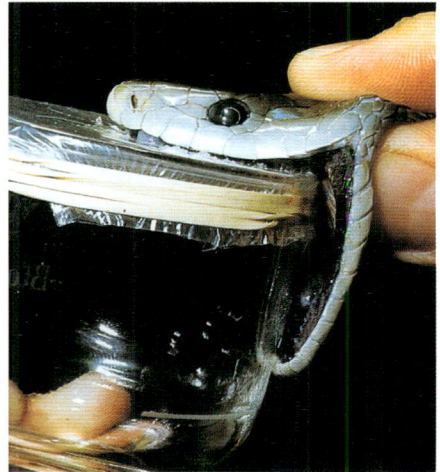

▲ **MILKING VENOM**
Venom is collected from a black mamba.

91

Green bush viper
(Atheris squamigera)

Focus on Vipers

Vipers are the most efficient poisonous snakes of all. Their long fangs can inject venom deep into a victim. The venom acts mainly on the blood and muscles of the prey. Vipers usually have short, thick bodies and triangular heads covered with small, ridged scales. There are two main groups of vipers. Pit vipers have large heat pits on the face, and other vipers do not.

TREE VIPER

The green bush viper lives in tropical forests, mainly in the trees. Its colouring means that it is well camouflaged against the green leaves. It lies in wait for its prey and then kills it with a quick bite. Once the prey has been caught, the snake must hold tight to stop it falling out of the tree.

BALLOON SNAKE

When threatened, the puff adder swells up like a long balloon. It does this by taking a lot of air into its lungs. Being larger makes it look even more dangerous. Puff adders also hiss loudly.

Puff adder
(Bitis arietans)

rattlesnake
(Crotalus)

QUICK JAB

This rattlesnake is exploring its surroundings with its forked tongue. When the rattlesnake strikes at its prey, the hinged fangs swing forward and lock into place. The viper gives its prey a quick injection of venom, then lets go. The prey soon dies, so there is no need for the snake to hold on to it.

HEAT DETECTORS

This Sumatran pit viper has a large heat pit on each side of its head, between the nostril and the eye. The heat pit is larger than the nostril. It can detect the heat given off by warm-blooded prey. By turning its head from side to side, a pit viper can work out the direction of its prey.

Sumatran pit viper
(Trimeresurus sumatranus)

SLOW SNAKE

Asp vipers are slow-moving snakes. They are active both by day and by night. Their main sources of food are mice, lizards and baby birds.

93

Defence

The predators of snakes include birds of prey, foxes, raccoons, mongooses, baboons, crocodiles, frogs and even other snakes. If they are in danger, snakes usually prefer to hide or escape. Many come out to hunt at night, when it is more difficult for predators to catch them. If they cannot escape, snakes often make themselves look big and fierce, hiss loudly or strike at their enemies. Some pretend to be dead. Giving off a horrible smell is another good way of getting rid of an enemy.

▼ **SMELLY SNAKE**

The cottonmouth is named after the white colour of the inside of its mouth, which it opens to threaten enemies. If it is attacked, it can also give off a strong-smelling liquid from near the tail.

◄ **EAGLE ENEMY**

The short-toed eagle uses its powerful toes to catch snakes. It eats large snakes on the ground. It carries small snakes back to the nest to feed its chicks.

Vine snake
(Oxybelis fulgidus)

◄ **SCARY MOUTH**

Like many snakes, this vine snake opens its mouth very wide to startle predators. The inside of the mouth is a bright red colour that warns off the predator. If the predator does not go away, the snake will give a poisonous bite with the fangs at the back of the mouth.

▶ PLAYING DEAD

This grass snake knows that most predators prefer healthy, living prey. So it protects itself by pretending to be dead. It rolls on to its back, opens its mouth and keeps quite still.

Cottonmouth
(*Agkistrodon piscivorus*)

◀ DRAMATIC DISPLAY

The hognose snake is harmless, but can make itself look dangerous. It flattens its neck to make a hood. It hisses loudly and strikes towards the enemy. Then it smears itself with smelly scent.

▶ HIDDEN SNAKE

The horned viper buries itself so that it cannot be seen by its enemies.

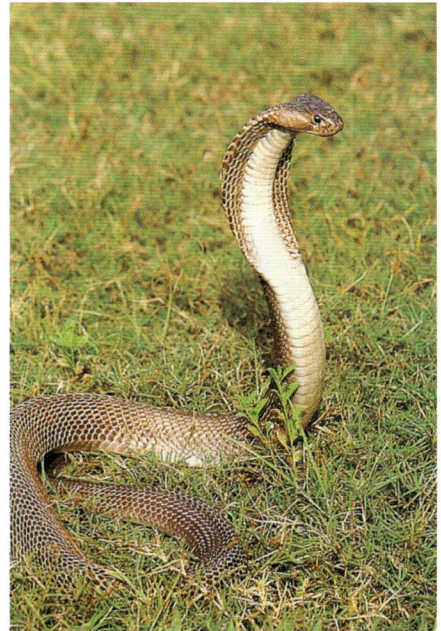

▲ LOOKING LARGER

The cobra spreads its hood wide to make itself look too big to swallow.

95

HOOD VARIETY

Like spitting cobras, the king cobra and the water cobra, this Egyptian cobra has a narrow hood. The Indian cobra and the Cape cobra of southern Africa have much wider hoods. The Egyptian cobra ranges over much of Africa and into Arabia

HOOD PATTERNS

Some cobras have eyespots on the back of their hoods to make them look more scary.

THE HOOD

The cobra's hood is made from flaps of skin supported by long ribs. Mostly, the skin rests flat against the body. But when it is alarmed, the cobra spreads its neck ribs, stretching the neck skin to form a hood.

Focus on the Cobra and its Relatives

Cobras are very poisonous snakes. Some of them can squirt deadly venom at their enemies. Cobra venom works mainly on the nervous system, causing breathing or heart problems. Cobras are members of the elapid snake family, which includes the African mambas, the coral snakes of the Americas and all the poisonous snakes of Australia.

LARGE COBRA
The king cobra is the largest venomous snake, growing to a length of 5.5m/18ft. They are the only snakes known to build a nest. The female guards her eggs and hatchlings until they leave the nest.

MIND THE MAMBA
The green mamba lives in trees. Other mambas, such as the black mamba, live mostly on the ground. Mambas are slim, long snakes that can grow up to 4m/13ft long. Their venom is very powerful and can kill a person in only ten minutes

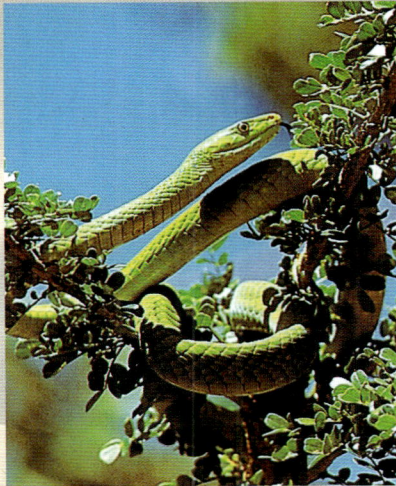

DO NOT DISTURB!
The Australian mainland tiger snake is a member of the elapid snake family. It is the world's fourth most poisonous snake. If it is disturbed, it puffs up its body, flattens its neck and hisses loudly. The diet of these snakes includes fish, frogs, birds and small mammals.

Rainbow boa
(*Epicrates cenchria*)

◄ **CHANGING COLOURS**

The rainbow boa is iridescently coloured. Light is made up of all the colours of the rainbow. When light hits the thin outer layer of the snake's scales, it splits into different colours. The colours we see depend on the type of scales and the way light bounces off them.

Colour and Camouflage

The colours of snakes come from the pigments in the scales and from the way light reflects off the scales. Dull colours help to camouflage a snake and hide it from its enemies. Bright colours startle predators or warn them that a snake is poisonous. Harmless snakes sometimes copy the warning colours of poisonous snakes. Dark colours may help snakes to absorb heat during cooler weather. Young snakes are sometimes a different colour from their parents, but no one knows why.

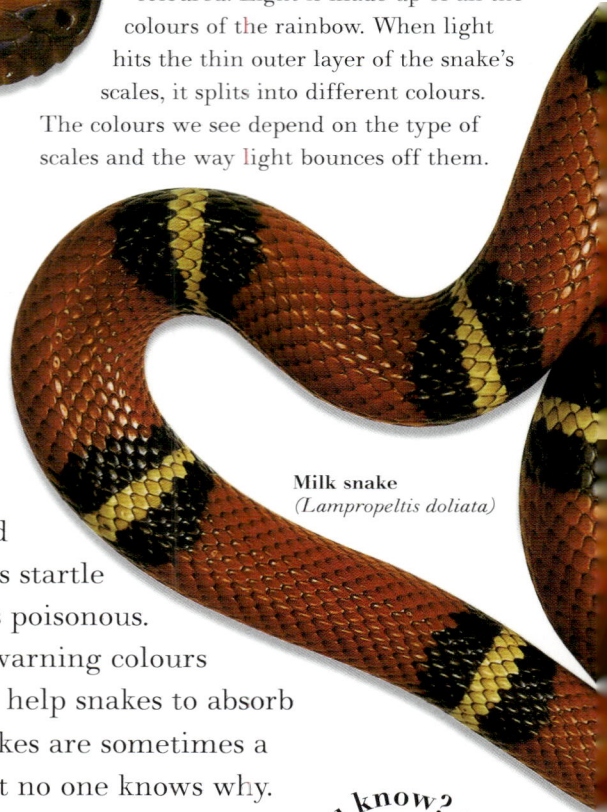

Milk snake
(*Lampropeltis doliata*)

Ring-necked snake
(*Diadophis punctatus*)

Did you know? Milk snakes always have black bands between the red and yellow – coral snakes have the red and yellow touching.

◄ **BRIGHT COLOURS**

This snake's red tail draws attention away from the most vital part of its body — the head.

◀ COLOUR COPIES

The bright red, yellow and black bands of this milk snake copy the colouring of the poisonous coral snake. The milk snake is not poisonous, but predators leave it alone — just in case. This colouring is found in milk snakes in the south-east of the United States.

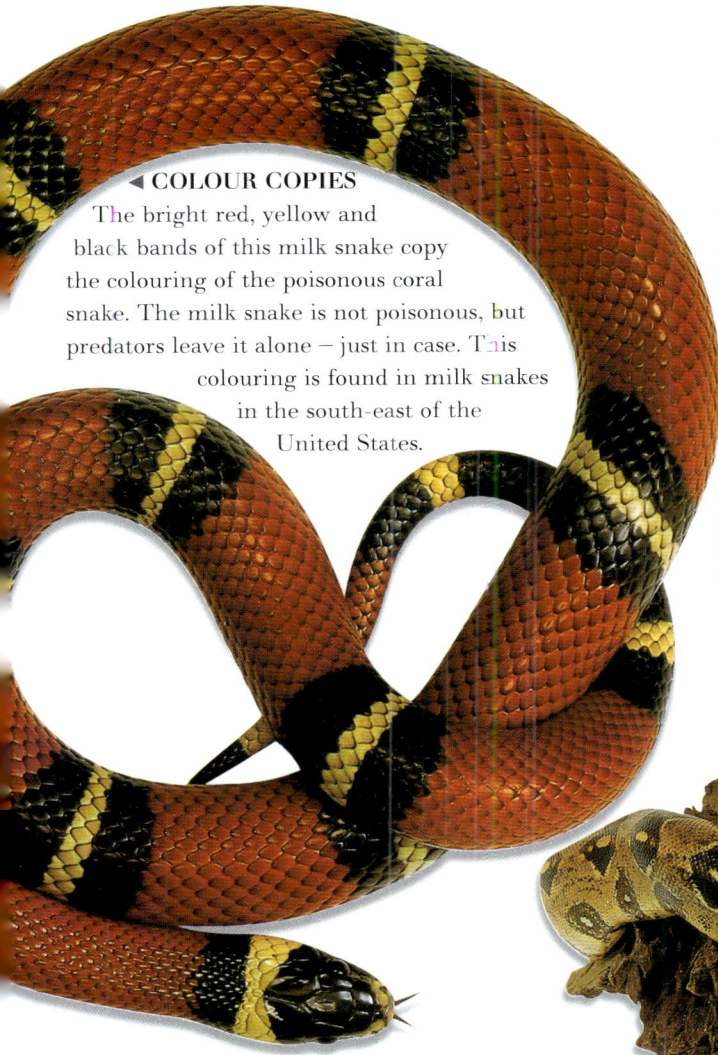

▼ NO COLOUR

White snakes, with no colour at all, are called albinos. In the wild, these snakes stand out against background colours and are usually killed by predators before they can reproduce.

▼ SNAKE MARKINGS

Many snakes are marked with colourful patches. These markings are usually caused by groups of different pigments in the scales.

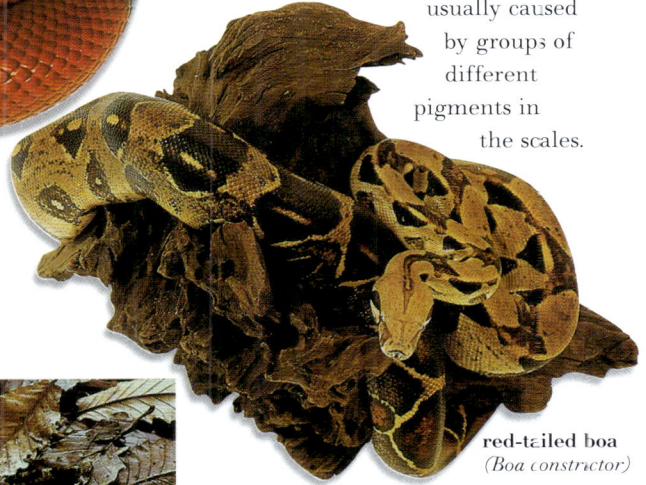

red-tailed boa
(*Boa constrictor*)

◀ CLEVER CAMOUFLAGE

Among the dead leaves of the rainforest floor, the gaboon viper becomes almost invisible. Many snakes have colours and patterns that match their surroundings.

Reproduction

Snakes do not live as families, and parents do not look after their young. Males and females come together to mate, and pairs may stay together for the breeding season. Most snakes are ready to mate when they are between two and five years old. In cooler climates, snakes usually mate in spring, so that their young have time to feed and grow before the winter starts. In tropical climates, snakes often mate before the rainy season, when there is plenty of food for their young. Male snakes find females by following their scent trails.

Flowerpot snake
(Typhlops braminus)

► FIGHTING
Male adders fight to test which one is the stronger. They rear up and face each other, then twist their necks together. Each snake tries to push the other to the ground. In the end, one of them gives up.

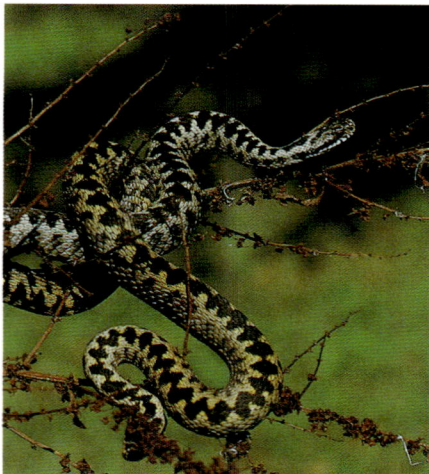

▲ NO MATE
Scientists believe that female flowerpot snakes can produce young without males. This is useful when they move to new areas, as one snake can start a new colony. However, all the young are the same, and if conditions change, the snakes cannot adapt and may die out.

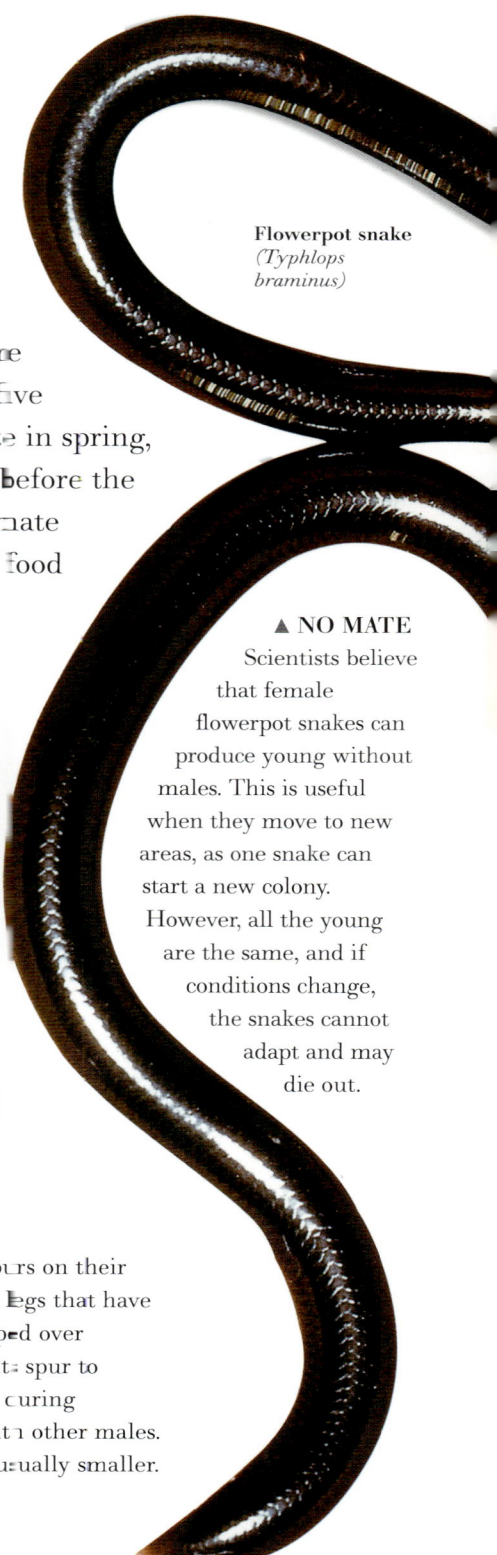

Spur

◄ SNAKE SPURS
Both boa and python males have small spurs on their bodies. These are the remains of back legs that have disappeared as snakes have developed over millions of years. A male uses its spur to scratch or tickle the female during courtship, or to fight with other males. Females' spurs are usually smaller.

▲ WRESTLING MATCH

These male Indian rat snakes are fighting to see which is the stronger. The winner stands a better chance of mating. The snakes hiss and strike out, but they seldom get hurt.

► SIMILARITIES AND DIFFERENCES

No one knows why the male and female of the snake shown here have such different head shapes. In fact, male and female snakes of the same species usually look similar because snakes rely on scent rather than sight to find a mate.

Male

(Langaha nasuta)

Female

◄ MATING

When a female anaconda is ready to mate, she lets the male coil his tail around hers. The male has to place his sperm inside the female's body to fertilize her eggs. The eggs can then develop into baby snakes.

101

Eggs

Some snakes lay eggs and some give birth to fully developed, or live young. Egg-laying snakes include cobras and pythons. A few weeks after mating, the female looks for a safe, warm, moist place to lay between six and 40 eggs. This may be under a rotting log, in sandy soil, under a rock or in a compost heap. Most snakes cover their eggs and leave them to hatch by themselves. A few snakes stay with their eggs to protect them from predators and the weather. However, once the eggs hatch, all snakes abandon their young.

▲ BEACH BIRTH
Sea kraits are the only sea snakes to lay eggs. They often do this in caves, above the water level.

▶ EGG CARE
This female python has piled up her eggs and coiled herself around them to protect them from predators. The female Indian python twitches her muscles to warm up her body. The extra heat helps the young to develop. Snake eggs need to be kept at a certain temperature to develop properly.

◀ LAYING EGGS
The Oenpellis python lays rounded eggs. The eggs of smaller snakes are usually long and thin to fit inside their smaller body. Some snakes lay long, thin eggs when they are young, but more rounded eggs when they grow larger.

Did you know? The mud snake lays over 100 eggs at a time.

▼ CHILDREN'S PYTHON MASS HATCHING

As they hatch, these children's pythons flatten their eggshells. A snake's eggshell is leathery, not brittle like the shell of a bird's egg. Birds' eggs would break into pieces if they were squashed. A snake's egg is not watertight, so it is laid in a moist place to stop it drying up.

Children's pythons (*Liasis childreni*)

▼ HIDDEN EGGS

Eggs are hidden from predators in the soil or under rocks and logs. Eggs are never completely buried, as the young need to breathe air that flows through the outer shell.

▲ HOT SPOTS

This female grass snake has laid her eggs in a warm pile of rotting plants.

103

Focus on Hatching out

About two to four months after the adults mate, the baby snakes hatch out of their eggs. Inside the egg, the baby snake feeds on the yolk, which is full of goodness. Once the snake has fully developed and the yolk has been used up, the snake is ready to hatch. All the eggs in a clutch tend to hatch at the same time. A few days later, the baby snake wriggles away to start life without any parents.

1 Eight weeks after being laid, these rat snake eggs are hatching. While they developed inside the egg, each baby rat snake fed on its yolk. A day or so before hatching, the yolk sac was drawn inside the snake's body.

2 The baby snake has become restless, twisting inside its shell. It is now fully developed and cannot get enough oxygen through its shell. A snake's egg has an almost watertight shell, but water and gases, such as oxygen, pass in and out of it through tiny holes (pores). As the baby snake prepares to hatch, it cuts a slit in the shell with a sharp egg tooth on its snout. This egg tooth will drop off a few hours after hatching.

3 After it has broken through the stretchy shell, the baby snake has a rest. It pokes its nose through the slit in the egg to breathe the air and take a first look at the strange and exciting world outside.

4 All the eggs in this clutch have hatched at the same time (a clutch is a set of eggs laid by a snake). After making the first slits in their leathery shells, the baby snakes will not crawl out straight away. They poke their heads out of their eggs to taste the air with their forked tongues. If they are disturbed, they will slide back inside the shell where they feel safe. They may stay inside the shell for a few days.

Did you know? *Some snakes lay as many as 100 eggs in one clutch.*

5 Eventually, the baby snake slithers out of the egg. It may be as much as seven times longer than the egg because it was coiled up inside.

Pope's tree viper
(Trimeresurus popeorum)

▲ TREE BIRTH

Tree snakes often give birth in the branches. The membrane around each baby snake sticks to the leaves and helps stop the baby from falling out of the branches to the ground.

▲ BIRTH PLACE

This female sand viper has chosen a quiet, remote spot to give birth to her young. Snakes usually give birth in a hidden place, where the young are safe from enemies.

► BABY BAGS

These red-tailed boas have just been born. They are still inside their see-through bags. The bags are made of a clear, thin, tough membrane, rather like the one inside the shell of a hen's egg.

Giving Birth

Some snakes give birth to fully developed or live young. Snakes that do this include boas, rattlesnakes and adders. The eggs develop inside the mother's body surrounded by see-through bags, called membranes. While the baby snake is developing inside the mother, it gets its food from the yolk of the egg. The babies are born after a labour that may last for hours. Anything from six to 50 babies are born at a time. At birth, they are still inside their membranes.

Did you know? Newborn anacondas are only 6cm/2¼in long.

► **BREAKING FREE**

This baby rainbow boa has just pushed its head through its surrounding membrane. Snakes have to break free of their baby bags on their own. Each baby has an egg tooth to cut a slit in the membrane and wriggle out. The babies usually do this a few seconds after birth.

Did you know? Baby boa constrictors are 30cm/12in long when they are born.

◄ **NEW BABY**

A red-tailed boa has broken free of its egg sac, which is in the front of the picture. The baby's colours are bright. Some newborn babies crawl off straight away, while others stay with their mother for a few days.

◄ **COLOUR CHANGE**

This vivid red baby is an emerald tree boa. As it grows up, it will turn green. Although boas and pythons are very similar snakes in some ways, one of the main differences between them is that boas give birth to live young while pythons lay eggs.

Did you know? Timber rattlesnake mothers defend their newborn babies for a few days.

emerald
tree boa
(*Epicrates
cenchria*)

Growth and Development

The size of baby snakes when they are born or when they hatch from their eggs, how much they eat and the climate around them all affect their rate of growth. In warm climates, snakes may double or triple their length in just one year. Some snakes are mature and almost fully grown after three to five years, but slow growth may continue throughout their lives. Young snakes shed their skin more often than adults because they are growing quickly. While they are growing, young snakes are easy prey for animals such as birds, raccoons, toads and rats.

▼ FAST FOOD
Like all young snakes, this Burmese python must eat as much as possible in order to grow quickly. Young snakes eat smaller prey than their parents, such as ants, earthworms and flies.

Mother European adder

▲ DEADLY BABY
This baby European adder can give a nasty bite soon after hatching. Luckily, its venom is not very strong.

Baby European adder

▲ MOTHER AND BABY
European adders give birth in summer. The young must grow fast so that they are big enough to survive winter hibernation.

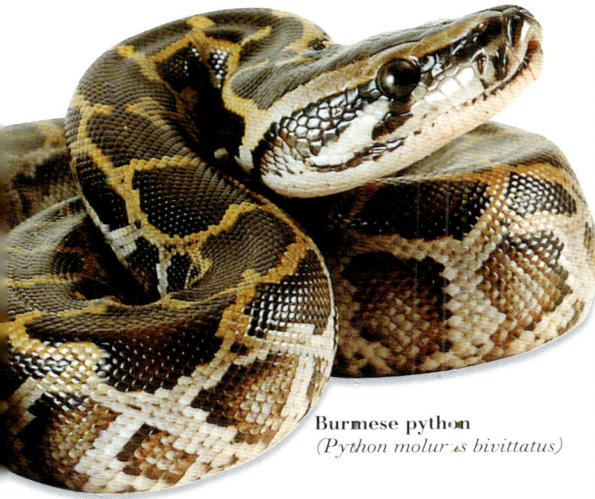

Burmese python
(Python molurus bivittatus)

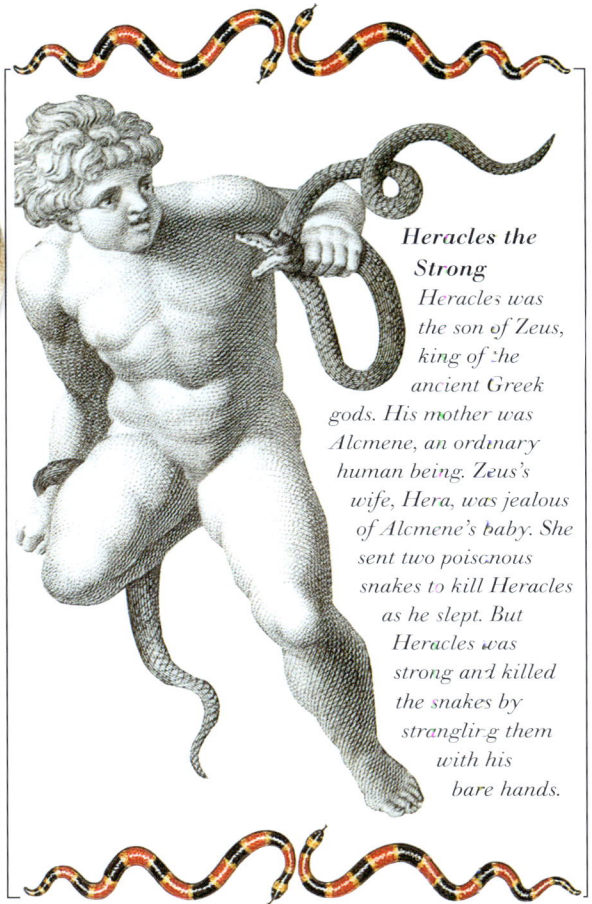

Heracles the Strong

Heracles was the son of Zeus, king of the ancient Greek gods. His mother was Alcmene, an ordinary human being. Zeus's wife, Hera, was jealous of Alcmene's baby. She sent two poisonous snakes to kill Heracles as he slept. But Heracles was strong and killed the snakes by strangling them with his bare hands.

Rattlesnake
(Crotalus)   Short rattle

▲ DIET CHANGE

Many young Amazon tree boas live on islands in the Caribbean. They start off by feeding on lizards, but as they grow, they switch to feeding on birds and mammals.

▶ RATTLE AGE

You cannot tell the age of a rattlesnake by counting the sections of its rattle because several sections may be added each year and pieces of the rattle may break off.

109

Where Snakes Live

Snakes live on every continent except Antarctica. They are most common in deserts and rainforests. They cannot survive in very cold places because they use the heat around them to make their bodies work. This is why most snakes live in warm places where the temperature is high enough for them to stay active day and night. In cooler places, snakes may spend the cold winter months asleep. This is called hibernation.

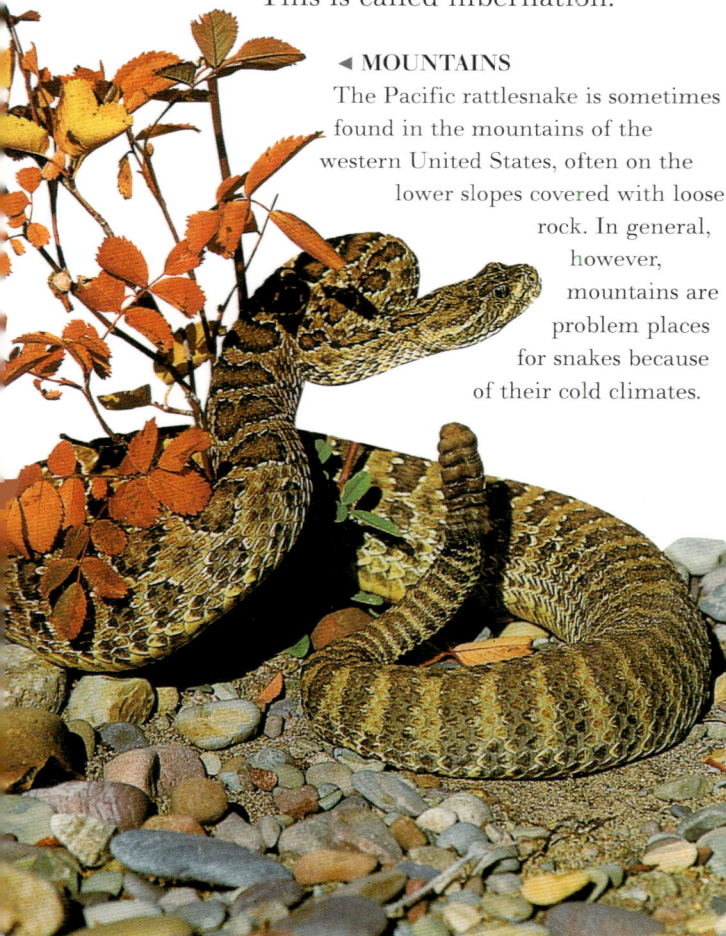

▲ GRASSLANDS
The European grass snake is one of the few snakes to live on grasslands, where there is little food or shelter.

◄ MOUNTAINS
The Pacific rattlesnake is sometimes found in the mountains of the western United States, often on the lower slopes covered with loose rock. In general, however, mountains are problem places for snakes because of their cold climates.

▲ WINTER SLEEP
Thousands of garter snakes emerge after their winter sleep.

◄ **TROPICAL RAINFORESTS**

The greatest variety of snakes lives in tropical rainforests, including this Brazilian rainbow boa. There is plenty to eat, from insects, birds and bats to frogs.

▲ **LIVING IN TREES**

The eyelash viper lives in the Central American rainforest. The climate in rainforests is warm all year round, so snakes can stay active all the time. There are also plenty of places to live – in trees, on the forest floor, in soil and in rivers.

Brazilian rainbow boa
(Epicrates cenchria)

► **BURROWERS**

Yellow-headed worm snakes live under tree bark. Many worm, or thread, snakes live underground where the soil is warm.

◄ **DESERTS**

This African puff adder lives in the Kalahari desert of southern Africa. Many snakes live in deserts because they can survive with little food and water.

111

Tree Snakes

With their long, thin, flat bodies and pointed heads, tree snakes slide easily through the branches of tropical forests. Some can even glide from tree to tree. Tree boas and pythons have ridges on their belly scales to give them extra gripping power. Many tree snakes also have long, thin tails that coil tightly around branches. Green or brown camouflage colours keep tree snakes well hidden among the leaves and branches.

▲ COLOUR AND PATTERN
This Amazon tree boa is coloured and patterned for camouflage. Many tree snakes are green or brown with patterns that break up the outline of their body shape. Some even have patterns that look like mosses and lichens.

▲ TREE TWINS
The green tree python lives in the rainforests of New Guinea. It looks similar to the emerald tree boa and behaves in a similar way, but they are not closely related.

◄ GRASPING
In a rainforest in Costa Rica, a blunt-headed tree snake has caught a lizard. It grasps its prey firmly so that it does not fall out of the tree.

Long-nosed whip snake *(Ahaetulla mycterizens)*

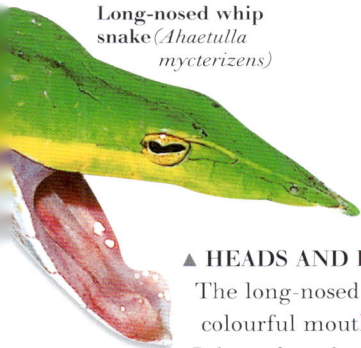

Did you know? Many snakes have long tails to grip tree trunks and branches.

▲ HEADS AND EYES

The long-nosed whip snake opens its colourful mouth to scare away a predator. It has a long head, with a pointed snout – an ideal shape for sliding through branches.

Cook's tree boa *(Boa cookii)*

▲ VIPER REFLEXES

The green eyelash viper has such speedy reflexes that it can catch birds as they fly through the trees. It has to hold on to its prey while its venom takes effect.

► BODY WEIGHT

Tree snakes have long, thin, light bodies. This helps them to stretch easily from one branch to another.

Focus on the Emerald

With their green coils looped around branches, emerald tree boas lurk among leaves in the rainforests of South America. These tree boas are good climbers, hanging head-first from branches to seize fast-moving prey in their teeth. To rest, they lie with their coils encircling a narrow branch, and their heads lying on top.

UPSIDE-DOWN MEALS

To catch a meal, emerald tree boas drape their coils over a horizontal branch and hang their heads down. Once the snake has a firm hold on its prey with its teeth, it coils around its victim. It slowly squeezes with its coils to stop the animal breathing. When the animal is dead, the emerald tree boa swallows it head-first, so that it slides down easily.

CLIMBING SKILLS

Tree boas are longer and slimmer than boas that live on the ground. This helps them to slide through the branches.

GRIPPING

The emerald tree boa's tail grips the branch. As the boa climbs, it reaches up with its front end and coils itself around a branch, then pulls up the rest of its body.

Tree Boa

COLOUR CHANGE

Young emerald tree boas are orange, pink or yellow when they are born. They gradually change to green in their first year by producing new colour pigments in their skin. No one is sure why the young are a different colour from the adults. They may live in different places from the adults and so need a different colour for effective camouflage.

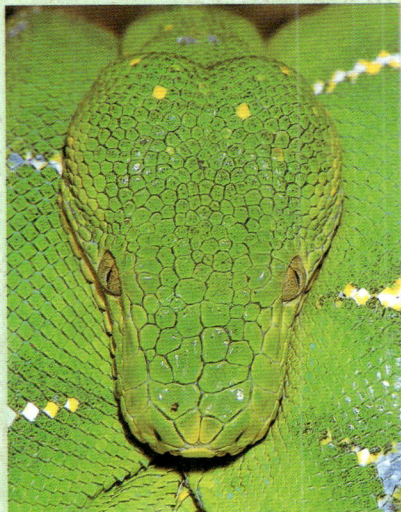

HOT LIPS

Emerald tree boas use pits on their lips to sense the heat given off by prey animals.

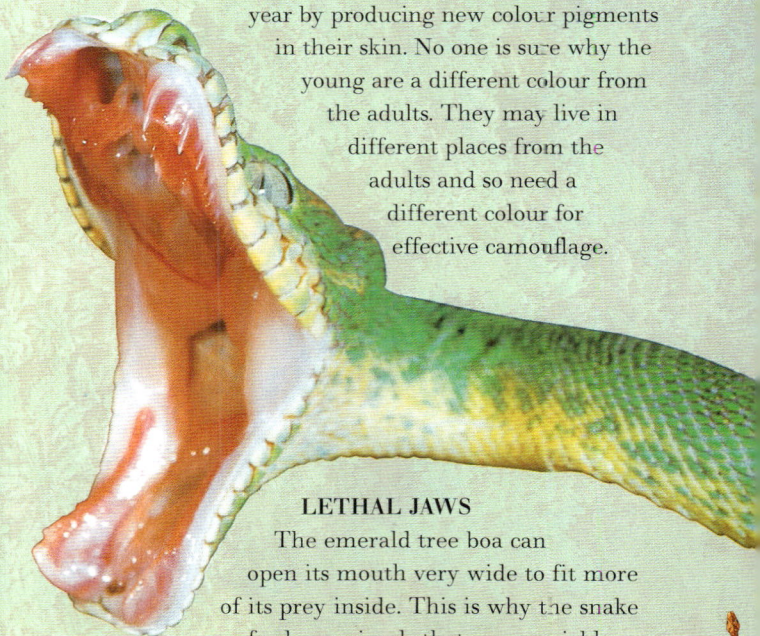

LETHAL JAWS

The emerald tree boa can open its mouth very wide to fit more of its prey inside. This is why the snake can feed on animals that move quickly, such as birds.

Desert Snakes

Deserts are full of snakes. This is partly because snakes can survive for a long time without food. They don't need energy from food to produce body heat because they get heat energy from their surroundings. It is also because their waterproof skins stop them losing too much water. Snakes push between rocks or down rodent burrows to escape the Sun's heat and the night's bitter cold.

◄ **SCALE SOUNDS**
If threatened, the desert horned viper makes a loud rasping sound by rubbing together jagged scales along the sides of its body. This warns predators to keep away.

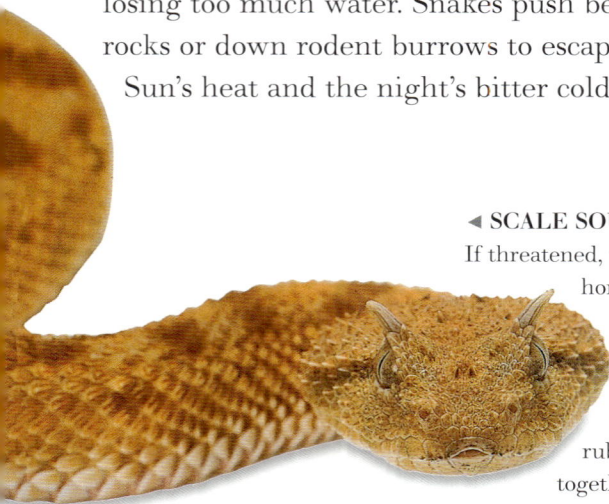

Horned viper
(Cerastes cerastes)

► **RATTLING**
A rattlesnake shakes its rattle to warn enemies. It shakes its tail and often lifts its head off the ground. It cannot hear the buzzing noise it makes — but its enemies can.

► **SAND SHUFFLE**

The desert horned viper shuffles under the sand by rocking its body to and fro. It spreads its ribs to flatten its body and pushes its way down until it almost disappears. It strikes out at its prey from this position.

◄ **SIDEWINDING**

Many desert snakes, such as this Peringuey's viper, travel in a movement called sidewinding. As the snake moves, only a small part of its body touches the hot sand at any time. Sidewinding also helps to stop the snake sinking down into the loose sand.

◄ **HIDDEN BOA**

The colours of this sand boa make it hard for predators and prey to spot among desert rocks and sand. The sand boa's long, round body shape helps it to burrow down into the sand.

The Hopi Indians

This Native North American was a Hopi snake chief. The Hopi people used snakes in their rain dances to carry prayers to the rain gods to make rain fall on their desert lands.

Water Snakes

Some snakes live in marshy areas or at the edge of freshwater lakes and rivers. Two groups of snakes live in salty sea water. They breathe air, but they can stay underwater for a long time. Glands on their heads get rid of some of the salt from the water. Sea snakes have hollow front fangs and are very poisonous. This is because a sea snake has to subdue its prey quickly in order to avoid losing it in the depths of the sea.

◄ SENSES
A sea snake's eyes and nostrils lie towards the top of the head. This means it can take a breath without lifting its head right out of the water, and the eyes can watch out for predators about to attack.

▼ CHAMPION SWIMMER
Northern water snakes are good swimmers, rarely found far from fresh water. They feed mainly on fish, frogs, salamanders and toads. At the first sign of danger, they dive under the water.

► BREATH CONTROL
Sea snakes have large lungs, enabling them to stay underwater for a few hours at a time.

◄ **HEAVY WEIGHT**
The green anaconda lurks in swamps
and slow-moving rivers, waiting for
birds, turtles and caimans to come
within reach of its strong coils. They
weigh up to 227kg/500lb.

Sea krait
(*Laticauda*
colubrina)

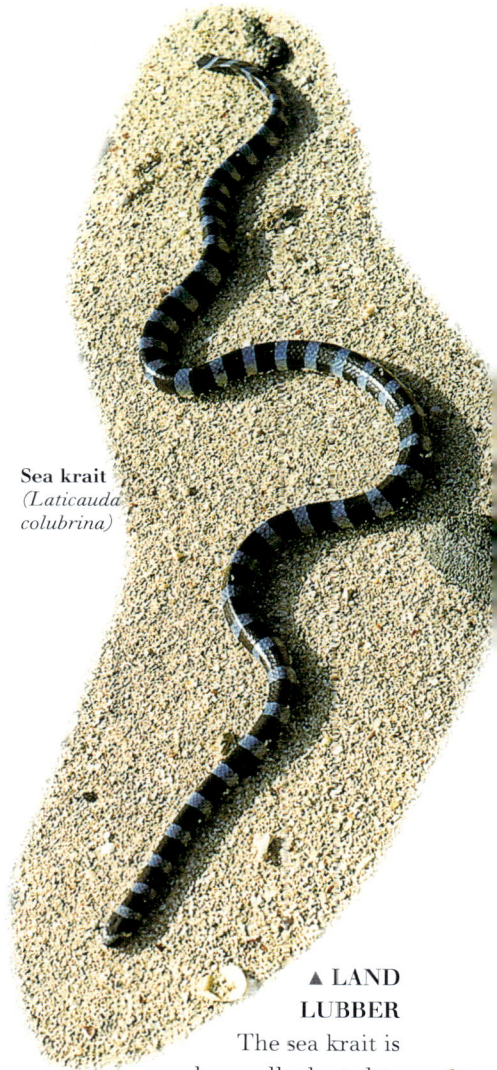

▲ **LAND
LUBBER**
The sea krait is
less well adapted to
the water and lays eggs on land.

Crocodiles

In Africa alone, crocodiles kill an estimated 1,000 people a year, yet female crocodiles are good, gentle and caring mothers. When adult, they are indiscriminate killers, taking anything that should step into the water. They also fast for long periods, when food is unavailable. It was probably these factors that helped them survive the "time of great dying" when their cousins the dinosaurs were wiped out about 65 million years ago.

What is a Crocodilian?

Crocodilians are scaly, armour-clad reptiles that include crocodiles, alligators, caimans and gharials. They are survivors from a prehistoric age – their relatives first lived on Earth with the dinosaurs nearly 200 million years ago. Today, they are the dinosaurs' closest living relatives, apart from birds.

Crocodilians are fierce predators. They lurk motionless in rivers, lakes and swamps, waiting to snap up prey with their enormous jaws and tough teeth. Their prey ranges from insects, frogs and fish to birds and large mammals, such as deer and zebras. Very few crocodilians regularly attack and kill humans. Most are timid. Crocodilians usually live in warm, tropical places in or near freshwater, and some live in the sea. They hunt and feed mainly in the water, but crawl on to dry land to sunbathe, nest and lay their eggs.

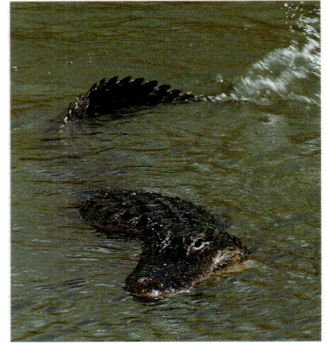

▲ SCALY TAILS
Like many crocodilians, an American alligator uses its long, strong tail to swim through the water. The tail moves from side to side to push the alligator along. The tail is the same length as the rest of the body.

Long, strong tail has flat sides to push aside water for swimming.

The Chinese Dragon
People in China have worshiped the dragon, a mythical creature, for centuries. The original stories surrounding the dragon may have been based on the real-life Chinese alligator. According to ancient texts, the dragon was a supernatural creature that could take on many different forms. It could change instantly from thick to thin, or long to short, and could soar into the heavens or plunge to the depths of the sea.

► CROCODILIAN CHARACTERISTICS
With its thick, scaly skin, huge jaws and powerful tail, this American alligator looks like a living dinosaur. Its eyes and nostrils are on top of the head so that it can see and breathe when the rest of its body is underwater. On land, crocodilians slither along on their bellies, but they can lift themselves up on their four short legs to walk.

▲ TALKING HEADS

Huge, powerful jaws lined with sharp teeth make Nile crocodiles killing machines. They are some of the world's largest and most dangerous reptiles. The teeth are used to attack and grip prey, but are no good for chewing. Prey has to be swallowed whole or in chunks.

► SHUT EYE

Although this spectacled caiman has its eyes shut, it is probably not asleep, but dozing. Two butterflies are basking in safety on the caiman's head. Predators will not dare to attack them because the caiman is still aware of what is going on around it, even though its eyes are shut.

► SOAKING UP THE SUN

Nile crocodiles sun themselves on a sandbank. This is called basking and warms the body. Crocodilians are cold-blooded, which means that their body temperature is affected by their surroundings. They have no fur or feathers to keep them warm, nor can they shiver to warm up. They move in and out of the water to warm up or cool down.

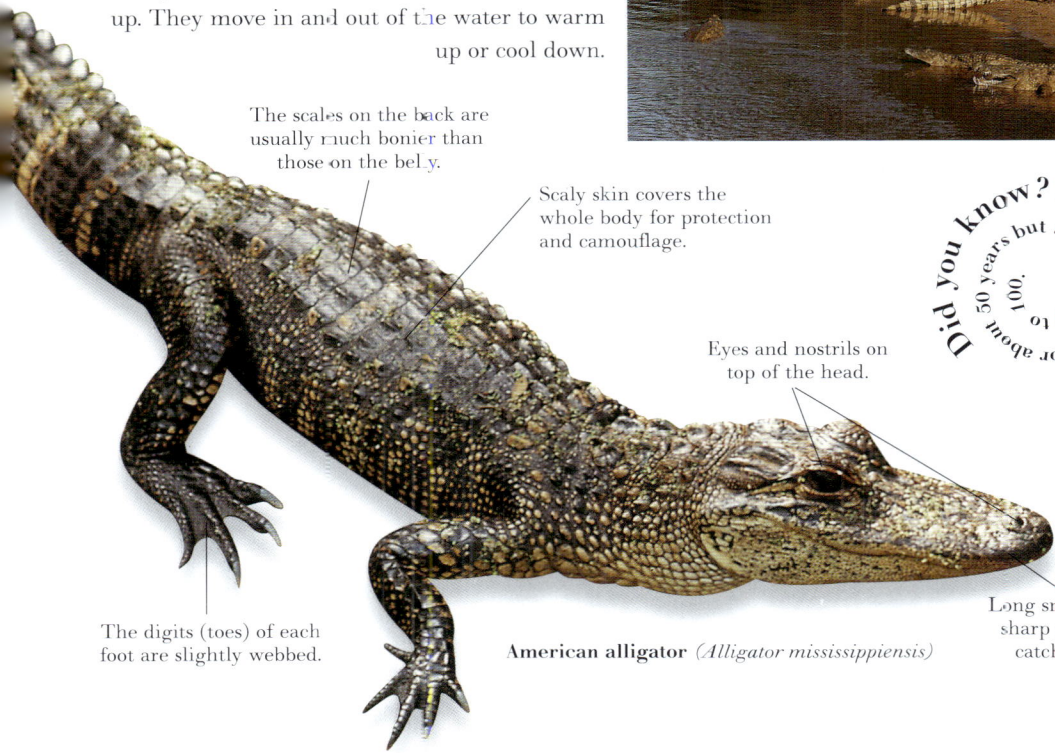

The scales on the back are usually much bonier than those on the belly.

Scaly skin covers the whole body for protection and camouflage.

Did you know? Most crocodilians live for about 50 years but some live up to 100.

Eyes and nostrils on top of the head.

The digits (toes) of each foot are slightly webbed.

American alligator (*Alligator mississippiensis*)

Long snout with sharp teeth to catch prey.

Croc or Gator?

There are 13 species (kinds) of crocodile; two species of alligator, six species of caimans; and two species of gharial. Gharials have distinctive long, slender snouts, but crocodiles and alligators are often more difficult to tell apart. Crocodiles usually have longer, more pointed snouts than alligators. Crocodiles also have one very large tooth sticking up from each side of the bottom jaw when they close their mouths.

▲ CAIMAN EYES

Most caimans have bonier ridges between their eyes than alligators. These ridges help strengthen the skull and look like the spectacles people wear to help them see. Caimans are usually smaller than alligators.

Chinese alligator (*Alligator sinensis*)

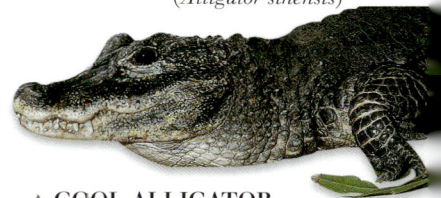

▲ WHERE IN THE WORLD?

Crocodiles are the most widespread crocodilian and live in Central and South America, Africa, southern Asia and Australia. Caimans live in Central and South America. Alligators live in the south-eastern United States and China. The gharial is found in southern Asia, while the false gharial lives in South-east Asia.

KEY

crocodiles

alligators/ caimans

gharials

GREENLAND
NORTH AMERICA
EUROPE
ASIA
Atlantic Ocean
AFRICA
Pacific Ocean
SOUTH AMERICA
Indian Ocean
AUSTRALIA

▼ A CROCODILE'S SMILE

With its mouth closed, a crocodile's fourth tooth in the lower jaw fits into a notch on the outside of the upper jaw. No teeth can be seen on the bottom jaw of an alligator's closed mouth.

▲ COOL ALLIGATOR

There are two species of alligator, the Chinese alligator (*shown above*) and the American alligator. Alligators are the only crocodilians that can survive cooler temperatures and live outside the tropics.

► DIFFERENT SNOUTS

Crocodilian snouts are different shapes and sizes because of the food they eat and the way they live. Gharials and crocodiles have narrow, pointy snouts suited to eating fish. Alligators, and caimans have wider, rounder snouts which can manage larger prey, such as birds and mammals. Their jaws are strong enough to overpower victims that are even larger than they are.

Gharial

Caiman

Crocodile

◄ OUT TO SEA

The enormous saltwater crocodile, often called the saltie, has the largest range of all the crocodilians. It is found from the east coast of India through South-east Asia to the Philippines, New Guinea and northern Australia. Saltwater crocodiles are one of the few species found far out to sea, but they do live in freshwater rivers and lakes as well.

► POT NOSE

There are two species of gharial – the gharial, or gavial – and the false gharial, that live in the rivers, lakes and swamps of southern Asia. The name comes from the knob on the nose of the male gharial, which is called a *ghara* (pot) in the Hindi language. Some experts say the false gharial is a species of crocodile and is therefore not really part of the gharial family.

Adult male gharials have a conspicuous knob at the tip of their snouts.

Gharial
(*Gavialis gangeticus*)

Large and Small

Can you imagine a crocodile that weighs as much as three cars? A big, 7m/23ft long saltwater crocodile is as heavy as this. It is the heaviest living reptile in the world. Other enormous crocodilians include Nile crocodiles, gharials and American alligators, which can reach lengths of 5.5m/18ft or more. Very large crocodiles and alligators are now rare because many are hunted and killed for their meat and skins before they grow to their maximum size. The smallest species of crocodilian are the dwarf caimans of South America and the African dwarf crocodile. These forest-dwelling reptiles grow to about 1.5m/5ft long.

▲ BIGGEST CAIMAN
The black caiman is the largest of the caimans. It can grow to over 6m/19½ft long and is the biggest predator in South America. Black caimans live in the flooded Amazon forest, around lakes and slow-flowing rivers. They hunt at night for capybara, turtles, deer and fish.

▲ A CROC IN THE HAND
A person holds a baby Orinoco crocodile (*top*) and a baby spectacled caiman (*bottom*). As adults, the Orinoco crocodile will be twice the length of the caiman, reaching about 5m/16ft. You can clearly see how the crocodile has a longer, thinner snout than the caiman.

Crocodile God
The ancient Egyptians worshipped the crocodile-headed god Sebek. He was the god of lakes and rivers, and is shown here with Pharaoh Amenhotep III. A shrine to Sebek was built at Shedet. Here, a Nile crocodile decorated with gold rings and bracelets lived in a special pool. It was believed to be the living god. Other crocodiles were also treated with great respect and hand-fed on meat, cakes, milk and honey.

◀ SUPER-SNOUTED CROCODILE

The mugger crocodile of India and surrounding lands has the broadest snout of all crocodiles, making it look more like an alligator. Adult males reach about 4m/13ft long. The name comes from its habit of snatching fish out of people's fishing nets.

◀ SMALLEST CROCODILIAN

Cuvier's dwarf caiman is about a fifth of the size of a giant saltwater crocodile, yet it would still only just fit on your bed. It lives in the rainforests of the Amazon basin in South America. It has particularly tough, armoured skin to protect it from rocks in fast-flowing rivers. It has a short snout and high, smooth skull. Its short snout does not prevent it from eating a lot of fish.

Did you know? Male alligators keep growing until they are 15 years of age.

▶ MONSTER CROC

The huge Nile crocodile is the biggest and strongest freshwater predator in Africa. It can grow up to 6m/19½ft long and eats any prey it can overpower, including monkeys, antelopes, zebras and people. Nile crocodiles probably kill at least 300 people a year in Africa. Despite its name, the Nile crocodile is not just found along the Nile, but also lives in rivers, lakes and swamps through most of tropical Africa.

A Scaly Skin

The outside of a crocodilian's body is completely covered in a suit of leathery armour. It is made up of rows of tough scales, called scutes, that are set into a thick layer of skin. Some scutes have small bony discs inside them. Most crocodilians have bony scutes only on their backs, but some, such as caimans, have them on their bellies as well. The tail never contains bony scutes, but it does have thicker tail scutes. As crocodilians grow, bigger scutes develop under the old ones. Crocodilians do not get rid of their old scaly skin in a big piece, like a snake, or in patches like a lizard. Old scutes drop off one at a time, just as humans lose flakes of skin all the time. On the head, the skin is fused directly to the bones of the skull without any muscles or fat in-between.

Tricky Alligator
A Guyanese myth tells how the Sun was tricked by an alligator into letting him guard his fishponds from a thief. The thief was the alligator and to punish him the Sun slashed his body, forming the scales. The alligator promised the Sun his daughter for a wife. He had no children, so he carved her from a tree. The Sun and the woman's offspring were the Carib people.

▲ COLOUR CHANGE
Most crocodilians are brightly coloured or patterned as babies, but these features usually fade as they grow older. They have more or less disappeared in the fully grown adult. The colours and patterns may help with camouflage by breaking up the outline of the body.

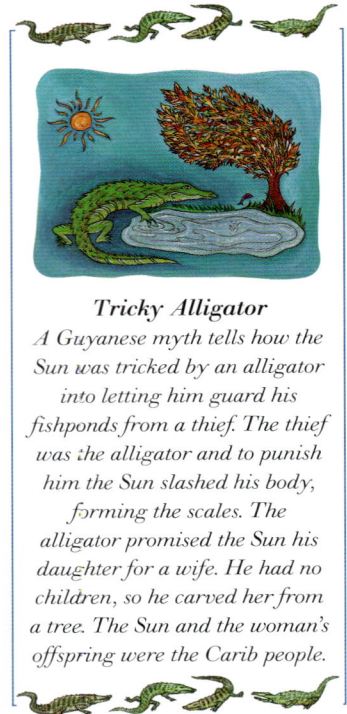

▲ NECK ARMOUR
Heavy, bony scutes pack tightly together to create a rigid and formidable armour on the back and neck of an African dwarf crocodile. Even the scutes on the sides of its body and tail are heavily armoured. This species lives in the dwindling rainforests of West and Central Africa. The small size and bony armour of the dwarf crocodile has saved it so far from being hunted for its skin.

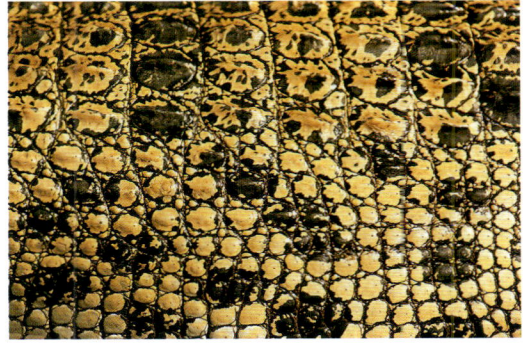

▲ MISSING SCALES

The gharial has fewer rows of armoured scutes along its back than other crocodilians. Adults have four rows of deeply ridged back scutes, whereas other crocodilians have two or four extra rows in the middle of the back. The scutes on the sides and belly are unarmoured.

▲ BONY BACK

The belly of a saltwater crocodile does not have bony plates in the scutes. You can see the difference in this close-up. Large, bony back scutes are shown at the top of the picture and the smaller, smoother belly scutes are at the bottom. The scutes are arranged in rows.

► EXTRA ARMOUR

This close-up shows the skin of a dwarf caiman – the most heavily armoured crocodilian. It has strong bones in the scutes on its belly as well as its back. This provides protection from predators. Even its eyelids are protected by bony plates.

Did you know? The scales of the black caiman are as tough as the head of a tool.

► ALBINO ALLIGATOR

An albino (white) crocodilian would not survive long in the wild. Its colours do not blend in well with its surroundings, making it easy prey. Those born in captivity in zoos or crocodile farms may survive to adulthood. True albinos are white with pink eyes. White crocodilians with blue eyes are not true albinos.

American alligator
(*Alligator mississippiensis*)

129

Bodies and Bones

The crocodilian body has changed very little over the last 200 million years. It is superbly adapted to life in the water. Crocodilians can breathe with just their nostrils above the surface. Underwater, ears and nostrils close and a transparent third eyelid sweeps across the eye for protection. Crocodilians are the only reptiles with ear flaps. Inside the long, lizard-like body a bony skeleton supports and protects the lungs, heart, stomach and other soft organs. The stomach is in two parts, one part for grinding food, the other for absorbing (taking in) nutrients. Unlike other reptiles, which have a single-chambered heart, a crocodilian's heart has four chambers, like a mammal. This allows the heart to pump more oxygen-rich blood to the brain during a dive. The thinking part of its brain is more developed than in other reptiles. This enables a crocodilian to learn things rather than act only on instinct.

▲ THROAT FLAP
A crocodilian has no lips so it is unable to seal its mouth underwater. Instead, two special flaps at the back of the throat stop water filling the mouth and flowing into the lungs. This enables the crocodile to open its mouth underwater to catch and eat prey without drowning.

Did you know? A saltwater crocodile can stay underwater for more than an hour.

◀ PREHISTORIC LOOKS
These American alligators look much like their crocodilian ancestors that lived with the dinosaurs long ago. Crocodilians are the largest living reptiles. The heaviest is the saltwater crocodile, reaching up to 1,100kg/2,425lb.

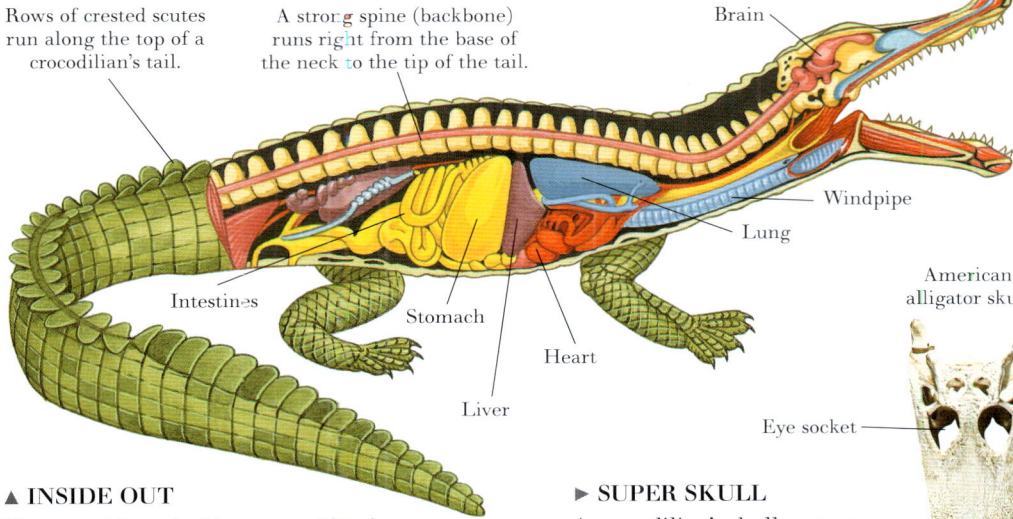

Rows of crested scutes run along the top of a crocodilian's tail.

A strong spine (backbone) runs right from the base of the neck to the tip of the tail.

Brain

Windpipe

Lung

Intestines

Stomach

Heart

Liver

American alligator skull

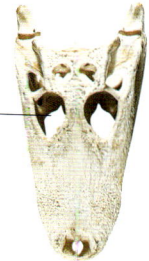

Eye socket

American crocodile skull

▲ INSIDE OUT

If you could see inside a crocodilian's body you would see a mixture of reptile, bird and mammal features. The crocodilian's brain and shoulder blades are like a bird's. Its heart, diaphragm and efficient breathing system are similar to those of mammals. The stomach and digestive system are those of a reptile, as they deal with food that cannot be chewed.

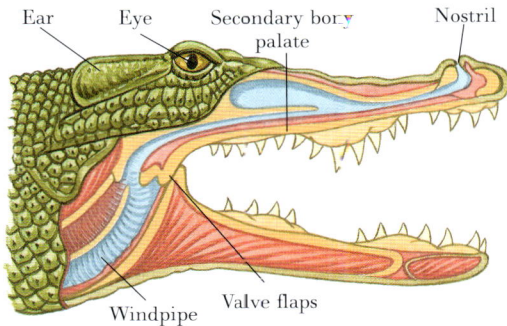

Ear   Eye   Secondary bony palate   Nostril

Windpipe   Valve flaps

▲ WELL DESIGNED

A view inside the head of a crocodilian shows the ear, eye and nostril openings set high up in the skull. The bones in the mouth are joined together to create a secondary bony palate that separates the nostrils from the mouth. Flaps of skin form a valve, sealing off the windpipe underwater.

▶ SUPER SKULL

A crocodilian's skull protects a brain that is more developed than any other reptile's. The skull is wider and more rounded in alligators (*top*), and long and triangular in crocodiles (*bottom*). Behind the eye sockets are two large holes where jaw muscles attach to the skull.

▶ STOMACH STONES

Crocodilians swallow objects, such as pebbles, to help break down their food. These gastroliths (stomach stones) churn around inside part of the stomach, helping to cut up food so it can be digested. Some very unusual gastroliths have been found, such as bottles, coins, a whistle and a vacuum flask.

131

Jaws and Teeth

The mighty jaws of a crocodilian and its impressive rows of spiky teeth are lethal weapons for catching prey. Crocodilians have two or three times as many teeth as a human. The sharp, jagged teeth at the front of the mouth, called canines, are used to pierce and grip prey. The force of the jaws closing drives these teeth, like a row of knives, deep into a victim's flesh. The short, blunt molar teeth at the back of the mouth are used for crushing prey. Crocodilian teeth are no good for chewing food, and the jaws cannot be moved sideways to chew either. Food has to be swallowed whole, or torn into chunks. The teeth are constantly growing. If a tooth falls out, a new one grows through to replace it.

▲ **MEGA JAWS**
The jaws of a Nile crocodile close with tremendous force. They sink into their prey with tons of crushing pressure. Yet the muscles that open the jaws are weak. A thick elastic band over the snout can easily hold a crocodile's jaws shut.

◄ **NEW TEETH FOR OLD**
Each tooth is set in a socket and held in place by connective tissue. Throughout a crocodilian's life, the old teeth fall out and new teeth underneath take their place. Teeth last up to two years before falling out. Alternate teeth are replaced together, so that not all the teeth in one part of the mouth are lost at the same time.

◀ **LOTS OF TEETH**

The gharial has more teeth than any other crocodilian, around 110. Its teeth are also smaller than those of other crocodilians and are all the same size. The narrow, beak-like snout and long, thin teeth of the gharial are geared to grabbing fish with a sweeping sideways movement of the head. The sharp teeth interlock to trap and impale the slippery prey.

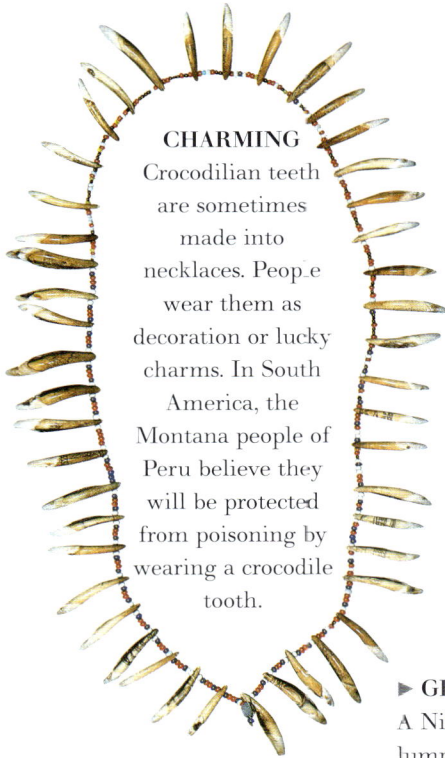

CHARMING

Crocodilian teeth are sometimes made into necklaces. People wear them as decoration or lucky charms. In South America, the Montana people of Peru believe they will be protected from poisoning by wearing a crocodile tooth.

▲ **BABY TEETH**

A baby American alligator is born with a full set of 80 teeth when it hatches from its egg. Baby teeth are not so sharp as adult teeth and are more fragile. They are like tiny needles. In young crocodiles, the teeth at the back of the mouth usually fall out first. In adults, it is the teeth at the front that are replaced more often.

▶ **GRABBING TEETH**

A Nile crocodile grasps a lump of prey ready for swallowing. If prey is too large to swallow whole, the crocodile grips the food firmly in its teeth and shakes its head hard so that any unwanted pieces are shaken off.

A Nile crocodile has 68 teeth lining its huge jaws.

Did you know? A Nile crocodile may use 45 sets of teeth by the time it is 4m / 13ft long.

On the Move

Have you ever seen a film of an alligator gliding through the water with slow, S-shaped sweeps of its powerful tail? Crocodilians move gracefully and easily in the water, using very little energy and keeping most of their body hidden under the surface. Legs lie close alongside bodies to make them streamlined, and cut down drag from the water. They may be used as rudders to change course. On land, the short legs of crocodilians make their walk look slow and clumsy, but they can move quite fast if they need to. Some can gallop at 18kph/11mph when running for short distances of up to 90m/295ft. Crocodilians also move by means of the belly slide. With side-to-side twists of the body, the animal uses its legs to push along on its belly. This tobogganing movement is useful for fast escapes, but is also used to slip quietly into the water.

▲ **BEST FOOT FORWARD**
The tracks of a saltwater crocodile in the mud show how its legs move in sequence. The right front leg goes forwards first, then the back left leg. The front left leg goes forward next and finally the right back leg. If the legs on the same side moved one after the other, the crocodile would overbalance.

▼ **THE HIGH WALK**
To move overland, crocodilians hold their legs underneath the body, lifting most of the tail off the ground. This is called the high walk. It is very different from the walk of a lizard, which keeps its legs sprawled out at the sides of its body. The tail is dragged behind the body in the high walk, but if the animal starts to run, the tail swings from side to side.
A special ankle joint lets crocodilians twist and turn their legs in the stately high walk.

▲ FLOATING AROUND

This Nile crocodile is floating near the surface of Lake Tanganyika, Tanzania, Africa. It is holding its feet out to the sides for balance. The toes and the webbing between them are spread out for extra stability. In the water, the crocodile floats with its tail down, but as it moves its body becomes horizontal.

▶ TAIL WALKING

Some crocodilians leap straight up out of the water. They seem to be walking on their tails in the same way that a dolphin can travel backwards on its strong tail. This movement is unusual. Large crocodiles will also spring upward, propelled by the back legs, to grab prey unawares.

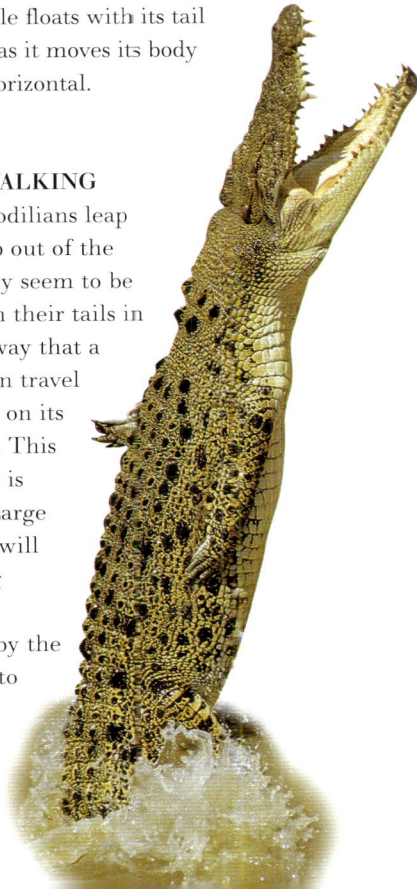

▶ FEET AND TOES

On the front feet, crocodilians have five separate digits (toes). These sometimes have webbing (skin) stretched between them. The back feet are always webbed to help them balance and move in the water. There are only four toes on the back feet. The fifth toe is just a small bone inside the foot.

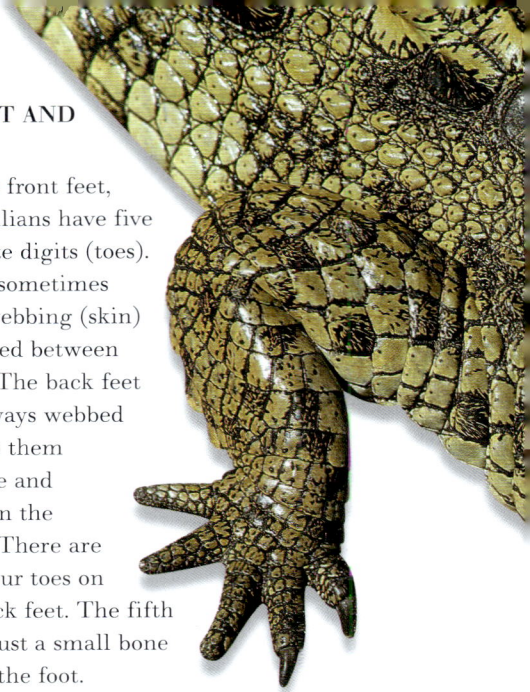

▲ THE GALLOP

The fastest way for a crocodilian to move on land is to gallop. Only a few crocodiles, such as the Johnston's crocodile shown above, make a habit of moving like this. In a gallop, the back legs push the crocodilian forward in a leap and the front legs stretch out to catch the body as it lands at the end of the leap. Then the back legs swing forward to push the animal forward again.

Temperature Check

Soon after the sun rises, the first alligators heave themselves out of the river and flop down on the bank. The banks fill up quickly as more alligators join the first, warming their scaly bodies in the sun's rays. As the hours go by and the day becomes hotter, the alligators open their toothy jaws wide to cool down. Later in the day, they may go for a swim or crawl into the shade to cool off. As the air chills at night, the alligators slip back into the water again. This is because water stays warmer for longer at night than the land.

Crocodilians are cold-blooded, which means their body temperature varies with outside temperatures. To warm up or cool down, they move to warm or cool places. Their ideal body temperature is 30–35°C/86–95°F.

▲ **MUD PACK**
A spectacled caiman is buried deep in the mud to keep cool during the hot, dry season. Mud is like water and does not get so hot or so cold as dry land. It also helps to keep the caiman's scaly skin free from parasites and biting insects.

◄ **SOLAR PANELS**
The crested scutes on the tail of a crocodilian are like the bony plates on armoured dinosaurs. They act like solar panels, picking up heat when the animal basks in the sun. The scutes also move apart fractionally to let as much heat as possible escape from the body to cool it down.

◄ **UNDER THE ICE**

An alligator can survive under a layer of ice as long as it keeps a breathing hole open. Only alligators stay active at the low temperatures of 12–15°C/53–59°F. However, they do not eat because it is too cold for their digestion to work.

▼ **OPEN WIDE**

While a Nile crocodile suns itself on a rock it also opens its mouth in a wide gape. Gaping helps to prevent the crocodile from becoming too hot. The breeze flowing over the wide, wet surfaces of the mouth and tongue dries its moisture and, in turn, cools off its blood. If you lick your finger and blow on it softly, you will notice that it feels a lot cooler.

▲ **ALLIGATOR DAYS**

Alligators follow a distinct daily routine when the weather is good, moving in and out of the water at regular intervals. They also enter the water if they are disturbed. In winter, alligators retreat into dens and become rather sleepy because their blood cools and slows them down.

► **MEAL BREAKS**

Being cold blooded is quite useful in some ways. These alligators can bask in the sun without having to eat very much or very often. Warm-blooded animals, such as mammals, have to eat regularly. They need to eat about five times as much food as reptiles to keep their bodies warm.

Crocodilian Senses

The senses of sight, hearing, smell, taste and touch are much more powerful in a crocodilian than in other living reptiles. They have good eyesight and can see in colour. Their eyes are also adapted to seeing well in the dark, which is useful because they hunt mainly at night. Crocodilians also have sharp hearing. They sense the sounds of danger or prey moving nearby and listen for the barks, coughs and roars of their own species at mating time. Crocodilians also have sensitive scales along the sides of their jaws, which help to feel and capture prey.

▲ **NOISY GATORS**

An American alligator bellows loudly during courtship. Noises such as hissing or snarling, are made at enemies. Young alligators call for help from adults. Small ear slits behind the eyes are kept open when the animal is out of the water. Flaps close to protect the ears when the animal submerges.

Did you know? Crocodiles shake their ear flaps up and down when they are angry.

▲ **SMELL DETECTORS**

A Nile crocodile picks up chemical signals through the nostrils at the tip of its snout. These smelly messages help it to detect prey and others of its kind. Crocodiles can smell food over long distances. They are known to have travelled as far as 3km/1¾ miles to feed on the carcass of a large animal.

Crocodile Tears
According to legend, crocodiles cry to make people feel so sorry for them that they come near enough for the crocodiles to catch them. Crocodiles are also supposed to shed tears of remorse before finishing their meal. It is said that people cry crocodile tears when they seem to be sorry for something, but really are not. Real-life crocodiles cannot cry but sometimes look as if they are.

138

▶ **TASTY TONGUE**

Inside the gaping mouth of an American crocodile is a wide, fleshy tongue. It is joined to the bottom of the mouth and does not move, so it plays no part in catching prey. We know that crocodilians have taste buds lining their mouths because some prefer one type of food to another. They can tell the difference between sweet and sour tastes. They also have salt glands on their tongues that get rid of excess salt. Salt builds up in the body over time if the animal lives in the sea or a very dry environment.

◀ **GLOW-IN-THE-DARK EYES**

A flashlight shone into a crocodile farm at night makes the dark glow eerily with a thousand living lights. The scientific explanation is that a special layer at the back of the eye reflects light back into the front of the eye. This makes sure that the eye catches as much light as possible. Above water, crocodilians see well and are able to spot prey up to 90m/295ft away. When they are under water, an inner, transparent lid covers the eye. This makes their eyesight foggy, rather like looking through thick goggles.

▶ **A PREDATOR'S EYE**

The eye of a spectacled caiman, like all crocodilians, has both upper and lower lids. A third eyelid at the side, called a nictating (blinking) membrane, moves across to clean the eye's surface. The dark, vertical pupil narrows to a slit to stop bright light damaging the eye. At night, the pupil opens wide to let any available light into the eye. A round pupil, such as a human's, cannot open so wide.

Food and Hunting

How would it feel to wait up to two years for a meal? Amazingly, a big crocodile can probably survive this long between meals. It lives off fat stored in its tail and other parts of its body. Crocodilians eat a lot of fish, but their strong jaws will snap up anything that wanders too close, from birds, snakes and turtles to raccoons, zebras, cattle and horses. They also eat dead animals. Young crocodilians eat small animals, such as insects, snails and frogs.

Most crocodilians sit and wait for their food to come to them, which saves energy. They also catch their meals by stealthily stalking and surprising prey. The three main ways of capturing and killing food are lunging towards prey, leaping up out of the water and sweeping open jaws from side to side through the water. Most crocodilians hunt at night. They eat every part of their prey, including the bones.

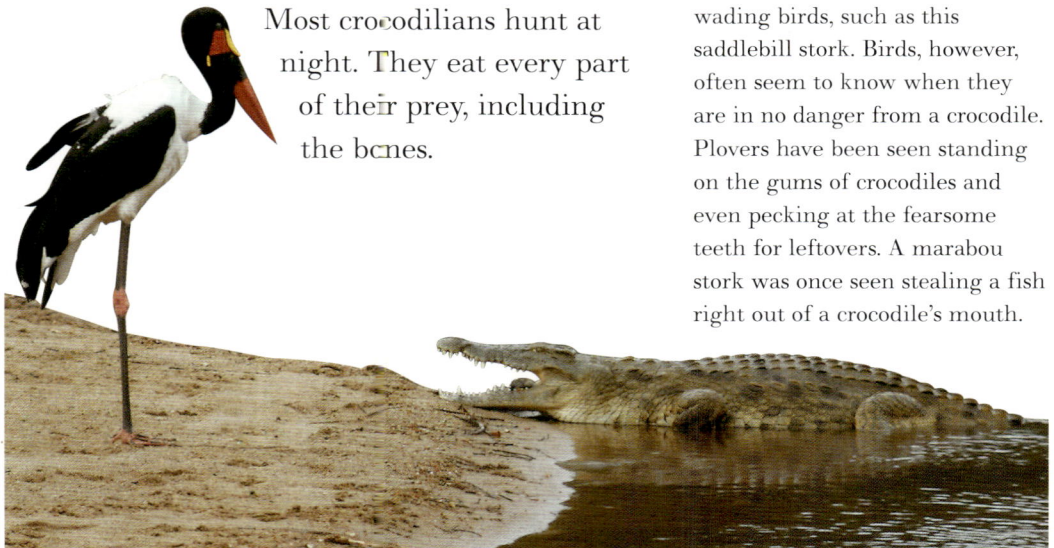

▲ SURPRISE ATTACK

A Nile crocodile lunges from the water at an incredible speed to grab a wildebeest in its powerful jaws. It is difficult for the wildebeest to jump back as the river bank slopes steeply into the water. The crocodile will plunge back into the water, dragging its prey with it in order to drown it.

▼ CHEEKY BIRDS

Large crocodiles feed on big wading birds, such as this saddlebill stork. Birds, however, often seem to know when they are in no danger from a crocodile. Plovers have been seen standing on the gums of crocodiles and even pecking at the fearsome teeth for leftovers. A marabou stork was once seen stealing a fish right out of a crocodile's mouth.

► **SMALLER PREY**

A dwarf caiman lies in wait to snap up a tasty bullfrog. Small species of crocodilian like this caiman, as well as young crocodilians, eat a lot of frogs and toads. Youngsters also snap up beetles, spiders, giant water bugs and small fish. They will leap into the air to catch dragonflies and other insects hovering over the water. Small crocodilians are also preyed upon by their larger relatives.

Crocodilians have varied diets and will eat any animal they can catch.

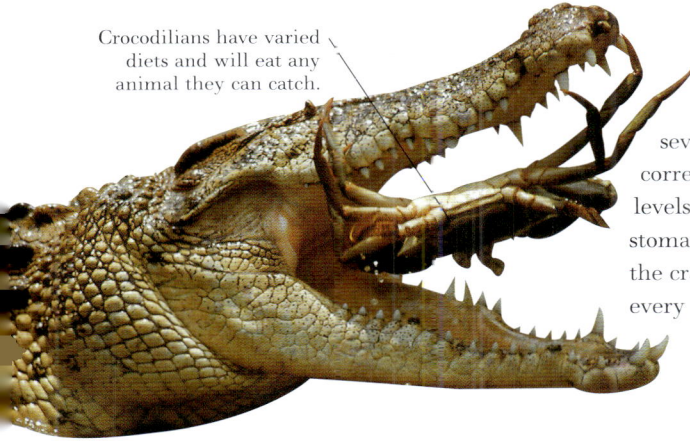

◄ **SWALLOWING PREY**

A crocodile raises its head and grips a crab firmly at the back of its throat. After several jerky head movements the crab is correctly positioned to be eaten whole. High levels of acid in the crocodile's stomach help it break down the crab's hard shell so that every part is digested.

Did you know? A Nile crocodile has a stomach that is about the size of a basketball.

► **FISHY FOOD**

A Nile crocodile swallows a fish head first. This stops any spines it has sticking in the crocodile's throat. About 70 per cent of the diet of most crocodilians is fish. Crocodilians with narrow snouts, such as the gharial, Johnston's crocodile and the African slender-snouted crocodile, feed mainly on fish. Fish are caught with a sideways, snapping movement that is easier and faster with a slender snout.

141

Focus on a

1 A Nile crocodile is nearly invisible as it lies almost submerged in wait for its prey. Only its eyes, ears and nostrils are showing. It lurks in places where it knows prey regularly visit the river. Its dark olive colour provides effective camouflage. To disappear completely it can vanish beneath the water. Some crocodilians can hold their breath for more than an hour while submerged.

A crocodile quietly drifting near the shore looks just like a harmless, floating log. This is just a disguise as it waits for an unsuspecting animal to come down to the river to drink. The crocodile is in luck. A herd of zebras comes to cross the river. The crocodile launches its attack with astonishing speed. Shooting forwards it snaps shut its powerful jaws and sharp teeth like a vice around a zebra's leg or muzzle. The stunned zebra is pulled into deeper water to be drowned. Other crocodiles are attracted to the large kill. They gather around to bite into the carcass, rotating in the water to twist off large chunks of flesh. Grazing animals constantly risk death-by-crocodile to drink or cross water. There is little they can do to defend themselves from the attack of such a large predator.

2 The crocodile erupts from the water, taking the zebras by surprise. It lunges at its victim with a quick burst of energy. It is important for the crocodile to overcome its prey quickly as it cannot chase it overland. The crocodile is also easily exhausted and takes a long time to recover from exercise of any kind.

Crocodile's Lunch

3 The crocodile seizes, pulls and shakes the zebra in its powerful jaws. Sometimes the victim's neck is broken in the attack and it dies quickly. More often the shocked animal is dragged into the water, struggling feebly against its attacker.

4 The crocodile drags the zebra into deeper water and holds it down to drown it. It may also spin around in a roll, until the prey stops breathing. The crocodile twists or rolls around over and over again, with the animal clamped in its jaws, until the prey is dead

5 A freshly killed zebra attracts Nile crocodiles from all around. A large kill is too difficult for one crocodile to defend on its own. Several crocodiles take it in turns to share the feast and may help each other to tear the carcass apart. They fasten their jaws on to a leg or lump of muscle and twist in the water like a rotating shaft, until a chunk of meat is torn loose and can be swallowed.

Communication

Crocodilians pass on messages to each other by means of sounds, body language, smells and touch. Unlike other reptiles, they have a remarkable social life. Groups gather together for basking, sharing food, courting and nesting. Communication begins in the egg and continues throughout life. Adults are particularly sensitive to hatchling and juvenile distress calls and respond with threats or actual attacks. Sounds are made with the vocal cords and with other parts of the body, such as slapping the head against the surface of the water. Crocodilians also use visual communication. Body postures and special movements show which individuals are strong and dominant. Weaker individuals signal to show that they recognize a dominant individual and in this way avoid fighting and injury.

▲ HEAD BANGER
A crocodile lifts its head out of the water, jaws open. The jaws slam shut just before they smack the surface of the water. This is called the head slap and makes a loud pop followed by a splash. Head slapping may be a sign of dominance and is often used during the breeding season.

The Fox and the Crocodile
In this Aesop's fable, the fox and the crocodile met one day. The crocodile boasted at length about its cunning as a hunter. Then the fox said, "That's all very impressive, but tell me, what am I wearing on my feet?" The crocodile looked down and there, on the fox's feet, was a pair of shoes made from crocodile skin.

▲ GHARIAL MESSAGES
The gharial does not head slap, but claps its jaws underwater during the breeding season. Sound travels faster through water than air, so sound signals are very useful for aquatic life.

▶ INFRASOUNDS

Some crocodilians make sounds by rapidly squeezing their torso muscles just beneath the surface of the water. The water bubbles up and bounces off the back. The sounds produced are at a very low level so we can hardly hear them. At close range, they sound like distant thunder. These infrasounds travel quickly over long distances through the water and may be part of courtship. Sometimes they are produced before bellowing, roaring or head slaps.

Did you know? The bellow of an alligator can be heard at least 150m/490ft away.

◀ I AM THE GREATEST

Dominant animals are usually bigger and more aggressive than submissive ones. They show off their importance by swimming boldly at the surface or thrashing their tails from side to side on land. Weaker individuals usually lift only their heads out of the water and expose their vulnerable throats. This shows that they submit and do not want to fight.

▶ GETTING TOGETHER

These caimans are gathering together at the start of the rainy season in Brazil. Crocodilians often come together in loose groups, for example when basking, nesting or sharing food. They tend to ignore each other once dominance battles have been established. During a long, dry spell, large numbers of crocodilians often gather together at water holes to share the remaining water. Young crocodilians stay in a close group for the first months of life as there is safety in numbers.

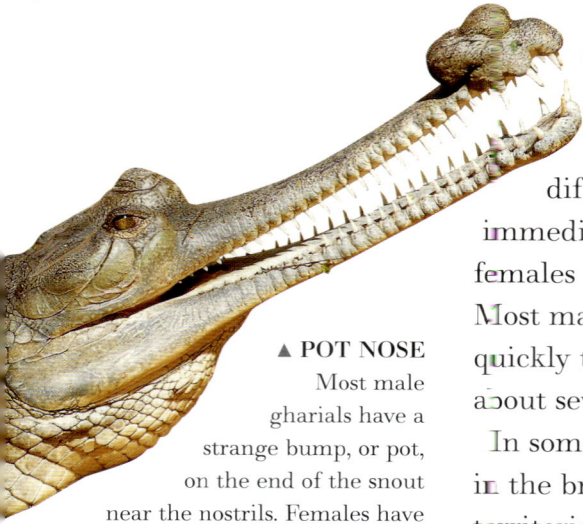

Choosing a Mate

Male and female crocodilians are often difficult to tell apart. Only male gharials are immediately recognizable, distinguished from females by the knob on the end of their snouts. Most males are larger, and grow and mature more quickly than females. They are ready to mate at about seven years old and females at about nine.

In some species, groups of adults gather together in the breeding season and set up special mating territories. In other species, mating takes place in long-established territories. Females often begin the courtship process. Courtship behaviour includes bellowing and grunting, rubbing heads and bodies, blowing bubbles, circling and riding on the partner's back.

▲ **POT NOSE**
Most male gharials have a strange bump, or pot, on the end of the snout near the nostrils. Females have flat snouts. No one is quite sure what the pot is for, but it is probably used in courtship. It may help the male to change hissing sounds into buzzing sounds as air vibrates inside the hollow pot.

◄ **COURTING COUPLE**
Crocodilians touch each other a lot during courtship, especially around the head and neck. Males will also try to impress females by bubbling water from the nostrils and mouth. An interested female arches her back, then raises her head with her mouth open. The two may push each other under the water to see how big and strong their partner is.

◄ SWEET-SMELLING SCENT

Crocodilians have little bumps under their lower jaws. These are musk glands. The musk is a sweet-smelling, greenish, oily perfume. It produces a scent that attracts the opposite sex. Musk glands are more noticeable in males. During courtship, the male may rub his throat across the female's head and neck. This releases the scent from the musk glands and helps to prepare the female for mating.

► FIGHTING MALES

Male crocodilians may fight each other for the chance to court and mate with females. They may spar with their jaws open or make themselves look bigger and more powerful by puffing up their bodies with air. Saltwater crocodiles are particularly violent and bash their heads together with a loud thud. These contests may go on for an hour or more, but do not seem to cause much permanent damage.

◄ THE MATING GAME

Courtship can last for up to two hours before mating occurs. The couple sink under the water and the male wraps his tail around his partner. Mating takes only a few minutes. The couple mate several times during the day. A dominant male may mate with up to 20 females in the breeding season. Females, too, mate with other males, but the dominant male tries to prevent this.

147

Focus on

Early in April or May, American alligators begin courtship rituals. Males fight each other to win their own territories. The biggest and strongest males win the best territories. Their musk glands give off a strong, sweet smell, attractive to females. Female alligators do not have territories. They visit the territories of several males and may mate several times. Once a female and a male have mated, they part. The female builds a nest in June or July and lays her eggs. In about 60 to 70 days, the young alligators begin to hatch and the female digs them out of the nest and carries them to water. She remains with her young for months or even years.

1 Male and female alligators do not live together all year round. They come together in spring to court and mate. The rest of the year they glide through the swamp, searching for food or basking in the sun. In winter they rest in cosy dens.

2 The American alligator is the noisiest crocodilian. Males and females make bellowing noises, especially in the breeding season. Males bellow loudly to warn other males to keep out of their territories and to let females know where they are. Each alligator has a different voice, which sounds like the throaty roar of a stalling motorboat engine. The sound carries for long distances in the swamp. Once one alligator starts to bellow, others soon join in and may carry on for half an hour.

Alligators

3 In the mating season bulls (males) test each other to see which is the biggest and strongest. They push and wrestle and sometimes fight violently. The strongest males win the best territories for food and water. Bellowing helps to limit serious fighting. Other males stay away from areas where they have heard a loud bull.

4 Alligators mate in shallow water. Before mating, there is a slow courtship made up of slapping the water and rubbing each other's muzzle and neck. Mating usually lasts only a minute or two before the pair separate. Alligators may mate with several partners in a season.

5 The female alligator uses her body, legs and tail to build a nest out of sand, soil and plants. It takes about two weeks to build and may be up to 75cm/30in high and 2m/6½ft across. In the middle the female digs a hole and lines it with mud. She lays between 20 and 70 eggs, which she then covers up. She stays near the nest site while the eggs develop, guarding them from raccoons and other predators.

Building a Nest

About a month after mating, a female crocodilian is ready to lay her eggs on land. First she builds a nest to keep her eggs warm. If the temperature stays below 28°C/82°F, the babies will die before they hatch. The temperature inside the nest determines whether the hatchlings are male or female. Females build their nests at night. Alligators, caimans and some crocodiles build nests that are solid mounds of fresh plants and soil. Other crocodiles, and gharials, dig holes in the sand with their back feet. Some species dig trial nests before they dig the real one. This may be to check that the temperature is right for the eggs to develop. Nest sites are chosen to be near water but above the floodwater mark. The females often stay close to the nest to guard it against predators, even while searching for food.

▲ SHARING NESTS
Turtles, such as this red-bellied turtle, sometimes lay their eggs in crocodilian nests to save them the hard work of making their own nests. The eggs are protected by the fierce crocodilian mother, who guards her own eggs and the turtle's eggs. Up to 200 red-bellied turtle eggs have been found in alligator nests.

◄ NEST MOUNDS
A Morelet's crocodile has scratched soil and uprooted plant material into a big pile to build her nest mound. She uses her body to press it all together firmly. Then she scoops out a hole in the mound with her back feet. She lays her eggs in the hole and then closes the top of the nest. As the plant material rots, it gives off heat, which keeps the eggs warm.

Did you know?
Male crocodilians do not help with making nests.

▼ IS IT A BOY OR A GIRL?

A saltwater crocodile, like all crocodilians, keeps its eggs at about 30–32°C/86–90°F inside the nest. The temperature during the first few weeks after the eggs are laid is crucial. This controls whether the babies are male or female. Higher temperatures, such as 32–33°C/90–91°F produce more males, while temperatures of 31°C/88°F or lower produce more females. Temperature also affects the babies' colour and patterns.

▲ A SANDY NEST

Nile crocodiles dig their nests on sandy river banks, beaches or lakesides. Females may compete for nest sites by trying to push each other over. Larger, heavier females usually win these contests. The female uses her back legs for digging, so the nest burrow is dug to a depth of about the same length as her back legs.

► NESTING TOGETHER

Female Nile crocodiles often nest together. A female may even return to the same breeding ground and nest site each year. Each female guards her nest, either by lying right on top of the nest or watching it from the nearby shade.

◄ NEST THIEF

The monitor lizard often digs its way into crocodile nests in Africa and Asia to eat the eggs. In Africa, these lizards may sometimes steal over half of all the eggs laid.

151

Developing Eggs

All crocodilians lay white, oval eggs with hard shells like those of a bird. The number of eggs laid by a single female at a time varies from about ten to 90, depending on the species and the age of the mother. Older females lay more eggs. The length of time it takes for the eggs to hatch varies with the species and the temperature, but takes from 55 to 110 days. During this time, called the incubation period, the weather can affect the babies developing inside the eggs. Too much rain can drown the babies before they are born as water can seep through the shells. Hot weather may cause the inside of the egg to overheat. This hardens the yolk so that the baby cannot absorb it and starves to death. Another danger is that eggs laid by one female are accidentally dug up and destroyed by another female digging a nest in the same place.

▲ EGGY HANDFUL

In many countries, people eat crocodilian eggs. They harvest them from nests for sale at the local market. This person is holding the eggs of a gharial. Each egg weighs about 100g/ 3½oz. The mother gharial lays about 40 eggs in a hole in the sand. She lays them in two tiers, separated from each other by a fairly thick layer of sand, and may spend several hours covering her nest.

► LAYING EGGS

The Indian mugger, or swamp, crocodile digs a sandy pit about 50cm/20in deep in a river bank and lays ten to 50 eggs inside. She lays her eggs in layers and then covers them with a mound of twigs, leaves, soil and sand. During the 50 to 75 day incubation, the female spends most of the time practically on top of the nest. When females lay their eggs, they are usually quite tame. Researchers have been able to catch the eggs as they are laid.

▶ INSIDE AN EGG

Curled tightly inside its egg, this alligator has its head and tail twisted around its belly. Next to the developing baby is a supply of yolk, which provides it with food during incubation. Researchers have removed the top third of the shell to study the stages of development. The baby will develop normally even though some of the shell is missing. As the eggs develop, they give off carbon dioxide gas into the nest. This reacts with air in the chamber and may make the shell thinner to let in more oxygen.

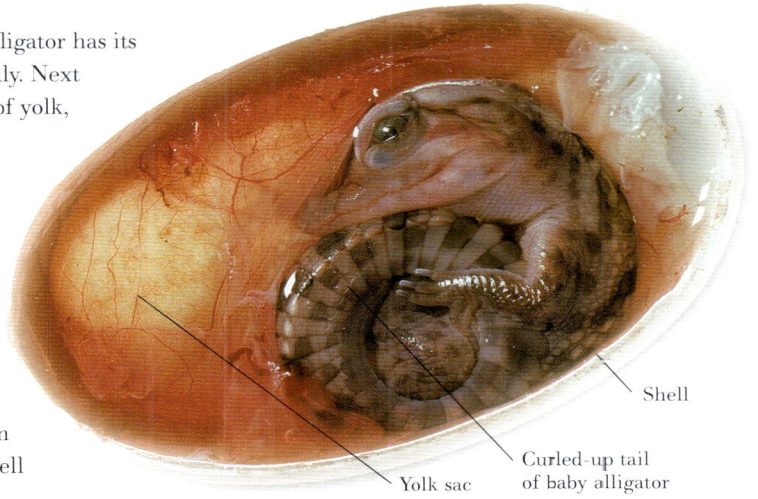

Shell

Curled-up tail
of baby alligator

Yolk sac

◀ CRACKING EGGS

A mother crocodile will sometimes help her eggs to hatch. When she hears the baby calling inside, she picks up the egg in her mouth. Holding it gently, she rolls the egg to and fro against the roof of her mouth, pressing gently to crack the shell. The mother may have to do this for around 20 minutes before the baby breaks free from the egg.

Did you know? A large crocodile may take an hour to lay 80 or more eggs.

▶ EGGS IN THE NEST

Saltwater crocodiles lay large, creamy-white eggs, up to twice the size of chicken's eggs. However, the eggs are more equally rounded at each end than chicken's eggs. It takes a female saltwater crocodile about 15 minutes to lay between 20 and 90 eggs in her nest. The eggs take up to 90 days to hatch.

Focus on

Baby crocodilians make yelping, croaking and grunting noises from inside their eggs when it is time to hatch. The mother hears the noise and digs the eggs from the nest. The babies struggle free of their eggshells, sometimes with help from their mother. While the young are hatching, the mother is in a very aggressive mood and will attack any animal that comes near. The hatchlings are about 28cm/11in long, lively and very agile. They can give a human finger a painful nip with their sharp teeth. Their mother carries them gently in her mouth down to the water. She opens her jaws and waggles her head from side to side to wash the babies out of her mouth.

1 As soon as a mother Nile crocodile hears her babies calling from inside their eggs, she knows it is time to help them escape from the nest. She scrapes away the soil and sand with her front feet and may even use her teeth to cut through any roots that have grown between the eggs. Her help is very important as the soil has hardened during incubation. The hatchlings would find it difficult to dig their way up to the surface without her help.

The hatchling punches a hole in its hard shell with a forward-pointing egg tooth.

2 This baby Nile crocodile has just broken through its eggshell. It used a horny tip on the snout, called the egg tooth, to break through. The egg tooth is the size of a grain of sand and disappears after about a week. The shell has become thinner during the long incubation. This makes it easier for the baby to break free.

Hatching Out

3 Struggling out of an egg is a long, exhausting process for the hatchling. When the babies are half out of their eggs, they sometimes take a break so they can rest before completely leaving their shells. After hatching, the mother crushes or swallows rotten eggs.

4 Even though they are fierce predators crocodilians make caring parents. The mother Nile crocodile lowers her head into the nest and delicately picks up the hatchlings, as well as any unhatched eggs, between her sharp teeth. She gulps them into her mouth. The weight of all the babies and eggs pushes down on her tongue to form a pouch that holds up to 20 eggs and live young. Male mugger crocodiles also carry the young like this and help hatchlings to escape from their eggs.

5 A young crocodilian's belly looks fat when it hatches. This is because it contains the remains of the yolk sac, which nourished it through the incubation period. The hatchling can swim and catch its own food straight away, but it continues to feed on the yolk sac for up to two weeks. In Africa, the wet season usually starts soon after baby Nile crocodiles hatch. This provides an abundance of food, such as insects, tadpoles and frogs for the hatchlings. They are very vulnerable to predators and are guarded by their mother for at least the first weeks of life.

Growing Up

Juvenile (young) crocodilians lead a very dangerous life. They are too small to defend themselves easily, despite their sharp teeth. Their bright colours also make them easy for predators to spot. All sorts of predators lurk in the water and on the shore, from birds of prey and monitor lizards to otters, pelicans, tiger fish and even other crocodilians. One of the reasons that crocodilians lay so many eggs is that so many young do not survive to reach their first birthday. Only one in ten alligators lives to the end of its first year. Juveniles often stay together in groups during the first weeks of life and call loudly to the adults for help if they are in danger. By the time the juveniles are four years old, they stop making distress calls and start responding to the calls of other young individuals.

▲ INSECT DIET
A spiky-jawed Johnston's crocodile is about to snap up a damselfly. Juveniles eat mainly insects. As they grow, they take larger prey, such as snails, shrimp, crabs and small fish. Their snouts gradually strengthen, so that they are able to catch bigger prey. At a few months old, they live rather like lizards and move quite a distance away from the water.

Did you know? 15 per cent of baby saltwater crocodiles do not survive a month.

◄ FAST FOOD
These juvenile alligators will grow twice as fast in captivity as they would in the wild. This is because they are fed regular meals and do not have to wait until they can catch a meal for themselves. It is also because they are kept in warm water — alligators stop feeding in cooler water. The best temperature for growth is 30–32°C/86–90°F.

▶ **BABY CARRIERS**

Juveniles stay close to their mother for the first few weeks, often using her back to rest on. No predator would dare to attack them there. Baby alligators are only about 25cm/10in long when they are born but grow quickly. When they have enough food to eat, male alligators grow about 30cm/12in a year until they are 15 years of age.

▲ **CROC CRECHE**

A Nile crocodile guards her young while they bask in the sun. A group of crocodilian young is called a pod. A pod may stay in the same area for as long as two years. At the first sign of danger, the mother rapidly vibrates her trunk muscles and the young immediately dive underwater.

▲ **TOO MANY ENEMIES**

The list of land predators that attack juvenile crocodilians include big cats, such as this leopard, ground hornbills, marabou storks and genet cats. Large wading birds, including herons, spear them with their sharp beaks in shallow water, while, in deeper water, catfish, otters and turtles all enjoy a young crocodilian as a snack. Only about two per cent of all the eggs laid each year survive to hatch and grow into adults.

▶ **NOISY POD**

A pod of juveniles, like this group of young caimans, is a noisy bunch. By chirping and yelping for help, a juvenile warns its brothers and sisters that there is a predator nearby. The siblings quickly dive for shelter and hope that an adult will come to protect them. If a young Nile crocodile strays from its pod, it makes loud distress calls. Its mother or any other female nearby, will pick up the youngster in her jaws and carry it back to the group.

On the Defensive

By the time a crocodilian has grown to about 1m/3¼ft long, very few predators will threaten it. The main dangers to adult crocodilians come from large animals, such as jaguars, lions, elephants and hippopotamuses, who attack to protect their young. Giant snakes called anacondas will attack and kill crocodilians for food. Adults may also be killed during battles with other crocodilians during the breeding season. People are the Number One enemy of crocodilians. They kill them for their skins, for food or because they are dangerous. Crocodilians are protected by their powerful jaws, strong tail and heavy armour. They can also swim away from danger and hide under the water, in the mud or among plants.

▲ KEEP AWAY!
An American alligator puffs up its body with air to look bigger and more threatening. It lets out the air quickly to make a hissing sound. If an enemy is still not scared away, the alligator will then attack.

► THE HIDDEN EYE
What sort of animal is peeping out from underneath a green carpet of floating water plants? It is hard to tell that there is a saltwater crocodile lurking just beneath the surface. Crocodilians feel safer in the water because they are such good swimmers. They may spend hours almost completely underwater, keeping very still, waiting for prey to come by or for danger to pass. They move so quietly and smoothly that the vegetation on top of the water is hardly disturbed.

► CAMOUFLAGE COLOURS

The colour of crocodilians blends in well with their surroundings. Many species change colour all the time. For example, at warmer times of the day, they may become lighter in colour. In cool parts of the day, such as the morning, they may look duller and are often mistaken for logs.

◄ CAIMAN FOR LUNCH

A deadly anaconda squeezes the life out of an unfortunate caiman. The anaconda of South America lives partly in the water and can grow up to 9m/30ft long. It can easily kill a caiman by twisting its strong coils around the caiman's body until the victim cannot breathe any more. The caiman dies slowly, either from suffocation or shock. However, anacondas only kill caimans occasionally – they are not an important part of the snake's diet.

Ticking Croc

One of the most famous crocodiles in literature is in Peter Pan, *written by J. M. Barrie in 1904. Peter Pan's greatest enemy is Captain Hook. In a fair fight, Peter cut off Hook's left hand, which is eaten by a crocodile. The crocodile follows Hook's ship, hoping for a chance to gobble up the rest of him. It makes a ticking noise as it travels because it swallowed a clock. At the end, Hook falls into the water. He is chased by the crocodile, but we do not find out if it eats him.*

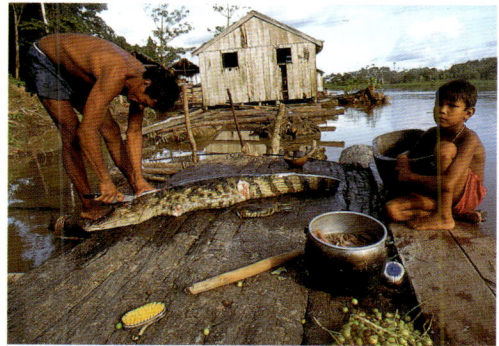

▲ HUMAN DANGERS

People have always killed small numbers of crocodilians for food, as this Brazilian family have done. However, the shooting of crocodilians through fear or for sport has had a far more severe impact on their population. Of the 22 species of crocodilian, 17 have been hunted to the verge of extinction.

159

Freshwater Habitats

A habitat is a place where an animal lives. Most crocodilians live in freshwater (not salty) habitats, such as rivers, lakes, marshes and swamps, in warm places. They tend to live in the shallow areas on the edge of the water because they need to be able to crawl on to dry land for basking and laying their eggs. The shallow water also has many plants to hide among and plenty of animals to eat. The temperature of the water does not vary so much as temperatures on dry land do. This helps a crocodilian keep its body temperature steady. Crocodilians save energy by moving about in water rather than on dry land, because the water supports their heavy bodies. Crocodilians also make an impact on their habitats. The American alligator, for example, digs holes in the river bed. These are cool places where alligators and other animals hide during the heat of the day.

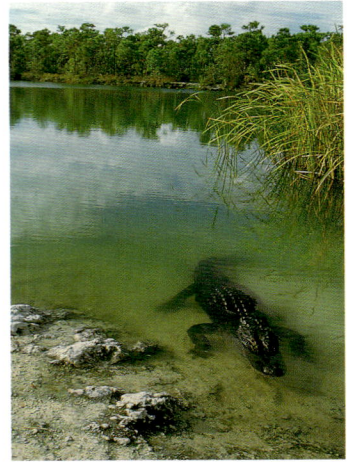

▲ GATOR HOLES
American alligators living in the Florida Everglades dig large gator holes in the limestone river bed. In the dry season, these holes stay full of water. They provide a vital water supply that keeps the alligators and many other animals alive.

▲ RIVER DWELLERS
The gharial likes fast-flowing rivers with high banks, clear water and deep pools where there are plenty of fish. It inhabits rivers, such as the Indus in Pakistan, the Ganges in India and the Brahmaputra of Bangladesh and Assam.

Aboriginal Creation Myth
Crocodiles are often shown in bark paintings and rock art made by the Aboriginals of Australia. Their creation myth, called the dream time, tells how ancestral animals created the land and people. According to a Gunwinggu story from Arnhem Land, the Liverpool River was made by a crocodile ancestor. The mighty crocodile made his way from the mountains to the sea, chewing the land as he went. This made deep furrows, which filled with water to become the river.

◄ **SEASONAL CHANGE**
During the dry season, caimans gather in the few remaining pools along a drying-up river bed. Although the pools become very crowded, the caimans seem to get along well together. In some parts of South America, caimans are forced to live in river pools for four or five months of the year. After the floods of the wet season, they can spread out again.

► **NILE CROCODILES**
Nile crocodiles warm themselves in the sun on a sandy riverbank. Despite their name, Nile crocodiles do not live only in the river Nile. At one time, these powerful crocodiles lived all over Africa, except in the desert areas. Nowadays, they still live in parts of the Nile, as well as the other African waterways, such as the Limpopo and Senegal rivers, Lake Chad and the Okavango swamp. There are also Nile crocodiles living on the island of Madagascar.

◄ **AUSTRALIAN HABITATS**
Australian crocodiles, such as Johnston's crocodile, often live in billabongs (waterholes) such as this one in the Northern Territory of Australia. A billabong is a branch of a river that comes to a dead end. They provide crocodiles with water and land as well as food to eat. Saltwater crocodiles are also found in such areas because they live in both fresh and salt water. People are advised not to swim or wade in the water and to avoid camping nearby.

161

Rainforest Dwellers

Three unusual crocodilians live in rainforest streams and swamps where they avoid competition with larger caimans and crocodiles. Cuvier's dwarf caiman and Schneider's dwarf caiman live in South America, while the African dwarf crocodile lives in the tropical forests of Central Africa. The bodies of these small crocodilians are heavily armoured. This may help to protect the South American caimans from sharp rocks in the fast-flowing streams where they live and from spiky plants in the forest. All three crocodilians may also need this extra protection from predators because of their small size. Rainforest crocodilians do not usually bask in the sun during the day, although the dwarf crocodile may sometimes climb trees to sun itself. All three crocodilians seem to spend quite a lot of time on land. Schneider's dwarf caiman lives in burrows dug in stream banks.

▲ MYSTERY CROC

Very little is known about the African dwarf crocodile. It is a secretive and shy animal that is active at night. It lives in swamps, ponds and small, slow-moving streams. After heavy rain, the dwarf crocodile may make long trips over land at night. Females lay about ten eggs, which take 100 days to hatch. They probably protect their young in their first weeks.

Did you know? Cuvier's dwarf caimans sometimes eat their own young.

◄ YOUNG COLOURS

A newly hatched Cuvier's dwarf caiman rests on a rock. Hatchling dwarf caimans have a yellowish-brown skull and black or brown cross bands on the body and tail. This gives good camouflage. For the first couple of days, they are also covered in slime. Then they enter the water for the first time.

Termite mound

Schneider's dwarf
Caiman eggs

Caiman nest

Termite
mound

Edge of nest

28°C/
82°F

28.5°C
83°F

29°C/84°F

30°C/86°F

32°C/90°F

34°C/
93°F

1 metre/39 inches

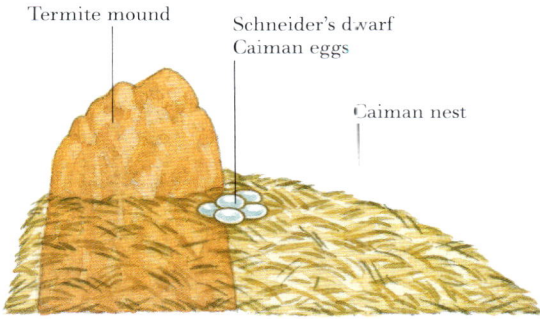

◄ HELPFUL NEIGHBOURS

Schneider's dwarf caiman lays its eggs beside termite mounds. Little sun reaches the forest floor, so the extra heat generated by the termites helps the caiman's eggs develop. Often, the termites cover the eggs with a rock-hard layer, so the parents must help their young break out.

▲ NOSE TO TAIL

Unlike other caimans, dwarf caimans do not have bony ridges around the eyes and snout. Because of this they are also known as smooth-fronted caimans. Shown here is Cuvier's dwarf caiman. Its short snout is not streamlined for swimming and it has a short tail, which may help it to move more easily on land.

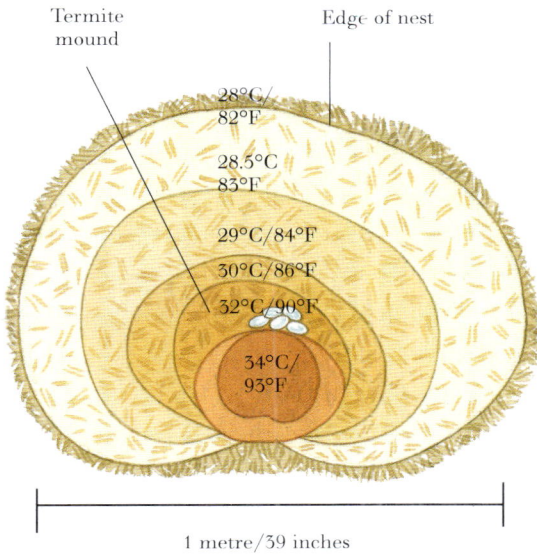

◄ TEETH AND DIET

The sharp, pointed teeth of Cuvier's dwarf caiman curve backwards in the mouth. This helps it grip the slippery skin of frogs or seize such prey as fish in fast-flowing waters. The Cuvier's diet is not well known, but it probably eats a variety of aquatic invertebrates (animals without a backbone), such as shrimp and crabs, as well as rodents, birds and snakes.

163

Focus on

Caimans are mostly small, agile crocodilians that live in Central or South America. Most do not grow more than 2.4m/7¾ft long, but the black caiman can be bigger than an alligator. Caimans look like alligators because their lower teeth do not show when their mouths are closed. They have sharper, longer teeth than alligators and strong, bony plates on the belly and back, including eight bony scutes on the back of the neck. This bony armour helps to protect them from predators, even humans (tough skin is unsuitable for leather goods). Many caimans are endangered, but some spectacled caimans are very adaptable. They have taken over habitats where American crocodiles and black caimans have been hunted to extinction.

MARKINGS FOR LIFE
A black caiman hatches from its egg. Its mother laid up to 65 eggs in the nest, which hatched six weeks later. Its strong markings stay as it grows.

SPECTACLED CAIMAN
The spectacled caiman is so called because of the bony ridges around its eye sockets and across the top of the muzzle. These look a little like eye glasses and may help to strengthen its skull as it seizes and kills prey.

BIG HEAD
The broad-snouted caiman has the widest head of any crocodilian, with a ridge running down the snout. About 2m/6½ft long, it lives in marshes or streams with dense vegetation.

Caimans

Young caimans and alligators have spots and bands across the body.

Black caiman
(Melanosuchus niger)

Bony scutes.

Unusual webbed front feet.

Short, low snout and jaws lined with 64 teeth.

MEMBERS OF THE GATOR CLAN

Caimans have short snouts, roughly circular eye sockets and wrinkled eyelids. Although caimans are closely related to alligators, they are quicker and move more like crocodiles.

EGG THIEF

Tegu lizards eat caiman eggs. In some areas, over 80 per cent of the nests are destroyed by these large lizards. Female caimans may nest together to help defend their eggs.

CAPABLE CAIMAN

The black caiman is the largest of all caimans. The one shown here has just snapped up a piranha fish. Black caimans can grow to over 6m/20ft long and have keen eyesight and hearing. They hunt for capybaras and fish after dusk. When black caimans disappear, the balance of life in an area is upset. Hunted for killing cattle, they are now an endangered species.

Saltwater Species

Most crocodilians live in fresh water, but a few venture into estuaries (the mouths of rivers), coastal swamps or the sea. American and Nile crocodiles and spectacled caimans have been found in saltwater habitats The crocodilian most often seen at sea is the saltwater crocodile, also known as the Indopacific or estuarine crocodile. It is found over a vast area, from southern India to Fiji in the Pacific Ocean, and although usually found in rivers and lakes, it has been seen hundreds of kilometres (miles) from the nearest land. Saltie hatchlings are even reared in seawater. This species has efficient salt glands on its tongue to get rid of extra salt without losing too much water. It is a mystery why freshwater crocodiles also have these glands, but it may be because their ancestors lived in the sea. Alligators and caimans do not have salt glands.

▲ SALTY TONGUE
Crocodiles have up to 40 salt glands on the tongue. These special salivary glands allow the crocodile to get rid of excess salt without losing too much water. These glands are necessary because crocodiles have kidneys that need plenty of fresh water to flush out the salt. At sea there is too little fresh water for this to happen.

► SCALY DRIFTER
Although it can swim vast distances far out to sea, a saltwater crocodile is generally a lazy creature. Slow, side-to-side sweeps of a long, muscular tail propel the crocodile through the water, using as little energy as possible. Saltwater crocodiles do not like to have to swim vigorously, so they avoid strong waves wherever possible. They prefer to drift with the tide in relatively calm water.

▶ NEW WORLD CROC

The American crocodile is the most widespread crocodile in the Americas, ranging from southern Florida in the United States to the Pacific coast of Peru. It grows up to 6m/20ft in length (3.4m/11ft on average) and lives in mangrove swamps, estuaries and lagoons as well as fresh and brackish coastal rivers. It has the least armour of any crocodilian and a hump on the snout between the eyes and nostrils.

◀ TRAVELLING CAIMANS

A group of baby spectacled, or common, caimans hides among the leaves of aquatic plants. This wide-ranging species lives in all sorts of habitats, including saltwater ones, such as salt marshes. They even live on islands, such as Trinidad and Tobago in the Caribbean.

◀ LOST ARMOUR

A saltwater crocodile has less protective armour on the neck and back compared to other crocodilians. This makes it easier for the crocodile to bend its body when swimming. Thick, heavy scales would weigh it down too much at sea.

▲ NILE CROCODILE

Although they typically live in rivers Nile crocodiles also inhabit salty estuaries and mangrove swamps. Sometimes they are found on Kenyan beaches and may be swept out to sea. Some have reached the islands of Zanzibar and Madagascar.

Living with People

Many people only ever see a crocodile or an alligator in a story book, on the television or at the cinema. These crocodilians are often huge, fierce monsters that attack and eat humans. Such images have given crocodilians a bad name. A few large crocodiles, such as Nile and saltwater species, can be very dangerous, but most are timid creatures that are no threat to humans. Some people even keep baby crocodilians as pets. Humans are a much bigger threat to crocodilians than they are to us. People hunt them for their skins to make handbags (purses), shoes and belts. Traditional Chinese medicines are made from many of their body parts. Their bones are ground up to add to fertilizers and animal feed. Their meat and eggs are cooked and eaten, while perfume is made from their sex organs, musk and urine.

▲ **ALLIGATOR DANGER**
The just-seen head of an American alligator reinforces why swimming is not allowed. Alligators lurking under the water do occasionally attack people. This usually happens only when humans have invaded its habitat or disturbed its nest or hatchlings.

▶ **CROCODILE DUNDEE**
One of the most dangerous and aggressive crocodilians is the saltwater crocodile, which appeared in the film *Crocodile Dundee*. In the film, Mick "Crocodile" Dundee, saves an American journalist from a surprise attack by a saltie. An adult saltie can grow up to 7m/23ft long and is likely to view a human entering its territory as a meal.

Krindlekrax

In Philip Ridley's 1991 story, Krindlekrax, *a baby crocodile from a zoo escapes into a sewer and grows enormous on a diet of discarded toast. It becomes the mysterious monster Krindlekrax, which lurks beneath the pavements of Lizard Street. It is eventually tamed by the hero of the book, weedy Ruskin Splinter, who wedges a medal down the crocodile's throat. He agrees to take the medal away if Krindlekrax will go back to the sewer and never come back to Lizard Street again.*

▲ SKINS FOR SALE

These saltwater crocodile skins are being processed for tanning. Tanning converts the hard, horny, preserved skin into soft, flexible leather that can be made into bags, wallets (billfolds), shoes and other goods. Some of the most valuable skins come from saltwater crocodiles because they have small scales that have few bony plates inside.

▲ ALLIGATOR WALKABOUT

An American alligator walks through a campsite, giving the campers a close-up view. Attacks out of the water are unlikely – the element of surprise is lost and alligators cannot move fast. Meetings like this are harmless.

A false, glass eye has been inserted into the head.

► TOURIST SOUVENIRS

A baby Siamese crocodile was killed so that its head could be made into a key ring as a tourist souvenir. Most tourists never manage to see a wild crocodilian, but if they buy souvenirs such as this, it means more animals will be killed for a cruel trade.

169

Rare Crocodilians

Almost half of all of crocodilian species are endangered, even though there is much less hunting today than in the past. Until the 1970s, five to ten million crocodilians were being killed each year — far too many for them to reproduce and build up their numbers again. Today, the loss of habitat is a greater threat than hunting for most crocodiles. Other problems include illegal hunting, trapping for food and medicine, and the harvesting of crocodile eggs. Many species are not properly protected in national parks and there are not enough crocodilians being reared on farms and ranches to make sure each species does not disappear for ever. The four most endangered species are the Chinese alligator, the Philippine, Siamese and the Orinoco crocodiles. Other species that live in only small populations are the Cuban crocodile, black caiman and the gharial.

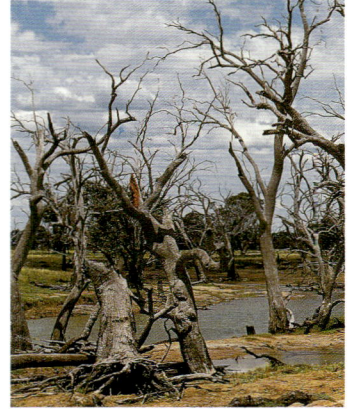

▲ **HABITAT DESTRUCTION**
The trees beside this billabong in Australia have died because there is too much salt in the water. Farmers removed many of the bush plants, which used to trap salt and stop it sinking down into the ground. Now much of the land is ruined by high levels of salt and it is difficult for crocodilians and other wildlife to live there.

▶ **FISHING COMPETITION**
People fishing for sport as well as for food create competition for crocodilians in some areas. They may also accidentally trap crocodilians under water in their fishing nets so that they cannot come up for air, and drown. In waterways that are used for recreation, such as angling, bathing and boating, crocodilians may be killed by the blades of a motorboat's engine and because they pose a threat to human life.

◄ CUBAN CROCODILE

This crocodile has the smallest range of any living crocodilian and is seriously endangered. It lives only on the island of Cuba and the nearby Isle of Pines. The growth of charcoal burning has drastically reduced the habitat of the Cuban crocodile. It has also moved into coastal areas and rivers, where it is more in danger from hunters.

Cuban crocodile
(Crocodylus rhombifer)

► SIAMESE CROCODILE

This endangered crocodile has almost died out in the wild. It was once found over large areas of South-east Asia, but wild Siamese crocodiles now live only in Thailand. They have become so rare because of extensive hunting and habitat destruction. They now survive mainly on crocodile farms.

▲ ILLEGAL HUNTING

This poacher has speared a caiman in the Brazilian rainforest. Hunting crocodilians is banned in many countries, but people still hunt illegally in order to make money. Their hides are so valuable that, even though this caiman's skin contains many bony scutes, it is still worthwhile taking the soft parts.

▼ UNWANTED CROCODILE

A small saltwater crocodile that strayed into somebody's garden is captured so it can be returned to the wild. Its jaws are bound together with rope to stop it biting the ranger. One of the biggest problems for crocodilians is the fact that more and more people want to live in the same places that they do.

Focus

WELL ADAPTED

Gharials have a light-coloured, slender body with extensive webbing between the toes on the back feet. Their long back legs are relatively weak. Gharials are well adapted for life in the water, but are not fast swimmers.

The gharial of northern India and the false gharial of South-east Asia are both endangered species. Their numbers have fallen through hunting for their skins, habitat loss and competition for their main food, fish. Many of the fast-flowing rivers in which they live have been dammed to provide irrigation and to generate electricity. Dams flood some areas and reduce the flow of water in others. They also damage the river banks where gharials nest. People collect their eggs for food and believe them to have medicinal properties. To save the gharial, young are reared in captivity and released into the wild. The false gharial, however, does not breed well in captivity.

CAPTIVE SURVIVAL

This gharial was bred in captivity and has been released into the wild. It has a radio tag on its tail so that scientists can follow its movements. In the 1970s, there were only about 300 wild gharials left. Captive breeding has increased numbers to over 1,500.

MEAL TIME

A gharial lunges sideways to snap up a meal from a passing shoal of fish. Predatory catfish are a favourite meal. When gharial numbers went down, more catfish survived to eat the tilapia fish that local villagers caught for food.

172

on Gharials

FALSE IDENTITY

The false gharial looks like the true gharial and is probably related to it. It lives farther south than the true gharial, from southern Thailand to Borneo and Sumatra. In the wild, adults do not seem to help young escape from the nest and many die as they fend for themselves after hatching. Habitat loss and an increase in land used for rice farming have made false gharials rare. In Indonesia, over-collection of juveniles for rearing on farms may also have reduced numbers.

SAFE HOUSE

A scientist collects gharial eggs so that they can be protected in a sanctuary. There, no predators will be able to get at them and the temperature can be kept just right for development. In the wild, about 40 per cent of eggs are destroyed by predators. Only about 1 per cent of the young survive to adulthood.

WATER SPORT

In the dry, low-water months of winter, gharials spend a lot of time basking on sand banks. Even so, they are the most aquatic crocodilian. They move awkwardly when leaving the water and do not seem able to do the high walk like other crocodilians. Female gharials do not carry their young to the water. This is probably because their snouts are too slender and delicate and their teeth too sharp.

Birds of Prey

Exceptional eyesight capable of spotting prey many miles away is the most important sense used by birds of prey. Powerful talons, a meat-ripping bill and an ability to soar with the minimum effort or power dive at an extremely high speed complete the weapons store of these skilled and formidable aerial predators.

What is a Bird of Prey?

There are nearly 9,000 different species (kinds) of birds in the world. Most of them eat plant shoots, seeds, nuts and fruit or small creatures, such as insects and worms. However, around 400 species, called birds of prey, hunt prey with their feet or scavenge carrion (the flesh of dead animals). Birds of prey are called raptors, from the Latin *rapere* meaning "to seize", because they grip and kill their prey with sharp talons and hooked beaks. The majority of raptors hunt by day. They are called diurnal birds of prey. Day hunters include eagles, falcons and hawks, and vultures (which are scavengers). Other raptors, such as owls, are nocturnal, which means they are active at night.

▼ **HANGING AROUND**

The outstretched wings of the kestrel (*Falco tinnunculus*) face into the wind as the bird hovers above a patch of ground in search of prey. The bird also spreads its broad tail to supplement the air-catching effect of its wings.

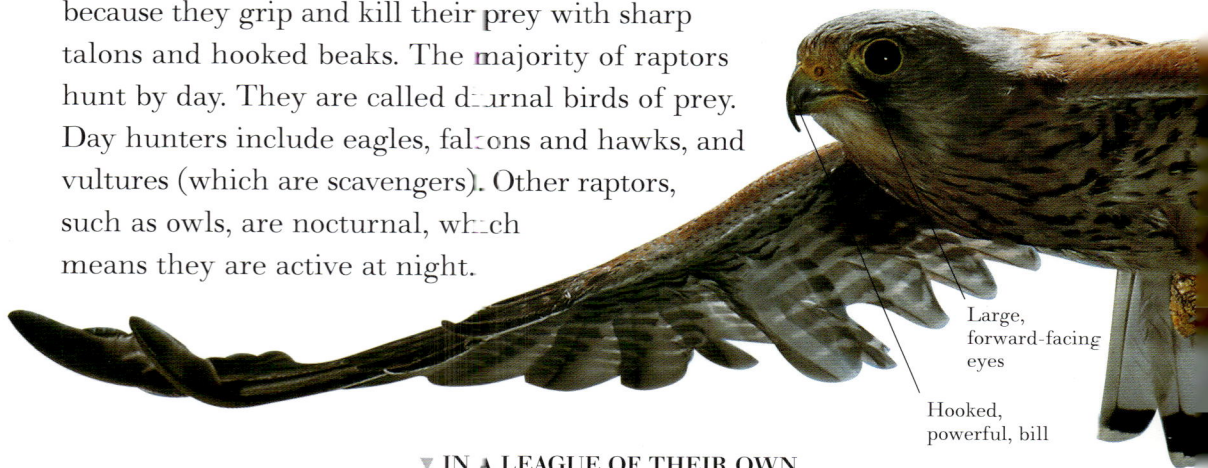

Large, forward-facing eyes

Hooked, powerful, bill

▼ **IN A LEAGUE OF THEIR OWN**

Five young tawny owls cluster together on a branch. Owls are not closely related to the other birds of prey. They usually hunt by night instead of during the day. However, they do share certain features with the other birds of prey. They have excellent eyesight for spotting prey, sharp, hooked bills (beaks) for ripping flesh, and strong legs, with pointed, curled claws (talons) for gripping their prey.

Tawny owls
(*Strix aluco*)

◄ HAWKEYE

The sparrowhawk has large eyes that face forward. The bill is hooked, for tearing flesh. These are typical features of daytime hunters.

Eurasian sparrowhawk
(*Accipiter nisus*)

Wings lift in the flow of air and support the bird's weight. The primary feathers on the wing fan out.

Long, sharp, curved talons

Tail guides the bird through the air and also acts as a brake

▲ BUILT FOR SPEED

The peregrine falcon is the one of the swiftest birds in the world, able to dive at up to 224 kph/139mph. Its swept-back wings help it cut through the air at speed. Their shape has been copied by the designers of fighter planes.

▼ THE EAGLE HAS LANDED

In the snow-covered highlands of Scotland, a golden eagle stands over a rabbit it has just killed. Eagles kill with their talons. They are so long, sharp and deeply curved that one swipe is usually enough to kill a rabbit.

Golden eagle
(*Aquila chrysaetos*)

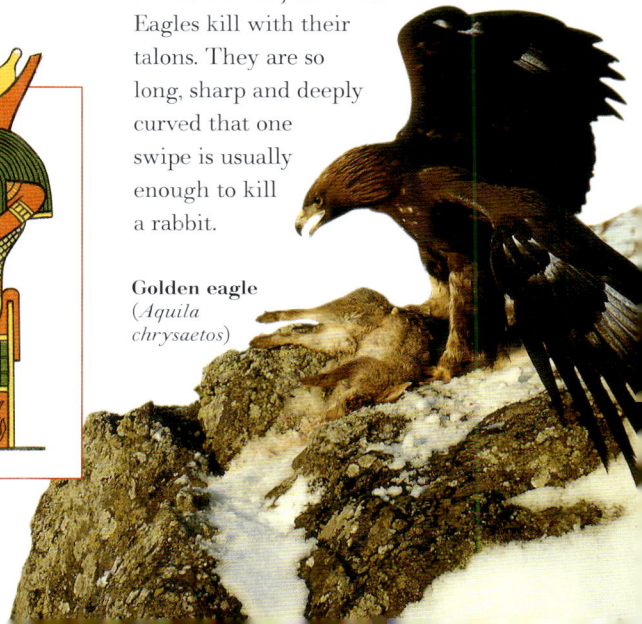

God of the Sky

Horus was one of the most important gods in ancient Egypt. He was the god of the sky and the heavens. His sacred bird was the falcon and Horus is often represented with a human body and a falcon's head. The Egyptian hieroglyph (picture symbol) for "god" in ancient Egyptian is a falcon.

Shapes and Sizes

There are huge differences in size among birds of prey. As many as 40 pygmy falcons could perch on the outstretched wings of one Andean condor. Pygmy falcons are the smallest birds of prey, measuring as little as 20cm/8in from head to tail. The Andean condor is the biggest bird of prey, with a wingspan of some 3m/10ft. In most species, the female is larger than the male. In fact, in some hawk and falcon species, females are up to 50 per cent bigger than males. This is called reverse sexual dimorphism. Most raptors look quite similar when they perch. When they fly, however, there is a great variation in wing size and shape. This usually reflects the different techniques they adopt when hunting prey and the nature of their habitat. For example, the huge wings of the Andean condor allow it to soar high above the Andes mountains.

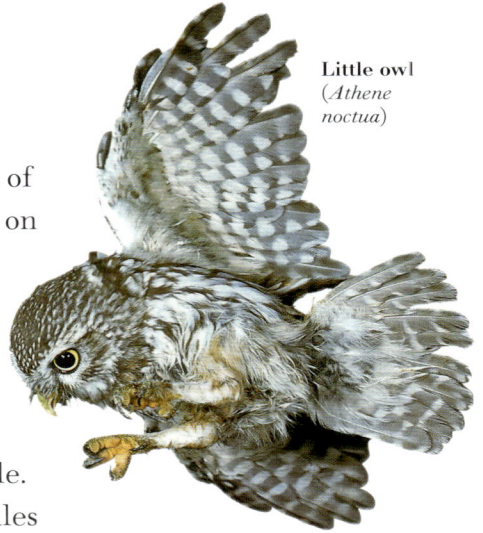

Little owl
(*Athene noctua*)

▲ **WELL-ROUNDED**
The little owl, like other owls, has a round head and broad, rounded wings. Its body, too, has a well-rounded shape, because of its fairly loose covering of feathers. It appears to have no neck at all. It is about 23cm/9in from head to tail.

▲ **AMERICAN SCAVENGER**
The turkey vulture (or turkey buzzard) is a small vulture that lives in North and South America. It grows up to 80cm/31in from head to tail.

▶ **DIFFERENT SIZES**
The female sparrowhawk can grow up to about 38cm/15in from head to tail. The male bird (*shown here*) is much smaller, reaching only about 28cm/11in from head to tail.

Eurasian sparrowhawk
(*Accipiter nisus*)

► **THE BIGGEST**

The magnificent Andean condor is the biggest of all birds of prey. The males grow up to 1.3m/ 4¼ft from head to tail and can weigh more than 12kg/26lb. The condor is a scavenger, feeding on dead animals rather than hunting live prey.

Andean condor (*Vultur gryphus*)

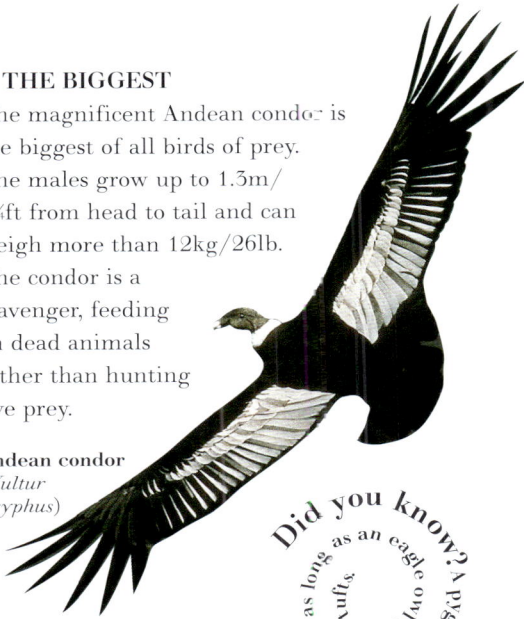

Did you know? A pygmy owl's body is as long as an eagle's ear tuft.

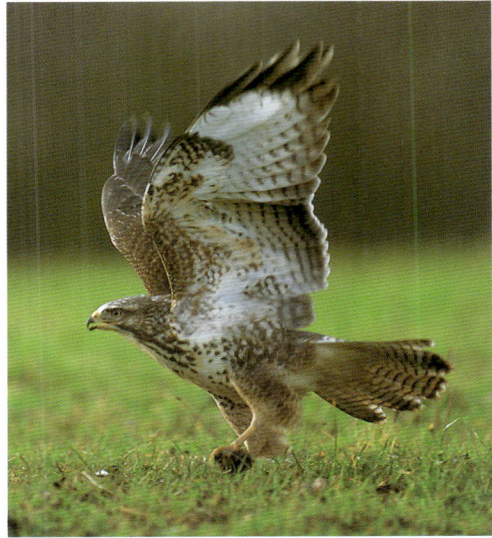

▲ **COMMON BUTEOS**

This common buzzard (*Buteo buteo*) is typical of the family of birds of prey known as buteos. Buteos are about 50cm/20in from head to tail and have long, broad wings up to 1.3m/4¼ft from wing tip to wing tip. This bird is commonly found gliding high above the grasslands and woodlands of Europe and Asia in search of small mammals and reptiles.

▲ **FISH-EATING EAGLE**

The bald eagle (*Haliaeetus leucocephalus*) is instantly recognizable by its snowy white head and tail. It is an impressive bird, growing up to 1m/39in from head to tail. Its long talons enable it to pluck fish from the surface of rivers and lakes in North America.

► **STANDING TALL**

The tallest and most unusual bird of prey is the secretary bird of Africa. It stands up to 1.2m/4ft tall, and its wings can span more than 2m/6½ft. It can soar in the sky like other birds of prey, but most of the time it walks on the ground on its long legs.

Secretary bird (*Sagittarius serpentarius*)

How the Body Works

Birds of prey are supreme fliers. Like other birds, they have powerful chest and wing muscles to move their wings. Virtually the whole body is covered with feathers to make it smooth and streamlined and able to slip easily through the air. The bones are very light and some have a honeycomb structure, which makes them lighter still. Birds of prey differ from other birds in a number of ways, particularly in their powerful bills and feet, which are well adapted for their life as hunters. Also unlike most other birds, they regurgitate (cough up) pellets. These contain the parts of their prey they cannot digest.

▲ **NAKED NECK**
A Ruppell's vulture feeds on a zebra carcass in the Masai Mara region of eastern Africa. Like many vultures, it has a naked neck, which it can thrust deep inside the carcass. As a result, it can feed without getting its feathers too covered in blood.

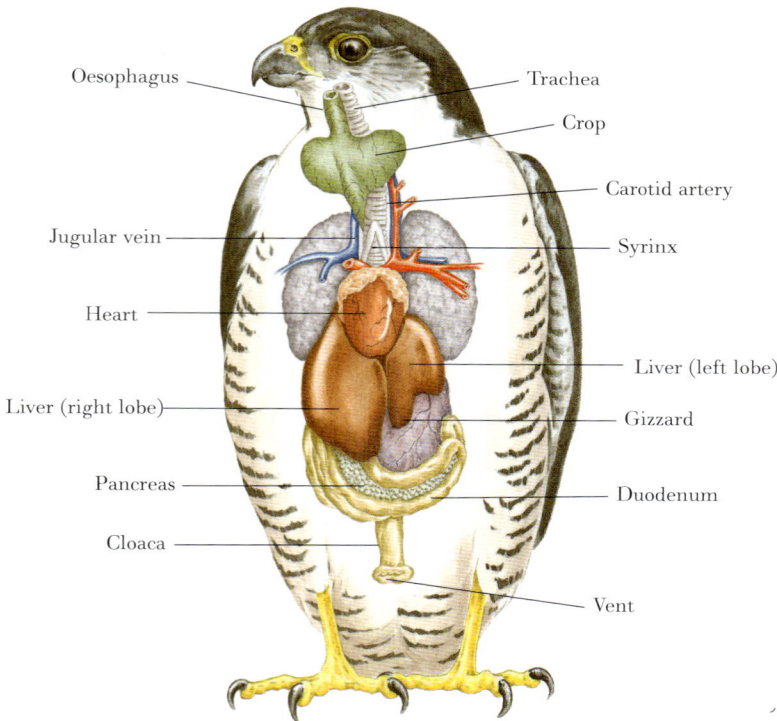

Oesophagus
Trachea
Crop
Carotid artery
Jugular vein
Syrinx
Heart
Liver (left lobe)
Liver (right lobe)
Gizzard
Pancreas
Duodenum
Cloaca
Vent

◄ **BODY PARTS**
Underneath their feathery covering, birds of prey have a complex system of internal organs. Unlike humans, most birds have a crop to store food in before digestion. They also have a gizzard to grind up hard particles of food, such as bone, and to start the process of making a pellet. Birds also have a syrinx (the bird equivalent of the human vocal cord).

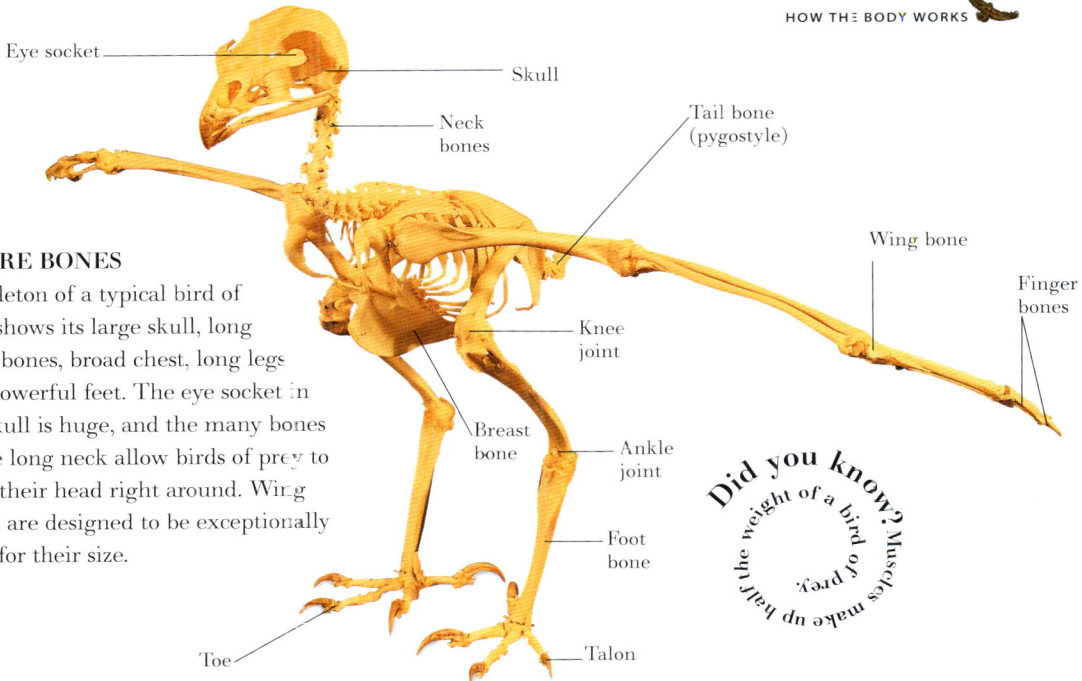

Eye socket

Skull

Neck bones

Tail bone (pygostyle)

Wing bone

Finger bones

► **BARE BONES**

A skeleton of a typical bird of prey shows its large skull, long wing bones, broad chest, long legs and powerful feet. The eye socket in the skull is huge, and the many bones in the long neck allow birds of prey to twist their head right around. Wing bones are designed to be exceptionally light for their size.

Knee joint

Breast bone

Ankle joint

Foot bone

Did you know? Muscles make up half the weight of a bird of prey.

Toe

Talon

▼ **BACK TO FRONT**

This peregrine falcon appears to have eyes in the back of its head. Its body is facing away, but its eyes are looking straight into the camera. All birds of prey can twist their heads right around like this, because they have many more vertebrae than mammals. They can see in any direction without moving the body, but they cannot move their eyeballs in their sockets.

Peregrine falcon
(*Falco peregrinus*)

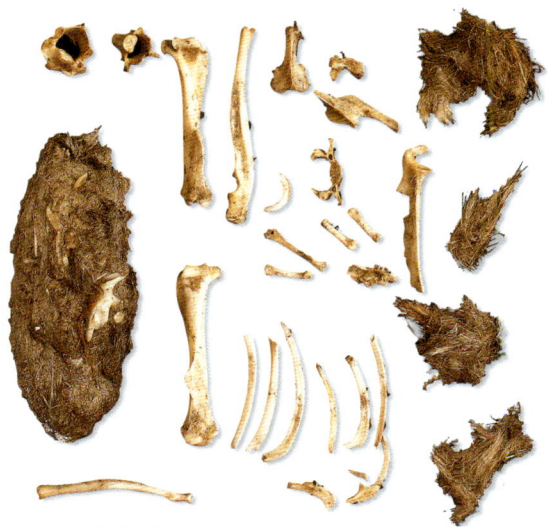

▲ **INDIGESTION**

On the left of the picture above is the regurgitated (coughed-up) pellet of a barn owl, and on the right are the indigestible parts it contained. The pellet is about 5cm/2in long. From its contents we can tell that the owl has just eaten a small mammal, as the pellet contains scraps of fur and fragments of bone.

181

The Senses

Humans rely on five senses to find out about the world. They are sight, hearing, smell, taste and touch. However, most birds live using just the two senses of sight and hearing. In birds of prey, sight is by far the most important sense for finding and hunting the prey they need to survive. Their eyes are exceptionally large in relation to the size of the head and they are set in the skull so that they look forward. This binocular (two-eyed) forward vision enables them to judge distances accurately when hunting. Owls have particularly large eyes that are well adapted for seeing in dim light. They are equally dependent on hearing to find prey in the dark. Some harriers and hawks use their keen sense of hearing to hunt, too. Birds' ear openings are quite small. They are set back from the eyes and cannot be seen because they are covered in feathers.

Common buzzard (*Buteo buteo*)

▲ OPEN WIDE

A common buzzard opens its mouth wide to make its distinctive mewing call. This bird has extremely large eyes in relation to its body, so it has excellent eyesight. The forward-facing eyes give it good stereoscopic (3D) vision and the ability to pinpoint the exact position of a mouse in the grass 100m/328ft away.

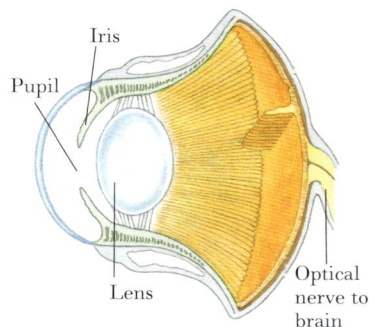

◄ NOT TO BE SNIFFED AT

The turkey vulture of North and South America, like all New World vultures, has nostrils that you can see right through. Its nose is very sensitive. This enables the turkey vulture to sniff carrion on the ground while it is flying above the forest canopy.

Turkey vulture (*Cathartes aura*)

Iris

Pupil

Lens

Optical nerve to brain

▲ OWL EYE

The owl has exceptional eyesight. Its eye is very long, unlike the spherical human eye. The tubular shape of the owl's eye allows it to spot its prey from far away.

Spotted eagle owl (*Bubo africanus*)

◄ FORWARD FACE

The African spotted eagle owl has big eyes. The pupil (middle) and lens are especially large to allow more light to enter and provide the owl with good night vision. The eyes are set in a flat facial disc. The ear-like projections on top of the owl's head are actually ornamental tufts of feathers used for display. The true ears are hidden under stiff feathers at either side of the facial disc. They are sensitive to the slightest noise, which helps the owl locate its prey in the dark.

► ON THE LOOKOUT

This large falcon, called a lanner, is soaring high in the sky on outstretched wings, looking down with its sharp eyes on the scene below. If the lanner sees a flying bird, it will fold back its wings and dive on the unsuspecting bird. The lanner will hit the bird at high speed and usually break its neck. Then it will either snatch the bird in mid-air or pick it up off the ground.

Montagu's harrier
(*Circus pygargus*)

◄ MONTAGU'S EYEBROW

Montagu's harrier is a slender, long-legged hawk with an owl-like facial ruff. The eyes are surrounded by a small bony ridge covered in feathers, called a supraorbital ridge. It probably helps protect the harrier's eyes from attack when the bird goes hunting and may also act as a shield against the sun's rays when it is flying.

183

Wings and Flight

The wings of most birds work in the same way. Strong pectoral (chest) muscles make the wings flap and drive the bird through the air. As it moves, the wings lift in the flow of air and support the bird's weight. The bird is now flying. All birds have differently shaped wings that are adapted to their way of life. Large birds of prey, such as vultures, spend much of their time soaring high in the sky. These birds have long, broad wings that glide on air currents. The smaller hawks, such as the sparrowhawk, have short, rounded wings and a long tail for rapid, zigzagging flight through woodland habitats. A bird's tail is also important for flying. It acts much like a ship's rudder, steadying the bird's body and guiding it through the air. It can be fanned out to give extra lift and also helps the bird to slow down when landing.

▲ **WING FINGERS**
An African fish eagle takes to the air. Like other eagles, it has broad wings and fingered wing tips, seen plainly here. The "fingers" reduce air turbulence around the wings, giving better lift.

Mauritius kestrel
(*Falco punctatus*)

◄ **AGILE BIRD**
The Mauritius kestrel has a broad tail and, for a falcon, fairly short wings. These two features help it to manoeuvre well in the woodland habitat in which it lives. It lives on the island of Mauritius, in the Indian Ocean.

▲ **DROPPING IN**
A sparrowhawk (*Accipter nisus*) is poised to seize a bird it has just spotted. It has short, rounded wings and a long tail. The sparrowhawk's wings beat rapidly and provide enough speed to surprise its unsuspecting prey.

Eagle of the Gods

In Greek mythology, the eagle was the favoured bird of the mighty Zeus. Zeus was god of the sky, lord of the winds and rains, and king among the gods. He is often depicted holding a thunderbolt in his right hand, with an eagle standing at his feet. Here we see him riding in a chariot, drawn by a pair of his sacred birds.

▼ LIKE AN ARROW

The sharply pointed wings tell us that this bird is a falcon. In fact, it is a lanner falcon. A bird can fly extremely fast with pointed wings because the wings cut through the air and offer less wind resistance. Lanner falcons hunt in open ground and use pure speed to catch slower-flying birds.

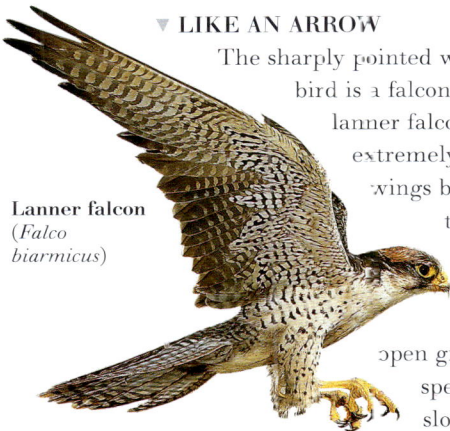

Lanner falcon
(*Falco biarmicus*)

▲ BUILT TO SOAR

A white-backed vulture soars high in the sky, with its broad wings fully outstretched, on the lookout for carcasses on the ground. In the right climate, the vulture can remain in the air for a long time, because its wings provide plenty of lift.

▶ READY, STEADY, GO

A young male kestrel takes off in a multiple-exposure photograph. First the bird thrusts its body forward and raises its wings. Its wings extend and beat downward, pushing slightly backward. As the air is forced back, the bird is driven forward. At the same time, air moving past the wings gives the bird the lift it needs to keep itself airborne.

185

Focus on

1 A Harris's hawk (*Parabuteo unicinctus*) perches on a branch on the lookout for prey, such as reptiles and small mammals. This native of South and Central America and the southern United States is also called the bay-winged hawk because of the rust-brown (bay) bars on its shoulders. It has the relatively short, rounded wings and long tail typical of most small hawks.

Most of the smaller species of hawk have developed wings that enable them to fly at fast speeds over short distances. Larger hawks have broader, longer wings. These allow the birds to soar and glide in the air while scanning the ground below for their prey. Every species favours a different flying technique. For example, sparrowhawks twist and turn with ease as they manoeuvre among the many trees in the woodlands in which they are found. High-speed photography allows us to follow the action as the Harris's hawk shown here takes to the air.

2 Now the hawk is getting ready to fly. It leans forward and begins to raise its wings. It tenses its leg muscles, ready to thrust itself from the perch. The bird's distinctive red thighs and white rump and the white patches on the underwing, are clearly visible.

3 The hawk lifts its wings, and the primaries (the flight feathers at the end of the wings) fan out. It pushes its legs against the perch to take off.

Hawk Flight

4 With a powerful downbeat of its wings and a final push with its legs, the hawk thrusts its body from the perch and begins to travel forward through the air. As the air flows past the wings, it makes them lift and so supports the bird's body. The tail fans out and downward to provide extra lift. The bird is now airborne.

5 The hawk continues beating its wings and gathers more speed. However, the bird's feet are hanging below the body, causing air resistance, or drag, which slows it down. Consequently, the bird will soon tuck its feet up under its body and become a perfectly streamlined, magnificent flying machine.

Did you know? Sacs in a bird's body fill with air to help it stay airborne.

Bill and Talons

The bill and talons of birds of prey are well adapted for killing and feeding on prey or scavenging on the remains of carcasses. Typically the bill is hooked and sharp. However, it is not generally used for killing, but for tearing flesh. Raptors also use their bills to pluck the feathers from birds they catch. Most birds of prey use their feet for the kill. Their toes are tipped with long, sharp, curved talons. When a bird swoops on its prey, the toes clamp around the prey's body and the talons sink into the flesh. The prey is quickly crushed to death. Small birds of prey, such as many falcon species, have less powerful leg muscles and may not always kill their prey this way. So the bird may have to finish it off with a bite. For this purpose, they have a notch (called a tomial tooth) in the upper part of the bill.

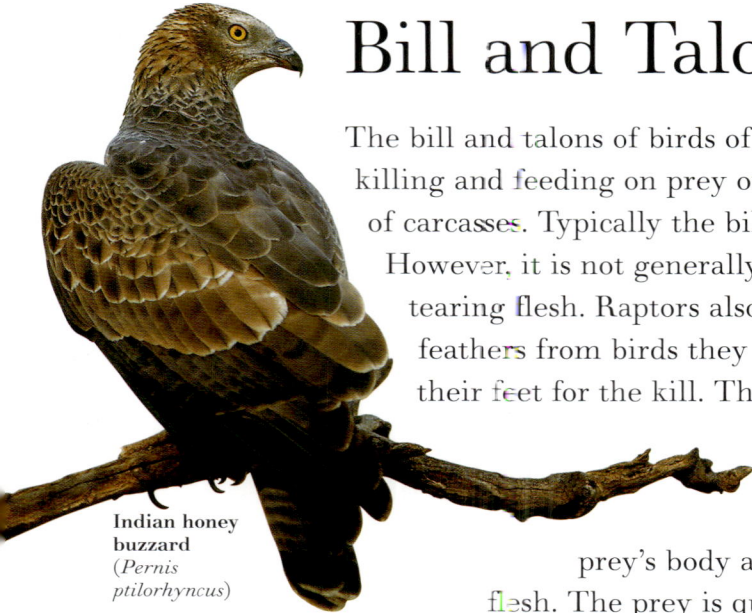

Indian honey buzzard
(*Pernis ptilorhyncus*)

▲ INSECT-EATER

The bill of the Indian honey buzzard is relatively small and delicate compared with that of most other birds of prey. The honey buzzard has no need for a strong bill because it feeds mainly on insects and the larvae of wasps and bees.

► EGG HEAD

The Egyptian vulture's hooked bill is too weak to break into a large carcass without the aid of other, larger vultures. However, its long bill is ideal for breaking eggs, one of its favourite foods. In contrast to this bird's fine head plumage, other vultures have bare heads and necks. This prevents them from covering their feathers with blood when they reach deep inside a carcass to feed.

▲ SPINDLY LEGS

Featherless legs

Sharp talons

The legs of the sparrowhawk are long and slender and lack feathers. Both the toes and talons are long. As it homes in on a small bird, the sparrowhawk thrusts its legs forward, with both feet spread wide. It then snaps its toes and talons around the prey's body and captures it in a deadly grip. The sparrowhawk then flies off to land and feed on its catch.

▲ FEATHER TROUSERS

Like most owls, the great horned owl of North America has soft feathers covering its legs and feet, as well as its body. They help keep its flight silent.

▲ FEET FIRST

The strong feet of the American bald eagle are geared to catching fish, the main part of the bird's diet. Its talons are sharp and curved. The American bald eagle's feet are powerful enough to cope with a struggling Pacific salmon, sometimes weighing as much as the bird itself.

Horrific Harpies
The harpy eagle is one of the most formidable birds of prey. It takes its name from the Harpies of Greek mythology. These were winged monsters that brought violent winds. They had women's heads, pale with hunger, and the bodies and sharp talons of eagles. They attacked people and stole or fouled their food.

Hunting on the Wing

Sparrowhawk
(*Accipiter nisus*)

Birds of prey hunt in different ways. Many smaller raptors and owls sit on a perch and simply wait for a meal to appear on the ground or fly past. This is called still hunting. Other birds search for prey by flying low over the open ground or in and out of cover, such as a clump of trees. Kestrels are among the birds that hover in the air while looking for prey and then swoop down suddenly on it. On the other hand, peregrines are noted for their spectacular dives, or stoops. With wings almost folded, they dive on their prey from a great height, accelerating up to hundreds of kilometres an hour. Their aim is to strike the prey at high speed to kill it instantly. The peregrine either snatches its prey from the air or picks it up off the ground.

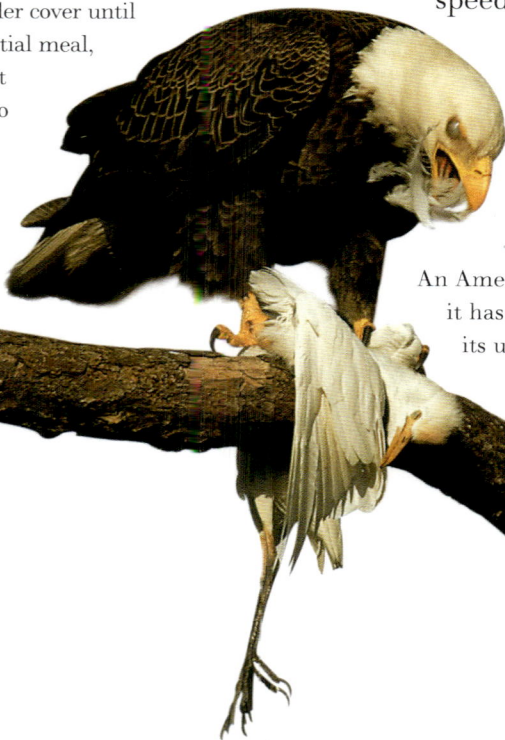

▲ SURPRISE, SURPRISE

The sparrowhawk uses surprise and speed to make a kill. It flies under cover until it spots a potential meal, then dashes out into the open to snatch up its unsuspecting prey at speed.

◄ PLUCKY EAGLE

An American bald eagle plucks a cattle egret it has just killed, making a change from its usual diet of fish. Most birds of prey pluck the feathers from birds they have caught before eating, as they cannot digest them. Owls are the only birds to swallow their prey whole.

Bald eagle
(*Haliaeetus leucocephalus*)

Buzzard
(Buteo buteo)

◀ **RABBIT RELISH**
A common buzzard stands guard over the rabbit it has just killed. Over grassland, the buzzard hunts on the wing, sometimes hovering like a kestrel. Where there are trees or rocks, it may perch on a high point for hours until it sights prey. The buzzard then swoops down quickly upon it.

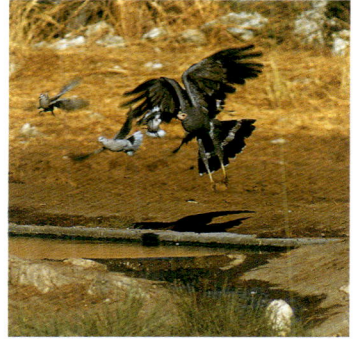

▲ **IN HOT PURSUIT**
An African harrier hawk chases doves along the riverbank. Such chases more often than not end in failure. This hawk is about the same size as a typical harrier, but it has longer wings.

▼ **IT'S A COVER-UP**
Spreading out its wings, a kestrel tries to cover up the mouse it is preparing to eat on its feeding post. This behaviour is known as mantling and is common among birds of prey. They do it to hide their food from other hungry birds, in case they try to rob them

▼ **MAKING A MEAL OF IT**
A kestrel tucks into its kill on its favourite feeding post. The bird holds the prey with its feet and claws and tears the flesh into small pieces with its sharp bill. It swallows small bones, but often discards big ones. Later it regurgitates (brings up) pellets containing the bits of its prey it was unable to digest.

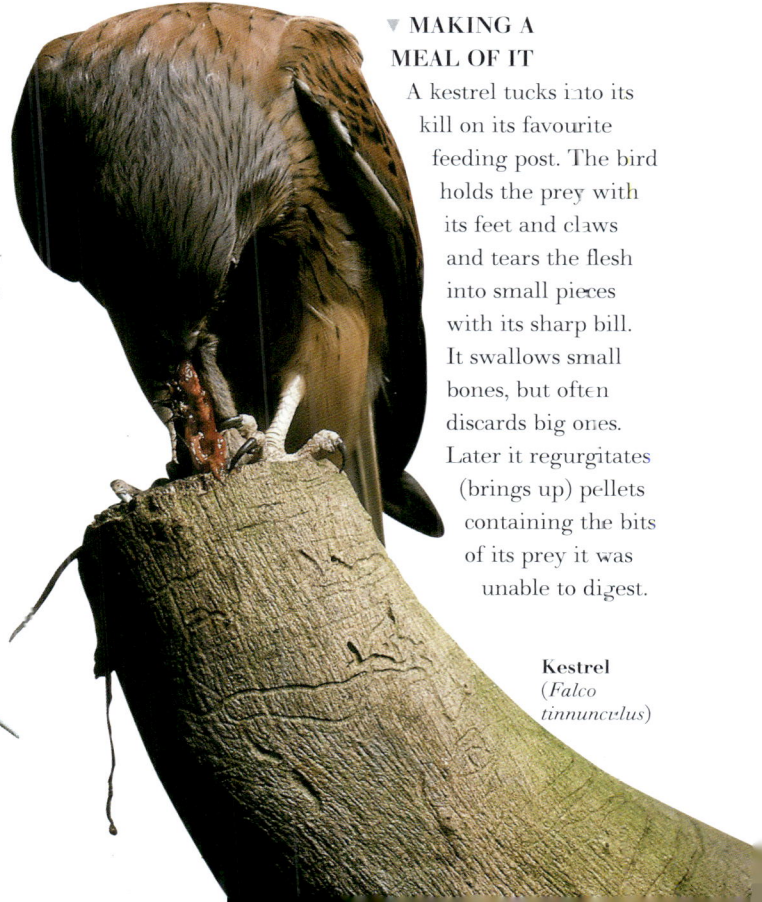

Kestrel
(Falco tinnunculus)

The Hunted

Birds of prey hunt all kinds of animals. Many prey on other birds, including sparrows, starlings and pigeons, which are usually taken in the air. Certain birds prey on small mammals, such as rabbits, lemmings, rats, mice and voles, and some of the larger eagles will even take larger mammals. The Philippine eagle and the harpy eagles of South America pluck monkeys from the rainforest canopy. These eagles are massive birds, with bodies 1m/39in long. Serpent eagles and secretary birds feast on snakes and other reptiles. Small birds of prey often feed on insects and worms. Most species will also supplement their diet by scavenging on carrion (the meat of dead animals) whenever they find it.

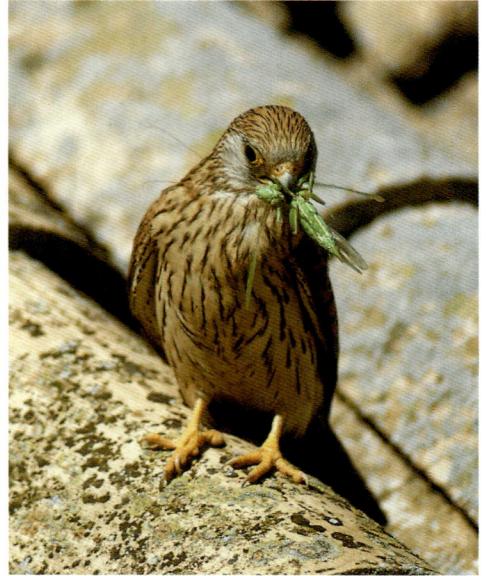

▲ **INSECT INSIDE**

A lesser kestrel prepares to eat a grasshopper it has just caught on a rooftop in Spain. This kestrel lives mainly on insects. It catches grasshoppers and beetles on the ground, and all kinds of flying insects while in flight. When there are plenty of insects, flocks of lesser kestrels feed together. Unlike the larger common kestrel, the lesser kestrel does not hover when hunting.

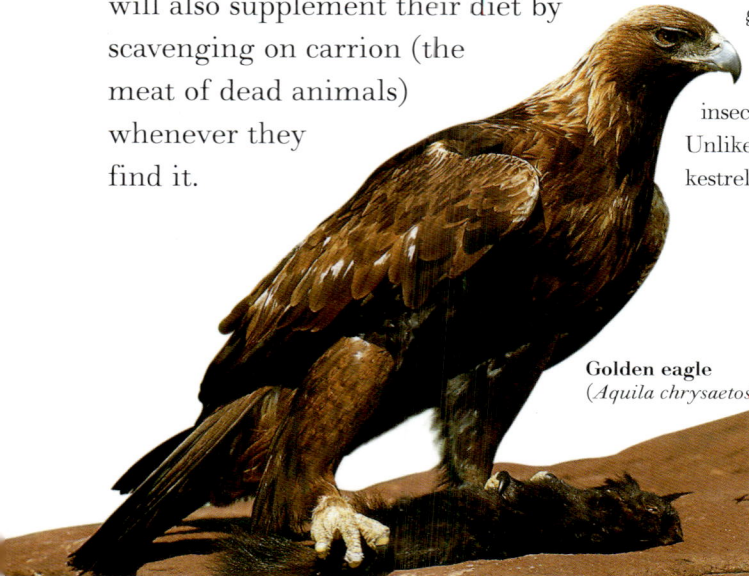

Golden eagle
(*Aquila chrysaetos*)

◄ **GOLDEN HUNTER**

A golden eagle stands guard over the squirrel it has just caught. The golden eagle usually hunts low down. It flushes out prey – mainly rabbits, hares and grouse – which it catches and kills on the ground. Whenever it gets the chance, it will also eat carrion.

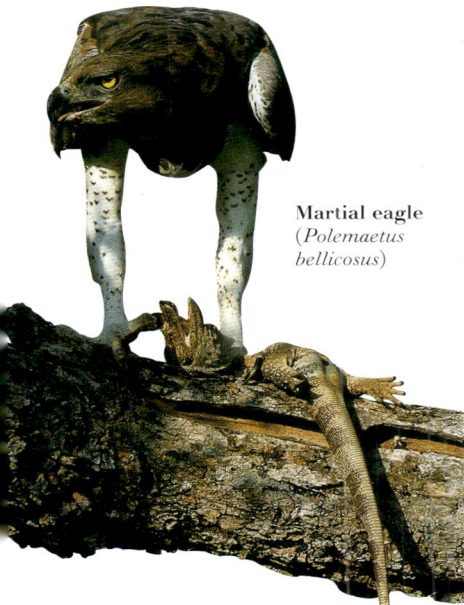

Martial eagle
(*Polemaetus bellicosus*)

▲ REPTILIAN SNACK

A martial eagle stands over its lizard kill in the Kruger National Park, South Africa. This is Africa's biggest eagle, capable of taking prey as big as a kuda (a small antelope).

Did you know? 12 species of birds of prey eat only insects.

▼ SNAIL SPECIALIST

A snail kite eyes its next meal. This is the most specialist feeder among birds of prey eating only freshwater snails. It breeds in the Everglades National Park, Florida, in the United States.

▲ COBRA KILLER

A pale chanting goshawk has caught and killed a yellow cobra. The chanting goshawks earned their name because of their noisy calls in the breeding season. The African plains are the hunting grounds of both the pale and the dark chanting goshawks, which feed mainly on reptiles, such as lizards and snakes.

Snail kite
(*Rostrhamus sociabilis*)

193

Feuding and Fighting

Birds often squabble over food. Some birds of prey harry (intimidate) other raptors that have already made a kill and try to force them to drop it. This behaviour is called piracy. Sometimes birds of prey are attacked by the birds that they often prey on. A number of small birds may join forces against a larger adversary and give chase, usually calling loudly. This is known as mobbing and it generally serves to confuse and irritate the raptor and also warns off other prey in the area.

Birds of prey must also defend their nests against predators. The eggs and chicks of harriers and other ground-nesting raptors are especially vulnerable to attack. Nesting adults will often fly at intruders and try to chase them off.

▲ SCRAP IN THE SNOW
On the snowy shores of the Kamchatka Peninsula, in North-east Russia, these sea eagles are fighting over a fish. A Steller's sea eagle, the biggest of all sea eagles, is shown on the right, with its huge wings outstretched. Its opponents, struggling in the snow, are white-tailed eagles. The two kinds of sea eagles are bound to meet and fight because they occupy a similar habitat and feed on similar prey – fish, birds and small mammals.

◄ FISH FIGHT
Two common buzzards fight over a fish they have both spotted. Buzzards do not go fishing like ospreys, but they will feed on dead fish washed up on river banks. Buzzards, like many other raptors, will eat carrion as well as their preferred food of small mammals, such as rabbits, and the worms and beetles they find on the ground.

Common buzzards
(*Buteo buteo*)

194

► **UNDER THREAT**

On the plains of Africa, a dead animal carcass attracts not only vultures, but other scavengers as well. Here, a jackal is trying to get a look-in, but a lappet-faced vulture is warning it off with outstretched wings.

Did you know? Hunters once used eagle owls as bait to attract mobbing birds into range.

Jay
(*Garrulus glandarius*)

▲ **CLEVER MIMIC**

When a jay spots a predator, such as a bird of prey, it gives out an alarm call or mimics the predator's own call to warn off other jays.

▲ **IN HOT PURSUIT**

An osprey has seen this pelican dive into the water and assumes that it now has a fish in its pouch. So it gives chase. Time and again, the osprey will fly straight at the pelican and scare it so much that it will finally release the fish from its pouch.

▼ **SAFETY IN NUMBERS**

A number of crows have ganged up to mob a steppe eagle. They are bold enough to perch dangerously close to their enemy, calling loudly to persuade it to move on. Although the eagle would be more than a match for its tormentors, it might fly off just to escape aggravation.

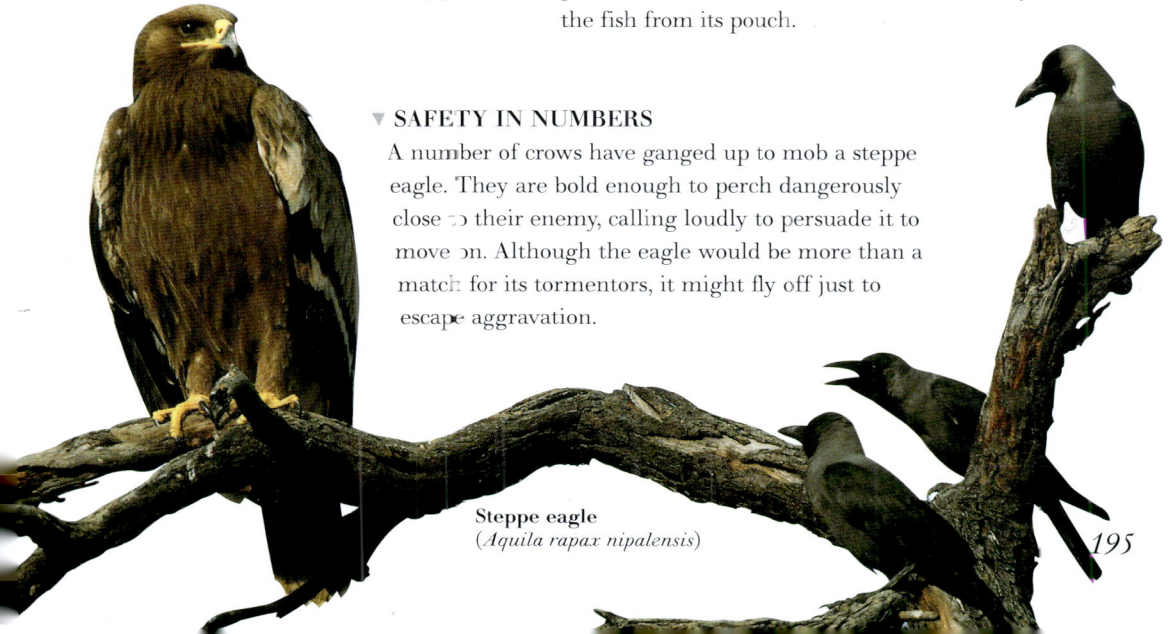

Steppe eagle
(*Aquila rapax nipalensis*)

195

The Night Hunters

Owls are the supreme night hunters, their bodies well adapted for hunting in the dark. For one thing, they fly silently. The flight feathers on their wings are covered with a fine down to muffle the sound of air passing through them. The owl's eyes are particularly adapted for night vision. They contain many more rods than the eyes of other species. Rods are the structures that make eyes sensitive to light. The owl's hearing is superb, too. The rings of fine feathers owls have around each eye help channel sounds into the ears. The ears themselves are surrounded by flaps of skin that can be moved to pinpoint exactly the sources of sounds. A few other raptors also hunt after sundown. They include the bat hawk of Africa and Asia, which eats bats, swallows and insects while in flight.

▲ **GET A GRIP**
Like all owls, the barn owl has powerful claws for attacking and gripping prey. The outer toe can be moved backward and forward to change grip.

Wise Owl
For centuries, owls have had a reputation for being wise birds. This came about because in Greek mythology, the little owl was the sacred bird of the goddess of wisdom, Athena. She gave her name to Greece's capital city, Athens. The best-known coin of the ancient Greek world was issued in Athens and featured an owl.

▲ **ROUNDHEAD**
Of all the owls, the barn owl has the most prominent round face — properly called a facial disc. This gives it a rather ghostly appearance. The disc is formed of short, stiff feathers.

▲ BIG OWL

A European eagle owl stands over a red fox left for it as bait. It looks around warily before beginning to eat. It is a fierce predator and will hunt prey as big as a young roe deer. It is a large bird, growing up to 70cm/27½in long, powerfully built, and with long ear tufts.

▼ MOUTHFUL

A barn owl carries off a mouse it has just caught. Owls carry prey in their bills, unlike the other birds of prey, which carry it in their claws. Barn owls are found throughout most of the world and in many kinds of habitat – moorland, desert, forest and farmland.

Barn owl
(*Tyto alba*)

▶ WHAT A HOOTER

A mouse is carried off by a tawny owl. The long hooting call of the tawny owl can be heard in woodlands, parks and gardens across Europe.

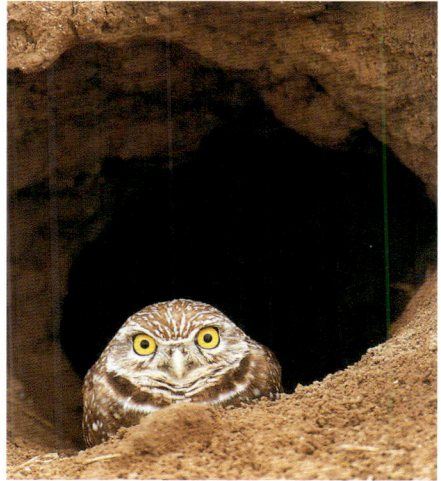

▲ PEEKABOO

A burrowing owl peers out of its nest hole. These small, long-legged birds live on the prairies and grasslands of the New World, from Canada to the tip of South America. They often take over the abandoned holes of other burrowers, such as prairie dogs.

Focus on

1 This owl is waiting for a rustle in the undergrowth. Suddenly it hears something. It swivels its head and its sensitive ears pinpoint exactly where the sound is coming from. Then it sees a mouse, rummaging among the leaf litter on the ground for grubs and insects.

2 Keeping its eyes glued on its potential meal, the owl launches itself into the air. It brings its body forward, pushes off the post with its feet and opens its wings. Just a few metres/yards away, the mouse carries on rummaging for food. It has heard nothing and is busy searching out a tasty insect in the leaf litter on the ground.

The barn owl is found on all continents except Antarctica. It is easily recognizable because of its white, heart-shaped facial disc. Its eyes are relatively small for an owl, but it can still see well at night. It hunts as much by ear as by eye. Its hearing is particularly keen because the feathers on its exceptionally well-developed facial disc channel sounds into its ears with great precision. The owl featured here is "still-hunting", watching for prey from a favourite perch. However, barn owls often hunt while flying. They cruise slowly and silently back and forth over their feeding grounds until they hear or spy prey, then swoop down silently for the kill.

the Silent Swoop

3 The owl makes a beeline for its prey
with powerful beats of its wings. Even
though it is travelling quite fast, it still
makes no sound. The owl has dense, soft
feathers covering its wings and legs. These
feathers silence the flow of air as it passes
through them. This helps the owl to
muffle its flight and to concentrate on the
sounds that the mouse makes as the bird
draws closer to its prey.

5 Now only a few
centimetres/inches above
the ground, the owl thrusts its
feet forward, claws spread wide,
and drops on to its prey. At the
same time, it spreads out its
wings and tail to slow down its
approach. The hunter's aim is
deadly. Its talons close around
the mouse and crush it to
death. Then the owl picks up
the dead mouse in its beak and
returns to its perch. The owl
will swallow the mouse
head first.

4 The mouse
at last
begins to sense
that something is wrong as the
owl approaches. For an instant it is
glued to the spot in fear. Then it
starts to run for its life. However, the
owl is more than a match for it. With
its rounded wings and broad tail, it is
able to twist and turn in the air with
ease, following every change of
direction of the scuttling mouse.

Fishing Birds

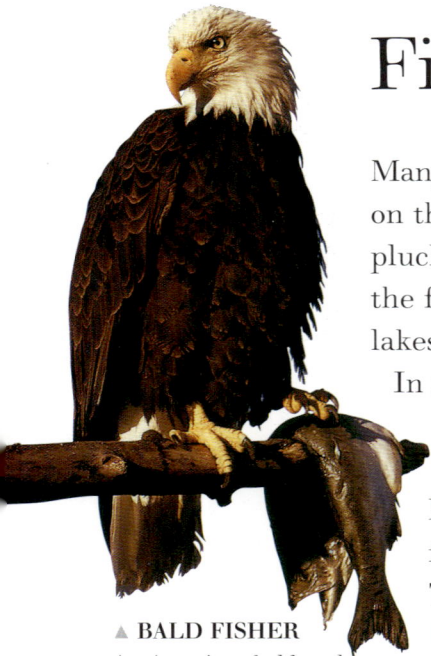

Many birds of prey will eat dead fish when they find them on the river bank and shore. However, some specialize in plucking live fish from the water. Outstanding among the fishing birds is the osprey, found around rivers and lakes throughout the world, except in the polar regions. In many areas, the osprey competes for its food with various species of sea or fish eagles, such as the magnificent bald eagle of North America. All these fishing raptors are large. They have strong, arched bills, long talons and rough scales on their feet, which help them grip their slippery prey. Their pale underparts imitate the bright sky and camouflage on the fish below.

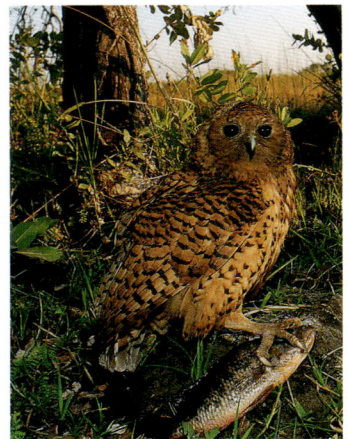

▲ **BALD FISHER**

An American bald eagle rests on a branch with a fish it has killed. It is the only fishing eagle in the Americas. The white feathers on its head and neck make the bird look bald fr

▲ **FISH OWL**

Some owls go fishing, too. This Pel's fishing owl, from Africa, is standing with its catch. Like other fishing owls, it has no ear tufts. Its talons are sharp and curved to catch slippery fish.

◄ **WELL CAUGHT**

An osprey kicks up spray as it grabs at a fish swimming just below the surface of the water. Sometimes ospreys take fish as heavy as 2–3 kg/4½–6½lb – much heavier than their own weight.

Steller's sea eagle (*Haliaeetus pelagicus*)

▲ FISHY DIET

An African marsh harrier grabs a fish from a river near Natal, South Africa. Most marsh harriers live mainly on amphibians, small mammals, reptiles and insects.

▲ BEST FOOT FORWARD

A Steller's sea eagle extends both legs. talons at the ready, as it swoops down to take a fish. This is the largest of the fishing birds of prey and it has an exceptionally fearsome bill.

It lives around the coasts of the Pacific Ocean in Russia and China, where its favourite food is Pacific salmon. It will also take geese and hares.

Did you know? Bald eagles catch fish that are heavier than their own weight.

▲ HIGH LOOKOUT

An osprey, or fish hawk, surveys the water below from its untidy treetop nest. This clever fisher supports a number of other birds, such as fish eagles and terns, that rob it of its catch.

▲ AFRICAN ADVENTURES

An African fish eagle goes in for the kill over a lake in central Africa. The eagle pushes its feet forward during the dive and spreads both wings wide to slow the descent. The bird then plucks the unfortunate fish from the surface of the water and returns to feed on a nearby perch.

Focus on

The osprey is outstanding among the fishing birds of prey. Its acceleration is fast and spectacular, beginning high in the air and ending dramatically in the water. Sometimes it will submerge itself completely, unlike other fishing raptors. It feeds in lakes and rivers and along estuaries and sea coasts. It takes freshwater fish, such as pike and trout. Marine sources of food include herring and flatfish. Although the osprey is a very skilful hunter, not all of its dives are successful. On average, it has to make three or four dives before it succeeds in making a kill. Ospreys may make up to four kills a day to feed themselves, but they need to catch more fish if they are very hungry or when they are feeding chicks in the nest.

1 The osprey soars over the lake, looking for fish swimming close to the water's surface. Once it spots its prey, the osprey falls like a stone out of the sky, gaining speed all the time. It opens out its wings to slow it down seconds before it hits the surface of the water. It brings its feet forward as it enters the water's surface.

2 The osprey's outstretched feet pierce the surface of the water and thrust toward the fish with open claws. The fish can be nearly 1m/39in down, and the osprey has to plunge right into the water to reach it. This time, however, the fish manages to avoid the hunter's clutches, and the bird looks as if it is taking a bath. In a shower of spray, the osprey struggles back into the air to try again.

202

Going Fishing

3 The next fish the osprey spies is swimming at the water's surface. Undeterred by the previous failure, the bird judges its dive well and soon the fish is gripped in the osprey's sharp talons. The spiny surface of the osprey's feet provides extra gripping force and prevents the slippery prey from getting free, no matter how much it wriggles.

4 With powerful beats of its wings, the osprey pulls the fish out of the water. Its feet hold the fish's body head first to cut down air resistance during the flight.

5 The osprey flies back to its perch. On the way, the bird might get attacked by pirates, birds that harry the osprey and force it to drop its catch, which they then pounce on.

6 With its catch in its claws, the osprey lands on its perch. There it uses its sharp bill to slice through the tough scales and skin of the fish to feast on the tasty flesh.

The Scavengers

Most birds of prey kill prey to eat, but many also scavenge on carrion (dead animals) when they find it. For example, the golden eagle feeds mainly on carrion during winter months, when its usual prey is scarce. However, one group of birds, called vultures, scavenges almost entirely on carrion. Vultures have sharp, sturdy bills for slicing through hides and tearing at meat and sinews. Some have heads, and often their necks, naked of feathers to prevent them from becoming caked with blood. Their feet are broad for walking, but weak and with flat claws, because they do not need them to kill. Vultures are noted for their high, soaring flight on long, broad wings. They ride on thermals – warm air currents rising from the ground. They can spot carrion many kilometres/ miles away with their excellent eyesight.

▲ **COASTING ALONG**
This Andean condor soars in search of carrion over cliffs on the Pacific coast of South America. Its diet also includes a lot of fish. It has longer wings than the Californian condor, with a wingspan of over 3m/10ft.

▼ **BEARDED BONEBREAKER**
The lammergeier is also named the bearded vulture owing to the black bristles on its face. It is famous for its habit of breaking bones by dropping them on rocks. It eats the bone fragments and the nutritious marrow inside.

Bearded vulture (*Gypaetus barbatus*)

▲ **CRACKING EGGS**
An Egyptian vulture uses a stone in its beak to crack the hard shell of an egg. It might be smaller than other vultures, but it seems more intelligent. It is the only tool-user among birds of prey. Ostrich eggs are among its favourite food.

◀ ON PATROL

European griffon vultures soar high in the sky using their long, broad wings. They keep a look-out for signs of carrion down below as they fly. Griffon vultures are common in the mountainous regions of southern Europe and northern Africa, often living in large flocks.

Did you know? Ruppell's vultures climb right inside a carcass to feed.

▶ SUNBATHING

A white-backed vulture stands with its wings wide open, sunning itself in the scorching heat of the African savanna. Many vultures do this, probably to allow their feathers to dry after bathing. They also do this to lose heat through the increased surface area of their spread wings.

▼ COLOURFUL KING

The king vulture has the most colourful and unusual head of all vultures. It is found in Central and South America, where it can be seen soaring over the rainforests and among the high peaks of the Andes mountains in search of carrion.

▲ TUCKING IN

A group of white-backed vultures tucks into the carcass of a freshly killed animal on the plains of Zimbabwe, southern Africa. These vultures soar and wheel high in the sky and are attracted to carrion when they see other vultures gathering around it. With their long, naked necks, they reach deeper inside carcasses to feed than some other vultures.

King vulture
(*Sarcoramphus papa*)

Going Courting

Males and females of most bird species usually get together once a year to mate and produce young. Then, as soon as the young birds mature into adults, they too go off to find a mate. Some birds of prey stay with their mate for life. However, courting still takes place every year. This helps strengthen the bond between the two birds. In courtship displays there is usually much calling to each other, with the birds close together. The male may offer the female prey it has caught. Since most birds of prey are superb fliers, however, the most spectacular courtship displays take place in the air. The birds may perform acrobatic dances, or fly side by side, then swoop at each other and even clasp talons. The male may also drop prey while in flight for the female to dive and catch in an extravagant game of courtship feeding.

▲ **THE MARRIED COUPLE**
Like most birds of prey, American bald eagles usually mate for life. They occupy the same nest year after year, gradually adding to it each time they return to breed.

◀ **TOGETHERNESS**
Secretary birds become inseparable for life once they have paired up. Their courtship flights are most impressive, as they fly through the sky with their long tails streaming behind them. The birds also sleep side by side in their nest. They use their nests as living quarters throughout the year, not just during the breeding season.

▲ BEARING GIFTS

A male barn owl has caught a mouse and presents it to his mate back in the nest. This behaviour is called courtship feeding. It helps strengthen the bond between the pair. It is also preparation for the time when the male will have to feed the female when she is nest-bound and incubating their eggs.

▼ BALANCING ACT

A pair of ospreys struggle to keep their balance as they mate on a high perch. While the female turns her tail to one side, the male lowers his tail and presses his cloaca (sexual organ) against hers. His sperm can then be transferred to her body, and she can lay fertilized eggs that will hatch into chicks.

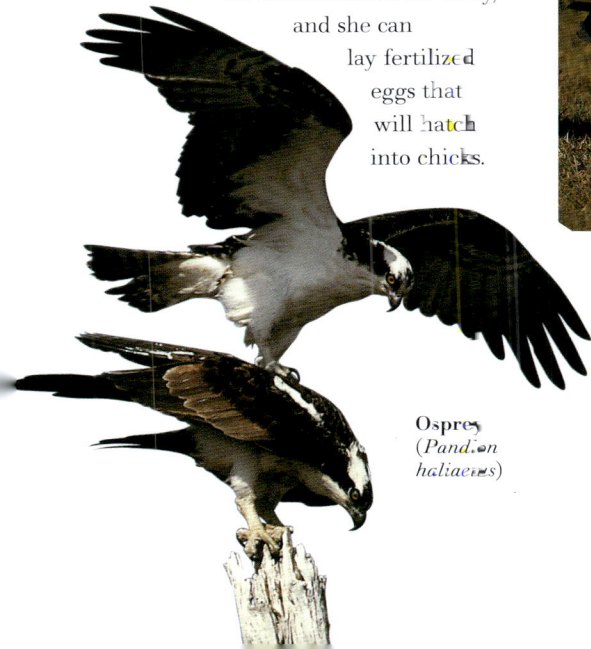

Did you know? Peregrines spend hours performing an amazing courtship flight.

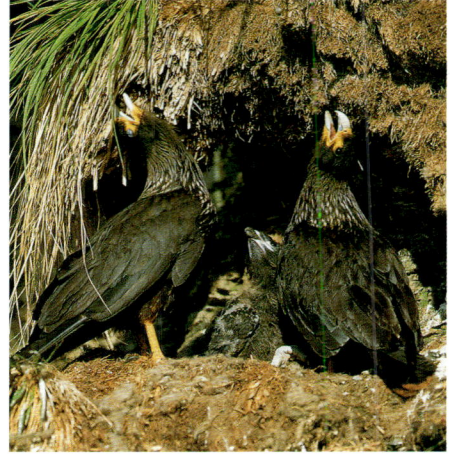

▲ CARACARAS ON DISPLAY

A pair of striated caracaras call to one another by their nest. They are no longer courting but raising young. Mated pairs display like this frequently to strengthen the bond between them. Caracaras can raise two broods (groups of chicks hatched together) a year in South America, but in Florida, they are usually single-brooded.

▲ FACE TO FACE

A pair of Egyptian vultures stand face to face on the ground in an elaborate courtship display. In addition to their ground-based display, the pair also perform spectacular aerial displays. They fly, climb and dive close together, often presenting their talons to each other.

Osprey
(*Pandion haliaetus*)

207

Building Nests and Laying Eggs

Courtship displays help the male and female birds to bond. They also help establish the pair's territory, the area in which they hunt. Within this territory, the birds build a nest in which the female lays her eggs. Birds of prey usually nest far apart, because they need a large hunting area. However, some species, including griffon vultures and lesser kestrels, nest in colonies. Birds of prey choose many different nesting sites, in caves and on cliffs, in barns and the disused nests of other birds, on the ground or high up in trees. The nests themselves may be simple scrapes on a ledge, no more than a bare place for the eggs to rest in. Other nests are elaborate structures built of branches and twigs. Many birds return to the same nest with the same mate every year, adding to it until it becomes a massive structure.

▲ CAMOUFLAGE COLOURS
This hen harrier is nesting on the ground among vegetation. The female, pictured brooding (sitting on her eggs), has the typical mottled-brown plumage of ground-nesting birds. This makes her hard to spot on the nest. The male often feeds the female in the air. He calls her to him, then drops the prey for her to catch.

Bonelli's eagle
(*Hieraaetus fasciatus*)

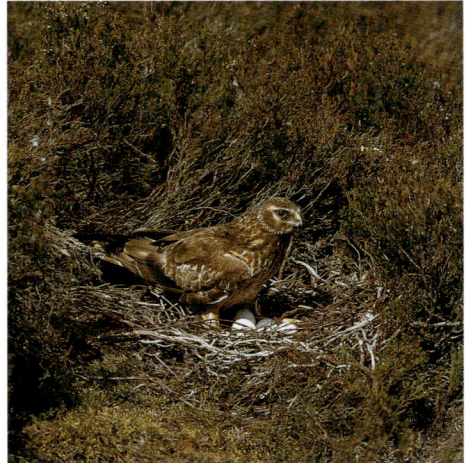

◀ SETTING UP HOME
A female Bonelli's eagle repairs her clifftop nest, keeping a careful watch over her young chick. If there are no cliffs in her territory, the female will build her nest at the top of a tall tree. The nests measure just under 2m/6½ft in diameter, and they are used year after year. You can see that scientists have ringed this chick's leg.

▶ GO AWAY!

With its wings spread wide to make it
look bigger, a barn owl adopts a
threatening pose to protect his nest.
The female has already laid several
eggs, which she will incubate for just
over a month. During this time the
male feeds her, usually with rats, mice
or voles, but sometimes with insects
and small birds. If food is plentiful, the
pair may raise two broods a year.

◀ IN A SCRAPE

On a cliff ledge, this peregrine falcon has
made a simple nest called a scrape,
clearing a small patch of ground to nest
on. Many peregrines use traditional
nesting sites, where birds have made
their homes for centuries. Others have
adapted to life in the city, making their
scrapes on the ledges of skyscrapers,
office buildings and churches.

◀ FULL UP

A secretary bird comes
in to land on the huge tree-top
nest of a colony of social weaver birds
in search of its own nesting
site. As this tree is full,
the bird will have to
choose another site
in which to nest.
It prefers low
thorny trees,
such as the
acacia. It
makes its nest
out of sticks, lining
it with soft grass.

Secretary bird
(*Sagittarius serpentarius*)

▲ SECOND-HAND

A disused raven's nest has been adopted by
this peregrine falcon. Peregrines do not
build their own nests, but often lay eggs in
nests abandoned by other birds. The eggs
are incubated by both parents. Falcon eggs
are pale reddish-brown, unlike those of most
other raptors, which are white or speckled.

209

Focus on

Once a pair of birds has mated, the female lays her eggs. The number of eggs laid depends on the species. Large raptors, such as eagles, lay one or two eggs. Smaller raptors, such as kestrels, may lay up to eight eggs. The eggs have to be incubated (kept warm) after they have been laid so that the baby birds can develop inside. This is done by one of the birds brooding (sitting on the eggs) in the nest all the time. Brooding is done usually by the female. The male's job is to bring the female food. Incubation times vary widely, from less than a month for small falcons to nearly two months for eagles and vultures.

1 A young Mauritius kestrel chick develops inside its egg, feeding on the nutrients surrounding it. Once the chick has grown enough, it begins to chip away at the shell with a projection on its bill called an egg tooth. In time, it makes a little hole, called a pip.

2 Pipping puts the chick in touch with the outside world, and its lungs breathe in the outside air. The chick rests for several hours and then starts hammering away with its egg tooth next to the first pip. After a while the chick twists around and starts hammering again. It does this until it has chipped right around the shell.

3 With the shell cracked, the chick starts its fight to break out. It presses its feet against the lower part of the shell and heaves with its shoulders against the upper part. Soon the top of the egg breaks off, and the head of the chick becomes visible.

Hatching Out

4 The chick kicks and heaves as it continues its fight to escape from the shell, resting frequently to regain its strength. Soon its head is free, then a wing and finally a leg. The chick prepares itself for a last push.

5 With all its remaining strength, the chick forces its body away from the shell. It lies almost motionless, wet and nearly naked, weak and helpless The chick will need to rest for several hours before it has the strength to beg for food. This can be a dangerous time for the chick. It might be trampled by clumsy parents.

6 When the newly hatched chick dries out, its body is covered with sparse, fluffy down. This early down is not enough to keep the chick warm, so it has to snuggle up to its mother in the nest. Gradually, a thicker cover of down grows, which can be seen on these two-week-old kestrel chicks. A full covering of downy feathers will keep them warm and allow their mother to leave the nest.

A Chick's Life

When chicks hatch out, they find it difficult to move. They are unable to stand and just sit on their ankles. Their bodies are covered with fine down, which cannot keep them warm, so they need their mother's warmth to stay alive. That is why she still does not move from the nest. The male continues to bring food, which she tears and feeds to the chicks. After a couple of weeks, a thicker down grows on the chicks' bodies to keep them warm and the female can leave the nest and go hunting again. Soon the chicks grow strong enough to stand up and move about. In species where the eggs hatch at different times, older chicks beg the most food and grow strongest. This can result in the death of the weaker chicks.

▲ **CHICK AND RAT**
A barn owl chick is feeding on a rat its parents have caught. The chick is about six weeks old, and already the well-defined face patch characteristic of all owls has begun to appear.

◄ **SITTING PRETTY**
A secretary bird and its chick rest in their nest in a thorny tree on the African savanna. First, the parents feed the chick on regurgitated liquids. Later, they regurgitate rodents, insects and snakes into the nest for the chick to eat. The chick is fully feathered in five weeks and stays in the nest for about a month longer.

◀ FEEDING TIME

In its nest high up in a tall tree, a female booted eagle feeds its chick. The chick is several weeks old and still covered in thick down, but its feathers are beginning to appear. Both parents feed the chick, often hunting the same prey together. The booted eagle is one of the smallest eagles, measuring about 50cm/20in from head to tail.

▼ LEMMING FEAST

A lemming is the next meal for this snowy owl chick. Lemmings are the staple (usual) diet of this owl. When lemmings are in plentiful supply, snowy owls may raise as many as eight chicks at a time. The eggs are laid over a considerable period of time, so there is a noticeable size difference between the young owls in large clutches.

Snowy owl (*Nyctea scandiaca*)

▲ THREE IN A HOLE

Three kestrel chicks peer out of their nest in a hole in a tree. By the time they are a month old, they will have left the nest and be flying. It will take them up to another five weeks to copy their parents and master the art of hovering in the air to scan for prey.

213

Raising the Young

Young birds of prey remain in the nest for different periods, depending on the species. The young of smaller birds, such as merlins, are nest-bound for only about eight weeks. The young of larger species, such as the golden eagle, stay in the nest for more than three months. Young vultures may stay for over five months. As the chicks grow, their thick down moults (molts) to reveal their proper feathers. They become stronger and start to exercise their wings by standing up and flapping them. Shortly before they leave the nest, they make their first flight. This greatest step in the life of a young bird is called fledging. It takes weeks or even months before the fledglings (trainee fliers) have learned the flying and hunting skills they need to catch prey. During this time, they are still dependent on their parents for all their food.

▲ TAKING OFF

A young kestrel launches itself into the air. It is fully grown but still has its juvenile plumage. Other adults recognize the plumage, so they do not drive the young bird away.

▼ GROWING UP

The pictures below show three stages in the early life of a tawny owl. At four weeks, the chick is a fluffy ball of down. At seven weeks, it is quite well feathered. At 12 weeks, it is fully feathered and can fly.

4 weeks old

7 weeks old

12 weeks old

Pygmy falcon (adult)

Pygmy falcon (juvenile)
(*Poliohierax semitorquatus*)

◀ **BIG PYGMY**

This pygmy falcon parent is still feeding its chick, which is as big as the parent. In the early stages of the chick's life, the male pygmy falcon supplies all the food, while the female keeps the chick warm in the nest. Then both adults feed the fledgling, until the young bird learns to catch insects for itself. This skill can take up to two months to master.

▶ **MONTH-OLD KESTREL CHICKS**

Two young kestrels huddle together near their nest in an old farm building. They are fully feathered and almost ready to take their first flight. However, it could be another month before they learn to hunt.

◀ **JUST PRACTISING**

This tawny owl is still unable to fly. It is flapping its wings up and down to exercise and strengthen the pectoral (chest) muscles that will enable it to fly. As these muscles get stronger, the young bird will sometimes lift off its perch. Eventually, often on a windy day, the owl will find itself flying in the air. On this first flight, it will not travel far. Within days, it will be flying just like its parents.

Tawny owl
(*Strix aluco*)

215

Open Country

Birds of prey are found almost everywhere in the world. However, each species prefers a different kind of habitat, in which it can hunt certain kinds of prey. This prevents too much competition for the food resources available. Many species prefer open country habitats. Imperial and golden eagles hunt in open mountainous country. On the bleak expanses of the Arctic tundra the gyrfalcon and snowy owl are the most successful predators. The vast savanna lands of eastern and southern Africa are the home of many vultures. Here, there are rich pickings on the carcasses of grazing animals killed by big cats, such as the cheetah and lion. Areas where farming is practised are common hunting grounds for kestrels and harriers.

▲ **GROUND NESTER**
A young Montagu's harrier spreads its wings in the nest. Like other harriers, it nests among thick vegetation. This harrier lives on open moors and farmland throughout Europe, northern Africa and Asia.

Did you know? The gyrfalcon is the largest falcon, up to 62cm/25in from head to tail.

◀ **TUNDRA HUNTER**
A gyrfalcon devours its prey. This bird lives in the cold, wide-open spaces of the Arctic tundra, in Alaska, northern Canada and northern Europe. The bird in the picture is a young bird with dark, juvenile plumage. The adult is much paler – grey above and white underneath. Some birds are almost pure white and blend in perfectly with their snowy habitat.

▲ VULTURES AT THE CAPE

The Cape vultures of southern Africa inhabit the clifftops and hilly regions around the Cape of Good Hope. They have broad wings that enable them to soar effortlessly on the warm air currents rising from the hot land below. Often, several birds soar together, watching out for a meal to share and guarding their territory against other vultures.

▼ KILLING FIELDS

A common buzzard feeds on carrion — a dead rabbit that it has recently found. Buzzards, or buteos, are found in open and lightly wooded country throughout the world. They live in both lowland and highland areas and feed mainly on small mammals.

◄ PLAINS WALKER

The secretary bird can be found in most savanna (open plains) or grassland, habitats in Africa south of the Sahara desert. Its long legs enable it to walk through all but the tallest grass. It avoids forests, but it does build its nest in trees.

▼ SUNNING ON THE SAVANNA

A juvenile bateleur eagle suns itself on a tree in the sparse savanna of Africa, keeping a watchful eye for small mammals and reptiles. It takes six years for a juvenile to reach full maturity.

Bateleur eagle
(*Terathopius ecaudatus*)

217

Woodlands and Wetlands

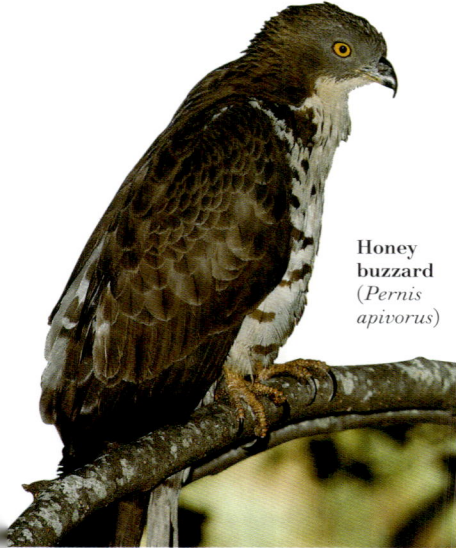

Honey buzzard (*Pernis apivorus*)

The world's woodlands make good hunting grounds for many different birds of prey. The sparrowhawk and goshawk and the common and honey buzzards all make their homes in woodland habitats. Many owls prefer a wooded habitat, nesting in both coniferous and broad-leafed trees. The most formidable forest predators, however, are the enormous South American harpy eagle and the Philippine eagle. They live in rainforests and hunt monkey prey high in the treetops. Freshwater and marine wetlands are the territory of the sea and fishing eagles and the osprey. Among the smaller birds of prey, peregrines hunt around sea cliffs, while marsh harriers hunt among the reed beds of freshwater marshes. In Africa and Asia, the fishing owls make their homes in woodlands close to the coast or by inland waterways.

▲ FOREST FEEDER

The honey buzzard is commonly found in the deciduous forests of Europe, where it feeds mainly on the larvae of bees and wasps. It is quite a small bird, with a delicate bill suited to its diet.

◄ IN THE MARSHES

Three marsh harrier chicks peep out of their reed nest in a swampy region of Poland. Marsh harriers are the largest harriers, measuring up to 55cm/21½in from head to tail. They hunt in the reed beds and on open farmland nearby. These fearsome hunters will eat birds, small mammals, reptiles, and amphibians.

◀ DOWN IN THE JUNGLE

The harpy eagle lives in the thick forests and jungles of Central and South America. It is an awesome predator, picking animals as big as sloths and monkeys from the trees, as well as birds, such as parrots. Harpy eagles grow up to 1m/39in from head to tail. They have huge talons to grip their heavy prey.

▲ DAYLIGHT OWL

A hawk owl perches on a tree stump. The hawk owl lives in the massive conifer forests of northern Canada and Alaska. It can often be seen in daylight.

▼ EAGLE AT SEA

This white-bellied sea eagle lives high on the clifftops of an island in Indonesia, South-east Asia. Like other sea eagles, it takes fish from both coastal and inland waters and also feeds on carrion. This bird will also eat poisonous sea snakes.

▲ FLEET FLIER

The sparrowhawk is found in the woodlands of Europe and Asia. It flies swiftly and close to the ground, using the dense vegetation as cover. However, it sometimes hunts like a peregrine, circling high and then diving steeply at its prey.

Orders and Families

There are more than 400 species of birds of prey. Each is different in size, colouring, behaviour and feeding pattern from every other species. Birds of prey fall into two major groupings, or orders. The diurnal raptors, the day-time hunters, belong to the order Falconiformes. The owls, the night-hunters, belong to the order Strigiformes. Within each order, similar kinds of birds are classed together in family groups. In the Falconiformes, there are five families. The secretary bird and the osprey have a family each. New World vultures form another family, and the falcons and caracaras another. But by far the largest family, containing more than 200 species, is the so-called accipiters, which include eagles, Old World vultures, kites, hawks and buzzards.

▲ NIGHT-HUNTERS

This great grey owl is one of about 130 species of owls. Most, but not all are nocturnal (night) hunters. Owls belong to the order Strigiformes and are not related to the other birds of prey.

Roman Eagle

To the ancient Romans, the eagle symbolized power, nobility, strength and courage. When the Roman army marched into battle, one soldier at the head of each legion (group of soldiers) carried a golden eagle on a standard (see left). The Roman name for the eagle was aquila. Today, this name is given to a family of eagles, including the magnificent golden eagle.

▶ THE CARACARAS

This striated caracara lives in the Falkland Islands. It is a member of a group within the falcon family. Caracaras are large, long-legged birds found from the southern United States to southern South America. Unlike true falcons, they often hunt on the ground.

▼ ALL ALONE

There is only one species of osprey the world over. This one is nesting in Maryland, in the eastern United States, where it is known as a fish hawk. Some of the largest colonies of ospreys are found in north-eastern Africa.

▲ TALL SECRETARY

The secretary bird looks like no other bird of prey, so it is not surprising that it has a family all to itself. Its distinctive features are a crest on its head, very long tail and legs and short, stubby toes.

▼ OLD WORLD VULTURES

These white-backed vultures live in southern Africa. They belong to a family of some 14 species of vultures, found in the "Old World", that is, Europe, Asia and Africa. Like all vultures, they live largely on carrion, often the remains of prey killed by big cats such as lions.

King vulture
(*Sarcoramphus papa*)

▲ VULTURES OF THE NEW WORLD

The king vulture displays its impressive 1.7m/5½ft wingspan. This bird is the most colourful and maybe the most handsome vulture of all. It is one of the seven species of "New World" vultures found in the Americas. The Andean and Californian condors are two other members of this group.

White-backed vulture
(*Gyps africanus*)

221

Focus on

Most eagles are very large, aggressive birds, preying on both small and large mammals, other birds and reptiles. Although some are hardly bigger than buzzards, they are, in general, fiercer and more active. Each eagle has a different lifestyle and hunting strategy. The golden eagle swoops down from on high mostly on mammal prey. The bald eagle takes mainly fish. The tawny eagle will eat anything. The most distinctive feature of the bateleur eagle is its acrobatic manoeuvres in the air. Its name comes from a French word meaning acrobat.

FAMILY LIFE

A bald eagle returns to its nest with a rock ptarmigan in its talons. Now it will tear strips of meat from its prey and feed them to its two offspring. These two eaglets are only a few weeks old and have just grown their thick second coat of down. They are still not strong enough to stand on their legs.

YOUNG AND OLD

For the first few years of its life, the bateleur eagle has drab brown juvenile plumage (*left*). But by the sixth year, it has acquired glorious adult plumage (*right*), which signals that it is now mature and ready to breed.

Bateleur eagle (juvenile)
(*Terathopius ecaudata*)

Bateleur eagle (adult)

Eagles

MARTIAL LORE

A martial eagle swoops down from the skies to deliver a deadly blow to a monitor lizard basking on the searing-hot African savanna. This heavy bird, with its huge wingspan of up to 2.5m/8¼ft, will often capture small animals, mostly reptiles, but it usually feeds on game birds. The martial eagle is persecuted by humans because it occasionally attacks domestic livestock, such as chickens and goats.

TAWNY SCAVENGER

The tawny eagle of Africa is mainly a scavenger. It often joins a flock of vultures to feed on the carcasses of prey killed by big cats, such as the zebra in this photograph. It also frequently steals prey from other raptors.

Golden eagle
(*Aquila chrysaetos*)

MASTER OF THE MOUNTAINS

A golden eagle opens its wings wide. They span nearly 2.5 m/8¼ft. This magnificent bird gets its name from the golden tinges on its head and neck feathers. It lives in remote mountains around the world and feeds on birds, mammals and carrion.

Kookaburra
(*Dacelo gigas*)

▲ **KOOKABURRA CATCH**
A snake makes a good meal for this Australian kookaburra. It eats more or less anything, from frogs to small mammals and other small birds.

Fellow Hunters

Birds of prey are probably the most feared hunters of the bird world. However, they are not the only birds that hunt live prey. Other birds catch insects and worms, amphibians and fish, and even small mammals and other birds. Most common are the insect-eaters, such as the bee-eater and the flycatcher. Wading birds, such as the oystercatcher, feed on worms and crustaceans, while herons eat amphibians and fish. Skimmers, pelicans and all kinds of seabirds live mainly on fish. Many seabirds prey on the chicks of other species, as do magpies on land. Many birds, especially those belonging to the crow family, will eat small mammals and carrion. However, none of these birds is classed as a bird of prey, for they lack the formidable sharp, hooked bill and lethal, taloned feet of the raptor.

▲ **BIG BILL**
The turkey-sized African ground hornbill loves to eat snakes, even very poisonous ones, such as cobras. It kills them by repeatedly squeezing up and down their bodies with the tip of its large, powerful bill.

▼ **HUNTER-SCAVENGER**
A harvest mouse has just been killed by this common crow. The crow will also eat insects and the eggs and young of other birds, as well as carrion. Other members of the crow family, such as jackdaws and magpies, have a similar diet.

Crow
(*Corvus corone*)

▶ STANDING IN WAIT

The great blue heron of North America stands absolutely still at the water's edge, scanning the water for fish as they swim by. When it sees a fish, the heron thrusts its long bill into the water lightning-fast and grabs it with deadly accuracy. It hits the fish on the ground to kill it, before swallowing it head first. Herons also eat frogs and mammals, such as voles.

◀ BROWN BULLY

A brown skua swoops down to take a giant petrel chick on the remote Atlantic island of South Georgia. Skuas are always on the lookout for eggs and chicks left in nests while the parent birds are away feeding. They are also known for harrying (chasing) birds that have just been fishing. They make them disgorge (throw up) their food and eat it themselves.

Did you know? Butcher birds impale their prey on sharp thorns.

▼ DEADLY DIVER

Perching on a branch, a kingfisher prepares to eat a recent catch. This bird feeds almost entirely on fish. It perches near the water's edge and dives in head first when it spots its prey. The kingfisher then beats the fish on a branch until it stops wriggling. Only then is it swallowed.

Kingfisher
(*Alcedo atthis*)

225

Under Threat

In the wild, birds of prey have few natural enemies except, perhaps, other birds of prey. In many habitats they are the top predator. They have only one thing to fear – humans. Over the centuries, people have hunted raptors as vermin (pests) because they have occasionally killed domestic livestock, such as birds raised for game. Recently humans have been killing birds of prey indirectly by using pesticides on seeds and crops. When birds catch contaminated animals, pesticides build up in their own bodies and eventually poison them, causing death. Many birds of prey are now protected by law. This, and the safer use of farm chemicals, has led to a recovery in the numbers of several species. However, the indiscriminate shooting of migrating birds is still a threat, as is the destruction of forest habitats in which they live.

▲ **TRIGGER HAPPY**
A shooting enthusiast takes aim. A dog stands nearby, ready to retrieve the fallen bird. Raptors are shot by irresponsible hunters every year, especially as they flock together when migrating.

▲ **GRIM WARNING**
A dead hawk is left dangling on a piece of rope. This age-old practice is used by gamekeepers and farmers to warn off other birds of prey or vermin (pests) such as crows.

◄ **PHILIPPINE EAGLE**
The Philippine eagle is one of the rarest of all birds of prey. This is because the dense tropical forest in which it lives is rapidly being destroyed for farming and for humans to live. The eagle gets its name from the Philippine Islands, in South-east Asia, where it lives. It eats mammals called lemurs, various kinds of birds and sometimes monkeys.

◀ DEADLY CHEMICALS

A sparrowhawk has been poisoned to death. It has preyed on smaller birds that have eaten seeds or insects sprayed with chemical pesticides. Gradually, the chemicals built up in the sparrowhawk's body until they made it ill, finally causing its death.

Did you know? Barn owls and kites are killed by eating poison-resistant rats.

Alice and the Griffin

A griffin sits next to Alice in a scene from Alice's Adventures in Wonderland. *The griffin is a mythical bird. According to Greek legend, it had the head and wings of an eagle but the body of a lion.*

▲ HIT AND RUN

A barn owl lies dead at the roadside, battered by a passing vehicle the night before. Motor vehicles kill thousands of birds every day and every night. At night, owls often hunt for small prey, such as mice and voles, in roadside verges and hedges. Their habit of slow-flying close to the ground puts them in danger from passing cars and trucks.

227

Bears and Pandas

Bears and pandas are unusual predators. They eat berries and bamboo, yet they are classified as carnivores, mammals that are predominantly meat-eaters. These bully-boys of the animal world are actually opportunists. They eat whatever is readily available whether it be meat or veg, and they get into serious trouble with the authorities when they dine on the "fast-foods" we leave at rubbish (garbage) dumps.

The Bear Facts

Bears may look large, cuddly and appealing, but in reality they are enormously powerful animals. Bears are mammals with bodies covered in thick fur. They are heavily built with short tails and large claws. All bears are carnivores (meat-eaters), but most enjoy a very mixed diet with the occasional snack of meat. The exception is the polar bear, which feasts on the blubber (fat) of seals. There are eight living species of bear: the brown bear, American black bear, Asiatic black bear, polar bear, sun bear, sloth bear, spectacled bear and the giant panda. They live in both cold and tropical regions of the world. Bears are loners and their nature is unpredictable, which makes them potentially dangerous to people.

WINNIE-THE-POOH

The lovable teddy bear Winnie-the-Pooh was created by A.A. Milne. Like real bears, he loves honey. Teddy bears became popular as toys in the early 1900s. The President of the United States, Theodore Roosevelt, refused to shoot a bear cub on a hunting trip. Toy bears went on sale soon after known as "teddy's bears".

◀ **BEAR FACE**
The brown bear shares the huge dog-like head and face of all bears. Bears have prominent noses, but relatively small eyes and ears. This is because they mostly rely on their sense of smell to help them find food.

▲ **BIG FLAT FEET**
A polar bear's feet are broad, flat and furry. The five long, curved claws cannot be retracted (pulled back). One swipe could kill a seal instantly.

Thick fur covers a
heavily built body.

◄ POINTS OF A BEAR

The brown bear is called the grizzly bear
in North America. Fully grown brown
bears weigh nearly half a tonne (ton).
They fear no other animals apart from
humans. They can chase prey at high
speed, but they rarely bother as
they feed mainly on plants.

A bear has a large head,
with small eyes and
erect, rounded ears.

The long, prominent,
dog-like snout
dominates the face.

▲ GIANT PANDA

China's giant panda, with its distinctive
black and white coat, is a very unusual
bear. Unlike most other bears which
will eat anything, pandas feed almost
exclusively on the bamboo plant.

A bear's main
strength is in its
massive shoulders
and front legs.

Its broad, flat feet
have long claws.

◄ ARCTIC NOMAD

Most bears lead a solitary life. The polar bear
wanders alone across the Arctic sea ice.
Usually it will not tolerate other
bears. The exceptions are
bears that congregate at
rubbish dumps or
mothers accompanied
by their cubs, as
shown here.

231

Sloth bear
(*Melursus*
ursinus)

Size of a Bear

The two largest bears are the powerful polar bear and the brown bears of Kodiak Island, Alaska. Kodiak bears grow up to 2.8m/9ft long and weigh up to 443kg/977lb on average, while polar bears have a maximum length of 3m/10ft and weigh as much as 650kg/1,433lb. Brown bears in Europe and Asia are smaller than grizzlies (American brown bears). The largest is the Kamchatka brown bear of eastern Russia. A full size adult grizzly weighs as much as a bison and even the smallest is bigger than a wolf. The smallest bear is the sun bear at 1.4m/4¼ft long and weighing 65kg/143lb. In-between are American and Asiatic black bears (1.7m/ 5½ft long, up to 120kg/265lb), the spectacled bear (2.1m/7ft long, up to 200kg/441lb) and the sloth bear (1.9m/6¼ft long, up to 115kg/253lb).

▲ SLOTH BEAR

Long curved claws, a mobile snout and long fur are the distinguishing features of the sloth bear. It lives in India and Sri Lanka and feeds mainly on termites, an insect, and fruit.

American black bear
(*Ursus americanus*)

▼ SPECTACLED BEAR

The spectacled bear gets its name from the distinctive markings on its face. It is the only bear found in South America.

Spectacled bear
(*Tremarctos ornatus*)

▲ AMERICAN BLACK BEAR

There are ten times as many black bears as brown bears living in the forests of North America. Black bears resemble small brown bears except that they lack a shoulder hump.

Polar bear
(Ursus maritimus)

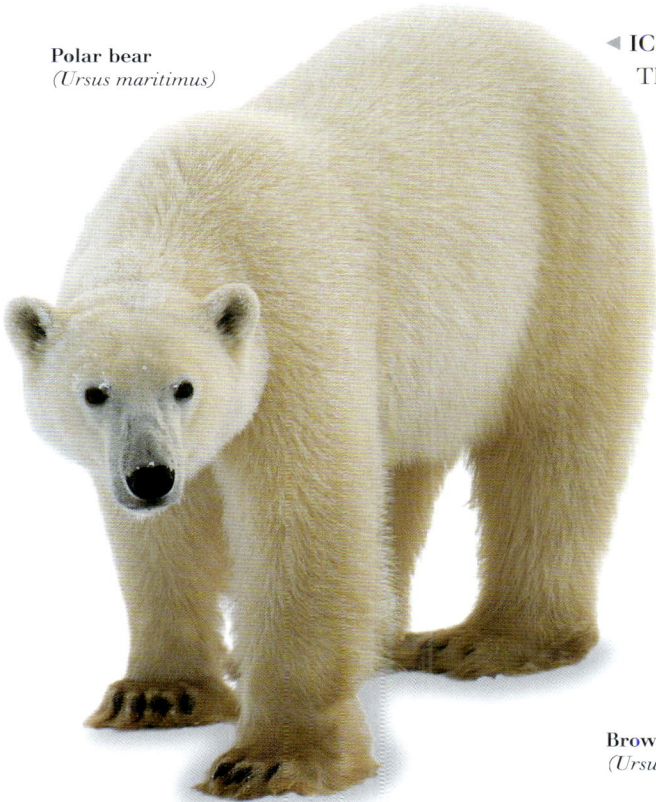

◄ **ICE GIANT**

The male polar bear is a giant among
bears. It is bigger than most brown bears,
but less robustly built, with a longer
head and neck. Female polar bears are
much smaller, weighing less than half
a fully grown adult male. Polar bears
live in the frozen wastes of the Arctic.
They can swim in the icy sea, protected
by insulating fur and layers of thick fat.

Brown bear
(Ursus arctos)

► **BIG BROWN BEARS**

The brown bear is the most widely found bear,
living in Europe, Asia and North America. Its size
varies in different parts of the world. This is
owing to diet and climate rather than any genetic
differences. For example, large Kodiak bears
catch a lot of protein-rich salmon.

Did you know? The heaviest Kodiak brown bears weigh up to 750kg / 1,653lb.

▼ **THE SUN BEAR**

The sun bear is the smallest of all the bears.
It lives in the thick forests of South-east
Asia. Because it lives in a hot tropical
climate, the sun bear also has
a short coat. Its feet have naked soles
and long, curved claws, which can grip
well when climbing trees.

Sun bear
(Helarctos malayanus)

233

Giant panda
(Ailuropoda melanoleuca)

Giant Pandas

Scientists have argued for many years about whether or not the giant panda is a bear. In 1869, the first Western naturalist to see a giant panda identified it as a bear. But a year later, scientists examined a panda skeleton and decided it was more like a raccoon. This was because the giant panda's skeleton shared some features with the red panda, an earlier discovery that had been grouped with the raccoon family. The giant panda certainly looks like a bear, but it does not behave like one. It does not hibernate, although it lives in places with very cold winters. It rarely roars like a bear, but tends to bleat. Recent genetic studies and comparisons with other animals, however, indicate that the panda's nearest relatives are bears and that the giant panda is indeed a bear.

▲ UP A TREE

Giant pandas sometimes climb trees to avoid enemies. They also scrape trees with their claws. This is a sign that says KEEP OUT to other pandas. They are about 1.7m/5½ft long and weigh up to 125kg/276lb. They are the only surviving members of the earliest group of bears to evolve. Fossils have only ever been discovered in Thailand and China.

▶ RED PANDA

The red panda is a member of the raccoon family and lives in the high bamboo forests of southern Asia. It has several similarities to the giant panda, including skull shape, tooth structure and a false thumb to hold bamboo.

Red panda
(Ailurus fulgens)

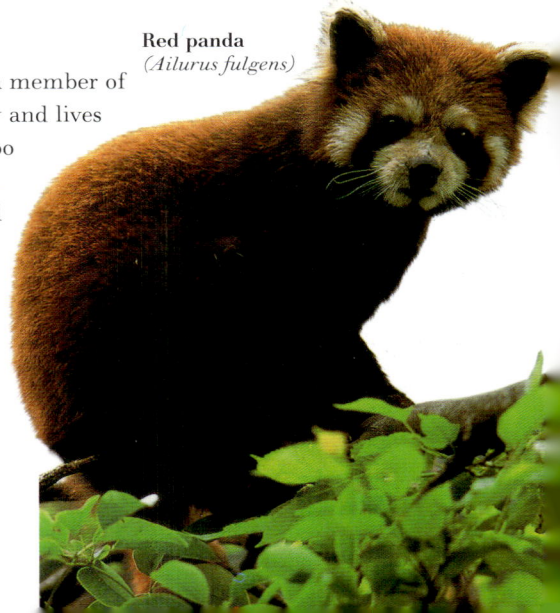

234

► **BAMBOO BEAR**

The giant panda of western China spends 10–12 hours a day eating bamboo. Its massive head contains large chewing muscles needed to break up the tough bamboo. It has a simple stomach and short gut, however, which are features of a carnivore and make digesting bamboo hard work. The giant panda's large shoulders and reduced hindquarters give it a curious, shambling walk.

Giant panda
(Ailuropoda melanoleuca)

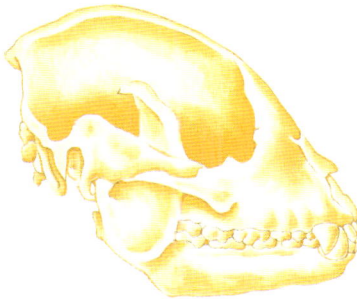

Raccoon *(Procyon lotor)*

▲ **FALSE THUMB**

The giant panda has a false thumb on its forepaw. This is a modified wrist bone used to hold narrow bamboo shoots. A giant panda's massive skull is quite distinct from the smaller, more slender skull of the raccoon. The raccoon (*Procyon lotor*) does not have a false thumb, unlike its relative the red panda.

▼ **AMERICAN BANDIT**

The inquisitive raccoon is a close relative of bears. It lives in North America and uses its front paws to capture small aquatic prey, such as freshwater crayfish. It also scavenges through the remains of human rubbish (garbage).

Raccoon
(Procyon lotor)

Bones and Teeth

Bears have a large and massive skull, a solidly built skeleton, relatively short and stocky limbs, a small tail and short feet. Each foot has five equal-sized digits (toes), with strong, curved claws for digging and tearing. The claws cannot be retracted (pulled back), so are constantly worn down. In most bears' jaws, the carnassial teeth (large meat-shearing teeth) common to all carnivores are reduced or even missing. Instead, bears have broad flat molars for crushing plant food. Only the polar bear has flesh-slicing carnassials to deal with its animal prey. The sloth bear is also unusual because it lacks the inner pair of upper incisors (front teeth). This helps it suck up insects from their nests.

▲ **A MIGHTY ROAR**
As this bear roars, it bares its large canine teeth. However, on average only 20 per cent of a brown bear's diet is made up of animal flesh. Instead, bears rely on their large molars to crush their vegetable food.

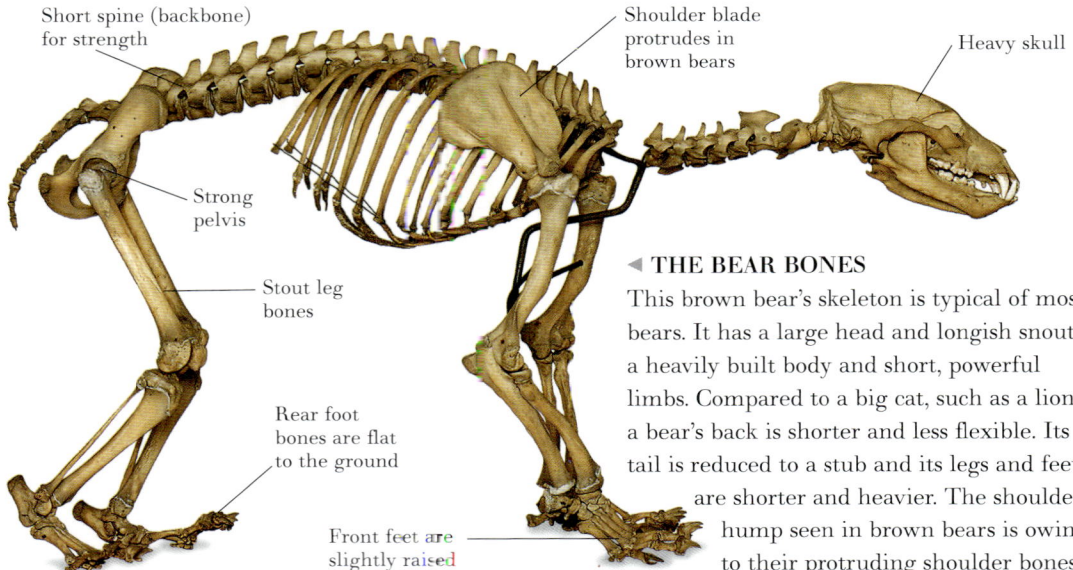

Short spine (backbone) for strength

Shoulder blade protrudes in brown bears

Heavy skull

Strong pelvis

Stout leg bones

Rear foot bones are flat to the ground

Front feet are slightly raised

◄ **THE BEAR BONES**
This brown bear's skeleton is typical of most bears. It has a large head and longish snout, a heavily built body and short, powerful limbs. Compared to a big cat, such as a lion, a bear's back is shorter and less flexible. Its tail is reduced to a stub and its legs and feet are shorter and heavier. The shoulder hump seen in brown bears is owing to their protruding shoulder bones.

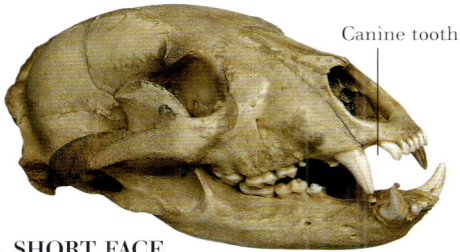

Canine tooth

Carnassial tooth

▲ SHORT FACE

This brown bear's skull is shorter and more robust than that of the polar bear. North American brown bears tend to have larger skulls than bears in other parts of the world.

▲ LONG FACE

This polar bear's skull is longer and more slender than that of other bears. Like other carnivores, it has prominent, dagger-like canine teeth and meat-slicing carnassials at the back.

▲ PRIMITIVE BEAR

The spectacled bear is grouped separately from other bears. Apart from the giant panda, it is the most primitive bear. Its short muzzle and the unique arrangement of teeth in its jaw give it a more rounded head shape than its fellow bears.

▲ GIANT PANDA

The giant panda has the most massive skull in relation to its size of all living bears. It has a round face and head with large jaw muscles to grind tough bamboo stems.

► SLENDER SWIMMING BEAR

The polar bear has a more elongated body than other bears. Its neck and skull are relatively long and slim. These are adaptations that help the bear to swim through the water by streamlining its body. It also has lower shoulders, well-developed hindquarters and large broad feet.

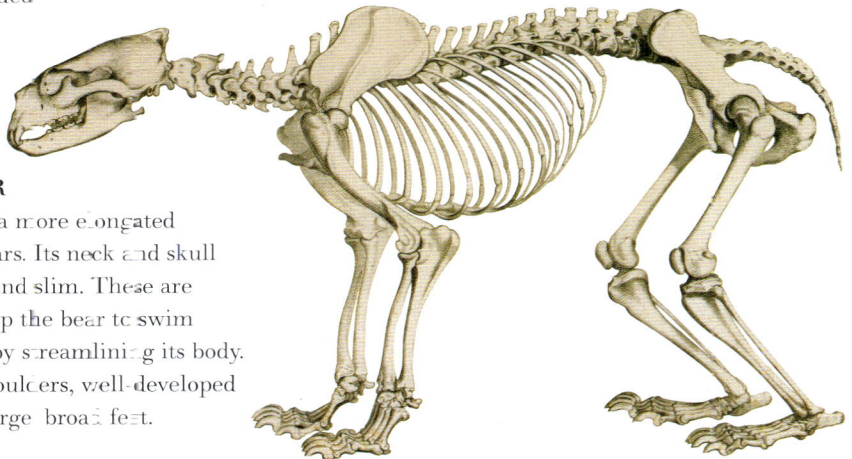

237

Strong Muscles

Bears are the bully-boys of the animal kingdom. Their strength is mainly in the muscles of their legs and shoulders. Unlike cats and dogs, which run on their toes for speed, bears walk on the flat soles of their broad feet, just as humans do. What bears lack in speed they make up for in strength. Their powerful, mobile limbs can be put to good use digging, climbing, fishing and fighting. They will attack others of their own kind and defend themselves ably from enemies. In a fight, a bear can do considerable damage and survives by sheer brute force. Male bears are generally much larger than females of the same species.

▲ **CLAWS DOWN**
The sun bear has particularly large, curved claws for climbing trees. It spends most of the day sleeping or sunbathing in the branches. At night it strips off bark with its claws, looking for insects and honey in bees' nests.

◀ **PUTTING ON WEIGHT**
This grizzly bear is at peak size. Most bears change size as the seasons pass. They are large and well-fed in autumn (fall), ready for winter hibernation. When they emerge in spring, they are scrawny with sagging coats.

BEOWULF
An Old English poem tells of the hero Beowulf (bear-wolf). He had the strength of a bear and went through many heroic adventures. Beowulf is famous for slaying a monster called Grendel. Here, Beowulf as an old man lies dying from the wounds inflicted by a fire-breathing dragon.

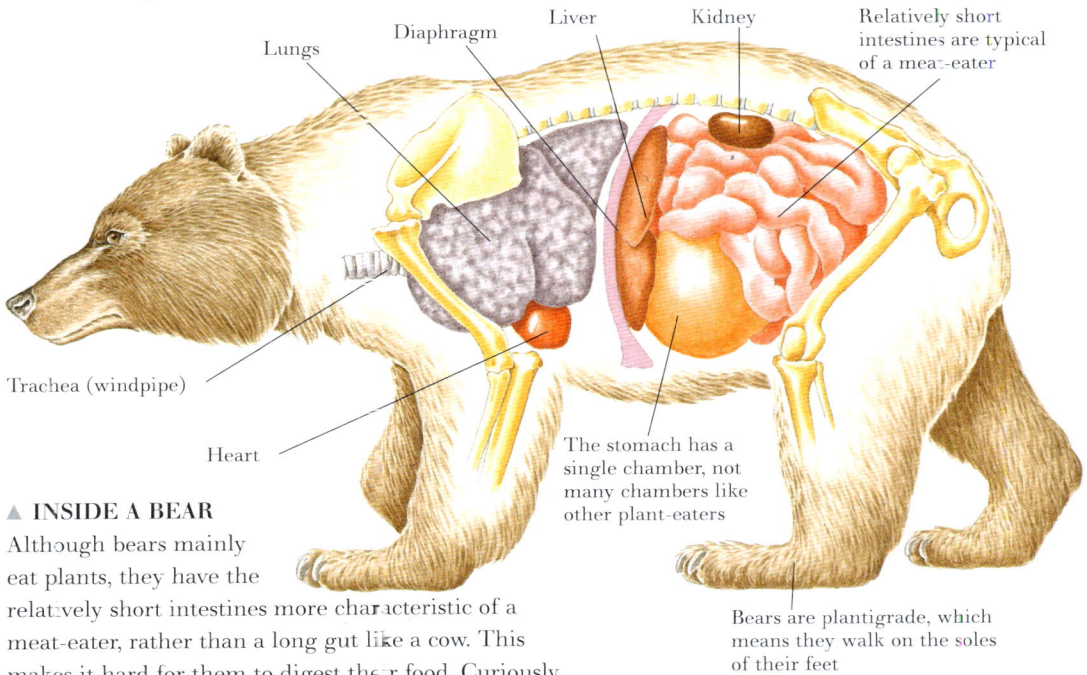

Lungs

Diaphragm

Liver

Kidney

Relatively short intestines are typical of a meat-eater

Trachea (windpipe)

Heart

The stomach has a single chamber, not many chambers like other plant-eaters

Bears are plantigrade, which means they walk on the soles of their feet

▲ INSIDE A BEAR

Although bears mainly eat plants, they have the relatively short intestines more characteristic of a meat-eater, rather than a long gut like a cow. This makes it hard for them to digest their food. Curiously, the bamboo-eating giant panda has the shortest gut of all. Because of this it can digest no more than 20 per cent of what it eats, compared to 60 per cent in a cow.

▲ SHORT BURSTS

Bears are not particularly agile and swift, but can run fast over short distances. The brown bear can charge at 50kph/31mph (lions reach about 65kph/40mph) and sometimes chases its food. A bear at full charge is a frightening sight and scares away enemies.

▲ SWEET TOOTH

The sun bear's long slender tongue is ideal for licking honey from bees' nests and for scooping up termites and other insects. Like all bears it has mobile lips, a flexible snout and strong jaws.

Warm Fur

All bears have thick fur all over their bodies, including the face. Ground-living bears even have fur between the pads of their feet, while the soles of tree-climbing bears are naked. A thick coat insulates well in the cold, but can cause overheating in summer, so many bears moult (molt). Most bears' coats tend to be brown, black, cinnamon (reddish-brown), grey or white, and some have face and chest markings. The most strikingly marked bear is the giant panda. Its startling black and white pattern blends in with the shadowy bamboo of its mountain home. This is particularly so at dawn and dusk, the panda's most active times. In winter, against snow, black rocks and trees, the panda is almost invisible.

▲ WHITE BEAR
The Chinese call the giant panda *bei-shung* (white bear). It is considered to be basically white with black ears, eye patches, legs and shoulders. Sometimes the black areas have a chestnut-reddish tinge.

BERSERKER
Among the most feared of Viking warriors were berserkers. They were named after the bear pelts or bearskin shirts they wore. Berserkers worked themselves up into a frenzy before battle. We still use the Norse word berserk to mean crazy or wild. This walrus ivory berserker is sort of a chess set from the island of Lewis off the west coast of Scotland. The berserkir is shown biting his shield and clasping his sword in the rage of battle.

▲ VELVET COAT
The sun bear has relatively short fur, a little like velvet. It is generally black with a grey to orange muzzle and pale feet. Some bears have white or pale orange-yellow, crescent-shaped markings on the chest.

▲ BEAR FOOT

The broad, flat paw of a brown bear has thick fur on the upper surface and some between the toes, too. Ground-living bears, such as the brown bear, use their claws to hold on to a salmon or to catch and kill a young deer

▼ SILVER TIP

The grizzly (American brown bear) gets its name from the way in which the long hairs of the shoulders and back are frosted with white. This gives the bear's coat a grizzled appearance. Brown bears, like the grizzly, are usually a dark brown colour, but they may also be any shade between light cream and black.

▲ FACIAL MARKINGS

The spectacled bear is generally dark brown or black. It has an unmistakable, spectacle-like pattern of white or yellowish hairs around the eyes and across the nose. These markings may extend to the chest.

▶ LONG HAIR

The sloth bear has long, black, shaggy fur. The longest hair is between the shoulders. The black fur can be tinged with brown or grey. There is a white, or yellow to chestnut-brown, patch in the shape of a U or Y on the bear's chest. Chest markings may act as a warning sign when the bear stands up.

Life on the Ice

The polar bear is perfectly adapted to life in the frozen Arctic, where winter temperatures can drop to -50°C/-58°F. Beneath its skin lies a thick layer of fat. The bear's entire body, including the soles of the feet, is covered in insulating fur made up of thick hairs with a woolly underfur. Each hair is not actually white, but translucent and hollow. This acts like a tiny greenhouse, allowing light and heat from the sun to pass through, trapping the warm air. Sometimes, such as in zoos, the hairs are invaded by tiny algae and the polar bear's coat has a green tinge. In the wild, the fur often appears yellow, the result of oil stains from its seal prey. Beneath the fur the skin is black, which absorbs heat. This excellent insulation keeps the polar bear's body at a constant 37°C/98.6°F.

RESPECT FOR THE ICE BEAR

The polar bear is the most powerful spirit in Arctic cultures. The Inuit believe that a polar bear has a soul. It will only allow itself to be killed if the hunter treats it properly after death. It is forbidden to hunt another bear too soon. Time must be left for the bear's soul to return to its family. Some Inuit offer a dead male bear a miniature bow and arrow, and a female bear a needle holder.

◄ **SEA-GOING BEAR**

Polar bears are excellent swimmers. They must swim frequently for their icy world is unpredictable. In winter, the Arctic Ocean freezes over. But with the arrival of storms and warmer weather the ice breaks up. Then the bear must swim between ice floes in search of seals. The thick layer of fat below the skin and dense, insulating fur allow a polar bear to swim in the coldest seas without suffering. In such cold water, a human being would be dead in a few minutes.

▲ COOLING DOWN

Polar bears are so well insulated they
are in danger of overheating on warm
days. To keep cool, they lie flat out on
the ice. At other times they lie on their
backs with their feet in the air.

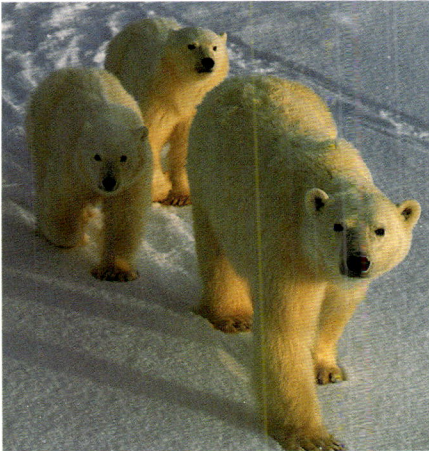

▲ WARM BEARS

The insulating fur and fat of a polar bear
is so efficient that little heat is lost. In
fact, if a scientist were to look at a polar
bear with an infra-red camera (which
detects heat given off by the body), only
the bear's nose and eyes would be visible.

▶ LAZY DAYS

Polar bears are most active at the start of
the day. During summer, when the ice
melts and retreats, bears may be prevented
from hunting seals. Then they rest, living
off their fat reserves and eating berries.

▲ BEAR SLUMBERS

A polar bear, like a human,
sleeps for seven or eight hours at a time.
This helps the polar bear to conserve energy and
heat. Polar bears are not at risk of attack when they
are sleeping, so they do not have to hide like other
animals. Most often, polar bears find a sheltered area
to protect them from the cold polar winds.

Using Brain and Senses

All bears are very intelligent. Size for size, they have larger brains than other carnivores, such as dogs and cats. They can remember sources of food and are very curious. Bears use their brains to find food or a mate and to stay out of trouble. They are mainly solitary plant-eaters, however, so they have little need to think up hunting tactics or ways of communication. They rely on smell (the part of their brains that detects scent is the largest of any carnivore), with small eyes and ears compared to their head size. Bears often appear short-sighted, although they have colour vision to recognize edible fruits and nuts. People can easily chance upon a bear and take it by surprise, prompting the startled animal to attack in self-defence.

▼ SCENT MARKING
An American black bear cub practises marking a tree by scratching. When it is older, the bear will leave a scent mark to indicate to other bears that the territory is occupied.

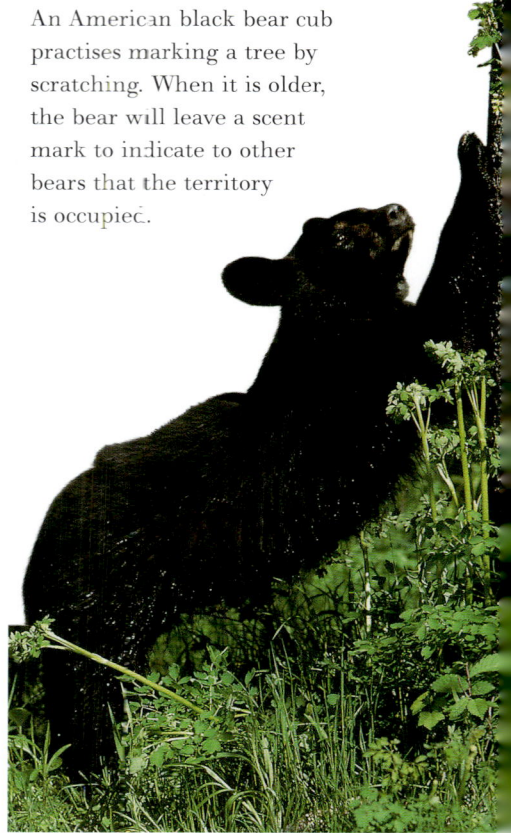

◄ TEMPER TANTRUM
A threatened bear puts on a fierce display. First it beats the ground or vegetation with its front feet. Then it stands up on its back legs to look larger. This is accompanied by a high-pitched snorting through open lips or a series of hoarse barks. The display of aggression finishes with snapping the jaws together.

▼ GETTING TO KNOW YOU

Polar bear cubs rub against their mother to spread her scent over themselves. Smell allows a mother and cubs to recognize each other. They also communicate with sounds. Distressed cubs make low-pitched snores that develop into high whines.

▲ FOLLOW YOUR NOSE

A brown bear relies more on smell than sight. It often raises its head and sniffs the air to check out who or what is about. It can detect the faintest trace of a smell, searching for others of its kind.

BRUNO THE BEAR

Aesop's Fables are a set of tales written by the ancient Greek writer Aesop. One fable features Bruno the bear. He is shown as stupid and easily deceived. Bears were considered slow-witted because they slept a lot. But Bruno was kind, unlike the cunning Reynard the fox. Bruno cared about others and forgave those who played pranks on him. Bruno was the forerunner of characters such as Winnie-the-Pooh.

▲ SNOWY SCENT TRAIL

Even in the Arctic, polar bears can pick up the trails of other bears and follow them. There are few objects around to use as scent posts for polar bears, so trails may be marked by dribbling urine on the ground.

Finding Food

Most bears eat whatever is available at different times of the year. They have binges and put on fat in times of plenty, then fast when food is scarce. Brown bears are typical of most bears in that they eat an enormous variety of food, from grasses, herbs and berries to ants and other insects. They also catch salmon and rodents and, on rare occasions, hunt down bigger game, such as caribou, seals and birds. Only polar bears eat almost entirely meat, especially young seals. In summer, however, as the ice melts and they are unable to hunt, polars supplement their diet with grasses and berries. All bears, even the bamboo-loving panda, also scavenge on the carcasses of prey left by other animals. They are attracted to easy food, and rummage through debris left behind at campsites and in dustbins (trash cans).

▶ HUNTING DOWN A MEAL

This American black bear has caught a white-tailed deer fawn. Both black and brown bears are successful hunters. They are able to ambush large animals and kill them by using their considerable bulk, strong paws and jaws. The size of the bear determines the size of its prey. Large brown bears may prey on moose, caribou, bison, musk ox, seals and stranded whales. Black bears are smaller than brown bears and take smaller prey, such as deer fawns and lemmings. Roots, fruit, seeds and nuts, however, form up to 80 per cent of brown and black bears' diets.

GOLDILOCKS

The famous story of Goldilocks and the Three Bears *was first told in 1837. In the story, the bears and their ability to organize themselves properly are used to make a strong moral point. In contrast, Goldilocks is shown as a foolish, unthinking girl, who gets a nasty fright.*

▶ WALRUS CITY

Polar bears arrive on the northern coast of Russia each year to hunt walruses that have come there to breed. Enormous adult walruses shrug off attacks, but the young walrus pups are more vulnerable.

▲ BEACHCOMBING

Brown bears are attracted to beaches beside rivers and in estuaries. They overturn stones to feed on aquatic creatures, such as crabs and crayfish, that are hiding underneath.

▲ FRUIT LOVERS

An American black bear snacks on the ripe berries of a mountain ash tree. It carefully uses its incisors (front teeth) to strip the berries from their woody stem.

▲ INSECT EATERS

Two sloth bear cubs learn to dig up termites. The sloth bear uses its sickle-shaped claws to break open ant hills, bees' nests and termite mounds. Because it feeds mainly on termites, it has an ingenious way of collecting its insect food. First it blows away the dust. Then it forms a suction tube with its mouth and tongue through which it can vacuum up its food.

247

Focus on

The giant panda specializes in eating bamboo, which forms over 99 per cent of its diet. Bamboo is plentiful and easy to harvest. Pandas consume the sprouts, stems and leaves. Digesting bamboo, however, is hard work. This is because the giant panda has a simple stomach and a short gut more characteristic of a carnivore. Most herbivores, such as cows, have several stomachs and very long intestines with bacteria inside that break down the plant tissue. The panda does not, so it must feed on huge quantities of bamboo (up to 40kg/88lb) every day in order to keep going. Much of the leaf and stem matter passes through undigested.

MEAT AND TWO VEG

While pandas spend most of their time eating bamboo, they do sometimes supplement their diet with meat when they can get it. They catch rats and beetles in the bamboo stands, and have been known to scavenge at leopard kills. But they make clumsy hunters and easy prey is scarce. In contrast bamboo is very abundant.

EARLY RISER

The giant panda is most active in the early morning and late afternoon. It spends 16 or more hours a day feeding and sleeps for up to four hours at a time. Most of the water a panda needs comes from bamboo. If it is thirsty, it scoops out a hollow by a stream. When this is full, the panda drinks all it can.

Bamboo Bears

ESSENTIAL FOOD

Umbrella bamboo and arrow bamboo are the giant panda's favourite food. Pandas also eat 28 other species of bamboo. They favour the leaves over the stems because these are the most nutritious parts and are easiest to digest. Pandas also eat other plants, such as juniper, vines, holly and wild parsnip.

FEEDING ALL YEAR

Since bamboo is green and nutritious throughout the year, even in winter, the panda has a continuous supply of food. Unlike other bears, whose food is scarce at certain times, the panda has no need to hibernate, even when snow is covering its mountain home. A thick fur coat protects it from the cold.

TABLE MANNERS

A panda usually feeds sitting upright on its haunches. This leaves its forelegs free to handle bamboo. It manipulates the long stems of bamboo using its extra thumb (actually a modified wrist bone) on its front paws. It strips away the woody outer covering with its teeth. Then it pushes the stem at right angles into the corner of its mouth. Here, the centre part is crushed by large back teeth and then swallowed.

Climbing Trees

Trees provide food for some bears and a place of safety for others. Sun bears, sloth bears and spectacled bears climb trees regularly in search of food, such as fruits, seeds and nuts, as well as birds' eggs. Black bears are also agile tree-climbers. Polar bears rarely encounter trees. Those that move into the forest during the summer months, however, rest in hollows dug among tree roots to avoid the heat. Brown bear cubs climb trees to escape danger, but adult brown bears are too heavy to be good climbers. A female sloth bear will carry her small cubs into a tree on her back, unless she is escaping from a leopard since they can also climb trees. Most bears also use trees to mark their territory. They scratch the bark and rub on scents to tell other bears they are there.

▶ **BEAR DANGER**

A mother American black bear sends her cubs up into a tree while she stands guard at its base. If the danger is from an adult brown bear, the female will flee and return later for her cubs when the grizzly has gone.

◀ **TREE-TOP HOME**

The sun bear seeks out termite and bees' nests, and will rip away bark to get at insects hidden underneath. Although the sun bear feeds mainly on insects, it also eats ripe fruit and preys on small rodents, birds and lizards.

▲ **BELOW THE BARK**

An adult, cinnamon-coloured American black bear is able to climb into a tree with ease using its short but sturdy claws. It can also lift bark to lick out insects with a long tongue.

▲ UP A TREE

Giant pandas stay mainly on the ground, but they will climb trees occasionally. They do so to sun themselves or to rest. Female pandas sometimes head up a tree to escape males, while males climb trees to advertise their presence.

▼ SAFE HAVEN

Black bears are normally found in forested areas. They have favourite trees located along trails where bears and other animals regularly pass. The bear marks the tree base with its scent and climbs into the branches where it is safe from brown bears.

Short, sturdy claws on a black bear's feet make tree climbing easy

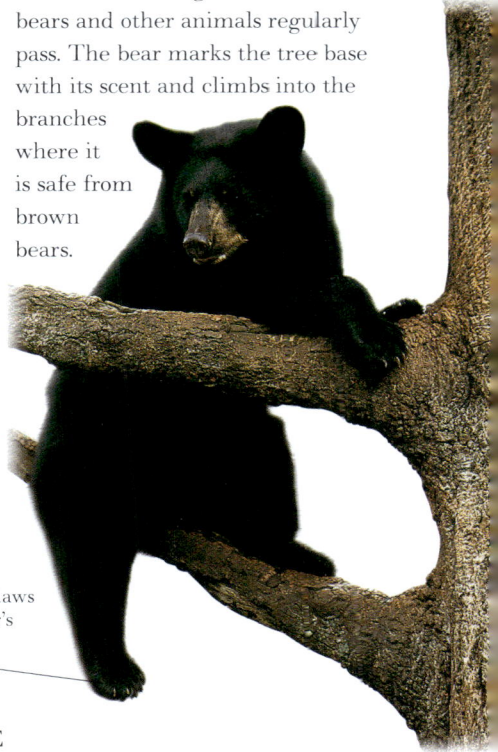

▲ HIGH SCHOOL

Black bear cubs stay close to their mother both on the ground and in a tree. They watch and learn from her how to climb and find food among the branches.

▼ TREE HOUSE

Spectacled bears pull branches together to make a feeding platform. From here the bears feed mainly on tough plants called bromeliads. They also eat fruits, nuts and honey and may take mice, rabbits and insects.

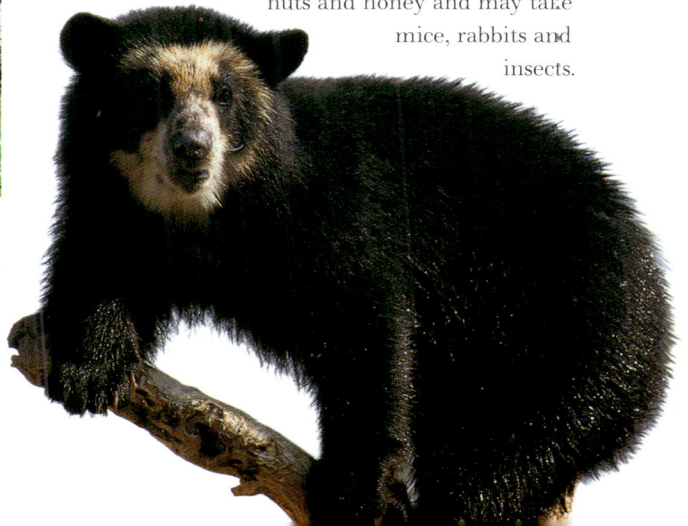

Gone Fishing

Brown and black bears sometimes overcome their reluctance to be with other bears when there is plenty of food available. This happens regularly on the rivers of the Northwest coast of North America. Here, thousands of salmon come in from the sea and head upriver to spawn. The bears fish alongside each other at sites, such as rapids, where the water is shallower and the salmon are swimming more slowly. An uneasy truce exists between the bears, although isolated fights do occur. The salmon runs take place at different times of the year, but the most important are those in the months leading up to winter. The bears catch the oil-rich salmon to obtain the extra fat they need for the long hibernation ahead.

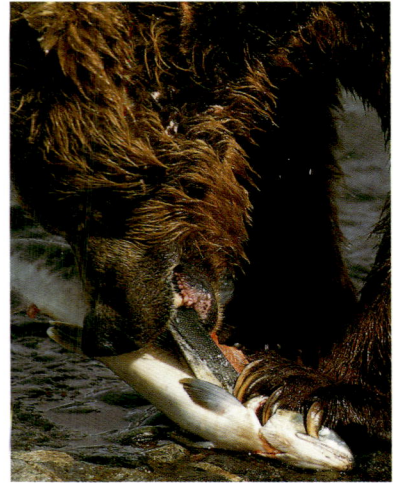

▲ **STRIPPED TO THE BONE**
Having caught a fish, the bear holds it firmly in its forepaws. Then it strips away the skin and flesh from the bones.

◀ **SALMON LEAP**
Sometimes salmon jump right into a bear's mouth. The bear stands at the edge of a small waterfall. Here the salmon must leap clear of the water to continue their journey upriver. All the bear needs to do is open its mouth.

◀ **COME INTO CONFLICT**

Sometimes the uncertain truce between bears breaks down and they fight for the best fishing sites in the river. Young bears playfight, but older ones fight for real. An open mouth, showing the long canine teeth, is a warning to an opponent. If the intruder fails to back down, it is attacked. Fights are often soon over because the bears are quick to return to the abundant source of fish.

▲ **FISHING LESSON**

Bear cubs watch closely as their mother catches a salmon. The cubs learn by example and will eventually try it themselves. It will be a long time before they are as skilful as their mother.

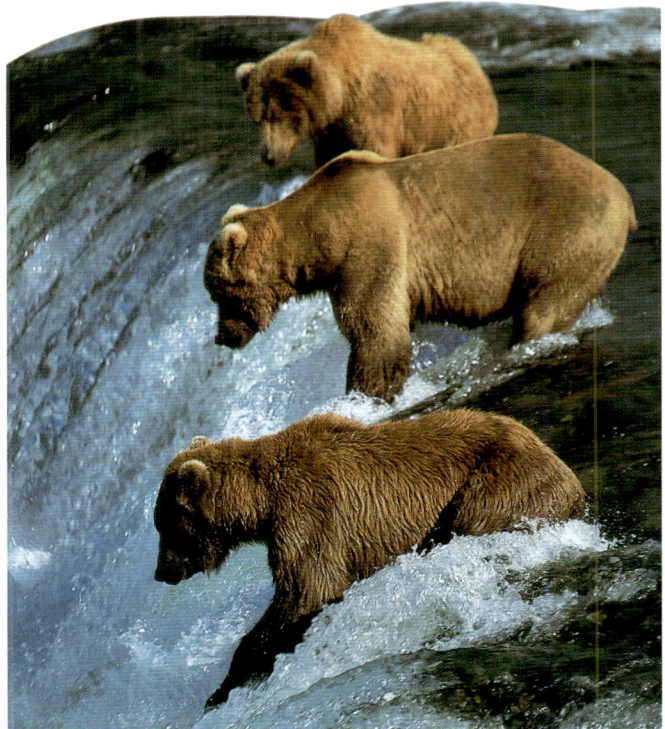

▲ **A SLOUTHE OF BEERYS**

A group of bears is called a sloth, so brown bears on a salmon river are a sloth of grizzlies. The term "a slouthe of beerys" was used in the Middle Ages. It came from people's belief at the time that bears were slow and lazy.

253

Focus on

Because it lives in one of the harshest and most unpredictable places on Earth, the polar bear is constantly on the look-out for food. There may be four or five days between meals. Their most common prey is the ringed seal, although harp, bearded and hooded seals or young walruses are also taken. In spring, a bear searches for seal nursery dens. It breaks through the roof of snow and ice to reach the seal pups inside by jumping down with its powerful forelegs. During the rest of the year, a bear searches for holes in the ice where seals come up to breathe. While its eyesight and hearing are similar to ours, a polar bear's sense of smell is far superior. It can smell a den or breathing hole from a kilometre away.

1 A polar bear uses stealth and surprise to catch its prey. The bear approaches its target slowly, moving silently across the ice and swimming between ice floes. Its broad paws act like paddles and propel it effectively through the water. Its hind legs trail in the water and steer like a ship's rudder. A polar bear can also swim underwater to reach its prey, erupting from the sea to surprise seals resting on the edge of the ice.

2 A polar bear will stand or lie motionless for hours beside a good place for hunting. This may be at a seal's breathing hole or den. In spring, cracks form in the ice where it begins to melt. At points along the ice, seals emerge to rest or bask in the sun. A bear sniffs out suitable hauling-out places and lies in wait. Often, the bear's patience is not rewarded, as only one in 50 attempts to catch prey is successful.

Seal Hunting

3 A harp seal pops up to breathe through a hole in the ice. Before surfacing it would have looked for signs of danger. A bear usually lies on its stomach with its chin close to the edge of the ice. This conceals it from sight until the seal surfaces.

4 When a seal surfaces, the bear scoops it out with a paw or grasps it around the head with its teeth and flips it out on to the ice. A powerful bite to the head crushes the seal's skull or breaks its neck and kills it instantly. The bear eats the fat and internal organs, but not the meat unless it is very hungry. It eats quickly since the smell of the kill might attract other bears.

5 Arctic foxes often follow polar bears across the ice in order to take advantage of their leftovers. Polar bears feed mainly on the seal blubber (fat), leaving behind most of the meat and bones. An average bear needs to eat 2kg/ 4½lb of seal fat a day to survive. They have huge stomachs, enabling them to eat much more. After the meal, a polar bear cleans its fur by swirling in the water or rolling in the snow.

Winter Shutdown

Black bears, brown bears and pregnant female polar bears hibernate. They do so because food is scarce, not because of the cold. Scientists argued for years whether bears truly hibernate or merely doze during the winter months. Now, according to recent research, the hibernation of bears is thought to be even more complete than that of small mammals. During hibernation, a brown bear's heart rate drops to about 35 beats per minute, half its normal rate. American black bears reduce their blood temperature by at least one degree. They do not eat or drink for up to four months. Bears survive only on the fat that they have stored during the summer. A bear might have lost up to 50 per cent of its body weight by the end of the winter.

▲ **FAT BEARS**

Before the winter hibernation a bear can become quite obese. Fat reserves make up over half this black bear's body weight. It needs this bulk to make sure that it has sufficient fat on its body to survive the winter fast. In the weeks leading up to hibernation, a bear must consume large quantities of energy-rich foods, such as salmon.

Did you know? Some hibernating bears sleep for 5½ months non-stop.

◄ **HOME COMFORTS**

A brown bear pulls in grass and leaves to cushion its winter den. American black bears and brown bears sleep in small, specially dug dens. These are usually found on the sunny, south-facing slopes of mountains.

▲ SNOW HOUSE

Female polar bears leave the drifting floes in winter and head inland to excavate a nursery den. They dig deep down into the snow and ice, tunnelling about 5m/16½ft into the ground. Here they will give birth to their cubs. In severe weather, a male polar bear rests by lying down and allowing itself to be covered by an insulating layer of snow.

▲ SCANDINAVIAN REFUGE

A hole dug by a brown bear serves as its winter den in this Swedish forest. Bears spend winter in much stranger places, such as under cabins occupied by people, under bridges or beside busy roads.

▲ READY FOR ACTION

If disturbed, a bear wakes easily from its winter sleep. Although it is dormant, a bear's body is ready for action. It is able to defend itself immediately against predators, such as a hungry wolf pack.

▲ WINTER NURSERY

In the early winter, one bear enters a den, but three might emerge in spring. Female polar bears, like most bears, give birth (usually to twins) while hidden away in their dens. The tiny cubs are born in the middle of winter, in December or January.

A Solitary Life

Bears do not like other bears. They prefer to be alone. When two bears meet there is sometimes a fight, but usually it is just a shouting match and display. Young bears have playfights, not serious contests but rehearsals for battles later in life. Bears will break off hostilities when food is plentiful. Brown bears tolerate each other at fishing rivers and polar bears scavenge together at whale carcasses and rubbish (garbage) dumps. But bears have to be constantly wary of other bears. Cannibalism (eating members of the same species) is more common in bears than in any other mammals. Male bears will fight and kill cubs. Deadly fights between adult male bears may end in one killing the other and then feeding on the loser's body.

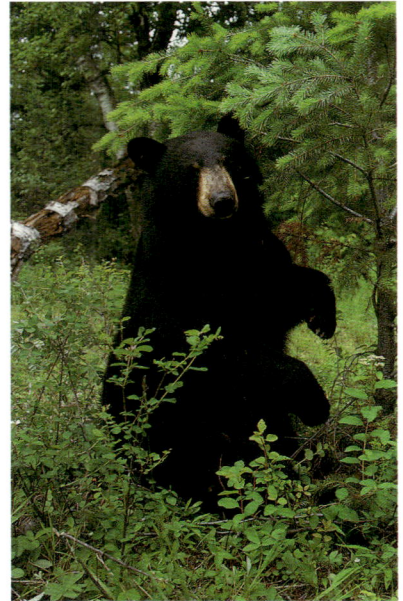

▲ CANNIBALISM

Adult American male black bears and male polar bears are cannibals. They eat mainly younger bears. However, this sort of behaviour is thought to be relatively rare.

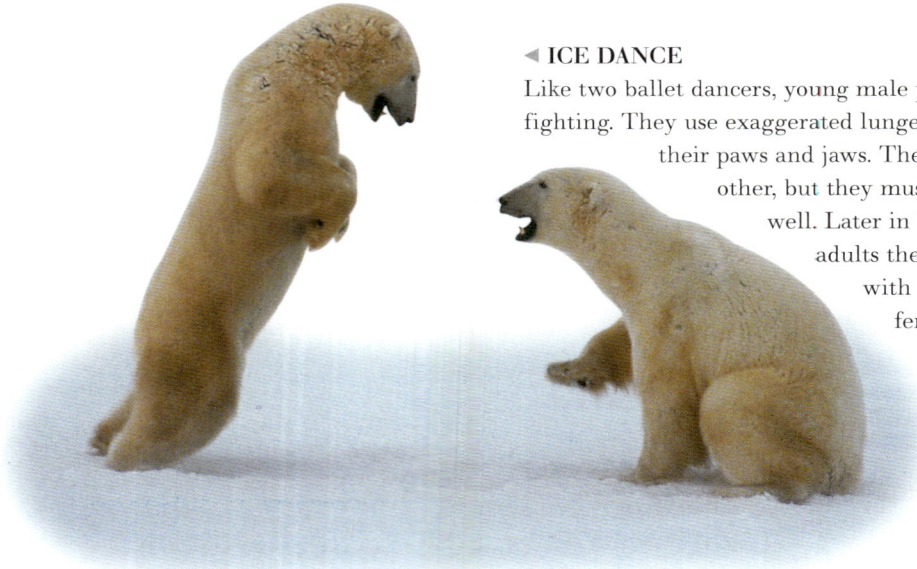

◄ ICE DANCE

Like two ballet dancers, young male polar bears play at fighting. They use exaggerated lunges and swipes with their paws and jaws. They do not hurt each other, but they must learn to fight well. Later in life as fully grown adults they will compete with other males for females during the breeding season. Fights between well-matched individuals can be violent and often bloody.

THE JUNGLE BOOK

Rudyard Kipling's famous story The Jungle Book *was first published in 1894. A young boy named Mowgli is brought up by wolves. He is befriended by Baloo the bear and Bagheera the panther who teach him the law of the jungle. The tiger Shere Khan plots to kill the man-cub.*

▲ TRAGEDY ON THE ICE

A mother polar bear stands over her cub, which has been mauled by a male. Male polar bears usually kill cubs for food. The female attacks and tries to drive the male away. Males are much bigger than females, but a female with cubs is a fierce opponent.

▲ FRIENDS AT THE FEAST

Brown bears gather to catch salmon at a popular site in Alaska. If they get too close to each other, the bears will contest their fishing rights. Usually the larger bears succeed in fishing the best sites.

▲ FISHING BREAK

Young brown bears take a break from learning to fish and practise fighting instead. They fight by pushing and shoving at each other, using their enormous bulk to overcome their opponent. They also try to bite each other around the head and neck.

Meeting a Mate

Brown and black bears mate in the summer between May and July. Males use their well-developed sense of smell to track down females in heat. Brown bears often group together near rich food sources in the mating season, so males have to fight each other for the right to mate. Courtship between male and female bears is very brief, but when the male finds the female is ready to mate, he tries to isolate her from other males. The female is pregnant for from six to nine months. The length varies, because, no matter the time of mating, all the cubs are born at roughly the same time in the new year. This is because female bears delay the development of the fertilized egg in their wombs until late summer.

▲ **COURTING COUPLE**
A male and female brown bear may stay together for over a week during courtship and mate several times. The act of mating stimulates the female to release an egg. The male keeps other male bears away to be sure he is the father of any offspring.

◀ **LOOK!**
Male giant pandas often climb trees to advertise to females they are willing to mate. They wail, yap and bark to attract attention. Their loud calls also attract other males. The most dominant male mates with the female first. Pandas mate in spring.

▲ **COURTSHIP DEADLOCK**
A male has to overcome the female's natural tendency to be wary of him. The two assess each other with some gentle sparring interrupted by brief stand-offs and a lot of sniffing.

▼ HEAVENLY SCENT

Bears rely on their keen sense of smell to find a partner. An Alaskan brown bear approaches a receptive female, checking her odour track on the ground. If she lets him approach, he sniffs her head, body and rear for signs that she is ready to mate. This period of courtship can last for up to 15 days, before the female is finally ready.

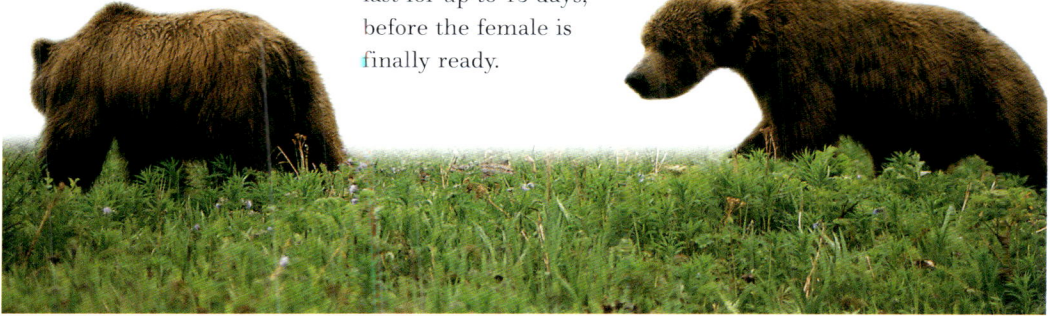

► ARCTIC ENGAGEMENT

Polar bears mate from late March to late May. They tend to congregate where there are plenty of seals. There are usually more males willing to mate than females. Like brown bears, a successful male tries to keep his temporary partner away from other male bears. They mate many times over a period of a week or more.

◄ MATING TIME

If a female brown bear is receptive, the male places his paw on her back. He mounts and grasps her in a bear hug, and bites the back of her head and neck. Mating is brief, lasting for only a few seconds up to about three minutes. The pair may mate up to 16 times in one day, and this may be repeated over several days. This makes sure that the female becomes pregnant by that particular male.

Nursery Dens

Most bears give birth hidden away from the outside world in dens. American black and brown bear cubs are born in winter, in January and February, when their mother is closeted in her winter den. A den can be a cave, in a hollow tree, under a tree that has been pushed over by the wind or in a self-made hollow. Usually, two to three cubs are born, naked and helpless. Newborn bear cubs are small compared to the size of their mother. This is because a female bear's gestation period is very short. The mother has also to rely only on her fat reserves to build up their tiny bodies. A mother bear is only able to feed her cubs if she has eaten enough food in the months before her winter hibernation.

▲ **BLIND AND HELPLESS**
Ten-day-old brown bear cubs nestle into their mother's fur for warmth. With their eyes and ears tightly closed shut, they are totally dependent on her. The cubs remain in the den until May or June when they are about four months old.

Did you know? polar bear cubs are no bigger than guinea pigs when born.

◄ **TWINS**
A polar bear mother tends her two young. The family leaves its den between late February and April depending on where they live. The further north they are, the later in the year they emerge.

▲ TRIPLETS

This American black bear has given birth to three healthy cubs. Females may have up to four cubs at one time. About the size of a rat and naked at first, the cubs grow quickly. They will leave the den in April or May.

▲ PANDA BABY

At Wolong breeding station in Sichuan, China, a baby giant panda is put in a box to be weighed. Giant pandas give birth to one or two cubs in a cave or tree hollow. If twins are born, the mother often rears only one, leaving the other to die.

◄ MOTHER'S MILK

Three-month-old polar bear cubs suckle on their mother's milk. The milk is rich in fats and the cubs suckle for up to a year. Polar bear cubs are born covered with fine hair.

► IN THE DEN

American black bears weigh less than 300g/10½oz when they are born in late January or early February. Their small size and lack of fur makes them vulnerable to the cold. The mother cleans and dries the cubs, then cuddles them close. The den is lined with branches, leaves, herbs and grasses to make a warm blanket. The mother spends a lot of time grooming her cubs and keeps the den scrupulously clean by eating their droppings.

Focus on

1 A bank of snow makes an ideal site for a polar bear's winter den. The pregnant female bear digs into the south side of the snowdrift. The prevailing northerly winds pile up snow on the other side.

From late October, a pregnant female polar bear digs a snow den. Usually it is on a slope facing south, some distance from the sea. This is where she will give birth to her cubs. The mother warms her den with heat from her body. A tunnel to the nursery chamber slopes upward so that warm air rises and collects in the chamber, which can be 20°C/68°F warmer than outside. She gives birth during the harshest part of winter from late November to early January, when permanent night covers the Arctic. The cubs grow fast. Around March the mother drives two holes through the walls of the den and helps the cubs to emerge for the first time.

2 This etching shows an artist's impression of the inside of a polar bear's snow hole. The female bear gave birth to her cubs about three months ago. The cubs are now strong enough to follow their mother toward the sea where she can hunt and feed.

3 The female polar bear emerges from her winter home for the first time in the middle of March. The den's southward-facing entrance and exit hole faces toward the Sun, which is low on the horizon in early spring. The mother and her cubs are warmed by the Sun's rays.

Snow Homes

4 Sitting upright in a snow hollow, a female polar bear nurses her cubs. She differs from other female bears in having four working nipples rather than six. Her cubs also stay with her longer than most bears. She protects them from male bears until they are three years old. During this time she will teach her cubs how to survive in the cold Arctic conditions and also how to hunt seals.

5 On first emerging, the family remains at the den site for a few days so that the cubs become used to the cold. They play outside in the snow during the short days and shelter in the den at night and during storms.

6 The cubs' first journey outside can be a long one. They may have to walk up to 22km/13½ miles to reach the sea ice where they will see their first seal hunt. The mother takes great care to avoid adult male bears who might try to kill her cubs.

Raising Cubs

Bear cubs spend the first 18 months to three years with their mother. If something should happen to her, they may be adopted by another mother with cubs the same age. The cubs learn everything from their mother. They learn to recognize the best foods and where and when to find them. They must also learn how to escape danger and how to find a winter den or shelter in a storm. Without this schooling, the young bears would not survive. Mothers and cubs can communicate by calling, particularly if they become separated or if a mother wants her offspring to follow her. During their development, cubs must keep out of the way of large male bears who might attack them.

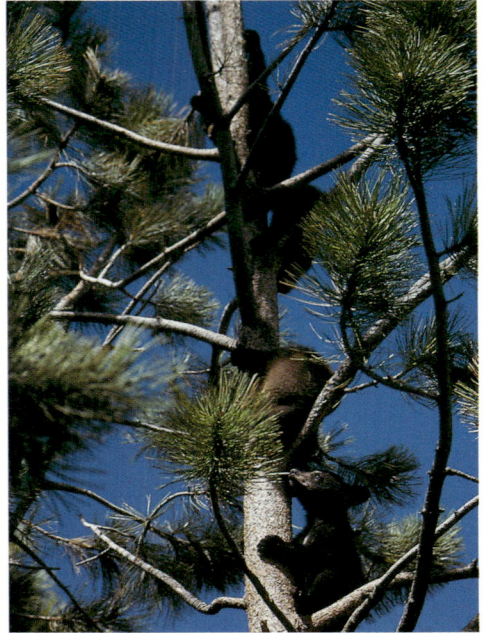

▲ **SAFE IN THE BRANCHES**
Black bear cubs instinctively know that they should head for the nearest tree when danger threatens. It is easier for a mother to defend a single tree than a scattered family.

▼ **MILK BAR**
A mother brown bear suckles her twins. Her milk is thick and rich in fats and proteins, but low in sugars. It has three times the energy content of human or cow's milk. The cubs are small at birth and must put on weight and grow quickly.

◄ LEAVING THE FAMILY

Young bears on their own, such as this brown bear, often become thin and scrawny. Despite being taught by their mothers where and how to feed, they cannot always find food. At popular feeding sites, such as fishing points, they are chased off by larger bears. When the time comes for young bears to look after themselves, the mother either chases them away or is simply not there when they return to look for her.

► LONG APPRENTICESHIP

Polar bear cubs are cared for by their mother for much longer than other bear cubs. They need to master the many different hunting strategies used by their mother to catch seals. These are not something that the cubs know instinctively, but rather skills that they must learn.

Did you know? Giant panda cubs are the first to leave their mothers at 18 months old

◄ FAMILY TRAGEDY

This polar bear cub is the victim in a tragic tug-of-war. A male bear has attacked the cub and its mother is trying to save it. Female polar bears fight ferociously to protect their young, but are often unsuccessful against larger opposition. Attacks like this, starvation, the cold and diseases mean that about 70 per cent of polar bear cubs do not live to their first birthday.

Where in the World are Bears?

Bears are found in a variety of habitats including the Arctic tundra, mountain slopes, scrub desert, temperate and tropical forests and tropical grasslands. Each species of bear, however, has its own preferred environment. The polar bear, for example, inhabits the lands and sea ice bordering the Arctic Ocean. It favours the shoreline areas where the ice breaks up and cracks appear, as this is where seals congregate. Most other bears are less specialized and have the uncanny ability to turn up wherever food is abundant. However, many of the wilderness areas where bears live are under threat. As more land is cultivated for farmland and forests all over the world are cut down, habitat loss is a major threat to many bears.

▲ IN THE BAMBOO FORESTS
The giant panda is restricted to areas of abundant bamboo forest. It was once much more widespread across eastern Asia, but now survives in just three provinces of western China – Gansu, Shanxi and Sichuan.

▼ MOUNTAIN BEAR
The spectacled bear lives in South America. It lives high in the Andes Mountains of Peru, Ecuador, Venezuela and Colombia. It is found in forests, including rainforests, cloud forests, and dry forests, as well as steppe (grassland) and rocky outcrops.

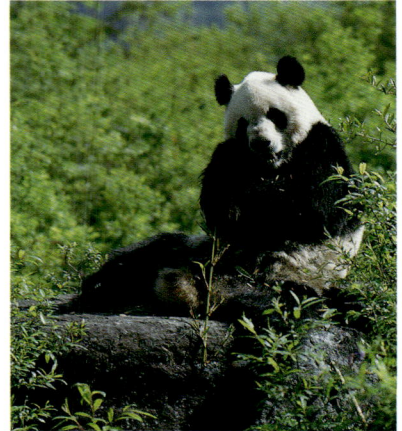

▲ BROWN BEAR
The brown bear is the most widespread of all bears. It is found in Europe, the Middle East, across Russia and northern Asia to Japan. North American brown bears live in Alaska and the Canadian Rockies.

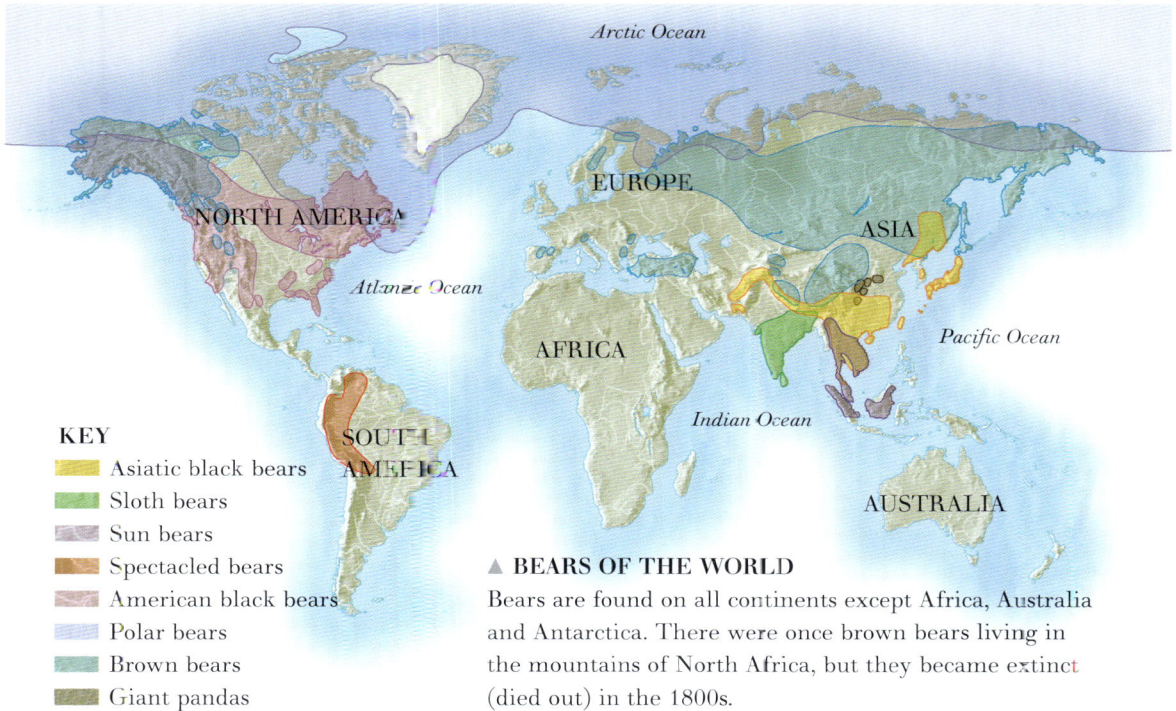

KEY

- Asiatic black bears
- Sloth bears
- Sun bears
- Spectacled bears
- American black bears
- Polar bears
- Brown bears
- Giant pandas

▲ BEARS OF THE WORLD

Bears are found on all continents except Africa, Australia and Antarctica. There were once brown bears living in the mountains of North Africa, but they became extinct (died out) in the 1800s.

▲ ASIATIC BLACK BEAR

The Asiatic black bear lives in mountainous regions over a wide area of southern and eastern Asia. It is found in northern India, Pakistan and on the islands of Japan and Taiwan.

▲ LIFE IN THE FOREST

The sloth bear (*above*) lives in dense, dry forests in India and Sri Lanka. The Malayan sun bear lives in similar lowland but tropical forests of South-east Asia. It is also thought to live in Yunnan in southern China, although no recent sightings have been reported.

269

Finding the Way

Bears have an uncanny knack of finding their way home even in unfamiliar territory. How they do this is only just beginning to be understood. For long distances, they rely on an ability to detect the Earth's magnetic field. This provides them with a magnetic map of their world and a compass to find their way around. When closer to home, they recognize familiar landmarks. In fact, bears have extraordinary memories, especially where food is involved. For example, a mother and her cubs are known to have trekked 32km/ 20 miles to a favourite oak tree to feast on acorns. Five years later, the cubs (now adults) were reported as being at the same tree.

STARS IN THE SKY
The Great Bear constellation in the northern hemisphere is known to astronomers as Ursa Major. In Greek mythology, it was said to have been made in the shape of a she-bear and placed in the heavens by Zeus. The Great Bear is also worshipped in Hindu mythology as the power that keeps the heavens turning. The Inuit believe these stars represent a bear being continually chased by dogs.

▲ ARCTIC NOMADS

Polar bears are capable of swimming long distances between ice floes at speeds of up to 10kph/6mph. They may travel thousands of kilometres/miles across the frozen Arctic Ocean and the surrounding lands in search of prey.

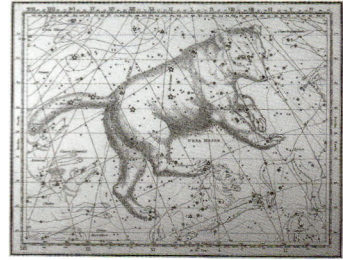

▲ BAD BEAR

A sedated polar bear is transported a safe distance out of town. Nuisance bears are often moved this way but they unerringly find their way back.

◄ TO AND FROM THE FOREST

The polar bears of Hudson Bay, Canada, migrate to the forests in summer and return to hunt on the sea ice in winter. On their return journey, they sometimes stop off at the town of Churchill. They gather at the dump to feed on leftovers, while they wait for ice to reform.

KEY

Bears return to ice in winter

Bears come ashore in June and July

Bears walk north in autumn (fall)

▲ REGULAR ROUTES

Polar bears move quickly even on shifting ice floes. A bear moving north, for example, against the southward-drifting ice in the Greenland Sea, can travel up to 80km/50 miles in a day.

▲ GOOD MEMORIES

Male brown bears live in large home ranges covering several hundred square kilometres. They must remember the locations of food and the different times of year it is available.

Focus on

Bears in some parts of the world are unique in terms of size or colour. Brown bears (grizzlies) on Kodiak, Shukak and Afongnak islands, Alaska, grow to a gigantic size. Across the Pacific, the brown bears of the Kamchatka Peninsula, Russia, are also giants. It is thought they reach their enormous size by including salmon as an important part of their diet.

Elsewhere, brown bears take the grizzly colour to an extreme and have fur resembling streaked hairstyles. American black bears show a very wide variation in colour. Many are not even black, ranging from white to red-brown. These variations may camouflage bears in different habitats. Black bears are invisible in dense forests, but lighter-coloured fur is an advantage in more open places.

BEAR GIANT
Standing on its hind legs, a Kodiak brown bear would tower over a person. It can weigh up to 750kg/ 1,653 lb – almost as big as a North American bison. The average weight for a male Kodiak bear, however, is about 300kg/ 661lb. These bears are so powerful, they can kill and carry an adult moose.

CINNAMON BEAR
Cinnamon-coloured American black bears have a coat that is reddish brown to blond. Bears in the west tend to be cinnamon or honey-coloured, whereas bears in the east are mainly black.

Super Bears

BLUE BEAR
Blue or glacier black bears are found in North-west Canada. They have a blue-grey tinge to their fur. Like all American black bears, no matter what their body colour is, they have a brown muzzle.

RUSSIAN BEAR
The giant brown bears of the Kamchatka Peninsula, eastern Russia, have a varied diet. They ea the seeds of conifer trees, fish for salmon, hunt for seals and birds and scavenge on stranded whales.

GHOST BEAR
One in ten black bears on Kermodes Island off North America's Pacific coast is snowy white. These bears are not albinos (animals that lack skin colour) or polar bears, but true black bears.

▲ SLOTH BEAR

Very little is known about the origins of the Indian sloth bear (*Melursus ursinus*). Few fossils (remains preserved in stone) have been found for this species of tropical bear. Sloth bears are thought to have evolved during an ice age that started about 1.6 million years ago.

Family Groups

The eight species of living bears belong to the family Ursidae. They all have the same general appearance, but in different parts of the world, each is adapted to a particular lifestyle. Bears in tropical places tend to be small and spend more time in the trees. Those in northern lands are larger and live mostly on the ground. To help them study bears, scientists divide the eight living species into three smaller groups, or subfamilies. The giant panda and spectacled bear are the sole survivors of two ancient subfamilies, the Ailuropodinae and Tremarctinae. The rest of the bears are grouped together in a third subfamily, the Ursinae. A bear's Latin name reveals how that particular species is grouped.

◄ BROWN BEAR

Brown bears (*Ursus arctos*) first appeared in China about 500,000 years ago. From here they migrated right across the northern hemisphere into North America and Europe.

▲ POLAR BEAR

The polar bear (*Ursus maritimus*) is the most recent bear to have evolved. Its closest relative is the brown bear. In zoos, polar bears and brown bears are sometimes interbred.

▲ GIANT PANDA

The giant panda (*Ailuropoda melanoleuca*) is the sole survivor of the earliest group of bears, the Ailuropodinae. It first appeared around 10 million years ago. Fossils of giant pandas have been found throughout China.

▶ ASIATIC BLACK BEAR

The Asiatic black bear evolved from the same ancestor as most other species of bear, *Ursus minimus*. It is found mainly in the hilly areas of southern Russia, Japan, and southern Asia. This bear is in danger of extinction in some areas, because it is still hunted for food and medicine.

▼ SUN BEAR

The sun bear (*Helarctos malayanus*) is another tropical bear about which very little is known. It too probably evolved during the last Ice Age. Today sun bears are under threat from pressures such as farming. The bears tear out the hearts of oil palms, which ruins the crop.

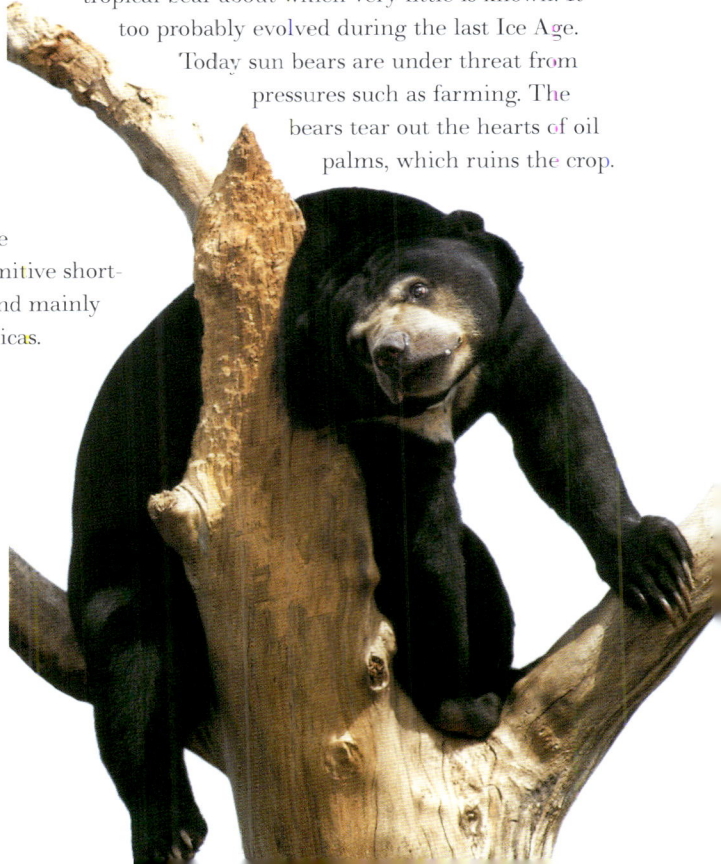

▼ SPECTACLED BEAR

The spectacled bear (*Tremarctos ornatus*) evolved about 2 million years ago. It is the last remaining member of a group of primitive short-faced bears (Tremarctinae) that were found mainly in the Americas.

Pandas on the Edge

Pandas are the rarest of all bears. Each year their habitat shrinks. There are just 25 pockets of panda forest remaining, each with no more than 50 wild pandas living there. This makes pandas extremely vulnerable. One threat is the flowering of bamboo. When bamboo flowers it dies back. Each species of bamboo flowers at a different time. In the past, pandas would leave their home range and travel to where other species of bamboo were not flowering. Today, pandas are trapped by the surrounding farmland and cannot move from one bamboo stand to another. The Chinese government is desperately trying to conserve the panda. Reserves have been set up to study panda behaviour and establish breeding programmes. The panda is regarded as a national treasure. Anyone killing a panda faces the death penalty.

▲ **FEEDING TIME**
A baby giant panda is bottle-fed at a panda breeding centre in China. By giving the babies a helping hand early in life, it is hoped more pandas may grow to adulthood. They may then be returned to their native bamboo forests.

Did you know? Baby pandas are blind, pink and weigh just 100g/3½oz at birth.

◄ **CAPTIVE BREEDING**
These are two of the 100 or so giant pandas in zoos and breeding centres worldwide. Unfortunately, pandas are slow to have young. Artificial insemination is used in attempts to breed more pandas in captivity.

▲ SYMBOL FOR CONSERVATION

The World Wide Fund for Nature adopted the giant panda as its logo. Its rarity and universally popular appeal has made the panda a natural ambassador for all living things facing extinction.

▲ ON DISPLAY

This giant panda is far from its natural home. The chances are that it has not been bred in a zoo, but taken from the wild. It is, however, safe from poachers who supply a lucrative market in panda skins.

◄ PANDA TRANSPORT

Chinese biologists in the Wolong Reserve, Sichuan, try to persuade a giant panda to enter a cage. They will move the panda to the breeding centre for further studies. It is only since the 1980s that scientists have started to understand the panda's biology.

► BACK TO THE WILD

Many pandas have been born in captivity, but less than a third of cubs have survived. It was hoped that captive-bred pandas could be returned to the wild, but the results are disappointing. This is because there is not enough vacant habitat to return captive pandas to. There are now 13 panda reserves and these cover about half the remaining habitat.

Focus on

Polar bears come into close contact with people each autumn (fall) at the isolated Canadian town of Churchill on the shores of Hudson Bay. The bears are on their way from the forests inland where they spend the summer, to the ice of the bay where they hunt. Often they arrive before the ice forms and cause a lot of trouble while they hang around with nothing to do. Some bears head for town and scare the local townsfolk. Others head for the town dump. The bears are chased away, but frequent offenders are tranquillized and transported somewhere safe. The bears, however, have become a tourist attraction. People come from all over the world to see the congregations of polar bears, which are more solitary in the wild.

LOOKING FOR TROUBLE
This bear has picked up the tantalizing scent of tourists. Many visitors arrive to see the bears each year. They travel about in great buses called tundra buggies, where they are safe from the powerful and inquisitive bears.

OVERSTEPPED THE MARK
A researcher cautiously tests a tranquillized polar bear to make sure it is fully sedated. He holds a gun in case the polar bear is not so sleepy as it seems and attacks. Polar bears at Churchill occasionally threaten people. They are tranquillized and moved a safe distance away or locked up in a trap until the ice refreezes.

278

Churchill

BEAR BACK

A polar bear keeps cool by rolling in a patch of snow while it waits for the ice to form on Hudson Bay. The days can be warm in the Arctic autumn (fall). Polar bears have thick fur and may overheat if they cannot cool down.

FAST FOOD

A bear scavenges through the town rubbish (garbage) dump. This is a favourite rendezvous spot. Household rubbish (garbage) provides easy food for hungry bears unable to hunt.

THE SIN BIN

A rogue bear is released from a bear trap. Unfortunately, bears have a well-developed homing instinct and often appear in town again. Persistent offenders are kept in a polar bear jail until the ice refreezes.

FREE FLIGHT

A sedated bear is carried away in a net strung under a helicopter. This is a quick way to move a large animal, but it is also very expensive.

DANGER
BEAR TRAP

Bears and People

Bears can be dangerous. They are attracted to food at campsites and dumps and here they come into contact with people. Fatal attacks by bears are rare. A person walking in bear country is seldom attacked, as long as the bear knows that they are there. Walkers are advised to make a lot of noise, clapping their hands and singing, for example, to warn any bears in the vicinity of their presence. Black bears tolerate people more readily than brown bears or grizzlies. Brown bears, because they have poor eyesight, might mistake people for a threat and charge. Whatever happens, a walker should never come between a mother bear and her cubs, as she will certainly fiercely defend them.

▲ **GREAT ESCAPE**

A hiker takes refuge in a tree after surprising a brown bear on a trail in Montana, United States. Adult brown bears do not climb trees. The man will have to wait for the bear to lose interest before he can descend.

◄ **BEGGING FOR FOOD**

People driving in national parks in the United States offer titbits to black bears, despite warnings not to. The animals have learned to associate cars with food. To get inside a car bears have been known to break windows or use their claws like a can-opener to slice through metal doors.

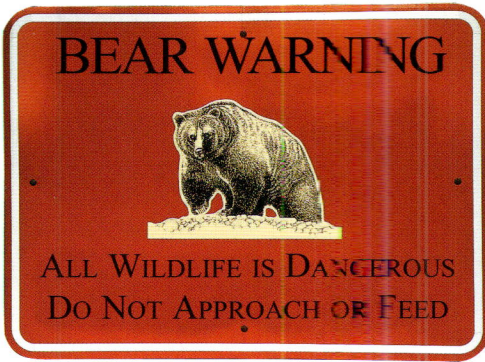

BEAR WARNING

ALL WILDLIFE IS DANGEROUS
DO NOT APPROACH OR FEED

▲ BEAR WARNING

Signs warn visitors to behave sensibly. Even so, a bear might attack. It acts aggressively at first, chomping its jaws together and hitting the ground. It then charges but usually stops at the last moment.

Did you know? Since 1900, there have been fewer than 150 attacks on people in the US.

▲ TRAPPED IN THE ZOO

A bear gnaws the bars of its tiny cage in a zoo in Tunisia. Bears are very popular animals, but they are often kept in terrible conditions in small zoos. This concrete-lined cage is totally bare and does not provide an interesting and stimulating home.

▲ LOOKING FOR FOOD

The tempting smells coming from a dustbin (trash can) are irresistible to a hungry bear. Unfortunately, bears begin to associate people with easy food. Harmless scavenging can become dangerous.

▲ DANGEROUS SITUATION

Bears and people cross paths occasionally. These people are too close to a brown bear for their own safety. If possible, bears should be given a wide berth. They will usually ignore or avoid people, and can be watched safely from a distance.

281

Big Cats

Most cats are loners. They have exclusive rights to a home range that contains all the food they need and they fight any intruders — cats or otherwise — to keep it for themselves. The exception is the lion. While solitary cats catch prey smaller than or the same size as themselves, a pride of lions works together to bring down an animal as big and formidable as a buffalo, considered by some to be the most dangerous animal in Africa.

What is a Cat?

Cats are native to every continent except Australia and Antarctica. All cats are mammals with fine fur that is often beautifully marked. They are skilled hunters and killers with strong agile bodies, acute senses and sharp teeth and claws. Cats are stealthy and intelligent animals and many are solitary and very secretive. Although cats vary in size from the domestic (house) cat to the huge Siberian tiger, they all belong to the same family, the Felidae. This means that both wild and domestic cats look alike and behave in very similar ways. In all, there are 38 different species of cat.

▲ **LONG TAIL**
A cat's long tail helps it to balance as it runs. Cats also use their tails to signal their feelings to other cats.

All cats have short, rounded heads.

Whiskers help a cat feel its surroundings.

The body of a cat is muscular and supple, with a broad, powerful chest.

▲ **BIG BITE**
As this tiger yawns it reveals its sharp teeth and strong jaws that can give a lethal bite. Cats use their long, curved canine teeth for killing prey.

BIG CATS
Cats are very specialized meat-eaters. They are the perfect carnivore, with excellent hearing and eyesight. Their curved, razor-sharp claws, used for catching and holding prey, are retractable. This means they can be pulled into the paws to protect them when running. The hair covering a cat's paws and surrounding the pads helps it move silently.

▲ NIGHT SIGHT

The pupils (dark centres) of cats' eyes close to a slit or small circle during the day to keep out the glare. At night they open up to let in as much light as possible. This enables a cat to see at night as well as during the day.

The Lion and the Saint

St Jerome was a Christian scholar who lived from about AD 331 to 420. According to legend, he found an injured lion in the desert with a thorn in its paw. Instead of attacking him, the lion befriended the saint when he removed the thorn. St Jerome is often shown with a lion sitting at his feet.

Very soft fur is kept clean by regular grooming with the tongue and paws.

A long tail helps the cat to balance when it runs and leaps on prey.

Did you know? Some Arctic cultures believe that cats represent the spirits of the dead.

Cats walk on their toes, not on the whole foot.

Large ears draw in sounds.

CATS' EARS ▶

A cat's ears are set high on its head. This gives a keen hunter the best possible chance of picking up sounds. The ears have a rounded shape, which enables sounds to be picked up from many directions. Cats can also rotate their ears to face towards the source of a sound.

The Big Cats

Scientists classify (arrange) the members of the cat family into related groups. The two main groups are small cats (the domestic cat and many wild cats) and the big cats (the tiger, lion, leopard, snow leopard and jaguar). The clouded leopard and the cheetah are each grouped separately, but many people regard them as big cats. Big cats differ from small cats not only because of their size. Big cats can roar, but small cats cannot. Small cats purr. They have a special bone, the hyoid, at the base of their tongues that enables them to breathe and purr at the same time. Big cats have elastic cartilage instead and can only purr when they breathe out. The puma is in fact a very large small cat. It is discussed here because of its size.

▲ **LION**
The lion is the only social cat and lives in a family group called a pride. Adult male lions, unlike other big cats, have a long, thick mane of hair. Female lions do not have manes.

▲ **PUMA**
The puma is also called the cougar or mountain lion. Although it is about the same size as a leopard, a puma is considered a small cat because it can purr. Pumas live in North and South America.

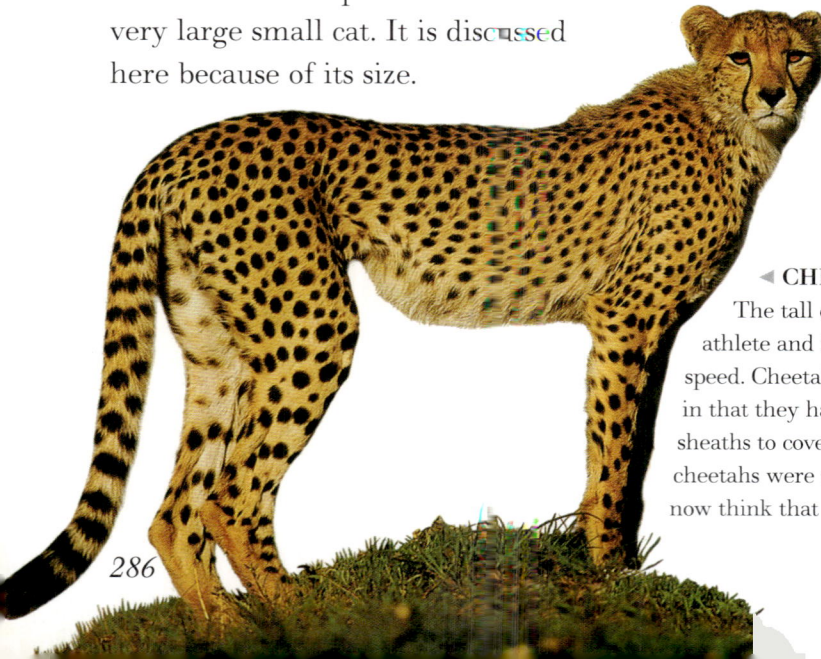

◄ **CHEETAH**
The tall cheetah is built like a slim athlete and is able to chase prey at great speed. Cheetahs are different from other cats in that they have retractable claws, but no sheaths to cover them. It was once thought that cheetahs were related to dogs, but scientists now think that their closest cousins are pumas.

▲ LEOPARD

The leopard is built for bursts of speed and for climbing trees. Heavier than a cheetah, this cat is not so large and bulky as a tiger or a lion. Its spotted coat helps to hide the cat as it hunts in wooded grassland. Black leopards are called panthers. They are the same species, but their spots are hidden.

▲ SNOW LEOPARD

Snow leopards are a different species from true leopards. These rare cats have very thick coats to keep them warm in the high mountains of central Asia. They have very long tails, which help them to balance as they leap from rock to rock in their mountainous surroundings.

▼ JAGUAR

The jaguar is sometimes confused with a leopard, but it is stockier and not so agile. It lives throughout South America in forested habitats where it needs strength to climb rather than speed to run.

▲ TIGER

The most powerful and largest of all the big cats is the tiger. A tiger reaches on average a length of over 2m/6½ft and weighs about 230kg/507lb. The biggest tigers live in the snowy forests of Siberia in Russia. A few tigers also live in tropical forest reserves and swamps in Asia.

Did you know? Although lions are called the King of the Jungle, they do not live there.

Bones and Teeth

The skeleton of a cat gives it its shape and has 230 bones (a human has about 206). Its short and round skull is joined to the spine (backbone), which supports the body. Vertebrae (bones of the spine) protect the spinal cord, which is the main nerve cable in the body. The ribs are joined to the spine, forming a cage that protects a cat's heart and lungs. Cats' teeth are designed for killing and chewing. Wild cats have to be very careful not to damage their teeth, because with broken teeth they would quickly die from starvation.

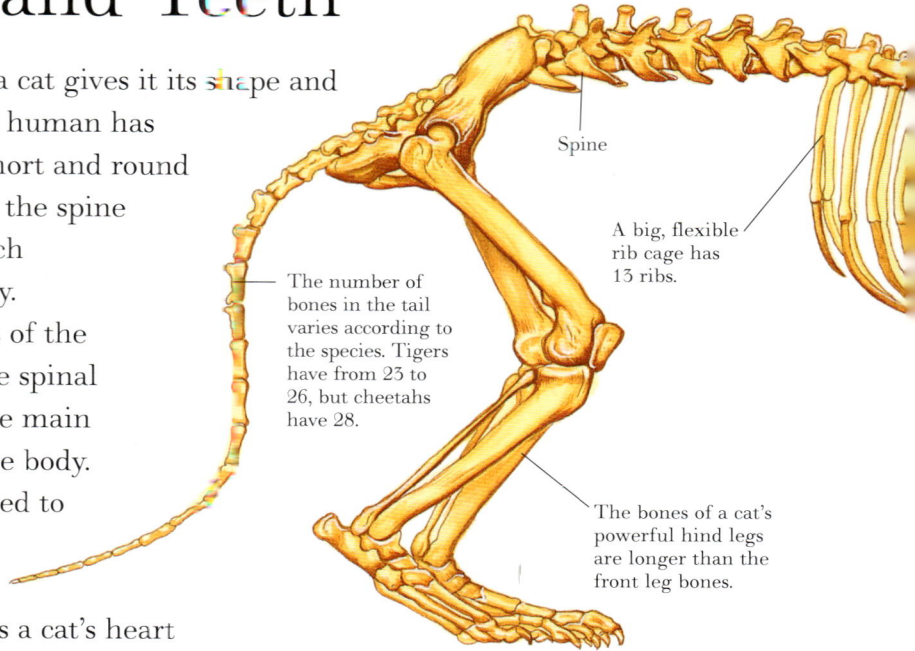

Spine

A big, flexible rib cage has 13 ribs.

The number of bones in the tail varies according to the species. Tigers have from 23 to 26, but cheetahs have 28.

The bones of a cat's powerful hind legs are longer than the front leg bones.

▲ THE FRAME

The powerfully built skeleton of a tiger is similar to all cats' skeletons. Cats have short necks with seven compressed vertebrae. These help to streamline and balance the cat so that it can achieve greater speeds. All cats have slightly different shoulder bones. A cheetah has long shoulder bones to which sprinting muscles are attached. A leopard, however, has short shoulder bones and thicker, tree-climbing muscles.

◄ CANINES AND CARNASSIALS

A tiger reveals its fearsome teeth. Its long, curved canines are adapted to fit between the neck bones of its prey to break the spinal cord. Like all carnivores, cats have strong back teeth, called carnassials. These do most of the cutting by tearing off pieces of meat.

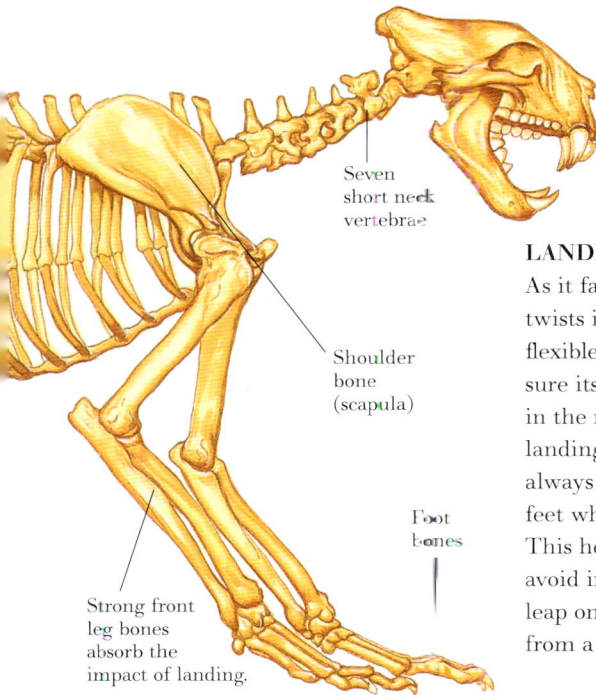

Seven
short neck
vertebrae

Shoulder
bone
(scapula)

Foot
bones

Strong front
leg bones
absorb the
impact of landing.

LANDING FEET ▶

As it falls, this cat
twists its supple,
flexible spine to make
sure its feet will be
in the right place for
landing. Cats almost
always land on their
feet when they fall.
This helps them to
avoid injury as they
leap on prey or jump
from a tree.

▼ CHEWING ON A BONE

Ravenous lions feast on the carcass of their latest
kill. Cats' jaws are hinged so that their jaw bones
can move only from side to side, not up and down.
Because of this, cats eat on one side of their mouths
at a time and often tilt their heads when they eat.

▼ CAT SKULL

Like all cats' skulls, this tiger's skull has a
high crown at the back giving lots of space
for its strong neck muscles. Big eye sockets
allow it to see well to the sides as well as to
the front. Its short jaws can open wide
to deliver a powerful bite.

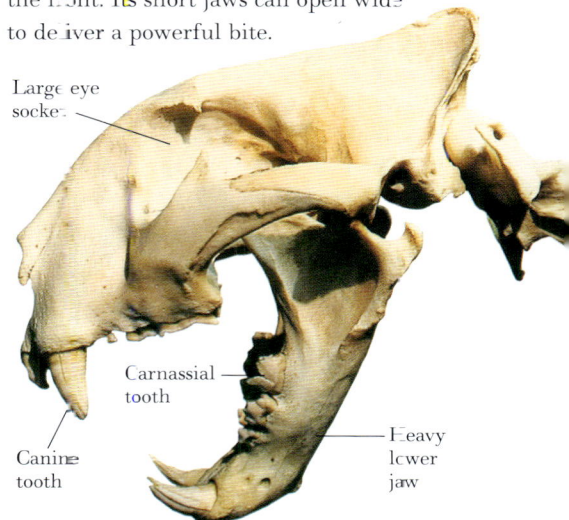

Large eye
socket

Carnassial
tooth

Canine
tooth

Heavy
lower
jaw

289

Muscles and Claws

Both inside and out, cats are designed to be skilled hunters and killers. Thick back and shoulder muscles help them to be excellent jumpers and climbers. Sharp, curved claws that grow from all of their digits (toes) are their weapons. One of the digits on a cat's front foot is called the dew claw. This is held off the ground to keep it sharp and ready to hold prey. Cats are warm-blooded, which means that their bodies stay at the same temperature no matter how hot or cold the weather is. The fur on their skin keeps them warm when conditions are cold. When it is hot, cats cool down by sweating through their noses and paw pads.

Heracles and the Nemean Lion
The mythical Greek hero Heracles was the son of the god Zeus and tremendously strong. As a young man he committed a terrible crime. Part of his punishment was to kill the Nemean lion. The lion had impenetrable skin and could not be killed with arrows or spears. Heracles chased the lion into a cave and strangled it with his hands. He wore its skin as a shield and its head as a helmet.

▶ **KNOCKOUT CLAWS**

Cheetahs have well-developed dew claws that stick out from their front legs. They use these claws to knock down prey before grabbing its throat or muzzle to strangle it. Other cats use their dew claws to grip while climbing or to hold on to prey. Cats have five claws, including the dew claw, on their front paws. On their back paws, they have only four claws.

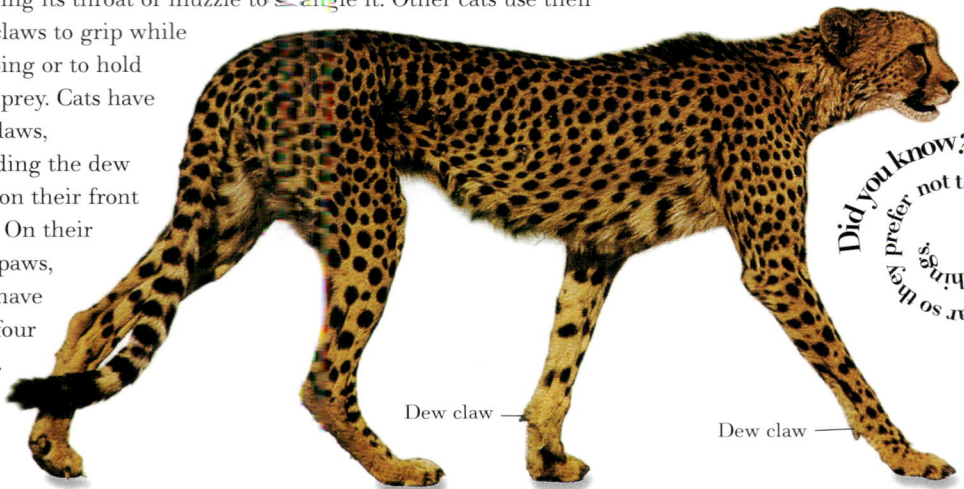

Did you know? Cats cannot digest sugar so they prefer not to eat sweet things.

Dew claw

Dew claw

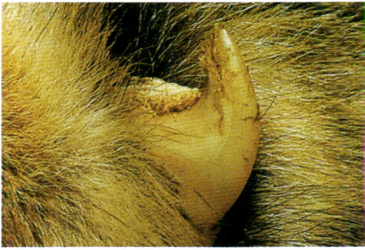

Underneath the skin, a lion's muscular body follows the lines of its skeleton. —

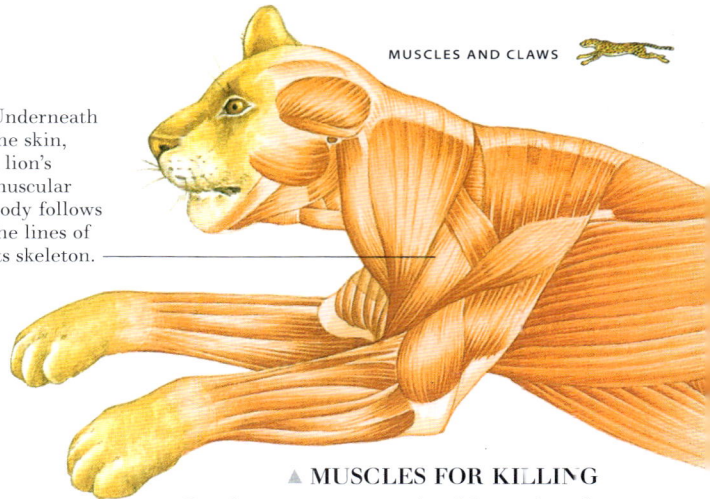

▲ TIGER CLAW

This is the extended claw of a tiger. Cats' claws are made of keratin, just like human fingernails. They need to be kept sharp all the time.

Oesophagus (gullet) Lungs Liver

Kidney

Anus (expels waste)

Trachea (windpipe)

Heart

Bladder

Artery

Intestines

Stomach

Vein

▲ MUSCLES FOR KILLING

Cats have very strong shoulder and neck muscles for attacking prey. The muscles also absorb some of the impact when the cat pounces.

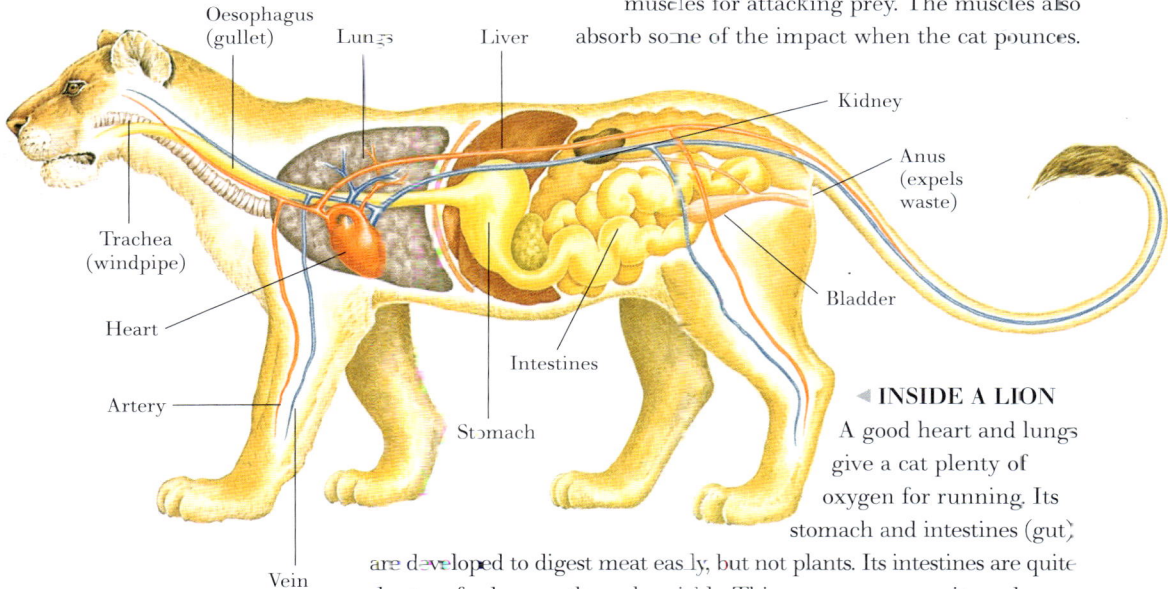

◀ INSIDE A LION

A good heart and lungs give a cat plenty of oxygen for running. Its stomach and intestines (gut) are developed to digest meat easily, but not plants. Its intestines are quite short so food passes through quickly. This means as soon as it needs more food, a cat is light enough to run and pounce. However, once a lion has had a big meal, it does not need to eat again for several days.

CLAW PROTECTION ▶

Cats retract (pull back) their claws into fleshy sheaths to protect them. This prevents them from getting blunt or damaged. Only cheetahs do not have sheaths.

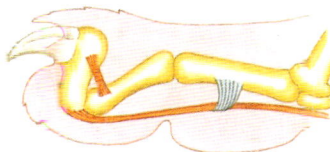

Flexed muscle

Sheathed claw is protected by a fleshy covering.

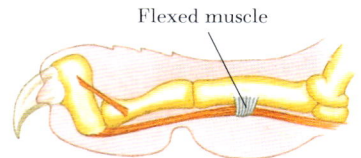

The claw is unsheathed when a muscle tightens.

Sight and Sound

To hunt well and not be seen or heard by prey or enemies, cats use their senses of sight, sound and touch. Cats' eyesight is excellent. Their eyes are adapted for night vision, but they can also see well in the day. Cats' eyes are big compared to the size of their heads. They have good binocular vision, which allows them accurately to judge how far away objects are. At night, cats see in black and white. They can see colours in the day, but not so well as humans can. Cats have very good hearing, much better than a human's. They can hear small animals rustling through the grass or even moving around in their burrows underground.

Did you know? A cat's pupils open wide when it is frightened and close up when it is angry.

▲ **CAUGHT IN BRIGHT LIGHT**
Cats' eyes are very sensitive to light. During the day in bright light, the pupils of the eyes close right down, letting in only as much light as is needed to see well. A domestic cat's pupils close down to slits, while most big cats' pupils close to tiny circles.

◄ **GLOWING EYES**
Behind the retinas (light sensitive areas) in this leopard's eyes is a reflecting layer called the *tapetum lucidum*. This helps to absorb extra light in the dark. When light shines into the eyes at night, the reflectors glow.

PREY IN SIGHT ▶

As it stalks through the long grass, a lion must pounce at just the right moment if it is to catch its prey. Binocular vision helps the cat to judge when to strike. Because its eyes are set slightly apart at the front of the head, their field of view overlaps. This enables a cat to judge the position of its prey exactly.

▲ ROUND-EYED

This puma's rounded pupils have closed down in daylight. In dim light, the pupils will expand wide to let in as much light as possible.

Large earflaps concentrate sound waves deep into each ear.

SHARP EARS ▶

Cats' ears are designed for them to hear very well. This Siberian lynx lives in snowy forests where the sound is often muffled. It has specially shaped, big ears to catch as much sound as possible.

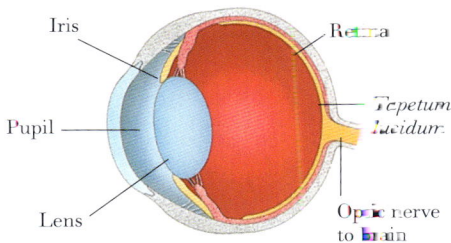

Iris

Retina

Pupil

Tepetum lucidum

Lens

Optic nerve to brain

▲ INSIDE THE EYE

The lens focuses light rays to produce a sharp image on the retina. Impulses from the retina are carried to the brain by the optic nerve. Cats have a membrane that can be pulled over the surface of the eye to keep out dirt and dust.

Touching, Tasting and Smelling

Like all animals, cats feel things with nerves in their skin, but they have another important touching tool – whiskers. These long, stiff hairs on the face have very sensitive nerve endings at their roots. Some whiskers are for protection. Anything brushing against the whiskers above a cat's eyes will make it blink. Cats use smell and taste to communicate with each other. A cat's tongue is a useful tool and its nose is very sensitive. Thin, curled bones in the nose carry scents inward to smell receptors. Unlike most animals, cats have special places on the roofs of their mouths to distinguish scents, especially of other cats.

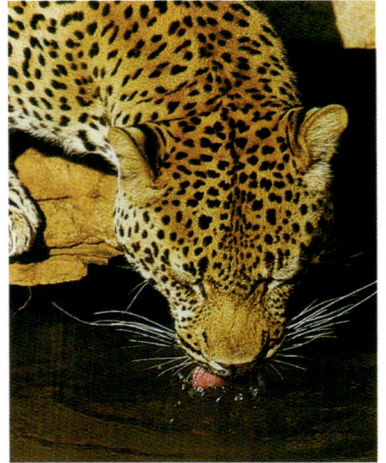

▲ **TONGUE TOOL**

A leopard curls the tip of its tongue like a spoon to lap up water. After several laps it will drink the water in one gulp. As well as drinking, the tongue is used for tasting, scraping meat off a carcass and grooming.

◄ **ROUGH TONGUE**

A tiger's bright pink tongue has a very rough surface. Cats' tongues are covered with small spikes called papillae. The papillae point backwards and are used by the cat, together with its teeth, to strip meat off bones. Around the edge and at the back of the tongue are taste buds. Cats cannot taste sweet things, but can actively recognize pure water.

The tiger raises its head and grimaces to taste the air.

Cats twitch their tails from side to side as they concentrate. When angry, the tail lashes to and fro.

WHO PASSED BY? ▶

By tasting the air a tiger uses his Jacobson's organ (the special scent centre on the roof of the mouth) to detect the scent left by another tiger. To get as much of the scent as he can, he wrinkles his nose, curls his lips upwards, bares his teeth and lifts his head. This action is known as flehmen. Males use it especially to locate females ready to mate.

Did you know? Hairballs coughed up by lions are worn as talismans in some parts of Africa.

▲ THE CATS' WHISKERS

This snow leopard's face is surrounded by sensitive whiskers. Cats use their whiskers to judge how far away objects are. The most important whiskers are on the sides of the face. These help a cat to feel its way in the dark, or when it is walking through tall grass.

▼ COAT CARE

The long, rough tongue of a lion makes a very good comb. It removes loose hairs and combs the fur flat and straight. Cats wipe their faces, coats and paws clean. They need to keep well groomed and spend a lot of time looking after their fur. Hair swallowed by grooming is spat out as hairballs.

295

Spots and Stripes

A cat's fur coat protects its skin and keeps it warm. The coat's colours and patterns help to camouflage (hide) the cat as it hunts prey. Wild cats' coats have two layers – an undercoat of short soft fur and an outercoat of tougher, longer hairs, called guard hairs. Together these two layers insulate the cat from extreme cold or extreme heat. Some guard hairs are sensitive and help a cat to feel its way. Cats have loose skin, making it difficult for an attacker to get a good grip and helping to prevent injury. The colours and patterns of a wild cat's coat depend on where it lives.

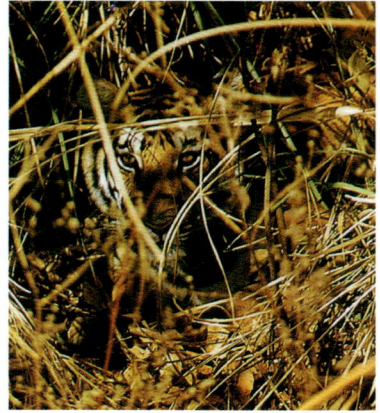

▲ **TIGER IN THE GRASS**

The stripes of a tiger's coat are the perfect camouflage for an animal that needs to prowl around in long grass. The colours and patterns help to make the cat almost invisible as it stalks its prey. These markings are also very effective in a leafy jungle where the dappled light makes stripes of light and shade.

Did you know? Domestic cats have a wider range of colours and markings than wild cats.

◀ **KING OF THE HILL**

King cheetahs were once thought to be different from other cheetahs. They have longer fur, darker colours and spots on their backs that join up to form stripes. Even so, they are the same species. All cheetahs have distinctive tear stripes running from the corners of their eyes down beside their muzzles.

▼ SPOT THE DIFFERENCE

Spots, stripes or blotches break up the outline of a cat's body. This helps it to blend in with the shadows made by the leaves of bushes and trees or the lines of tall grass. In the dappled light of a forest or in the long grass of the savanna, cats are very well hidden indeed.

A leopard's spots are in fact small rosettes.

The tiger has distinctive black stripes.

A jaguar has rosettes with a central spot of colour.

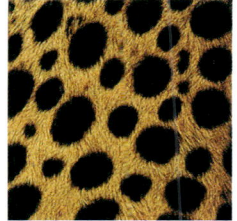

The cheetah has lots of spots and no rosettes.

▲ NON-IDENTICAL TWINS

Many big cats of the same species come in variations of colour, depending on where they live. These two leopard cubs are twins, but one has a much darker, blackish coat. Black leopards are called panthers. (Black jaguars and even pumas are sometimes called panthers.) Some leopards live deep in the shadows of the forest, where darker colouring allows them to hide more easily. Panthers are most common in Asia.

◄ WHITE FOR SNOW

A snow leopard has a shaggy, off-white coat with darker spots. This colouring helps the snow leopard to stay well hidden in the rocky, mountainous terrain where it lives. It moves around early in the morning or late afternoon, blending with its habitat as it looks for prey.

A snow leopard's pale, thick coat has dark irregular spots and streaks. This helps it to hide between the rocks and snow.

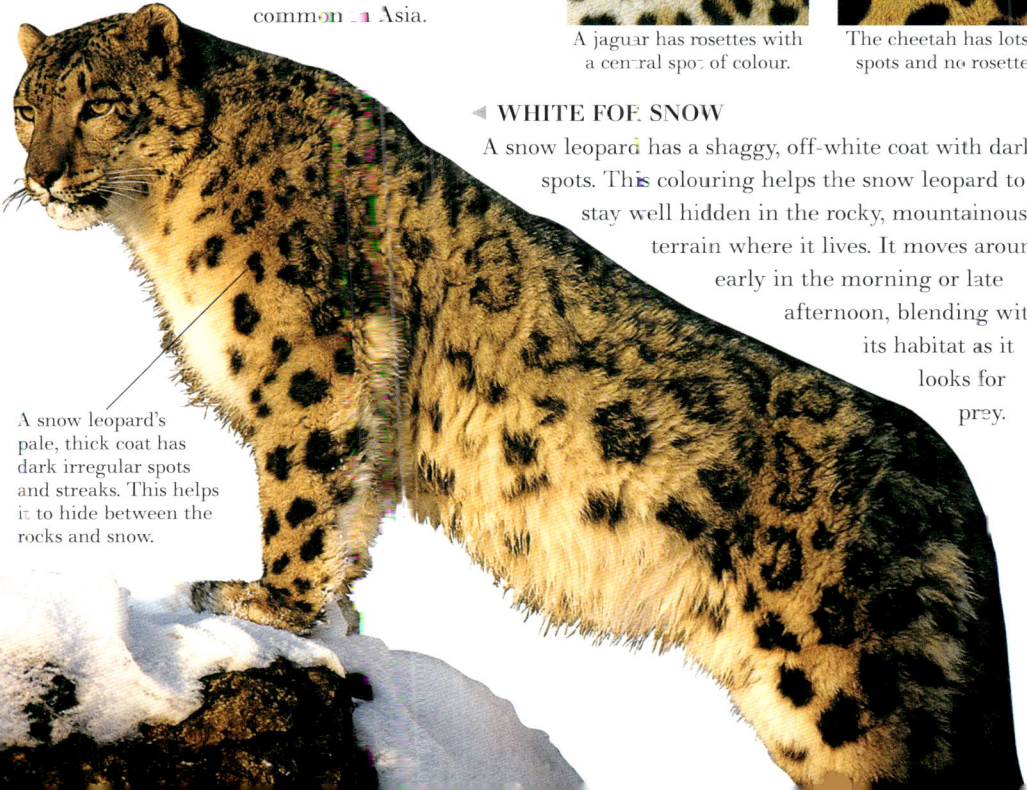

On the Move

Cats run and jump easily and gracefully. They have flexible spines and long, strong hind legs. With long, bouncy strides, they can cover a lot of ground very quickly. Big cats are not good long-distance runners, they are sprinters and pouncers. They use their long tails for balance when climbing trees and running fast. All cats can swim very well, but some do not like the water and will only swim to escape danger. Others, such as tigers and jaguars, live near water and often swim to hunt their prey.

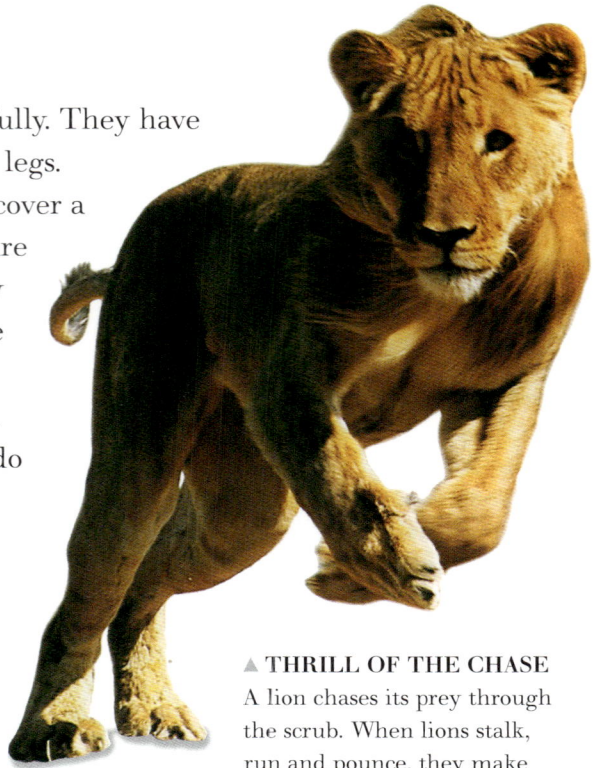

▲ THRILL OF THE CHASE
A lion chases its prey through the scrub. When lions stalk, run and pounce, they make use of their flexible backs, strong back legs, powerful chests and cushioning pads under their paws. Cats' back legs are especially powerful. They provide the major thrust for running. Cats can outpace their prey over short distances before launching into a final jump.

◄ TREE-CLIMBING CAT
Leopards spend a lot of time in trees and are designed for climbing. They have very powerful chests and front legs. Their shoulder blades are positioned to the side to make them better climbers. A leopard can leap 3m/10ft without difficulty and, in exceptional circumstances, can leap over 6m/20ft.

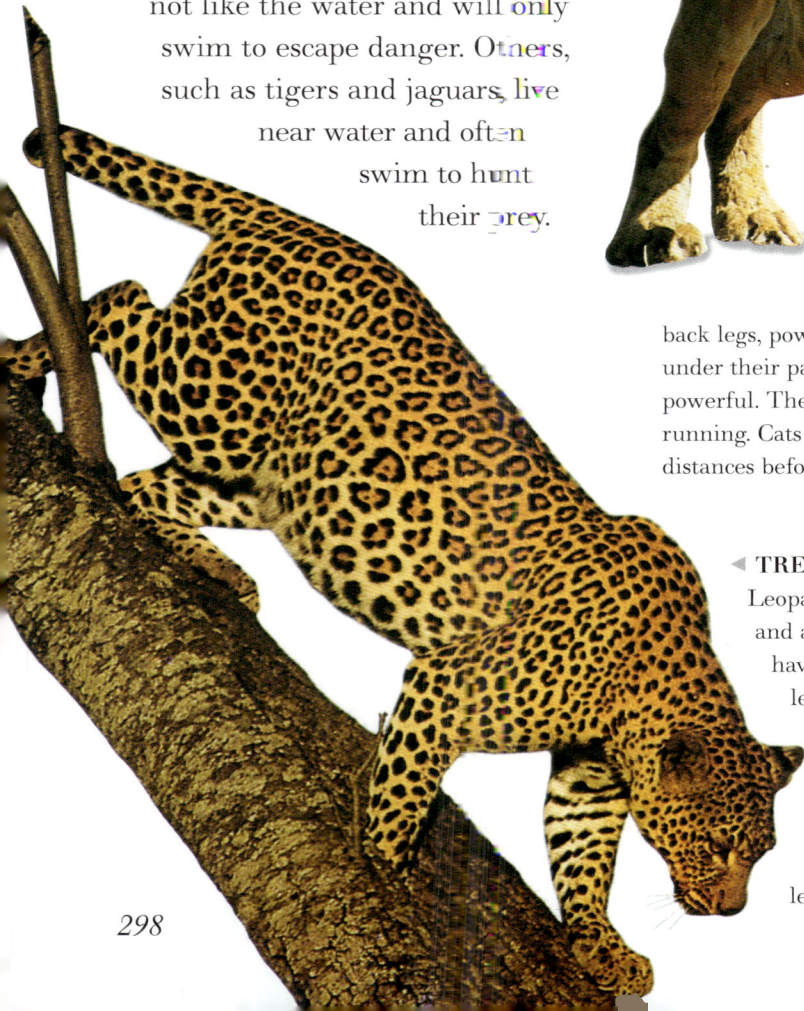

◀ SOFT PADDING

The thick pads under a lion's paw are like cushions. They allow the lion to move very quietly and also act as shock absorbers for running and jumping. Hidden between the pads and fur are the lion's claws, tucked away safely until they are needed.

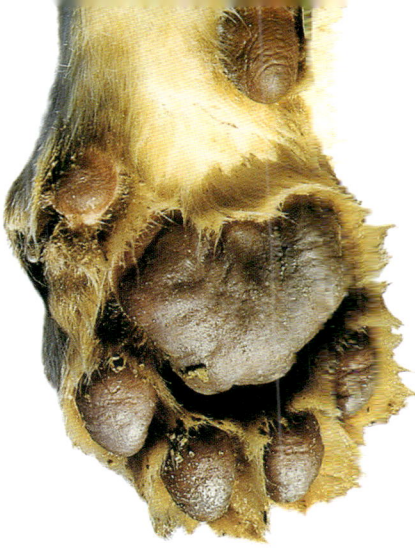

GRACE AND AGILITY ▶

A bobcat leaps with great agility off a rock. All cats have flexible backs and short collarbones to help make their bodies stronger for jumping off things. Bobcats are similar to lynxes. Both cats have an extensive coating of fur on their feet to give them extra warmth. The fur also prevents them from slipping on icy rocks.

Did you know? In the 1500s, rich people kept cheetahs as hunting animals like dogs.

As it leaps, a bobcat pinpoints its landing position. The front feet land separately in quick succession.

◀ KEEPING COOL CAT

A Bengal tiger swims gracefully across a river. Many tigers live in warm climates, such as India and South-east Asia. As well as swimming to get from one place to another, they often look for pools of water to bathe in during the heat of the day. They are one of the few cats that actively enjoy being in or near water. Tigers are superb swimmers and can easily cross a lake 5km/3 miles wide.

299

Focus on the

A cheetah can run at 115kph/71mph over short distances — a speed equivalent to a fast car. This makes it the world's fastest land animal. The cheetah's body is fine-tuned for speed. It has wide nostrils to breathe in as much oxygen as possible and specially adapted paws for running fast. Most cheetahs today live in east and southern Africa, with a small number living in Asia — in Iran and Pakistan. They live in many different kinds of habitats, from open grassland to thick bush and even in desert-like environments.

1 A pair of cheetahs creep up stealthily on a herd of antelope. Cheetahs hunt their prey by slinking towards the herd, holding their heads low. Cheetahs are not pouncing killers, like other cats. Instead, they pull down their prey after a very fast chase. In order to waste as little energy as possible, cheetahs plan their attack first. They pick out their target before starting the chase.

2 The cheetah begins its chase as the herd of antelope starts to move. It can accelerate from walking pace to around 70kph/43mph in two seconds. Cheetahs have retractable claws, but unlike other cats they have no protective sheaths. The uncovered claws act like the spikes on the bottom of track shoes, helping the cheetah to grip as it runs. Ridges on their paw pads also help to improve grip.

3 At top speed a cheetah makes full use of its flexible spine and lean, supple body. A cheetah's legs are very long and slender compared to its body. It can cover several metres in a single bound.

Hunting Cheetah

4 As the cheetah closes in on the herd, the antelope spring in all directions. The cheetah changes direction without slowing down. If a cheetah does not catch its prey within about 400m/1,312 ft, it has to give up the chase. Cheetahs usually hunt in the morning or late in the afternoon, when it is not too hot. They have short lifespans in the wild, because their speed declines with age, making it difficult to catch prey.

5 As the cheetah closes in on its prey it may have to make several sharp turns to keep up. The cheetah's long tail gives it excellent balance as it turns. The cheetah knocks its victim off balance with a swipe of its front paw. It uses its big dew claw to pull the victim to the ground.

6 Once the prey animal is down, the cheetah grabs the victim's throat. A sharp bite suffocates the antelope. Cheetahs are not strong enough to kill by biting through the spinal cord in the prey's neck like other cats. The cheetah will hang on to the victim's throat until the antelope is dead.

Communication

All big cats communicate with one another. They tell each other how old they are, whether they are male or female, what mood they are in and where they live. Cats communicate by signals such as smells, scratches and sounds. The smells come from urine and from scent glands. Cats have scent glands on their heads and chins, between their toes and at the base of their tails. Every time they rub against something, they transfer their special smell. Cats make many different sounds. Scientists know that cats speak to each other, but still do not understand much about their language. Cats also communicate using body language. They use their ears to signal their mood and twitch their tails to show if they are excited or agitated.

▲ **A MIGHTY ROAR**

The lion's roar is the loudest sound cats make. It is loud enough for all the neighbourhood lions to hear. Lions roar after sunset, following a kill and when they have finished eating. Lions make at least nine different sounds. They also grunt to each other as they move around.

HISSING LEOPARD ▶

An angry leopard hisses at an enemy. Cats hiss and spit when they feel threatened or when they are fighting an enemy. The position of a cat's ears also signals its intentions. When a cat is about to attack, it flattens its ears back against its neck.

▲ EAR SIGNALS

Many wild cats, such as the tiger, have white markings on the back of their ears. They turn their ears to show the markings to an enemy when they are angry.

▲ MARKS FOR SHOW

Cats like to scratch things to clean their claws and stretch their limbs. At the same time they leave a scented mark for others to both see and smell. When this lioness scratches, she leaves her own personal scent from the glands between her toes on the scratch marks.

▲ CAT SPRAY

A king cheetah marks its territory by spraying urine at points along its trails. Scent marks left by a male tell other males to stay away. The scent left by a female will tell a male passing through her range if she is ready to mate.

BABY TALK ▶

Mothers talk to their cubs a lot. The sounds are quiet so that enemies do not hear. The softest and safest sound of all is purring.

Did you know? When they are close together, lions chirrup, meow and yowl to each other.

Hunting Prey

All cats, big and small, are carnivores – they eat meat. Their bodies are not designed to digest plants. Big cats must hunt down and kill their own food. Most big cats, however, are only too happy to eat someone else's meal and steal kills from other animals whenever they can. Cheetahs are an exception and eat only animals they have killed themselves. To catch and kill their food, big cats must hunt. Some, like cheetahs, patrol their neighbourhoods, looking for prey. Others, such as jaguars, hide in wait and then ambush their victims. Many cats, such as leopards, do both.

King Solomon

Solomon ruled Israel in the 900s BC and was reputed to be a very wise ruler. His throne was carved with lions because of his admiration for these big cats who killed only out of necessity. In law, if a man was said to have fallen into a lion's den, it was not proof of his death.

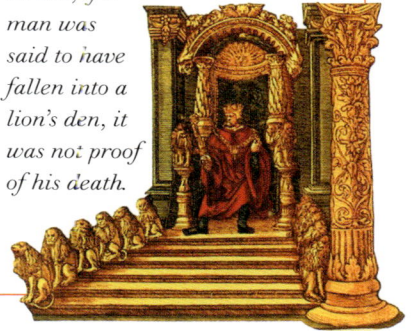

◄ **THE MAIN COURSE**
A big lion can kill large, powerful animals such as this buffalo. A big cat usually attacks from behind or from the side. If the prey is too big to grab right away, the cat will knock it off balance, hold on to it and bite into its neck.

CHOOSING A MEAL ►
A herd of antelope and zebra grazes while keeping watch on a lioness crouched in the grass. She lies as close to the ground as possible, waiting to pounce. Finally, when focused on a victim, she will bring her hind legs back into position and dart forwards.

▲ WARTHOG SPECIAL

Four cheetahs surround an injured warthog. The mother cheetah is teaching her three cubs hunting techniques. The cheetah on the right is trying a left paw side swipe, while another tries using its dew claw. Cheetahs love to eat warthogs, but also catch antelope and smaller animals.

▲ CAT AND MOUSE

A recently killed capybara (a large rodent) makes a tasty meal for a jaguar. Jaguars often catch their food in water, such as fish and turtles. On land they hunt armadillos, deer, opossums, skunks, snakes, squirrels, tortoises and monkeys.

Did you know? Cheetahs will only chase prey if it runs. If it stops, so does the cheetah.

SLOW FOOD ▶

If a lion has not been able to hunt successfully for a while, it will eat small creatures such as this tortoise. Lions usually hunt big animals, such as antelope, wildebeest, warthogs, giraffe, buffalo, bush pigs and baboons. They work together in a group to hunt large prey.

Killing Prey

The way a big cat kills its prey depends on the size of the cat and the size of its meal. If the prey is small with a bitesize neck, it will be killed with a bite through the spinal cord. If the prey has a bitesize head, the cat will use its powerful jaws to crush the back of its skull. Large prey is killed by biting its throat and suffocating it. Lions often hunt together and use a combined effort to kill large prey. One lion may grab the prey's throat to suffocate it, while other lions attack from behind.

Did you know? Lions try to flip porcupines on to their backs to avoid the sharp spines.

▼ OLD AGE
When big cats get old or injured it is very difficult for them to hunt. They will eventually die from starvation. This lion from the Kalahari Desert in South Africa is old and thin. It has been weakened by hunger.

◄ FAIR GAME
A warthog is a small, delicious meal for a cheetah. The bigger the cat, the bigger its prey. A cheetah is quite a light cat, so to kill an animal the cheetah first knocks it over, then bites the prey's neck to suffocate it.

▲ A DEADLY EMBRACE
A lioness immobilizes a struggling wildebeest by biting its windpipe and suffocating it to death. Lions are very strong animals. A lion weighing 150–250kg/330–551lb can kill a buffalo more than twice its weight. Female lions do most of the hunting for their pride.

SECRET STASH

A cheetah carrying off its prey, a young gazelle, to a safe place. Once it has killed, a cheetah will check the area to make sure it is secure before feeding. It drags the carcass to a covered place in the bushes. Here it can eat its meal hidden from enemies. Cheetahs are often driven off and robbed of their kills by hyenas and jackals or even other big cats.

A SOLID MEAL

These cheetahs will devour as much of this antelope as they can. Big cats lie on the ground and hold their food with their forepaws when they eat. When they have satisfied their hunger, cheetahs cover up or hide the carcass with grass, leaves or whatever is available in order to save it for later.

LIONS' FEAST

A pride of lions gather around their kill, a zebra. They eat quickly before any scavenging hyenas and vultures can steal the meat. Each lion has its place in the pride. Even if they are very hungry, they must wait until it is their turn to eat. Usually the dominant male lion eats first.

Focus on the Lone

Leopards are one of the most widespread of all the big cats, but are also the most secretive. They live in many different habitats throughout Africa and southern Asia, in open, rocky country as well as in forests. Not much is known about them because they are nocturnal animals, coming out to hunt at night. They sometimes creep up on prey on the ground, then pounce. At other times they ambush their prey from a tree.

CAT NAP

Leopards usually sleep all day in a tree, especially when it is very hot. Their spotted coats are excellent camouflage in the patchwork of light and shade in the forest. They are so good that, when they are resting, they are especially hard to see.

LONE LEOPARD

Leopards are loners. They come together only when a female signals to a male that she is ready to mate. After mating they separate again. The mother brings up the cubs until they are able to fend for themselves.

Leopard

BRUTE STRENGTH

A leopard drags its dead victim across the ground. Leopards have strong jaws, chests and front legs so that they can move an animal as big as themselves.

AMBUSH

Leopards like to ambush prey. They climb on to a low branch and wait for an animal to walk underneath. Then they jump down and grab it. The leopard uses its great strength to drag its victim high up into the tree. Prey includes pigs, antelope, monkeys, dogs and many other animals.

TOP MEAL

This leopard has dragged its kill up into a tree. This is to prevent the carcass from being stolen. Other big carnivores that live in the same area cannot climb trees so well as leopards. Once the prey is safe, a leopard can finish its meal.

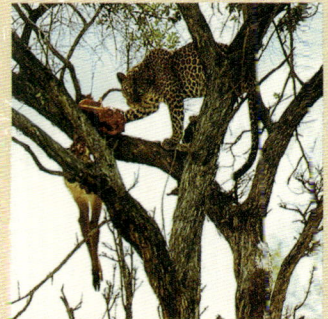

Living Together

Most big cats live alone. They hunt alone and the females bring up their cubs alone. Big cats come together only when they want to mate. They are solitary because of the prey that they hunt. There is usually not enough prey in one area for a large group of big cats to live on. Lions are the exception. They live in family groups called prides. (Male cheetahs also sometimes live in groups with up to four members.) All wild cats have territories (home ranges). These territories are a series of trails that link together a cat's hunting area, its drinking places, its look-out positions and the den where it brings up its young. Females have smaller home ranges than males. Males that have more than one mate have territories that overlap with two or more female home ranges.

Did you know? Big cats' territories range from a few kilometres to over 1,000km/620 miles.

▲ BRINGING UP BABY

Female snow leopards bring up their cubs on their own. They have up to five cubs who stay with their mother for at least a year. Although snow leopards are loners, they are not unsociable. They like to live near each other and let other snow leopards cross their territories.

◄ THE LOOKOUT

A puma keeps watch over its territory from a hill. Pumas are solitary and deliberately avoid each other except during courtship and mating. The first male puma to arrive in an area claims it as his territory. He chases out any other male that tries to live there.

▲ A PRIDE OF LIONS

The lions in a pride drink together, hunt together, eat together and play together. A pride is usually made up of related females and their young. Prides usually try not to meet up with other prides. To tell the others to keep out of its territory, the pride leaves scent markings on the edge of its range.

Daniel and the Lions' Den

A story in the Bible tells how Daniel was taken prisoner by Nebuchadnezzar, king of Babylon. When Daniel correctly interpreted the king's dreams he became a favourite of the king. His enemies became jealous of his position and had him thrown into a lions' den, a common punishment for prisoners at the time. But instead of eating Daniel, the lions befriended him. They were tamed by his great faith in God.

▲ FAMILY GROUPS

A cheetah mother sits between her two cubs. The cubs will stay with her until they are about 18 months old. The female then lives a solitary life. Males, however, live in small groups and defend a territory. They only leave their range if there is a drought or if food is very scarce.

▲ WELL GROOMED

Cats that live together groom each other. They do this to be friendly and to keep clean. They also groom to spread their scent on each other, so that they smell the same. This helps them to recognize each other and identify strangers.

Focus on

Lions are the second largest of the big cats after tigers. They like to live in open spaces, sometimes in woodland, but never in tropical forests. Lions are usually found on the savanna (grassy plains) and on the edges of deserts. Female lions live together in prides (family groups) of up to 12 lionesses and their cubs. The size of the group depends on how much food there is available. Male lions may live together in groups, called coalitions, which look after one or more prides. The coalitions defend their prides, fighting off any other males who want to mate with the females of their pride.

FATHER AND SON

Male lions are the only big cats that look different from the females. They have long shaggy manes to look larger and fiercer and to protect their necks in a fight. A male cub starts to grow a mane at about the age of three. At that age he also leaves the pride to establish his own territory.

THE FAMILY

A pride of lions rests near a waterhole. The biggest prides live in open grasslands where there are large herds of antelope, wildebeest and buffalo. If a foreign male takes over a pride, the new lion kills all the cubs under six months old. This is to make sure all the cubs are his.

a Pride

NURSERY SCHOOL

Young lions play tag to learn how to chase things and defend their pride. The pride does not usually allow strange lions to join the family group. Young lions need to be prepared in case other lions come to fight with them.

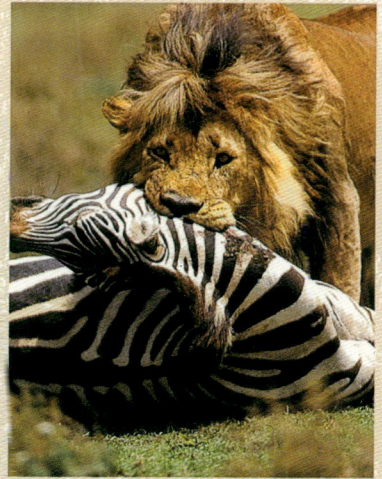

FIRST AT THE TABLE

Male lions usually eat first, even though the females do most of the hunting. A male can eat up to 30kg/66lb of meat at one time, but will not eat again for several days.

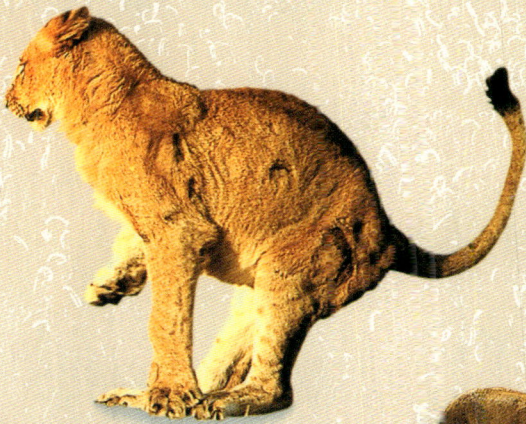

CAT SCRAP

Two lionesses fight each other to decide who will be first to eat. There is usually a dominant female in each pride, even when there are males around. This chief female rules the family.

MOTHER AND CUBS

Lionesses give birth to a litter of between one and six cubs. The cubs start learning to hunt when they are about 11 months old, but stay with their mother for over two years. In dry areas, lions live in small prides because less food is available.

Lionesses help to raise the young together. They even suckle each other's cubs.

Finding a Mate

Big cats roam over large areas, so it can be quite difficult for them to find a partner. When they are ready to mate, they use scent markers. These are like advertisements to all the other cats in the district. A female also calls loudly in the hope that a nearby male will come to her. Often more than one male will follow a female. This almost always leads to fights between the interested males. The winner of the fight then begins to court the female. In a pride of lions, one male establishes his dominance over the group. In this way he avoids having to fight every time a female is ready to mate. Many big cats will mate several times a day for up to a week to make sure that the female is pregnant.

▲ COURTSHIP

A male lion rubs against a female and smells her all over. He knows that the lioness is ready to mate from her scent. Having fought off rivals, he must now persuade the lioness to mate with him. He courts her by being attentive. Their courtship may last for several days before they mate.

Did you know? Pumas are also called mountain screamers after the female's mating call.

◀ THE HAPPY COUPLE

When the female is ready to mate, she crouches on the ground with her hindquarters slightly raised. The male sits behind and over her and sometimes holds the scruff of her neck between his jaws. Large cats, such as lions, may mate up to 100 times in two days. Smaller cats, such as cheetahs, are more vulnerable to predators and so mate for a shorter time.

KEEPING HIM IN HIS PLACE ▶

After mating, the lioness is aggressive and often lashes out at the lion. As soon as the two have mated the male jumps back very quickly. He remains close by her side to stop other males from approaching. Once she has calmed down, she rolls on her back and they mate again. Each mating lasts only a few seconds.

Did you know? A wild big cat may have up to 5 litters in an average lifespan of 12 years.

▼ ANIMAL ATTRACTION

Two courting tigers often make a great deal of noise. They roar, meow, moan and grunt as they mate. Female tigers mate every other year. The male stays close by the female for a few days until he is sure she is pregnant. Then the pair separate and live on their own again.

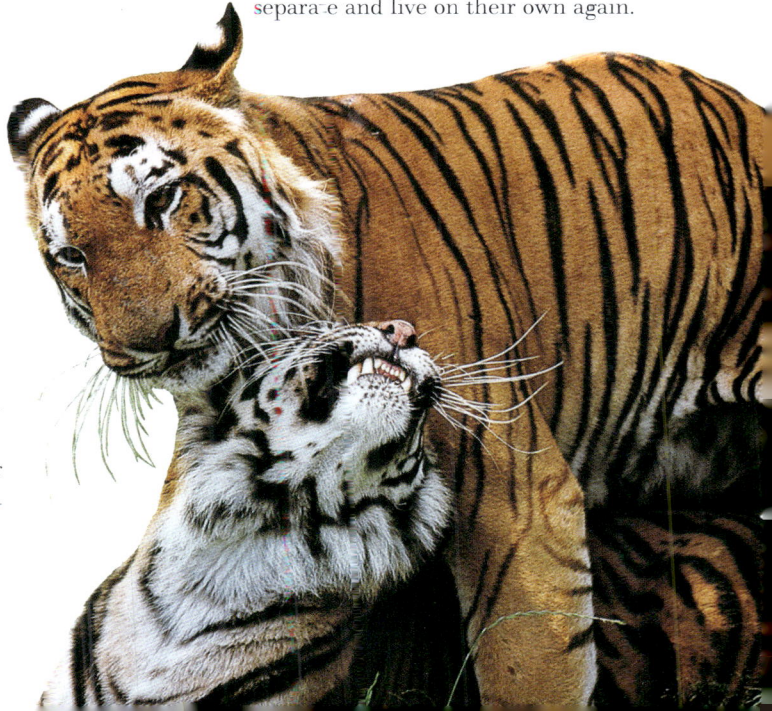

▲ LEAN AND HEALTHY

This lioness is only just pregnant. She has not put on much weight and can still hunt efficiently. At the end of her pregnancy (about three to four months) she will hunt small, easy-to-catch prey. Lionesses in a pride also get to share in the pride's kill.

Giving Birth

The cubs (babies) of a big cat are usually born with spotted fur and closed eyes. They are completely helpless. The mother cat looks after them on her own with no help from the father. She gives birth in a safe place called a den. For the first few days after birth, she stays very close to her cubs so that they can feed on her milk. She keeps them warm and cleans the cubs by licking them all over. The cubs grow quickly. Even before their eyes open they can crawl, and they soon learn to hiss to defend themselves.

▲ SNOW CUB

Snow leopard cubs have white fur with dark spots. They are always born in the spring and open their eyes one week after birth. The cubs begin to follow their mothers around when they are about three months old. By winter, they will be almost grown up.

MOTHERLY LOVE ▶

Tiger cubs are capable killers by the time they are 11 months old. They stay with their mothers, however, until they are two or even three years of age. In the wild, the mother does all she can to protect her young, but often at least half of the litter dies. Predators may kill the cubs or sometimes they starve to death if the mother cannot catch enough food.

◀ IN DISGUISE ▶

A cheetah cub is covered in long, woolly fur. This makes it look similar to the African honey badger, a very fierce animal, which may help to discourage predators. The mother cheetah does not raise her cubs in a den, but moves them around every few days.

A cheetah cub, unlike the adult, has a mane of fur. This may help to disguise it as it hides in the long grass.

▲ BRINGING UP BABY

Female pumas give birth to up to six kittens (babies). The mother has several pairs of teats for the kittens to suckle from. Each kitten has its own teat and will use no other. They will suckle her milk for at least three months and from about six weeks they will also eat meat.

▲ ON GUARD

Two lionesses guard the entrance to their den. Lions are social cats and share the responsibility of keeping guard. Dens are kept very clean so that there are no smells to attract predators.

▲ MOVING TO SAFETY

If at any time a mother cat thinks her cubs are in danger, she will move them to a new den. She carries the cubs one by one, gently grasping the loose skin at their necks between her teeth.

317

Focus on

The number of cubs in a big cat's litter depends on the species and where it lives. Most big cats have two or three cubs, but cheetahs have five or more. All cubs are born helpless, but it is not long before their eyes open and they can wobble around, learning to balance on their uncertain legs. Within a few weeks they begin to play with their mothers and each other. There is a lot to find out, but they learn very quickly. By the time they are six months old they will have learned how to keep themselves safe, what food tastes good and how to catch it. They will start to understand the language of smells and sounds. For the next year and a half they will stay close to their mothers, practising their new skills until they are experts.

PLAY TIME

A cub plays with its mother's tail. As soon as cubs can see, they begin to play. Play helps to build up muscles, improve co-ordination and develop good reflexes. It is valuable early preparation for learning how to hunt when the cubs are older.

SAFETY FIRST

For the first two years of their lives, cubs remain close to their mothers. She protects them and helps them when they make mistakes. A mother may rear all of her cubs successfully in a good year. She may lose most or even all of her cubs, depending on her skills as a parent and the availability of food.

BATH TIME

Cubs must learn to clean themselves, but while they are still young their mother washes them with her tongue. As she licks, she spreads her scent on the cubs so that all of her family have the same smell.

Cute Cubs

FAMILY BLISS

Lion cubs are spotted all over to help hide them from predators. The spots gradually fade as the lions grow older. Adult lions have only very faint spots on their legs and stomachs. Lion cubs are lucky because they have many companions to play with. Cubs of solitary cats have to grow up without much company. Some do not even have any brothers or sisters. Lion cubs learn through play how to get along with other lions.

MOVING HOME

To move her cubs a lioness carries each one gently in her mouth. Not only do the cubs have loose skin at their necks, but also the lioness has a special gap in her mouth behind the canines. This allows her to lift the cub off the ground without biting it.

LION LESSONS

These cubs are working together to kill an injured warthog. One grabs the neck, while the other starts tearing at the hind leg. The mother lioness watches over them. She is the cubs' teacher. They must learn to hunt as soon as possible, and this warthog is a small animal for them to begin with. The lioness brought down the warthog so that the cubs could learn to kill it.

Growing Up

Growing cubs have to learn all about life as an adult so that they can look after themselves when they leave their mother. She teaches them as much as she can and the rest they learn through play. Cub games depend on their species, because each type of cat has different things to learn. In playfighting cheetahs use their paws to knock each other over. This is a technique they will need for hunting when they are older. Cubs need to learn how to judge distances and when to strike to kill prey quickly, without getting injured or killed themselves. Their mother introduces them to prey by bringing an animal back to the den to eat. Mothers and cubs use very high-pitched sounds to communicate. However, if she senses danger, she growls at them to tell them to hide.

▲ **PRACTICE MAKES PERFECT**
These cheetah cubs are learning to kill a Thomson's gazelle. When the cubs are about 12 weeks old, a mother cheetah brings back live injured prey for them to kill. They instinctively know how to do so, but need practice to get it right.

▼ **FOLLOW MY LEADER**
Curious cheetah cubs watch an object intently, safe beside their mother. At about six weeks the cubs start to go on hunting trips with her. They are able to keep up by following her white-tipped tail through the tall grass.

THE CLASSROOM ▶

A group of lion cubs relaxes in the shade on a fallen tree. From here they watch the adults hunt, as if in a big, open-air classroom. Female cubs often stay in the pride, but young males are chased off by the dominant male.

◀ SCRATCH AND SNIFF

Three young lions sniff at the shell of a tortoise. Cubs learn to be cautious when dealing with unfamiliar objects. First the object is tapped with a paw, before being explored further with the nose. Cubs' milk teeth are replaced with permanent canine teeth at about two years old. Not until then can they begin to hunt and kill big animals.

TAIL TOY ▶

A mother leopard's tail is a good thing for her cub to learn to pounce on. She twitches it so the cub can develop good co-ordination and timing. As the cub grows, it will practise on rodents and then bigger animals until it can hunt for itself. Once they leave their mothers, female cubs usually establish a territory close by, while males go farther away.

Enemies of Big Cats

Big cats are perfect killing machines and are feared by all their prey. They do, however, have enemies. Big cats have to watch out for other carnivores taking their food or attacking their cubs. Wolves are a problem for pumas, wild dogs are a threat to tigers, and hyenas and jackals prey on the cubs of African big cats. Even prey animals can be a danger to big cats. Buffaloes are very aggressive and can attack and kill a young lion. Humans, however, are the main enemies of wild cats. As people move farther into the wilderness to build homes and farms, they destroy the precious habitats of the big cats. People kill the big cats' prey, leaving them with less to eat. They also hunt big cats for their beautiful and valuable fur coats.

▲ **SCAVENGING HYENAS**
A spotted hyena finishes off the remains of a giraffe. Hyenas live in Africa and western Asia. They eat whatever they can find. This is often carrion (the remains of dead prey) that animals such as big cats have killed for themselves. They will also kill cubs. Hyenas have strong jaws and bone-crunching teeth and look for food at night.

Did you know? Despite their dog-like appearance, hyenas are more closely related to cats.

◀ **PACK POWER**
Wolves live in Europe and North America. They live in the mountains as well as on open plains and hunt in packs of up to 20 animals. Wolves usually eat deer, elk, moose or small animals such as hares.

BIG CAT THREAT ▶

Leopards live in the same areas as cheetahs, but they are very hostile towards them. In fact, if they get a chance, leopards prey on cheetahs and their cubs. In turn, leopards have to be very wary of lions. Lions will attack and kill a leopard to protect the pride or their territory. Big cats do not like others because of competition for food in an area.

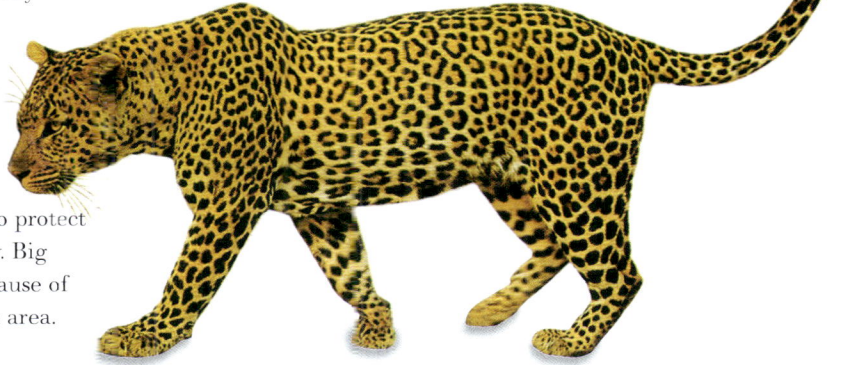

▼ DOG-LIKE JACKALS

Jackals (a relative of the dog) are half the size of hyenas and live in Africa. They will eat most things and will steal a big cat's kill. If they come across an unprotected den, they quickly kill and eat all the cubs.

▲ HUMAN TRAPS

Experts examine a tiger trap. Poachers (people who kill animals illegally) often use traps to catch big cats. When the trap snaps shut, the animal is stuck until it dies or until the poacher returns to kill it. These traps cause great pain. A cat may try to chew off its trapped leg to escape.

◀ INTRUDER PERIL

Sometimes big cats become cannibals and eat their own kind. These cheetahs are eating another cheetah that has invaded their territory. Male lions also eat all the young cubs in a pride when they take over dominance from another male.

Mountain Cats

To live in the mountains, cats need to be hardy and excellent rock climbers. They also have to cope with high altitudes where the air is thin and there is less oxygen to breathe. Big cats that live in the mountains include leopards and the rare snow leopard. Small cats include the puma, mountain cat, bobcat and lynx. Mountain climates are harsh and the weather can change very quickly. To survive, mountain cats need to use their wits and to know where to find shelter. They mate so that their cubs are born in the spring. This is to make sure that they will be almost grown by the time winter closes in.

▲ **MOUNTAIN CAT**
The mountain cat is a secretive, shy creature and seldom seen. It is about 50cm/20in long and has soft, fine fur. It is also known as the Andean mountain cat, since it lives in the Andes mountains of Chile, Argentina, Peru and Bolivia. This cat is found at altitudes of up to 5,000m/16,400ft above sea level.

This map shows the world's major mountain ranges. The puma, mountain cat and lynx live in the Americas. Lynx also live in Europe and Asia, while the snow leopard lives in Asia.

◄ **MOUNTAIN LION**
A puma keeps watch over its vast territory. Pumas are also known as mountain lions and cougars. Male pumas can grow to 2m/6½ft long and weigh 100kg/220lb. They are good at jumping and can easily leap 5m/16½ft on to a high rock or into a tree. Pumas are found over a wide area, from Canada to the very tip of South America. They live along the foothills of mountains, in forests on mountain slopes and all the way up to 4,500m/14,800ft above sea level.

WINTER LYNX ▶

Lynx live in mountainous regions of Europe, Asia and North America. They have unusually short tails and tufted ears. Lynx are well designed to live in very cold places. In winter they grow an especially long coat, which is light coloured so that they are well camouflaged in the snow. The bobcat of North America looks similar to the lynx.

◀ **PUMA CHASE**

A snowshoe hare darts this way and that to shake off a puma. To catch the hare, the puma must make full use of its flexible back and its long balancing tail. Pumas hunt by day as well as by night.

LONG-TAILED SNOW LEOPARD ▶

The snow leopard is one of the rarest big cats, found only in the Himalaya and Altai mountains of central Asia. It can live at altitudes of 6,000m/ 19,700ft, the highest of any wild cat. Snow leopards feed on wild goats, hares and marmots. Their bodies measure just over 1 m/39in long, with tails that are almost as long. They wrap their bushy tails around themselves to keep warm when they are sleeping. Snow leopards are agile jumpers and are said to be able to leap a gap of 15m/49ft. Their long tails help them to balance as they jump.

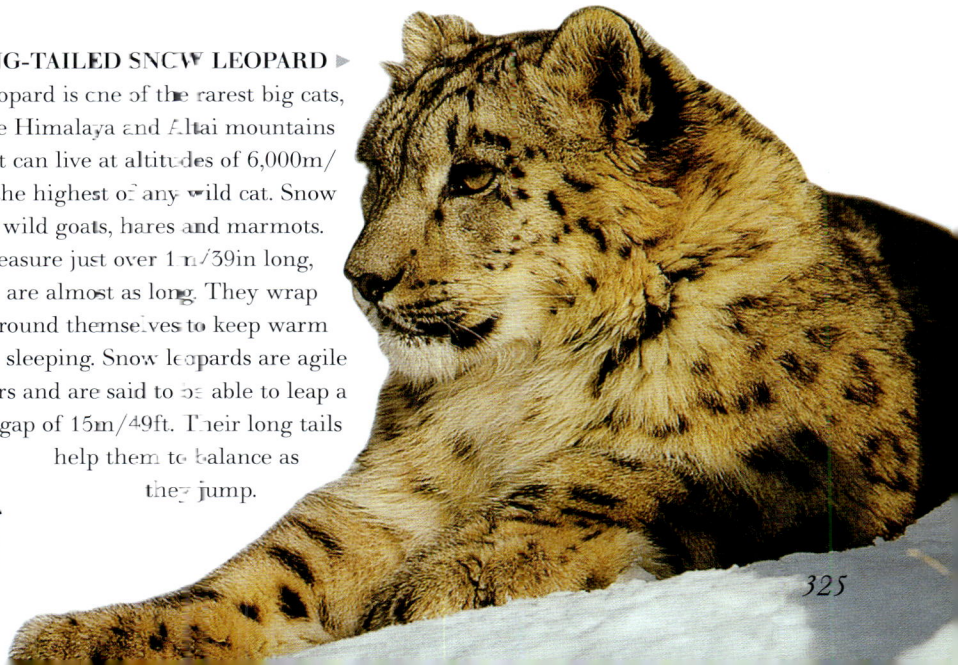

Did you know? A female snow leopard makes her den cosy by lining it with her own fur.

325

Forest Dwellers

Dense, wet rainforests are home to lots of small creatures, such as insects and spiders. These animals and forest plants provide a feast for birds, snakes, frogs and small mammals, which in turn are a banquet for big cats. Jaguars, tigers, leopards and clouded leopards all live in rainforests. Small cats include ocelots and margays. Although there is plenty of food in a forest, the dense trees make it a difficult place to hunt. There is little space among the trees and prey can escape easily in the thick undergrowth.

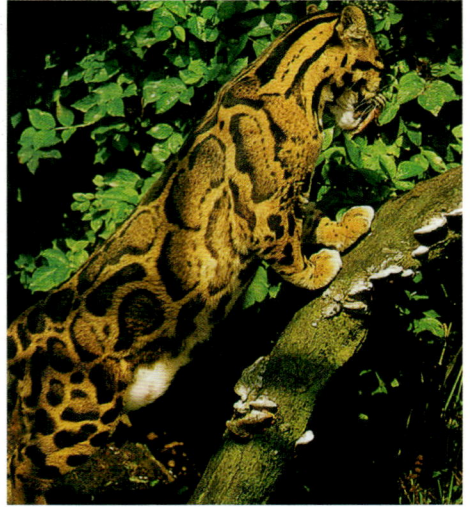

▲ CLOUDED LEOPARD

The clouded leopard is a shy and rarely seen Asian big cat. It lives in forests from Nepal to Borneo, spending most of its time in the trees. The Chinese call the clouded leopard the mint leopard because of its unusual leaf-like markings. Male clouded leopards reach about 1m/39in long, with an equally long tail, and weigh about 30kg/66lb. They are perfectly built for tree climbing, with a long, bushy tail for balance and flexible ankle joints.

This map shows where the world's tropical rainforests are located. They lie in a band on either side of the Equator.

JAGUAR ▼

Although jaguars live in grasslands and semi-deserts, they prefer the thick forests of South and Central America. They are the third largest big cat, growing to 2.4m/7¾ft in length and weighing up to 120kg/265lb.

Did you know? The jaguar was the symbol of the Sun for the Maya of Central America.

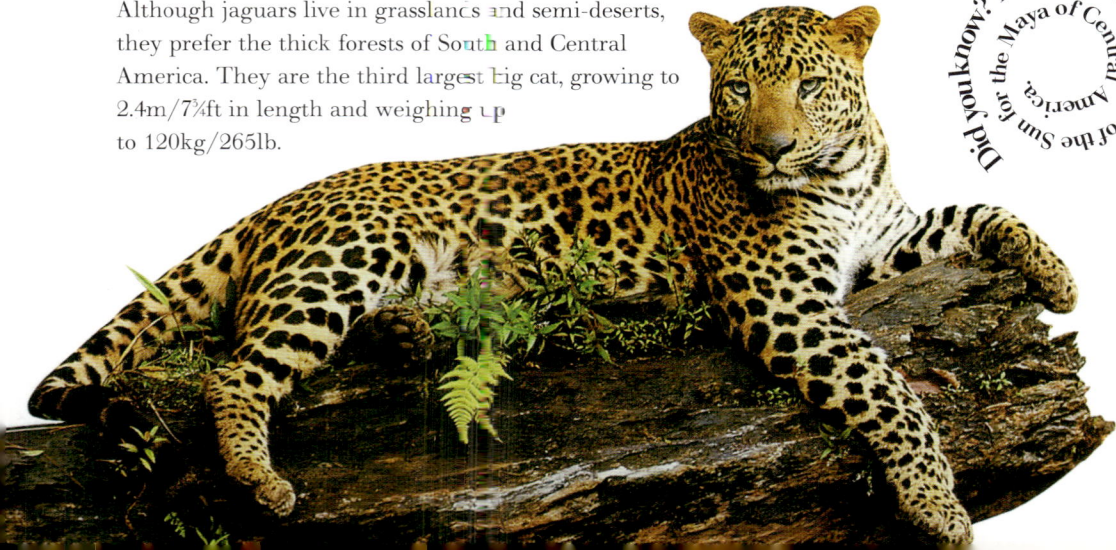

The sleek margay is very striking in appearance, with beautifully marked fur and large eyes.

▲ SUMATRAN TIGER

A tiger walks stealthily into a jungle pool on the island of Sumatra. Tigers are good swimmers and a forest pool is a good place to hunt as well as to cool off from the tropical heat. Tigers often hide the carcasses of their prey in water or the dense undergrowth.

▲ MARGAY

Margays live in the tropical forests of Central and South America. They are the best of all cat climbers, with broad, soft feet and exceptionally flexible ankles and hind legs. They feed largely on birds and so need to be good at moving around in the tops of trees.

▲ JAVAN LEOPARD

At one time, many leopards lived in the tropical rainforests of Asia. But now like this Javan leopard, they are endangered. They are threatened by over-hunting and the destruction of their forest habitat.

◄ BLACK JAGUAR

Forest jaguars are darker than their grassland cousins. Some can be black and are so well camouflaged that they can disappear in the shadows of their forest habitat.

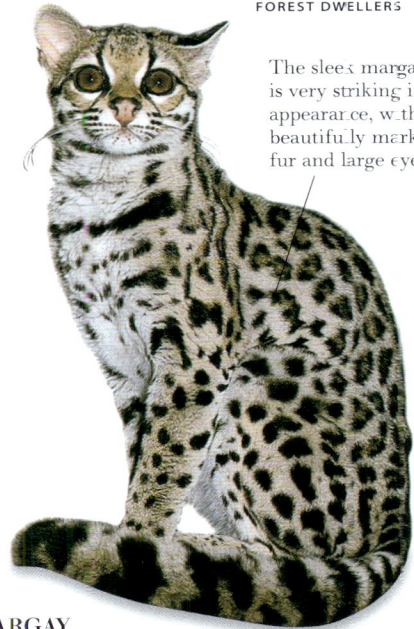

▲ A TURTLE TREAT

A jaguar catches a river turtle in a pool. Jaguars are such good swimmers that they hunt some of their prey in water. They love to eat fish and turtles. Their jaws are powerful enough to crack open a turtle's shell like a nut. They have been known to kill cayman (a type of crocodile).

Focus on

Tigers are the largest of all the big cats, and the largest of all tigers is the Siberian tiger. An adult male can reach up to 2.6m/8½ft long and weigh as much as 270kg/595lb. Siberian tigers live in the snow-covered forests of Siberia, which is part of Russia, and in Manchuria in China. They are also sometimes known as Amur tigers. Although there is only one species of tiger, they can differ significantly in their appearance. Siberian tigers have a relatively pale coat with few stripes. Bengal tigers from India, however, have shorter fur and are more strikingly marked. As humans destroy more of their habitats, the number of tigers in the wild is declining dramatically. Today, there are only about 400 Siberian tigers left in the wild.

SOLITARY SIBERIAN
Siberian tigers live alone in huge territories of over 1,000 square km/386 square miles. They do not like to fight, but a tiger will kill another if it invades its territory.

LUNCH TIME
A group of Siberian tigers devours a black ox. Despite being solitary animals, tigers do sometimes share food. The only other time they come together is to mate. Tigers have been known to roar when they have killed a big animal, just as lions will often roar when they have successfully caught their prey.

OPEN WIDE
A Siberian tiger shows its long, sharp canine teeth in a wide yawn. Canines are used to catch and kill prey. Tigers ambush prey and kill it by biting the neck or strangling it.

Siberian Tigers

ICY TONIC

A mother shows her 18-month-old cub how to get water from melted ice. Tigers have up to four cubs in a litter, every other year. They stay with her for at least two years.

COURTING COUPLE

When a female is ready to mate, she sprays, roars and grunts to tell the male. When tigers want to be friendly, they blow sharply through their nostrils and mouths, rub their heads together and gently bite each other's necks.

A PALE ICE QUEEN

Siberian tigers, like this female, have a lot of white fur. This makes it more difficult for prey and enemies to see them in the snow. They are powerfully and heavily built, with bodies slung close to the ground.

On the Savanna

Savannas are open, flat areas of grassland. Apart from grasses, the main plants of the savanna are small bushes and clumps of trees. Savanna is the ideal habitat for big herds of grazing animals, such as antelope, zebra and buffalo. In Africa, these herds migrate for thousands of kilometres each year in search of fresh grass and water. They are followed by lions, cheetahs and leopards who prey on the herds. The savanna of South America is home to jaguars. Rodents, such as mice, gerbils and marmots, also thrive on the savanna and these are a good food source for smaller cats, such as the serval.

This map shows where the world's savannas (tropical grasslands and dry woodlands) are located. The largest region of savanna lies in Africa.

▶ **LION IN THE GRASS**

A lion walks through the long, dry grass of the African savanna. Its sandy colouring perfectly matches its habitat. Lions hunt their quarry using the cover of grass. Often, only the tips of a lion's ears are seen as it slowly stalks its prey.

Did you know? Cats sleep for longer than most other animals. Lions sleep for 20 hours a day.

◀ **CHEETAH ON THE LOOKOUT**

A cheetah stands on the top of a small mound on the Kenyan savanna. Cheetahs are perfectly adapted for life on the plains. The surrounding open, flat terrain lets them make the most of their ability to chase down prey. From its vantage point, a cheetah uses its excellent eyesight to search for prey. It also keeps watch for any other cheetahs who might have invaded its home range.

◀ VIEW FROM A BRANCH

Leopards like to live in areas of grassland where there are trees. Here they can sleep hidden during the heat of the day. They can also enjoy the afternoon breeze and avoid the insects that live in the grass below. Leopards also prefer to eat up in a tree, out of the reach of scavengers.

Leo the Lion

People born between July 24 and August 23 are born under the astrological sign of Leo (the lion). They are said to be brave, strong and proud, just like lions.

▲ AT THE WATERHOLE

During the dry season in the African savanna, many grazing animals gather near waterholes to drink. Thomson's gazelle, zebra and giraffe are shown here. Lions congregate around the waterholes, not only to drink, but also to catch prey unawares. Their favourite prey is antelope, buffalo, zebra and warthog, but they also eat giraffe.

SPEEDY SERVAL ▶

Servals are small cats that live on the savanna of western and central Africa. They like to live near water where there are bushes to hide in. The servals' long legs enable them to leap over tall grass when they hunt small rodents. They also climb well and hunt birds. With their long legs, servals can run quickly over short distances and so escape from predators.

331

Desert Cats

Hot deserts are very dry places. Although they are hot during the day, at night they are very cold. Few plants and animals can survive in such a harsh environment, but cats are very adaptable. Cheetahs, lions and leopards live in the Kalahari and Namib deserts of southern Africa. As long as there are animals to eat, the cats can survive. Even the jaguar, a cat that loves water, has been seen in desert areas in Mexico and the southern United States. But they are only visitors in this tough, dry land and soon go back to the wetter places they prefer. The best-adapted cat to desert life is a small variety known as the sand cat. It lives in the northern Sahara Desert, the Middle East and western Asia.

Did you know? Lions follow along dry riverbeds in the desert, looking for waterholes.

▲ **DESERT STORM**

Two lions endure a sandstorm in the Kalahari Desert of southern Africa. The desert is a very hostile place to live. There is very little water, not much food and the wind blows up terrible sandstorms. Despite these hardships, big cats, such as these lions, manage to survive.

This map shows where the world's hot deserts and nearby semi-desert areas are located.

▼ **A HARSH LIFE**

An old lion drinks from a waterhole in the Kalahari Desert. Even when a big cat lives in a dry place, it still needs to find enough water to drink. This is often a difficult task, requiring the animals to walk long distances. In the desert, prey is usually very spread out, so an old lion has a hard time trying to feed itself adequately.

▲ CHEETAH WALK

A group of cheetahs walk across the wide expanse of the Kalahari Desert. They lead lives of feast and famine. In the rainy season, lush vegetation grows and enormous herds of antelope can graze. The cheetahs have a banquet preying on the grazing herds. But they go very hungry as the land dries up and prey becomes scarce.

Big ears near the soft, high-pitched squeaks of rodents.

◄ SAND CAT

Dense hair on the pads of the sand cat's feet protect it as it walks on hot ground and help it to walk on loose sand. All the water the cat needs comes from its food, so it does not need to drink.

Very thick, soft fur protects from the heat and cold.

▲ ADAPTABLE LEOPARD

A leopard rolls in the desert sand. There are very few trees in the desert, so leopards live among rocky outcrops. Here they can drag their prey to high places to eat in safety. The desert can be a dangerous place. With so little food around, competition can be fierce, especially with hungry lions. Big cats will eat small prey such as insects to keep from starving.

Egyptian Cat Worship
The Ancient Egyptians kept cats to protect their stores of grain from rats and mice. Cats became so celebrated that they were worshipped as gods. They were sacred to the cat-headed goddess of pleasure, Bast. Many cats were given funerals when they died. Their bodies were preserved, wrapped in bandages and richly painted.

333

Killer Cats

Humans can sometimes become the prey of big cats. People have been afraid of big cats for thousands of years. From 20,000-year-old cave paintings we know that people lived in contact with big cats and almost certainly feared them. More recently, there have been many reports of big cats killing people. Lions and tigers become bold when they are hungry and there is little other food around. First, they prey on livestock, such as cattle. When the cattle are gone, the big cats might kill people. Leopards, who do not have a natural fear of humans, may have their killer instinct triggered by an injury.

▲ **LION BAITING**
The Romans used lions (and bears) for gladiator fights in their amphitheatres (outdoor arenas). When the Romans wanted to kill prisoners, they would feed them to hungry lions. The lions had to be starving and made angry by their handlers, otherwise they would not kill the prisoners. Most captive lions will not kill people.

◀ **WRESTLING A TIGER**
Tigers are considered the most dangerous of all the big cats. This picture, called *A Timely Rescue*, shows a rather heroic view of killing a tiger. Once a tiger has become used to the taste of human flesh, it will strike at any time. Tigers have killed thousands of people over the centuries. During the early 1900s, tigers killed 800 to 900 people a year in India.

Did you know? In the early 1900s, one Indian leopard killed 125 people in eight years.

▲ TIPPU'S TIGER

This mechanical toy of a tiger attacking a British soldier was made in 1790. It is called Tippu's Tiger and was made for the Sultan of Mysore The Sultan resisted the British takeover of India, and his toy makes growling and screaming noises.

◄ HUNTER WITH A HEART

Jim Corbett was a famous hunter who lived in India in the early 1900s. Unlike most hunters of his day, he did not kill big cats for sport. He shot tigers and leopards that had been eating people.

Jaguar Knights

In the 1500s in Central America Aztec warriors were divided into military orders. Some of the most prestigious were the jaguar knights who ranked just below the emperor. They wore entire wild cats' pelts, with the still-attached heads worn as helmets. They thought that by wearing the pelt they could take on the cat's strength and stealth.

▲ EDUCATION FOR CONSERVATION

Nearly 100 tigers and 50 leopards live in the Corbett National Park in India. The Park runs programmes to teach children all about the big cats and their habitat. The more we know about big cats, the better able we are to respect them.

Wolves

We consider wolves to be the outcasts of the natural world, yet it is the wolf that gave rise to Man's best friend the dog. Even the most docile of domestic pets has a hint of wildness in it, for although we bred the dog from the wolf, we cannot breed the wolf out of the dog. In the wild, the wolf's extraordinarily keen senses and the ability to co-operate are the hallmarks of a successful hunter.

What is a Wolf?

Wolves are the wild members of the dog family, canids, with gleaming yellow eyes and lean, muscular bodies. The 37 different species of canids include wolves, jackals, coyotes, foxes and wild and domestic dogs. Canids are native to every continent except Australia and Antarctica. All of them share a keen sense of smell and hearing, and are carnivores (meat-eaters). Wolves and wild dogs hunt live prey, which they kill with their sharp teeth. However, many canids also eat vegetable matter and even insects. They are among the most intelligent of all animals. Some, such as wolves, are social in habit and live together in groups.

Large, triangular ears, usually held pricked (erect)

Powerful shoulders and supple body

▲ PRODUCING YOUNG

A female wolf suckles (feeds) her cubs. All canids are mammals and feed their young on milk. Females produce a litter of cubs, or pups, once a year. Most are born in an underground den.

BODY FEATURES ▶
The wolf is the largest wild dog. It has a strong, well-muscled body covered with dense, shaggy fur, a long, bushy tail and strong legs made for running. Its muzzle (nose and jaws) is long and well developed and its ears are pricked up. Male and female wolves look very similar, although females are generally the smaller of the two.

◄ KEEN SENSES

The jackal, like all dogs, has very keen senses. Its nose can detect faint scents and its large ears pick up the slightest sound. Smell and hearing are mainly used for hunting. Many canids also have good vision.

Thick, coarse fur helps to protect the wolf from extremes of temperature

The Big, Bad Wolf

Fairy tales often depict wolves as wicked, dangerous animals. In the tale of the Three Little Pigs, the big, bad wolf terrorizes three small porkers. Eventually he is outwitted by the smartest pig, who builds a brick house that the wolf cannot blow down, and all the pigs are safe.

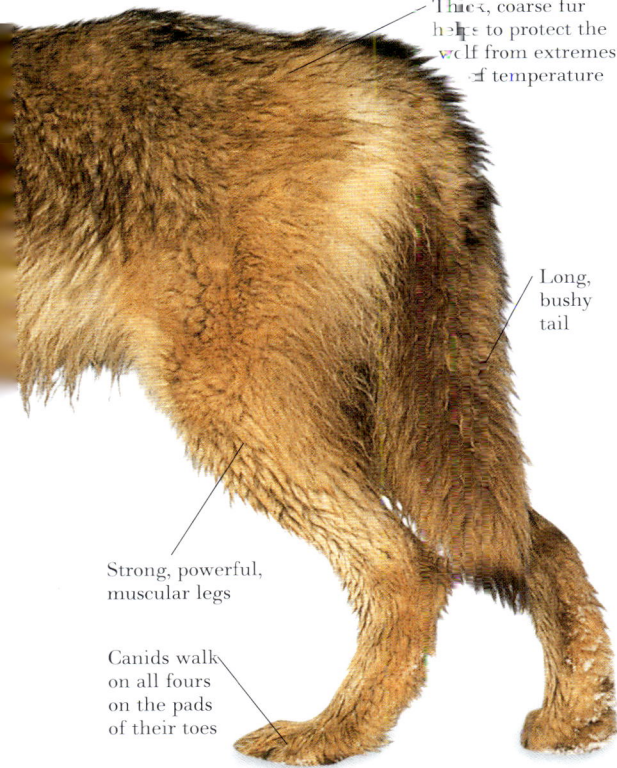

Long, bushy tail

Strong, powerful, muscular legs

Canids walk on all fours on the pads of their toes

▲ LIVING IN PACKS

Wolves and a few other wild dogs live in groups called packs of about eight to 20. Each pack has a hierarchy (social order) and is led by the strongest male and female.

EXPERT HUNTERS ►

A wolf bares its teeth in a snarl to defend its kill. Wolves and other canids feed mainly on meat, but eat plants, too, particularly when prey is scarce.

The Wolf Family

Wolves were once common throughout the northern hemisphere, right across North America, Europe and Asia. In the past, people hunted them mercilessly. In many areas they died out altogether. Across the north, wolves from various regions may look quite different, but they are all one species, *Canis lupus*. However, there are many subspecies (different types). Two of the main types are the grey wolf, also known as the timber wolf, and the Arctic, or tundra wolf. Many other subspecies are named after the area or habitat they come from, such as Mexican and steppe wolves. The same type of wolf may be known by different names in different areas. For example, the Arctic wolf is the same as the tundra wolf. The wolf's closest relatives are the coyote, the jackal, the dingo and the domestic dog.

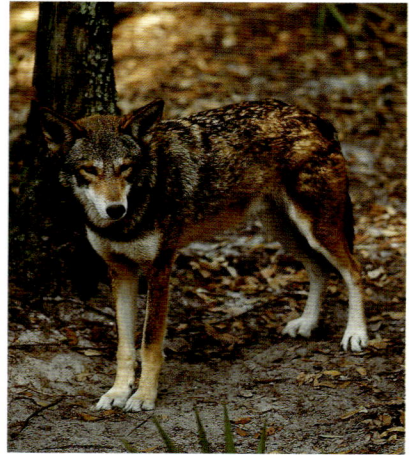

▲ **NEARLY EXTINCT**
The red wolf (*Canis rufus*) is found only in the south-eastern United States. It was once widespread, but became extinct in the wild. Today's red wolves stem from captive-bred wolves. They have longer legs and larger ears than the grey wolf and are named after the reddish fur on their heads, ears and legs. The grey wolf is thought to be a hybrid (cross) between the coyote and the wolf.

▼ **MOUNTAIN HOME**
The Simien wolf is found only in the Simien Mountains of Ethiopia, East Africa. It is about the same size as a coyote (1m/39in long) and has a mainly reddish-brown coat, with pale fur on its belly and throat. The Simien wolf was once thought to be a kind of jackal, but is now known to be a small wolf.

Did you know? Wolves kill prey animals as large as bison and as small as mice.

Simien wolf
(*Canis simensis*)

Dingo
*(Canis
familiaris)*

◄ DOG WITH NO BARK

The dingo lives in Australia and South-east Asia. It is now wild, but its ancestors are descended from tame dogs that Aboriginal people brought to the region from Asia more than 8,000 years ago. Dingoes are found mainly in dry areas, such as the dusty Australian interior. They live in small families and sometimes join other dingo families to hunt.

JACKAL ►

Jackals (*Canis lantrans*) are found on the grassy plains and in the woodlands of Africa, south-eastern Europe and southern Asia. They live in pairs and stay with the same mate for life. There are three species of jackal – side-striped and black-backed jackals (found only in Africa) and golden jackals.

Black-backed jackal
(Canis mesomelas)

◄ DOMESTIC DOG

You may not have seen a wolf in the wild, but you will know one of its relatives, for all domestic dogs are descended from the wolf. Dogs were the first animals to be tamed by people over 12,000 years ago. Now there are over 400 breeds of dog, including the miniature poodle.

**Miniature
poodle**
*(Canis
familiaris)*

▲ COYOTE

The coyote (*Canis latrans*) is found in North and Central America. It mainly lives on prairies (grassy plains) and in open woodlands and is also known as the prairie or brush wolf. Full-grown coyotes are half the size of grey wolves. They live alone, or in pairs and small family groups.

Wild Dogs

In addition to the wolf's immediate family, five species of wild dog are distantly related to wolves and to each other. Foxes are also canids but are not closely related to wild dogs or wolves. Of the wild dogs, the bush dog and maned wolf are both found in South America. The dhole and raccoon dog come from eastern Asia. The African hunting dog lives in central and southern Africa. Like other canids, the bodies of these animals are adapted to suit their way of life and their environment. Raccoon dogs and bush dogs are short-legged species that make their homes in underground burrows. Maned wolves and African hunting dogs have long legs to help them see over the long grass and scrub of savannas (grasslands) and woodlands. Human settlements are currently expanding in the areas where these wild dogs live and threatening their existence.

Bush dog
(*Speothos venaticus*)

▲ STURDY HUNTER

The bush dog inhabits forests and marshes in Central and South America. It is stocky, with a brown coat and paler fur on its neck and head.

◄ FOXY CORGI

The dhole (*Cuon alpinus*) can be found in India and China, on the islands of Sumatra and Java and also in parts Russia. Adult dholes reach about 1m/39in long, but have short legs. With their reddish coats, they look a little like corgis with long, bushy tails. Dholes live in packs and do much of their hunting during the day.

Classification Chart			
	Kingdom	*Animalia*	all animals
	Phylum	*Chordata*	animals with backbones
	Class	*Mammalia*	hair-covered animals that feed their young on milk
	Order	*Carnivora*	mammals that eat meat
	Family	*Canidae*	all dogs
	Genus Species	*Cuon alpinus*	dhole

▲ CLASSIFICATION OF WILD DOGS

All wolves and wild dogs are canids (members of the dog family). Wolves and their close relatives belong to the genus (group) *Canis*, but the wild dogs shown here each belong to a different genus. The African hunting dog's scientific name (*Lycaon pictus*) is completely different from the dhole's (*Cuon alpinus*).

HAPPY IN A CROWD ▶

The African hunting dog lives on the grassy plains south of the Sahara Desert. This wild dog has a mottled coat, long legs and rounded ears. It grows to about 1.1m/43in long. African hunting dogs are social animals and live in packs. Males and females look very much alike and live to around the age of ten years old.

▲ MASKED HUNTER

The raccoon dog (*Nyctereutes procyonoides*) is found in eastern Europe, Siberia, China and Japan. It reaches only 55cm/22in long and has a chunky build. Its summer coat is grey-brown, with darker eye patches like a raccoon's mask. Its winter coat is white. These dogs live alone or in small groups.

African hunting dog (*Lycaon pictus*)

◀ SHY LONER

The maned wolf (*Chrysocyon brachyurus*) lives in grasslands and swampy regions in eastern South America. Despite its name, this animal is not a wolf. Although its long legs have earned it the nickname ' the fox on stilts", it is not a fox either. Maned wolves have mostly reddish fur with darker legs and a mane of long hair at the neck. They grow to about 1.2m/4ft long. Solitary and shy, the wolves usually hunt at night.

343

Focus on

The skeletons of dogs buried with their owners in ancient tombs show that dogs have been domesticated for at least 12,000 years. All domestic dogs are descended from the wolf. The first dogs were probably bred from wolves tamed by hunters. These may have been captured as cubs and brought back to camp to help with hunting. Later, ancient peoples began to develop different breeds of dogs by selecting animals with definite features that they valued. From these beginnings developed the 400 different breeds we know today. Domestic dogs come in an amazing variety of shapes and sizes, from the tiny chihuahua to the huge St Bernard. Modern breeders divide the breeds into six main families: hounds, gundogs, working dogs, terriers, toys and utility (useful) dogs.

ANCIENT BREED
The pharaoh hound is one of the world's oldest dog breeds. It was developed in Egypt around 4,000 years ago as a swift hunting dog. Other breeds, such as the fierce mastiff, were developed as guard dogs. By Roman times, around 500BC, many of the breeds we know today had already been developed.

WORKING DOG
Border collies are working dogs and are used to herd sheep. The Border collie came from the Borders, an area on either side of the boundaries of England and Scotland. Working dogs have been bred to perform many useful tasks, from guarding homes to pulling sledges. This group includes corgis, boxers, mastiffs and huskies.

Domestic Dogs

BRED TO FETCH AND CARRY

A golden retriever fetches a duck shot by its owner. Retrievers, setters, labradors and pointers are all gundogs, bred to help with hunting game birds. These naturally reliable and obedient dogs make good pets.

SPEEDY DOG

A greyhound's body is built for speed, with long legs, a flexible back and small, pointed head. It is bred in many countries for racing. People have bred sporting dogs for centuries. In the past, dogs were often bred for cruel sports, such as bear-baiting. Today these sports are against the law in many countries.

BURROWING EXPERT

The wire-haired fox terrier was very popular in England during the 1800s. The name terrier comes from the Latin *terra* (earth). All terriers were bred to hunt animals in burrows, such as foxes, rabbits, rats and badgers.

HUNTING HOUNDS

A pack of foxhounds follow the scent of their quarry, a fox. Various breeds of hound have been developed to hunt different animals, including wolves, deer, rabbits, badgers and foxes. Foxhounds, beagles and bloodhounds track their prey by scent. Wolfhounds were bred to hunt wolves and deer. Afghan hounds were bred to chase antelope (similar to deer) and hunt by sight.

Body Shapes

Like all mammals, wolves and dogs are vertebrates (animals with backbones). The backbone protects the spinal cord, the main nerve of the body. The bones in the skeleton support the body and give it a distinct shape. The skeletons of wolves and dogs are different from other mammals. They have long skulls with large teeth, longish necks, and long, strong leg bones. Narrow collar bones help to make them slim and streamlined for speed over the ground, while their joints at the shoulders and hips pivot freely, giving them great agility. Wolves, foxes and wild dogs also generally have long tails. Many have a well-defined tail shape that can help to identify the animal at a distance.

Backbone (spine)

Tail bones

Toe bones

Elastic ligaments and tendons connect the bones together

▲ TALL AND GRACEFUL

The maned wolf has longer leg bones than a true wolf. It uses them to hunt in the tall grass of its homeland. Its leg bones are weaker than a wolf's so it often lacks the power and strength to run down swift-moving prey. It has a short tail.

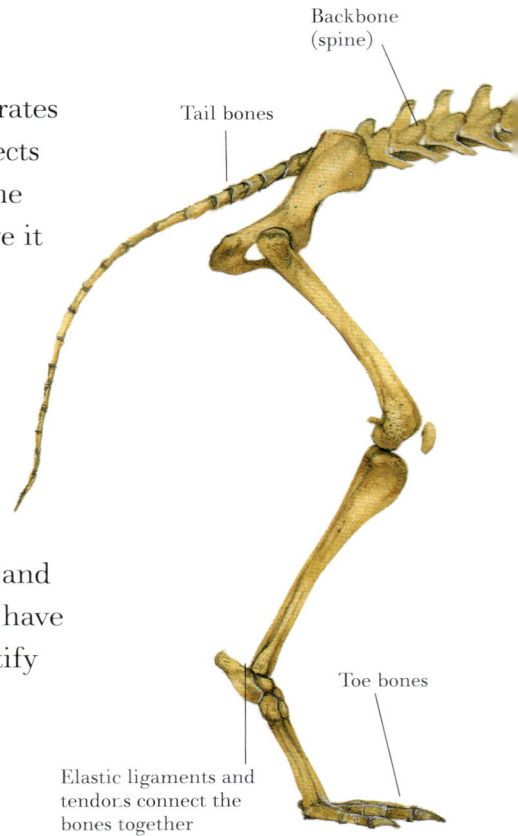

▲ BUILT FOR POUNCING

A fox's skeleton looks small and delicate compared to a wolf's. The leg bones are shorter in relation to its body size. Foxes spend much of their lives crouching and slinking through the undergrowth rather than running down prey.

Skull

Shoulder blade

Ribs protect vital organs

Seven strong, stout neck bones give the wolf the strength to bring down large prey

Soft breastbone allows the chest to expand as the animal breathes in

Elbow joint

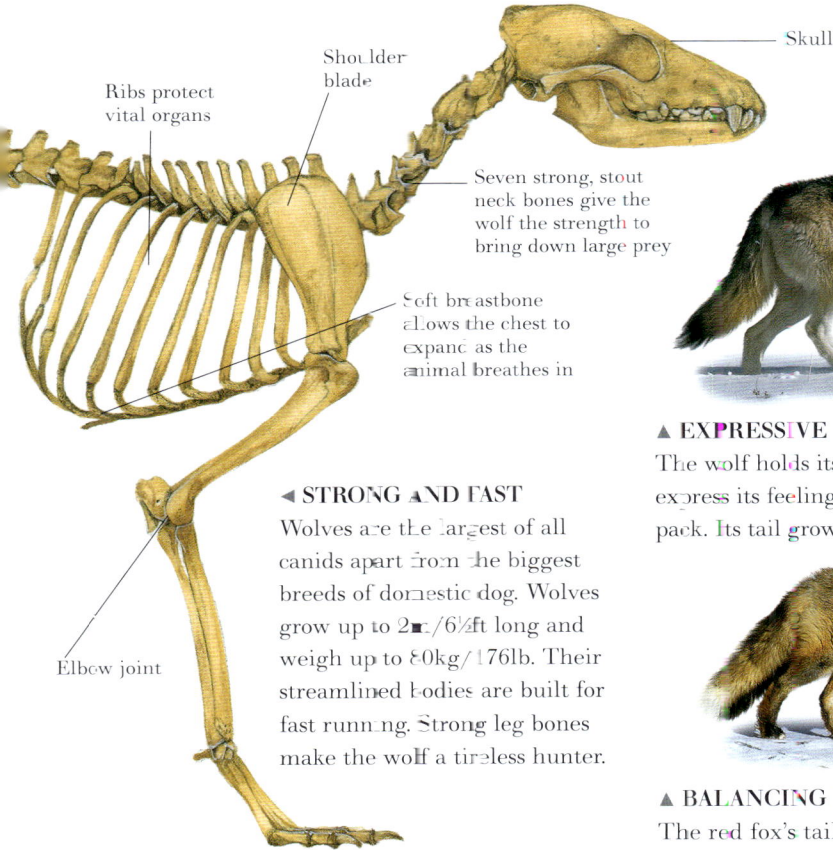

◄ STRONG AND FAST

Wolves are the largest of all canids apart from the biggest breeds of domestic dog. Wolves grow up to 2m/6½ft long and weigh up to 80kg/176lb. Their streamlined bodies are built for fast running. Strong leg bones make the wolf a tireless hunter.

▲ EXPRESSIVE TAIL

The wolf holds its tail in different positions to express its feelings and show its position in the pack. Its tail grows up to 48cm/19in long.

▲ BALANCING BRUSH

The red fox's tail, known as a brush, is long and bushy. It grows up to 50cm/20cm long and helps to balance the animal when it is running and jumping.

Strong Like the Wolf

Native Americans admired the strength, courage and intelligence of wolves and wild dogs. Plains tribes, such as the Blackfoot and Mandan, formed warrior-bands called Dog Societies to honour the loyalty shown by wild dogs to other dogs in their pack. This Hidatsa shaman (medicine man) is dressed for the Dog Dance. Dances were performed in celebration and for good luck.

▲ TAIL TALK

The African hunting dog's tail is short compared to most canids, about 30–40cm/ 12–16in long. Its white tip stands out clearly and is used to signal members of the pack.

Body Parts

Muscular, fast-running wolves and wild dogs are built for chasing prey in open country. Thick muscles and long, strong legs enable them to run fast over great distances. The long skull helps the wolf to seize prey on the run. The wolf has a large stomach that can digest meat quickly and hold a big meal after a successful hunt. Wolves, however, can also go without food for more than a week if prey is scarce. Teeth are a wolf's main weapon, used for biting enemies, catching prey and tearing food. Small incisors (front teeth) strip flesh off bones. Long fangs (canines) grab and hold prey. Towards the back, jagged carnassial teeth close together like shears to chew meat into small pieces, while large molars can crush bones.

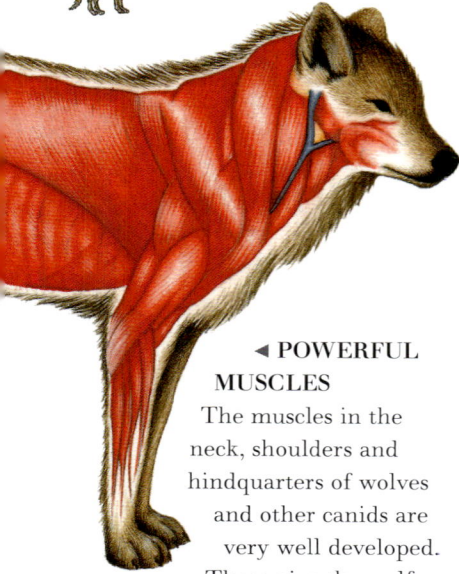

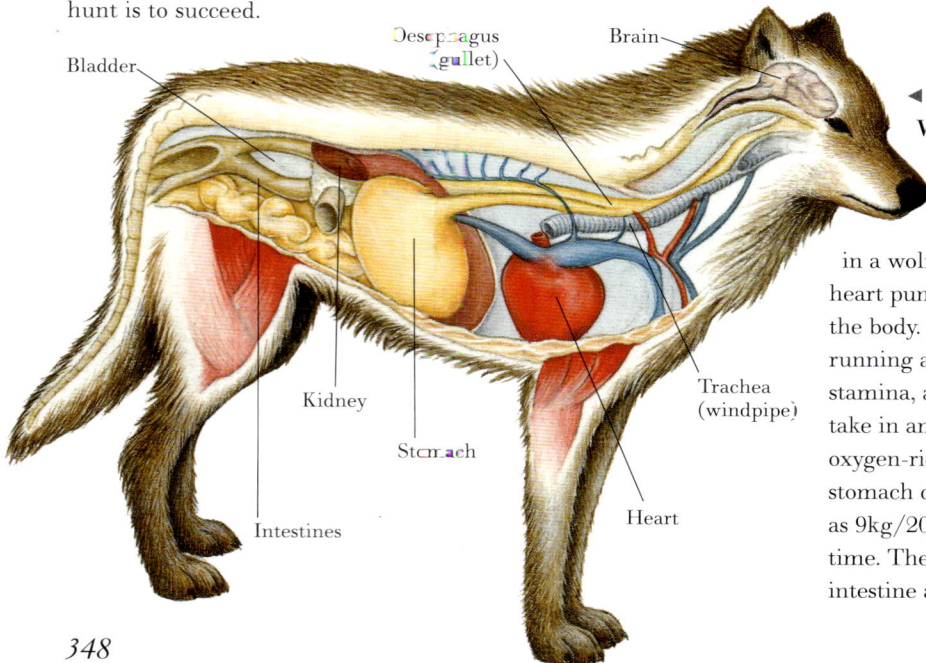

◀ **POWERFUL MUSCLES**

The muscles in the neck, shoulders and hindquarters of wolves and other canids are very well developed. These give the wolf strength and long-distance stamina as well as speed. Muscle-power alone is not enough, however, to catch prey. Wolves also need to use their cunning and stealth if the hunt is to succeed.

◀ **INSIDE A WOLF**

This diagram shows some of the main organs in a wolf's body. A strong heart pumps blood around the body. For long-distance running a wolf needs lots of stamina, and its large lungs take in ample supplies of oxygen-rich air. A wolf's stomach can hold as much as 9kg/20lb of food at a time. The stomach and intestine absorb nutrients.

Bladder

Oesophagus (gullet)

Brain

Kidney

Stomach

Trachea (windpipe)

Intestines

Heart

▼ WOLF'S SKULL

A wolf's head has a broad crown and a tapering muzzle. The bones of the skull are strong and heavy. They form a tough case that protects the animal's brain, eyes, ears and nose. The jaws have powerful muscles that can exert great pressure as the wolf sinks its teeth in its prey.

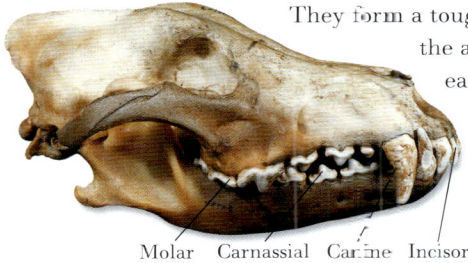

Molar   Carnassial   Canine   Incisor

▼ BAT-EARED FOX SKULL

The bat-eared fox has a delicate, tapering muzzle. Its jaws are weaker than a wolf's and suited to deal with smaller prey, such as insects. This fox has 46–50 teeth, which is more than any other canid. Extra molars at the back of the animal's mouth enable it to crunch up insects, such as beetles, which have a tough outer casing on their bodies.

Molar   Carnassial   Canine   Incisor

▲ TIME FOR BED

A wolf shows its full set of meat-eating teeth as it yawns. Wolves and most other canids have 42 teeth. In wolves, the four large, dagger-like canines at the front of the mouth can grow up to 5cm/2in long.

COOLING DOWN ▶

Like all mammals, the wolf is warm-blooded. This means its body temperature remains constant whatever the weather, so it is always ready to spring into action. Wolves do not have sweat glands all over their bodies as humans do, so in hot weather they cannot sweat to cool down. When the wolf gets too hot, it opens its mouth and pants with its large tongue lolling out. Moisture evaporates from the nose, mouth and tongue to cool the animal down.

On the Move

Wolves are tireless runners. They can lope along for hours on end at a steady pace of 38kph/24mph without resting. They have been known to cover an amazing 200km/124 miles in a day searching for food. Compared to cheetahs, which can reach speeds of 115kph/71mph over short distances, wolves are not fast runners. They can, however, put on a burst of speed to overtake fleeing prey.

Wolves and most other canids have four toes on their back feet and five toes on their front feet. The fifth toe on the front foot is called the dew claw, a small, functionless claw located a little way up on each front leg. They are more like pads than claws. They also have tough pads on the underside of their toes to help absorb the impact shock as the wolf's feet hit the ground.

▲ **SPEEDING COYOTE**
Like wolves, coyotes are good long-distance runners. They run on their toes, like all canids. This helps them to take long strides and so cover more ground. If necessary, coyotes can trot along for hours in search of food.

Did you know? Studies of wolves show one pack travelled 1,125km/700 miles in 40 days.

◄ **IN MID-LEAP**
Strong leg muscles enable a wolf to leap long distances – up to 4.5m/14¾ft in a single bound. Wolves and other canids are agile and can leap upward, sideways and even backward. As the wolf lands, its toes splay out to support its weight and prevent it from slipping.

Grey wolf
(*Canis lupus*)

LONG TOE ▶

This close-up of the bones in a maned wolf's foreleg shows the long toe bones that are used for walking. The bones in the foreleg, after the ankle joint and before the toes, are fused together for greater strength. Of all the canids, only the African hunting dog does not have dew claws.

Ankle joint

Bones in the foreleg are fused together

Toe bone

IN THE SWIM ▶

Bush dogs make their homes near streams and rivers and spend much of their lives in water. They are strong swimmers, and water creatures such as capybaras (a type of rodent) form part of their diet. Wolves, dingoes and most other canids can also swim well.

▲ WOLF TRACK

Clawmarks show up clearly in a line of wolf prints in a snowy landscape. Unlike cats, wolves and wild dogs cannot retract (draw in) their claws. When walking, the wolf places its paws almost in a straight line, to form a single track. The pawprints of a running wolf are more widely spaced.

A KEEN CLIMBER ▶

Wolves and wild dogs are quick on the ground, but they cannot climb trees. Some foxes, however, climb well. The grey fox of North America is an expert climber. It scrambles up trees to steal birds' eggs and chicks. It also climbs to get a good view over surrounding countryside when searching for prey.

Grey fox

(*Urocyon cinereoargenteus*)

Fur Coats

Black-backed jackal
(Canis mesomelas)

Wolves and other members of the dog family have thick fur coats. This dense layer of hair helps to protect the animal's body from injury and keeps it warm in cold weather. Wolves and other canids that live in cold places have extra-thick fur. Dingoes, jackals and wild dogs that live in warm countries close to the Equator have sparser fur. The fur is made up of two layers. Short dense underfur helps to keep the animal warm. Long guard hairs on top have natural oils that repel snow and rain to keep the underfur dry. A wild dog's fur coat is usually black, white or tan, or a mixture of these colours. Markings and patterns on the fur act as camouflage to disguise these animals, so they can creep up unseen on their prey.

▲ JACKAL COLOURS

The three species of jackal can be distinguished by their different markings. As its name suggests, the black-backed jackal has a dark patch on its back, as well as brown flanks and a pale belly. The golden jackal is sandy-brown all over. The side-striped jackal is so named because of the light and dark stripes that run along its sides.

◄ WAITING FOR SPRING

Two raccoon dogs shelter under a bush waiting for the snow to melt. They already have their summer coats of grey with pale and dark patches. This will help to camouflage them among the summer grasses and vegetation. In autumn (fall), they will moult (molt) these coats and grow a pure-white coat, ready for the winter snow.

◄ MANES AND RUFFS

The maned wolf gets its name from the ruff of long hairs on its neck. This may be dark or reddish-brown in colour. Wolves also have a ruff of longer hairs which they raise when threatened to make themselves look larger.

Arctic wolf
(Canis lupus tundarum)

▲ HANDSOME CAMOUFLAGE

African hunting dogs have beautiful markings, with tan and dark grey patches on their bodies, and paler, mottled fur on their heads and legs. The patterns work to break up the outline of their bodies as they hunt in the dappled light of the bush.

▲ WARM COAT

The Arctic wolf has very thick fur to keep it warm in icy temperatures. Its winter coat is pure white so that it blends in with the snow. In spring the thick fur drops out and the wolf grows a thinner coat for summer. This coat is usually darker to match the earth without its covering of snow.

Grey wolf
(Canis lupus)

VARYING COLOURS ►

Grey wolves vary greatly in colour, from pale silver to buff, sandy, red-brown or almost black. Even very dark wolves usually have some pale fur, often a white patch on the chest.

Sight and Sound

Wolves have excellent hearing. They can hear the sound of a snapping twig up to 3km/1¾ miles away and are alert to the smallest noise that might give away the presence of potential prey. Wolves hear a wider range of sounds than humans. They can hear ultrasounds (very high-pitched noise) that are too high for human ears to catch. This means they can track down mice and other rodents in the dark. Sight is less important than hearing for hunting. Wolves are good at spotting movement, even at a great distance, but find it harder to see objects that keep still. Canids that hunt at night rely on sound and smell rather than sight. African hunting dogs and dholes, however, hunt by day, often in open country, and have keener sight.

▲ PRICKED EARS
Wolves cock (turn) their ears in different directions to pinpoint distant sounds. Even a tiny noise betrays the hiding place of a victim.

Coyote
(Canis latrans)

▲ LISTENING IN
An African hunting dog's large, rounded ears work like satellite dishes to gather sound. Keen hearing is vital in the hunt and allows pack members to keep in touch among the undergrowth.

HOWLING HELLO ▶
Coyotes and other wild dogs keep in touch with distant members of their group by howling. The coyote call is actually a series of yelps that ends in a long wail.

◀ **BARKING MAD**

Some domestic dogs, such as this German shepherd, have been bred to bark loudly to warn their owners of approaching strangers. Wolves also bark if they meet an intruder near the den, but more quietly and less aggressively.

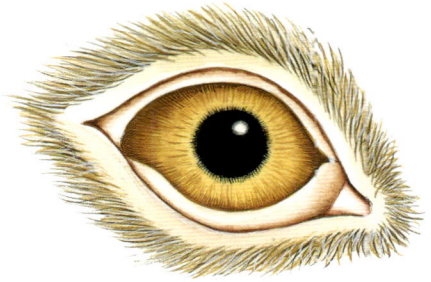

▲ **A THIRD EYELID**

Wolves' eyes have a third eyelid, called a nictating (blinking) membrane. This membrane is inside their upper and lower eyelids and sweeps over the surface of the eye when the wolf blinks. It protects the eyes from dust and dirt that might otherwise damage it.

◀ **GLOWING EYES**

Wolves have round, yellow eyes. In dark conditions, a layer at the back of the eye, called the *tapetum lucidum*, intensifies what little light there is. This allows a wolf to see at night. The layer also reflects light, making the wolf's eyes glow in the dark if a strong light is shone into them.

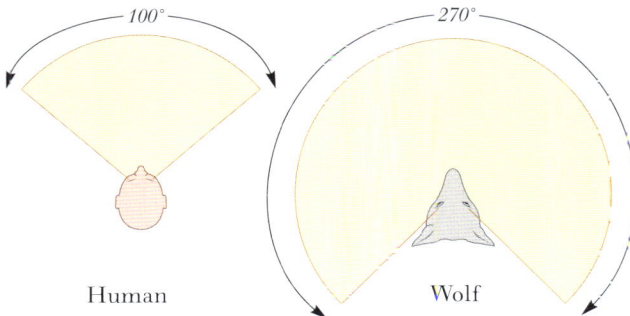

◀ **WOLF VISION**

Wide-set eyes in the front of its face give a wolf a very wide field of vision. As the view from each eye overlaps, binocular vision (using both eyes at the same time) allows a wolf to focus at close range and pounce on its prey.

100°

Human

270°

Wolf

355

Smell, Touch and Taste

Of all the senses, smell is the most important for wolves and wild dogs. These animals are constantly surrounded by different scents and their keen sense of smell can distinguish them all. They follow the scent trails left behind by other animals in their quest for food and can pick up even faint whiffs of scent on the wind. This helps them to work out the direction of distant prey. Canids that hunt in packs use scent to identify and communicate with other pack members. They also communicate by sight and touch. Like other mammals, wolves and wild dogs have taste buds on their tongues to taste their food. They eat foods they find the tastiest first. The tongue is also used to lap up water.

▲ TRACKING PREY

Nose to the ground, a wolf follows a scent trail. From the scent a wolf can tell what type of animal left it, whether it is well or ill, how far away it is and whether another wolf is following the trail.

▶ ON THE SCENT

Bloodhounds were specially bred as tracker dogs. They have a very acute sense of smell and can follow a scent that is several days old. They keep their noses very close to the ground. Their drooping ears help to channel scent into the nose.

▲ PLEASED TO MEET YOU

When two wolves meet they sniff the glands at the base of the tail. Pack members all have a familiar scent. Scent is also used to signal mood, such as contentment or fear, or if a female is ready to breed.

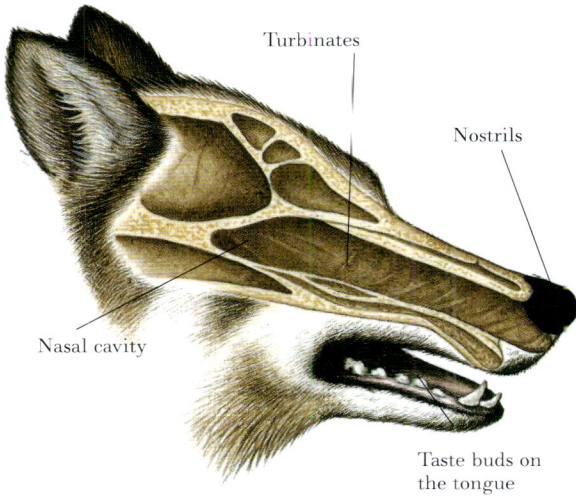

Turbinates

Nostrils

Nasal cavity

Taste buds on
the tongue

▲ INSIDE THE SNOUT

Inside a wolf's snout is a large nasal cavity used
for smelling. Scent particles pass over tubes of
very thin bone in the roof of the nasal cavity.
These tubes, called turbinates, are connected to
a nerve network that sends signals to the brain.

▼ SENSITIVE NOSE

The wolf's leathery outer nose is set
right at the end of
its snout. Two
nostrils draw air
laden with scents into
the nasal cavity. The
wolf may flare its
nostrils to take in extra
air. The animal may
lick its nose before
scenting, because a
damp nose helps its
sense of smell. Long,
sensitive whiskers on
either side of the
snout are used for
touching things
at close range.

▲ TOUCHY-FEELY

Wolves use touch to bond with each other.
They rub bodies, lick one another and thrust
their noses into each other's fur when they
meet. Pack members playfight by wrestling
with locked jaws or chasing around in circles.

▲ WELL GROOMED

A wolf nibbles at the tufts of hair
between its paw pads. It is
removing ice that might cut and
damage the paw. Wolves groom
(clean) their fur to keep it in good
condition. Licking and running
fur through the teeth helps to
remove dirt and dislodge fleas.

357

Living Together

Wolves are very social animals. A few may live alone, but most live in packs. A wolf pack may contain as few as two or as many as 36 animals. Most packs have between eight and 24 members. The main purpose of the pack is to hunt. A team of wolves together can hunt down and kill much larger and stronger prey than a wolf would be able to on its own. Only the strongest, healthiest pair in the pack will actually mate. Every pack member then helps to feed and bring up the cubs. Bush dogs, dholes and African hunting dogs also live in packs, while jackals and, sometimes, coyotes and raccoon dogs live in smaller family groups. Maned wolves and foxes usually live alone.

▲ TWO'S COMPANY
A pair of jackals drinks from a waterhole in South Africa. Some jackals are solitary, but most pair up for life. The cubs are reared in small, close-knit family groups. Older brothers or sisters often help their parents to rear the small cubs.

Did you know? Foxes produce alarming screams when looking for a mate.

WOLF PACK ▶
A wolf pack is led by the strongest, most experienced animals. The rest of the pack often consists of their children – young cubs and older, half-grown wolves. The young wolves follow their leaders until they are old enough to leave the pack.

maned wolf
*(Chrysocyon
brachyurus)*

▲ A FAMILY AFFAIR

Dholes live in family packs of between five and 12 animals. Sometimes several families join together to form a very large dhole pack called a clan. Hunting in a big group helps these relatively small wild dogs to tackle large prey, such as wild cattle and buffalo.

▲ EACH FOR ITSELF

The maned wolf is mostly solitary, living and hunting on its own. Males and females pair up during the breeding season. The male helps to feed and rear his pups – as do all canids, except for the domestic dog.

◄ COYOTE COUPLE

Most coyotes live and hunt alone, in pairs or in small family units. Sometimes, several of these small groups band together to make a bigger hunting party to go after large prey.

DOG SOCIETY ►

African hunting dogs are the next most social canids after wolves. They hunt co-operatively and all pack members help to raise the pups of the breeding pair. The males in the pack are all brothers. Females often join from a different pack.

Focus on

A wolf pack has a strict social order and each member knows its place. The senior male and female, known as the alpha male and female, are the only animals to breed. The alpha male takes the lead in hunting, defends the pack members from enemies and keeps the other animals in their place. In most packs, a second pair of wolves, called the beta male and female, come next in the ranking order. The other pack members are usually the offspring of the alpha pair, aged up to three years old.

LEADER OF THE PACK

An alpha male wolf greets a junior pack member. Wolves use different body positions and facial expressions to show rank. The leader stands upright with tail held high. The junior has his ears laid back and his tail tucked between his legs.

IT'S A PUSHOVER

A junior wolf rolls over on its back in a gesture of submission to a more dominant pack member. A junior wolf can also pacify a stronger animal by imitating cub behaviour, such as begging for food.

SHOWING WHO IS BOSS

A wolf crouches down to an alpha male. The young wolf whines as it cowers, as if to say, "You're the boss". The leader's confident stance makes him look as large as possible.

a Wolf Pack

"I GIVE IN"

A male grey wolf lays its ears back and sticks its tongue out. Taken together, these two gestures signal submission. A wolf with its tongue out, but its ears pricked, is sending a different message, showing it feels hostile and rebellious.

REJECTED BY THE PACK

Old, wounded or sickly wolves are often turned out of the pack to become lone wolves. Although pack members may be affectionate with each other, there is no room for sentiment. Young wolves may also leave to start their own packs. Lone wolves without the protection of a pack are much more vulnerable to attack and must be more cautious.

SCARY SNARL

A grey wolf bares its canine teeth in a snarl of aggression. Studies have shown that wolves use up to 20 different facial expressions. Junior wolves use snarling expressions to challenge the authority of their leaders The alpha male may respond with an even more ferocious snarl. If it does so, the junior wolf is faced with a choice. It must back down, or risk being punished with a nip.

Home Territory

Territories are areas that animals use for finding food or for breeding. An animal will defend its territory against others that might provide competition. Wolf packs use their territories as hunting grounds and also as safe places to raise their cubs. Wolf territories vary in size, depending on how much food is available to feed the pack. Small territories cover about 100 sq km/62 sq miles. Large territories may be 10 or even 100 times this size. At the heart of the territory is the rendezvous, a meeting place where the wolves gather. This place also acts as a nursery where older cubs are left to play. The borders of the territory are patrolled by the pack on a regular basis and marked with urine. Strong-smelling urine sprayed at marker sites lasts several days, while howling also serves as a long-distance warning. The pack will defend its territory fiercely if a rival pack tries to enter.

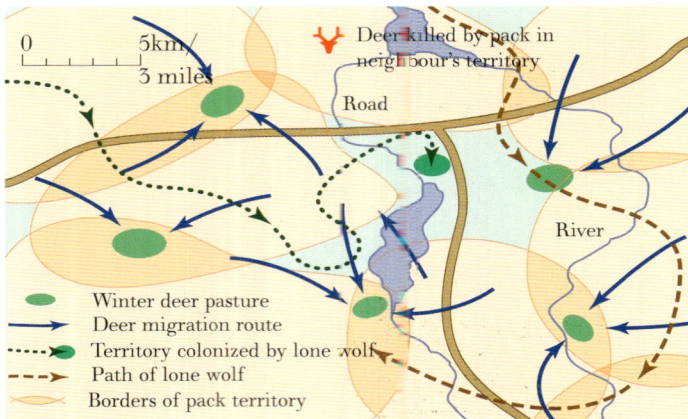

▲ **KEEP TO THE TRAIL**

A pack of wolves runs along a snowy trail in single file. Each wolf treads in the tracks of the one in front. This saves a lot of energy that would be wasted if each animal broke a separate trail through the deep snow. Wolves use well-worn paths inside their territories. These connect meeting places with lookout points and good ambush sites.

◄ **NEIGHBOURING TERRITORIES**

Several wolf territories may lie close to each other. Where food is plentiful, for example where deer breed, territories may overlap (*see diagram*). Rivers, towns and roads form natural boundaries. There may be a neutral 1km/½ mile wide no-go area between territories. If food becomes scarce, however, wolves will enter this zone.

0   5km / 3 miles

Deer killed by pack in neighbour's territory

Road

River

● Winter deer pasture
→ Deer migration route
⋯► Territory colonized by lone wolf
–► Path of lone wolf
▨ Borders of pack territory

▲ SCENT SIGNAL

A wolf smells a rock that another pack member has marked with urine. The scent lingers for several days after the animal has moved on. A wolf smelling this signal can tell how many animals have passed this way and whether they belong to its pack. Wolves from a rival pack will mark the other side of the rock to reinforce territory boundaries.

▲ BORDER DISPUTE

A wolf snarls at a wolf from another pack on the boundary between their territories. When food is scarce, packs are more likely to trespass or raid each other's territory. In times of plenty, scent signals keep trespassers out, so border disputes are rare.

◄ SCENT-MARKING

A dhole marks the edge of its territory by spraying urine on a patch of grass. Some canids, such as African hunting dogs and foxes, leave piles of droppings too. In a wolf pack, it is usually the alpha male that marks the boundaries.

KEEP-OUT CALL ►

Three wolves raise their heads in a group howl. Each animal howls a slightly different note, making an eerie harmony. The sound carries over a long distance — 10km/6 miles or more. If it reaches a rival pack, the other wolves may howl back. Howling is also used to rally the pack, for example before a hunt.

363

A Meaty Diet

Wolves and their relatives are carnivores (meat-eaters). They kill prey for fresh meat, but also eat carrion (dead animals). When no meat is available, wolves eat plants, such as fruit and berries, and also grass to aid digestion. Large herd animals, such as musk oxen, moose, deer and caribou, are the favourite targets of the wolf pack. All canids target other kinds of prey if a particular creature becomes scarce. For example, they hunt a wide range of smaller animals, including birds, hares, mice and beavers.

Wolves swim well and chase fish, frogs and crabs, but still spend much of their lives with empty bellies. When food is scarce, they sometimes approach towns and villages, where they rifle through rubbish (garbage) or kill domestic sheep, goats, cattle and horses.

▲ NOT-SO-FUSSY FEEDERS
Raccoon dogs of eastern Asia are omnivores — they eat all kinds of different foods, including rodents, fruit and acorns. They are strong swimmers and catch frogs, fish and water beetles in streams and rivers. They also scavenge carrion and scraps from rubbish (garbage) dumps.

▼ COYOTE PREY
Two coyotes tear at the carcass of a moose. Coyotes usually hunt small prey, such as mice, but sometimes they band together to go after larger creatures. Teams of coyotes also gang up on other predators and steal their kills.

◄ FAST FOOD

A pack of dholes makes quick work of a deer carcass. Each one eats fast to get its share. A hungry dhole can eat up to 4kg/9lb of meat in an hour. Mammals form a large part of a dhole's diet, but if meat is scarce they will also eat berries, lizards and insects.

▲ MEAT AND FRUIT-EATER

A maned wolf lopes off in search of prey. Without a pack to help it hunt, it looks for easy prey, including armadillos and small rodents, such as agoutis and pacas. It also feeds on birds, reptiles, frogs and insects, fruit and sugar cane.

▲ BEACH SQUABBLE

Two black-backed jackals squabble over the carcass of a seal pup. Jackals eat almost anything – fruit, frogs, reptiles and a wide range of mammals, from gazelles to mice. Jackals also scavenge kills from other hunters.

CACHING FOOD ►

A wolf looks for a suitable place in the snow to bury a freshly caught hare. After a pack has killed a large beast, or when a lone hunter has eaten its fill, it hides the remains of its food. Then, when food is scarce, the wolf can return to the hidden cache and retrieve its kill.

Did you know? All canids are quick feeders, but dholes in particular bolt their food down at a great rate.

Grey wolf
(Canis lupus)

Going Hunting

Wolves and wild dogs do not all hunt at the same time of day. Maned wolves, bush dogs and raccoon dogs are mainly nocturnal (active at night). They rely on smell and hearing to find their prey. Dholes and African hunting dogs are daytime hunters, and track their prey by sight as well as smell and sound. Wolves hunt at any time of day or night. Members of a wolf pack work together like players in a sports team. Each animal has particular strengths that help the group. Some wolves are good trackers, others are particularly cunning, fast or powerful, and so help to bring down large animals, such as moose. Wolves spend a lot of time searching for food. A hunt may last for several hours, but nine out of ten hunts are unsuccessful and the wolves go hungry. If they strike lucky, they might kill a beast large enough to provide meat for all the pack.

Little Red Riding Hood
In the story of Little Red Riding Hood, *a cunning wolf eats Red Riding Hood's grandmother. The wolf then steals the old woman's clothes to prey on the little girl. Fortunately a wood cutter rescues Red Riding Hood in the nick of time. As he kills the wolf, the grandmother emerges alive from inside the wolf.*

Pack of wolves

STEP 1

Baby moose

Mother moose

Wolves surround moose

STEP 2

Moose panic

◀ **WOLF PACK IN ACTION**
Wolves use skill as well as strength to hunt large creatures, such as moose. A moose calf is an easier target than a full-grown animal. The wolves stalk their prey, fanning out and running ahead to surround the victim. Pack members dash forward to panic the animals and separate the mother from her baby. Once the young calf is separated, the wolves run it down and kill it with a bite to the neck.

DINGO KILL ▶

Two dingoes have just caught a kangaroo. In the Australian outback, dingoes hunt a wide range of creatures, from tiny grasshoppers and lizards to large prey, such as wild pigs and kangaroos. Sheep, introduced by settlers in the 1800s, are a favourite target.

◀ GROUP KILL

A large pack of wolves has killed a white-tailed deer. This amount of meat will not satisfy the group for long. Where food is scarce, territories are often much larger than in places where the hunting is easy. The pack will always hunt the largest game it can find.

Did you know For peak condition, a wolf needs to eat 4kg/9lb of meat a day.

Coyote
(*Canis latrans*)

CLEVER TACTICS ▶

A coyote plays with a mouse it has surprised in the snow. Coyotes often hunt mice, leaping high in the air to pounce on their victims. Coyotes have a more varied diet than wolves, feeding on fruit, grass, berries and insects, as well as mammals, such as rabbits, deer and rodents. They take to water to catch fish and frogs, and also steal sheep and chickens, which makes them unpopular with farmers.

▲ TEAMWORK

Working as a team, dholes hunt large prey, such as sambar (a type of deer). Dholes whistle to keep in touch with one another as they surround their prey. Teamwork also helps the pack to defend the kill from scavengers, such as vultures.

367

Focus on African

African hunting dogs eat more meat than any other canid. One in every three of their hunts ends in a kill, a very high success rate. They live on the savanna (grassy plains) of central and southern Africa, which is also home to vast herds of grazing animals, such as zebra, wildebeest and gazelle. The pack wanders freely over a huge area of savanna, looking for herd animals to prey on. They rely on sight to find their quarry, so they hunt during daylight hours or on bright moonlit nights. They mainly hunt at dusk or dawn, when the air is coolest, and rest in the shade during the hottest time of day.

1 A pack of wild dogs begins to run down their quarry, a powerful wildebeest. On the open plains of the Serengeti in East Africa, there is little cover that would allow the dogs to sneak up on their prey. The hunt is often therefore a straightforward chase. A junior dog may lead the hunt at first. The pack also targets many kinds of antelope, such as kudu and gazelle.

2 The dogs run along at an easy lope at first. They have tested out the wildebeest herd to find an easy target. They look for weak, injured or young and inexperienced animals that will make suitable victims. This wildebeest is an older animal whose strength may be failing.

Hunting Dogs

3 A hunting dog tries to seize the wildebeest's tail. Hunting dogs with different strengths and skills take on different roles during the hunt. The lead dogs are super-fit and strong. They dodge out of the way if the wildebeest turns to defend itself with its sharp hooves and horns. Fast runners spread out to surround the victim and cut off its escape.

4 As the wildebeest tires, two dogs grip its snout and tail, pinning it down. Hunting dogs can run at 50kph/31mph for quite a distance, but their prey is much swifter. While the lead dogs follow the fleeing animal's twists and turns, backmarkers take a more direct line, saving their strength. The rear dogs take over the chase as the leaders tire.

5 More dogs arrive and the strongest move in for the kill. While some dogs hold their victim by the snout and flanks, others jump up to knock it off balance. The dogs attack their victim's sides and rump and soon the animal is bleeding freely. It begins to weaken through shock and loss of blood.

6 The wildebeest crashes to the ground and the dogs rip at its underparts to kill it. There is little snapping and snarling as they eat, but the kill is fiercely defended if a scavenger, such as a jackal, comes close. Half-grown cubs feed first, then the carcass is ripped apart and bones, skin and all are eaten. Back at the den young cubs are fed with pre-chewed meat.

Finding a Mate

Wolves and wild dogs breed once a year, towards the end of winter. The cubs are born roughly two months later, in the spring. The size of the litter varies from species to species. Maned wolves give birth to the fewest young, usually only two cubs. Each pregnant wolf produces between three and eight cubs per litter. African hunting dogs have the largest litters: up to 16 pups at a time.

About six weeks after mating, a female wolf prepares a den in a cave, a hollow tree trunk or an underground burrow. Here her cubs will be born. The pack gathers outside the den as she begins to give birth. They howl as if to encourage the mother as the young are born.

▲ PURE PEDIGREE
In some parts of Australia, dingoes live in packs, in which only the dominant female breeds. In other areas, they live in smaller family groups. Because there are no other wild dogs to breed with, dingoes are in fact the most pure bred dogs in the world. They are directly descended from prehistoric domestic dogs.

Did you know? Wolf cubs take about 63 days to develop in their mother's womb before they are born.

COURTING COUPLE ▶
A male wolf sniffs his partner to find out if she is ready to mate. Tensions run high in the wolf pack during the breeding season, as all the adult wolves are ready to breed. The alpha male and female must dominate the rest to make sure they are the only ones to mate. The alpha female temporarily drives the other females from the pack. Once the alpha pair have mated, all the wolves can relax.

◄ **MATING WOLVES**

When they mate, the male wolf mounts the female and grasps her sides with his front paws. The female becomes ready to mate as the periods of daylight grow longer. This means that her pups will be born in spring, as the weather warms up and food becomes plentiful. In North America, in the south of their range, if mating is in February, the cubs will be born in late April or May. Farther north, wolves give birth in May or June.

LOCKED TOGETHER ►

Directly after mating, canids often stay tied (locked together) for many minutes. Tying helps to ensure that the alpha male is the father of the cubs, rather than an alpha male from a rival pack that may mate with the alpha female afterwards. It also helps strengthen the bond between parent wolves.

◄ **DINGO DEN**

A rocky cave overlooking a stony desert makes a good den site for this mother dingo. The cave will be a safe, cool and shady place for the cubs to be born.

▲ **GIVING BIRTH**

A mother wolf licks her newborn cub to clean it and stimulate it to begin breathing. Wolf cubs are born at intervals of about 15–30 minutes and it may take up to six hours for a large litter to be born.

371

Newborn Cubs

At birth, the young of wolves and dogs are tiny and helpless. Newborn wolves are only about 21cm/8¼in long from the tip of their short noses to the end of their thin, little tails. With eyes tightly closed, they cannot see or hear, or even stand on their weak legs. They squirm around and huddle close to their mother for warmth. Like all mammals, their first food is their mother's rich milk, which she encourages them to suck from the moment they are born.

After one or two weeks, the cubs' eyes open and they take notice of their surroundings. They take their first wobbly steps and scramble over each other in the den. At about five weeks, the cubs begin to take solid food as well as milk. Half-chewed meat, stored in the stomach of an adult wolf, is brought to the den and coughed up when the cubs beg for food.

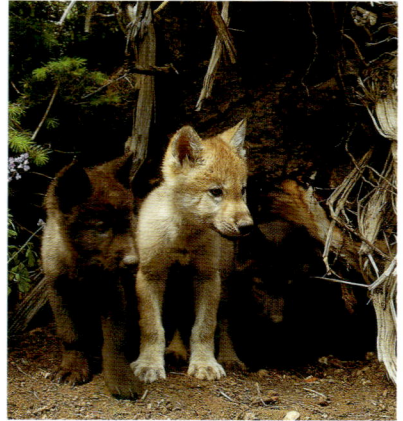

▲ AT THE DEN

Wolf cubs take a first look at the big world outside their den. For nearly eight weeks their only experience has been the burrow – a 4m/13ft long tunnel dug in soft earth with room for an adult wolf to creep along. The cubs sleep in a cosy chamber at the end, while their mother sleeps in a hollow nearer the entrance.

Did you know? Young wolf cubs need to feed every few hours and drink 300ml/10fl oz of milk a day.

NURSING MOTHER ▶

The mother wolf hardly leaves her cubs for the first weeks of their lives. Her mate and the other members of the pack bring food so she does not need to leave the den to go hunting. As a nursing mother, she is always hungry and needs large quantities of food to produce enough milk to feed her hungry cubs.

▼ CUBS IN DANGER

These wolf cubs are about six or seven weeks old. Not all cubs are born in a den. Some are born in a hollow sheltered from the wind or in a nest flattened in long grass. There are many dangers for cubs in the open. They may be snatched by predators, such as bears or eagles. Many do not survive.

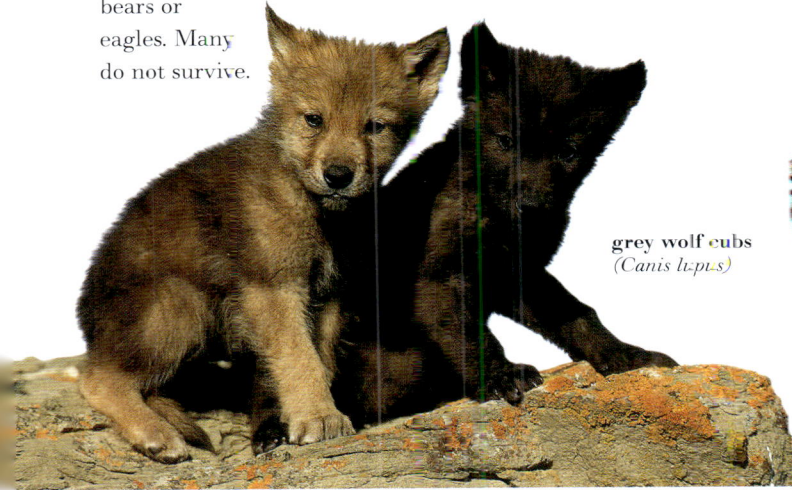

grey wolf cubs
(*Canis lupus*)

Romulus and Remus

According to ancient Roman legend, Romulus and Remus were twin brothers who were abandoned as babies on a remote hillside. A she-wolf found them and brought them up, feeding them on her milk. Both brothers survived and Romulus went on to found the city of Rome.

▲ HUNGRY PUPPIES

An African hunting dog suckles her pups. They suck milk from two sets of nipples on her underside. Female hunting dogs often have more nipples than other canids because they have the biggest litters and therefore the most mouths to feed. As the pups' sharp teeth begin to hurt, she will wean them on to meat.

▲ RARE CUBS

In the mountains of Ethiopia, a Simien wolf guards her litter of five cubs. Simien wolves have similar breeding habits to other wolves, but are much rarer. These cubs look healthy, so have a good chance of surviving long enough to breed as adults.

373

Growing Up

At eight weeks old, wolf cubs are very lively. Their snouts have grown longer, their ears stand up and they look much more like adult wolves. They bound about on long, strong legs. Now weaned off milk, they live on a diet of meat brought by the adults. As they leave the safety of the den, the other pack members gather around and take great interest in the cubs. The cubs' new playground is the rendezvous, the safe place at the heart of wolf-pack territory where the adults gather. This is usually a sheltered, grassy place near a stream where the cubs can drink. Here, they develop their hunting skills by pouncing on mice and insects. In playfights they establish a ranking order that mirrors the social order in the pack.

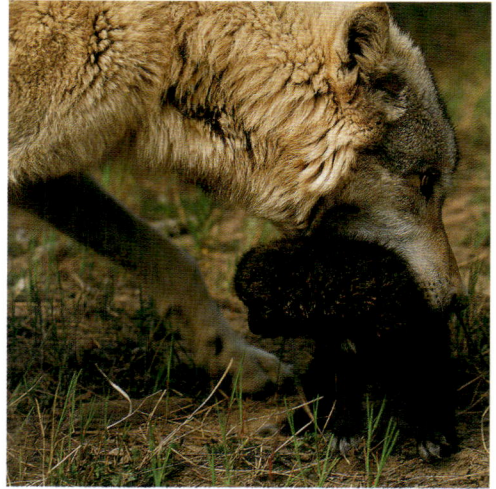

▲ CARRIED AWAY

A wolf carries a cub to safety by seizing the loose skin at the scruff of its neck in its teeth. This adult is most likely the cub's mother or father, but it may be another member of the pack. All the adult wolves are very tolerant with the youngsters to begin with. Later, as the cubs grow up, they may be punished with a well-placed nip if they are naughty.

Did you know?
Father wolves make squeaking noises to call their cubs.

SHARING A MEAL ►

A young African hunting dog begs for food by whining, wagging its tail and licking the adult's mouth. The adult responds by arching its back and regurgitating (bringing up) a meal of half-digested meat from its stomach. The pups grow quickly on this diet. At the age of four months, they are strong enough to keep up with the pack when they go hunting.

▼ PRACTICE MAKES PERFECT

Two Arctic fox cubs practise their hunting skills by pouncing on one another. Wolf cubs playfight to establish a ranking order. By the age of 12 weeks, one cub has managed to dominate the others. He or she may go on to become leader of a new pack.

Wolfchild

Rudyard Kipling's Jungle Book, *which was published in 1894, is set in India. The book tells the story of Mowgli, a young boy who is abandoned and brought up by wolves in the jungle. When Mowgli becomes a man he fights his arch-enemy, the tiger Shere Khan. Kipling's tale was inspired by many true-life accounts of wolf-children who grew up in the wild in India during the 1800s.*

▲ YOUTHFUL CURIOSITY

Young maned wolves investigate their surroundings. Females usually bear three cubs at most. Newborn young have grey-brown fur, short legs and snouts. Later they develop long legs and handsome red fur.

ALMOST GROWN ▶

These two young wolves are almost full-grown. Cubs can feed themselves at about ten months, but remain with the pack to learn hunting skills. At about two or three years old, many are turned out. They wander alone or with brothers or sisters until they find a mate and start a new pack.

Icy Wastes

Wolves were once widespread throughout the northern hemisphere. As human settlements have expanded, so wolves have been confined to more remote areas, such as the far North. The Arctic is a frozen wilderness where very few people live. Wolves and Arctic foxes are found here. On the barren, treeless plains, known as the tundra, harsh, freezing winter weather lasts for nine months of the year. Both land and sea are buried beneath a thick layer of snow and ice. Few animals are active in winter, so prey is scarce. During the brief summer, the ice and snow melt, flowers bloom and birds, insects and animals flourish, so prey is abundant. Arctic wolves and foxes rear their cubs in this time of plenty. Another harsh, remote habitat, the windswept grass steppes of Asia, is home to the small steppe wolf.

Arctic Legend

Native Americans named natural phenomena after the animals that lived around them. The Blackfoot called the Milky Way the Wolf Trail. In northern Canada, the Cree believed the Northern Lights, shown below, shone when heavenly wolves visited the Earth. In fact these spectacular light shows in the Arctic are caused by particles from the Sun striking the Earth's atmosphere.

◄ **WHITE WOLF**
Arctic wolves are larger than most other wolf species. They scrape under the snow to nibble plant buds and lichen if they are desperate for food.

Arctic wolf
(Canis lupus tundarum)

Did you know? The largest Arctic wolf territories cover 13,000 km/8,000 miles – an area about the same size as Northern Ireland.

▲ WARM FUR

This Inuit girl is wearing a hood trimmed with wolf fur. The fur is warm and sheds the ice that forms on the hood's edge as the wearer breathes. The Inuit and other peoples of the far north traditionally dressed in the skins of Arctic animals. Animal skins make the warmest clothing and help to camouflage the wearer when hunting.

▲ ARCTIC HUNTER

A grey wolf feeds hungrily on a caribou carcass. In the icy north, wolves need very large territories to find enough prey. They will follow deer for hundreds of kilometres/miles as the herds move south for the winter.

◄ ARCTIC HELPER

One crack of a whip brings a team of huskies under control. Tough and hardy huskies, with their thick fur coats, are the working dogs of the far north. They are used by the Inuit and other Arctic peoples to pull sledges and help to hunt.

SNOWY BED ►

A grey wolf shelters in a snowy hollow to escape a blizzard. With its thick fur, it can sleep out in the open in temperatures as low as 46°C/-50.8°F. Snow drifting over its body forms a protective blanket.

In the Forest

South of the treeless Arctic tundra, a belt of dense evergreen forests rings the northern hemisphere. It covers large parts of Canada, northern Europe and Russia. South of this belt lie the broad-leaved woodlands of temperate (warm) regions. Yet farther south, tropical rainforests grow in the hotter regions around the Equator.

Wolves and other canids flourish in forests and woods where there is a plentiful supply of prey and dense undergrowth in which to hide and stalk. Wolves are perhaps most at home in temperate northern regions, where large game such as deer abound. In tropical rainforests, most creatures live high in the tree-tops, where wild dogs cannot reach them. However, canids, such as bush dogs and raccoon dogs, are found near streams and rivers, which also teem with life.

▲ WOODLAND JACKAL
A side-striped jackal keeps a wary look-out for danger. In Africa, the three different kinds of jackal are found in different types of terrain. Side-striped jackals keep mostly to woods and swampy areas. Golden and black-backed jackals live in more open countryside.

◄ HIDDEN HUNTERS
In dark pine forests and dappled broad-leaved woodlands, the grey or blackish coats of wolves blend in with the shadows. This helps them to creep up on deer, moose and other forest prey. Dense foliage also protects the wolves from the worst of the north's drenching rain.

Raccoon dog
(Nyctereutes procyonoides)

◄ SOUND SLEEPERS

Raccoon dogs live in thickly wooded river valleys in eastern Asia. They are the only canids that hibernate in winter. In autumn (fall), raccoon dogs gorge themselves on fruit and meat to put on a thick layer of fat. Then they retreat to their burrows. They sleep right through the harsh winter and wake in spring.

JUNGLE PACK ►

A dhole moves through the thick undergrowth of a forest in India. Packs of dholes hunt deer, such as chital and sambar. They call to one another to surround their prey as it moves through the dense jungle. The pack will guard its kills against bears, tigers and scavengers.

◄ RODENTS BEWARE

Bush dogs live in the dense forests and marshlands of South America. In the wetlands, their main prey are aquatic rodents, such as pacas and agoutis. These fierce dogs will even plunge into the water to hunt capybaras – the world's largest rodents, 1.3m/ 4¼ft long.

Did you know? Raccoon dogs are the only canids that cannot bark.

A SCARCE BREED ►

A wolf surveys the snowy landscape in the Abruzzo region of central Italy. Wolves are common in remote forests in Canada and Russia, but in western Europe they are scarce. They survive in small pockets of wilderness, hiding in the hills by day and creeping down to villages to steal scraps at night.

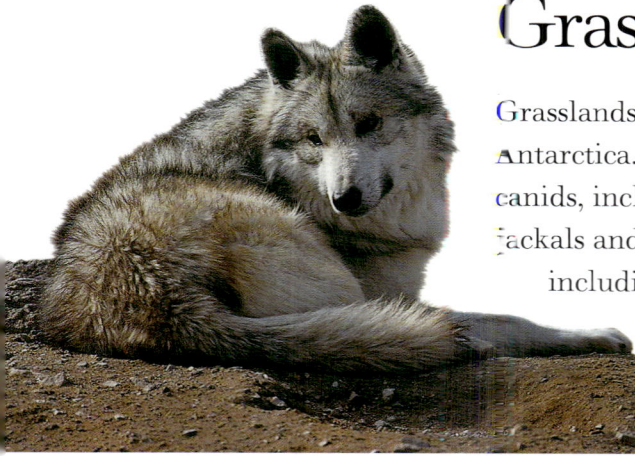

Grassland and Desert

Grasslands are found on every continent except Antarctica. Savanna (grassland) is home to several canids, including maned wolves, black-backed jackals and African hunting dogs. Other canids, including coyotes, dingoes and several kinds of fox, live in deserts. In these harsh, barren places, the sun beats down mercilessly by day, but at night the temperature plummets. Scorching daytime temperatures may cause animals to overheat. Desert foxes keep cool during the hot days by hiding under shady rocks or in dark burrows, emerging to hunt only at night. Another big problem for desert animals is lack of water. Wild dogs and foxes can survive for long periods with little water, or derive most of the liquid they need from their food.

▲ **DESERT WOLVES**
Wolves are found in deserts and dry areas in Mexico, Iran and Arabia. With little vegetation to provide cover, they stalk prey by hiding behind boulders or rocky outcrops. Desert wolves often have pale or sandy fur, to blend in with their surroundings.

▲ **GIVING OFF HEAT**
A black-backed jackal's large ears contain a network of fine veins. Blood flowing through these veins gives off heat, keeping the animal cool.

◄ **HUNTERS OF THE OUTBACK**
A pair of dingoes waits at a rabbit warren in central Australia. Dingoes have lived wild in the outback for more than 8,000 years. Their reddish-brown coats, with paler fur on their legs and bellies, are perfect camouflage in the desert landscape.

▲ OUTCAST DOGS

Feral dogs are the descendants of domestic dogs that have become wild. In Asia they are known as pariah (outcast) dogs. Feral dogs are very adaptable and change their behaviour to suit any situation. In India, pariah dogs hang around villages and sneak in to scavenge scraps.

▲ SMALLER PACKS

A pack of African hunting dogs tears a carcass apart. In the past, hunting dogs were numerous and widespread throughout central and southern Africa. Packs were large, containing 100 animals or more. Now these wild dogs are much more scarce and their packs are also smaller, usually containing between six and 30 animals.

The Jackal-headed God

In ancient Egypt, Anubis, the god of the dead, was shown with a human body and the head of a jackal. This god was believed to be responsible for the process of embalming, which preserved the bodies of the dead. Anubis often appears in wall paintings and sculptures found in burial places. Here he is shown embalming the body of an Egyptian king.

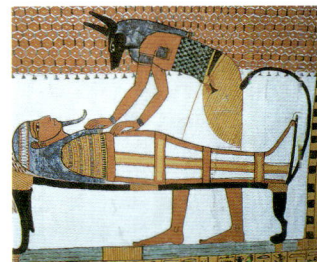

▲ SLY HUNTER

A maned wolf hunts in the long grass in Argentinian marshland. Despite its long legs, this canid is not a fast runner. It also lacks the stamina needed to chase prey over great distances. Instead, it stalks animals such as rodents, by slowly sneaking up on them before making a sudden pounce.

Focus on

The name coyote is from the ancient Aztec word *coyotl*, which means barking dog. These canids are found in most parts of North and Central America, from Costa Rica right up to Alaska and northern Canada. Coyotes eat the same sorts of food as wolves and the two species are rarely found together. Coyotes are only half the size of wolves, with bodies measuring about 95cm/37in long. They can be recognized by their narrow muzzles, large, pointed ears and long legs. Their tails have a black tip. Coyotes were once thought to be solitary animals, but research has shown that they often live in pairs or small family groups.

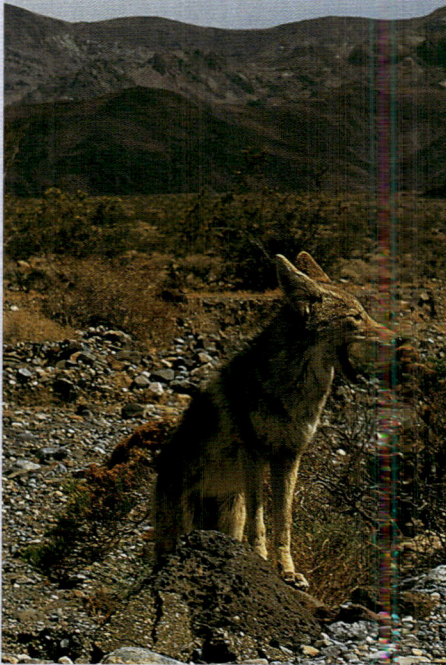

COYOTE COUNTRY

A coyote prowls the rocky desert landscape of Death Valley in California. Coyotes are also known as prairie wolves because they are usually associated with grassy habitat. In fact they inhabit all kinds of different terrain, including mountains, forests, woodlands and desert.

TERRITORIAL MARKING

A coyote marks the boundary of its territory by spraying urine. Coyotes also howl to keep other coyotes off their patch. Like wolves, coyotes use their territory both for hunting and for breeding. Coyote territories, however, are generally much smaller than wolf territories — usually 14–65 sq km/ 5½–25 sq miles in size.

Coyotes

CUNNING HUNTERS

Birds, such as this pheasant, make a tasty meal for coyotes. Coyotes often work in pairs to surround ground-nesting birds or grazing rabbits. They also team up to flush burrowing animals, such as ground squirrels, from their underground homes

GROWING UP

Two cubs sniff at a freshly killed pheasant brought by their mother. When the cubs are very young, the father brings all the food while the mother stays in the den. Later, she goes out to hunt as well. Most young coyotes leave their parents at the age of one year. A few youngsters stay on to help their parents rear a new litter of cubs.

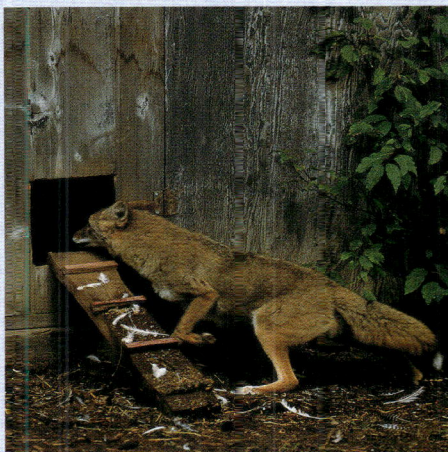

CLOSE TO HOME

A coyote cub surveys the world from the safety of its den entrance. Dens may be abandoned skunk or badger burrows. Coyotes mate in late winter. Around nine weeks later, the female gives birth to about five cubs. The young feed only on their mother's milk until the age of three weeks, when they start to eat meat as well.

CHICKEN RAID

A coyote peers into a chicken coop, hoping to steal a hen. Coyotes mainly feed on rabbits and rodents. In a way coyotes are actually useful to farmers. They kill large numbers of the unwanted small animals that graze on farmland pasture.

FOCUS on

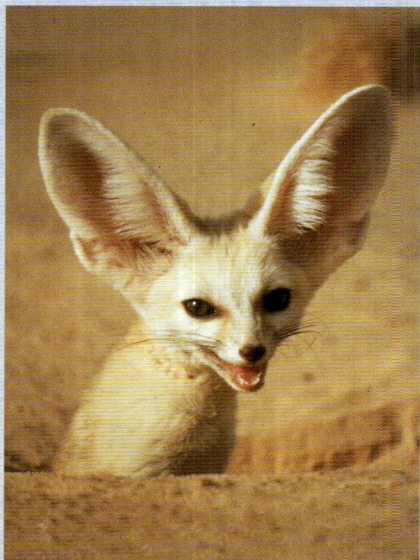

BIG EARS
The fennec is the world's smallest fox, but it has the biggest ears. Fennec foxes live in the sandy deserts of Africa and Arabia. Their very large ears help to give off heat and keep the animals cool in the scorching desert. The fox rests in its cool, sandy burrow by day, and comes out to hunt rodents, lizards and insects at night.

With their large, pointed ears and long snouts, foxes look a lot like coyotes, but have shorter legs. There are more than 20 species of fox. They are found in most places, but are not native to Australia, South-east Asia or Antarctica. Like other canids, foxes are very adaptable and live in a wide variety of habitats, from the frozen Arctic and bare mountainsides to scorching deserts and crowded cities. Foxes eat almost anything, including small mammals, birds, reptiles, insects, worms and fruit. Most are solitary hunters that keep other foxes away from their territories. In the breeding season, they yelp harshly to find a mate. Litters of up to six cubs are born in a burrow or rocky crevice.

Arctic fox in winter coat
(Alopex lagopus)

Arctic fox in summer coat
(Alopex lagopus)

SNOWY WANDERER
Arctic foxes roam over the freezing, wind-swept Arctic tundra. They feed on lemmings (rodents) and sometimes follow polar bears to steal the leftovers from their kills.

BRAND NEW COAT
In spring, the Arctic fox's thick white fur falls out. A new dark brown coat grows in its place. This blends in well with the rocks and plants of the tundra after the snow has melted.

Foxes

Crab-eating fox
(Cerdocyon thous)

NIGHT RAIDER

Red foxes live in woods and open country in North America, Europe and Asia, and were introduced into Australia after 1780. They kill their prey by springing upwards and then pouncing to trap it in their front paws. Red foxes have moved into towns, where they find food by raiding rubbish (garbage) at night.

CRAB-EATING FOX

The crab-eating fox lives in the grasslands, woods and swamps of South America. As well as crabs these foxes hunt a wide range of other animals, including lizards, frogs, rodents and chickens. They also steal reptiles' eggs. The species earned its rather misleading name because the first animal to be spotted by a scientist had a crab in its mouth.

COLPEO

A pair of colpeo foxes rest by a rocky outcrop in the Andes Mountains of Bolivia. This South American fox lives mainly on grasslands and in mountains. Its tawny-black fur provides camouflage among the boulders, where it hunts for mice, birds, eggs and snakes.

Colpeo fox
(Duscyon alpaeus)

Dangers

Wolves and wild dogs may be powerful predators, but they face many threats in the wild. Their natural enemies include the largest creatures that they hunt, such as moose, bison and musk oxen. Their sharp hooves and horns can fatally wound a predator. One careless slip and a wolf may be gored or trampled to death. Wolves and wild dogs are also threatened when their habitats are disturbed or destroyed. In many areas, the territories where wild dogs can roam freely are getting smaller and smaller. Land is needed for crops or to graze herds of sheep and cattle. Forests are cut down for timber or to make way for new roads and towns. The survival of wolves and wild dogs is also threatened by deadly diseases, such as distemper, anthrax and rabies.

▲ HUNTING THE HUNTERS

A lioness has killed an African hunting dog. Groups of lions are known to stalk and ambush hunting dogs while they feed on a kill or drink at waterholes. Hyenas and jackals also prey on hunting dogs. They sneak up to the den and steal young pups if the adult dogs are not keeping a careful watch.

▼ DEFENCE TACTICS

On the Arctic tundra, large, shaggy musk oxen form a defensive ring around their young. Their long, fierce horns face outward, keeping young and weak members of the herd safe from wolves.

◄ DANGEROUS TARGET

A moose browses among the tall lakeside shrubs in Wyoming, United States. Moose are powerful beasts. An adult male stands 2m/6½ft tall at the shoulder and weighs as much as ten wolves. Its antlers and hooves can inflict great damage. A moose can crack a wolf's skull with one kick or gore it with its antlers and toss it high in the air. Wolves must be very wary when hunting such dangerous prey.

DINGOES KEEP OUT ►

A dingo attacks a sheep, snapping at its hindquarters. Farmers have built a fence across 5,300km/3,300 miles of south-eastern Australia to keep dingoes out of sheep country. Any dog caught inside the fence is shot.

▲ DEADLY RABIES

A black-backed jackal lies dying of rabies. Rabies is a fatal disease that attacks the brain and nervous system. It is passed on by saliva from an infected bite. Wild dogs have been wiped out in many areas to prevent rabies spreading to humans, even though a vaccine is available.

▲ KEEP OFF THE ROAD

African hunting dogs roam along a newly built road that cuts across their territory in the bush. They are scavenging for road-kills, but may well become victims themselves. The rapid human development of the dogs' territory threatens their way of life and very survival.

Wolves and People

Wherever wolves and wild dogs come into contact with people, the animals are regarded as dangerous pests who will – given the chance – kill livestock. They are poisoned, trapped and shot, not only for their skins, but for sport. Wolves were once the most widespread carnivores in the northern hemisphere. Now they survive in a much reduced area, often in small, scattered groups. Several species are endangered, including the Simien wolf, the red wolf and the African hunting dog. Much of the land where these animals once lived is now being farmed. Dholes and bush dogs have also become very rare as their forest habitat is destroyed. Some species, such as the Falkland Island wolf, a kind of fox, are already extinct.

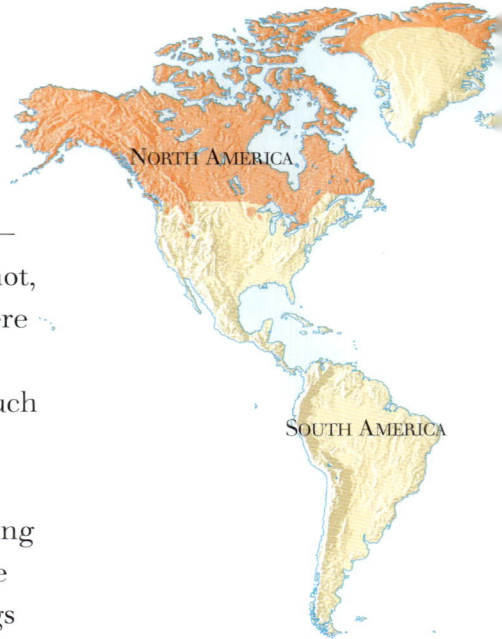

NORTH AMERICA

SOUTH AMERICA

grey wolf territories

▲ WOLF HUNT

In the Middle Ages, domestic dogs were often used to kill wolves, as this Dutch engraving of 1880 shows. The last wolves were wiped out in England by 1500 and in Ireland by 1800.

Tame Wolf

This book is a first edition of the popular novel White Fang by American writer Jack London. Set in northern Canada, it describes how a wolf, named White Fang, is tamed and becomes a pet. In general, it is not against the law to keep a wolf as a pet, but countries with restrictions require owners to have a special permit. The Call of the Wild by the same author describes how a pet dog joins a wolf pack and becomes wild.

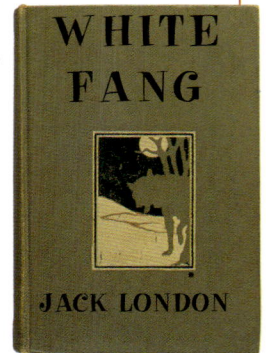

WHITE FANG

JACK LONDON

◀ NOWHERE TO RUN

A hunter in Colorado, United States, shoulders a coyote he has shot. In country areas, farmers shoot or poison coyotes because they steal sheep and other livestock and spread disease. Elsewhere, when coyotes and other wild dogs enter towns to scrounge scraps, they risk being shot as pests.

▲ WOLF TERRITORY

Grey wolves once had the greatest range of any wild land mammal. In the past, wolves were once common right across North America, throughout Europe, the Middle East and most of Asia. Their present range shows they have been exterminated in most of Mexico and the United States, in almost all of western Europe and over much of Asia.

▼ AN UNKIND LUXURY

Fox fur was very fashionable in the early 1900s, mainly for coats and for trimming garments. The fox fur stole (scarf) shown here uses the pelt (fur and skin) of an entire animal. In the past, furs were worn mainly to keep warm in winter. Today, however, man-made fabrics are as warm as fur, making it unnecessary and cruel to kill these animals for their pelts.

▲ UNDER THREAT

A Simien wolf howls high in the Ethiopian mountains. As the human population grows, more land is farmed and the animal's range is restricted. Simien wolves are shot for fur and killed by farmers as pests. There may now be only 500 Simien wolves left in the wild.

389

Sharks

The shark more than any other predator triggers a primeval fear in humans of being eaten alive, yet very few sharks attack people let alone eat them. In reality, the shark is a super-sophisticated hunter, each species adapted to its place in the ocean and its own food supply. None is really interested in us as food.

What is a Shark?

There are about 400 different kinds of shark in the world. Some are as big as whales, others as small as a cigar. Whatever their size, they all eat meat. Some sharks eat tiny plants and animals called plankton. Others hunt down fish, squid and even seals. Many sharks will also feed off the remains of another's meal or eat animal carcasses. They live at all depths, in every ocean, from tropical waters to cold polar seas. Some sharks can survive in the fresh water of rivers and lakes. Like other fish, sharks take oxygen from the water as it passes over their gills. Although some sharks like to live alone, others survive as part of a group.

▼ CLASSIC SHARK
This blue shark (*Prionace glauca*) is how most people imagine sharks. However, there are many different families of sharks in the seas and oceans and with a variety of body shapes.

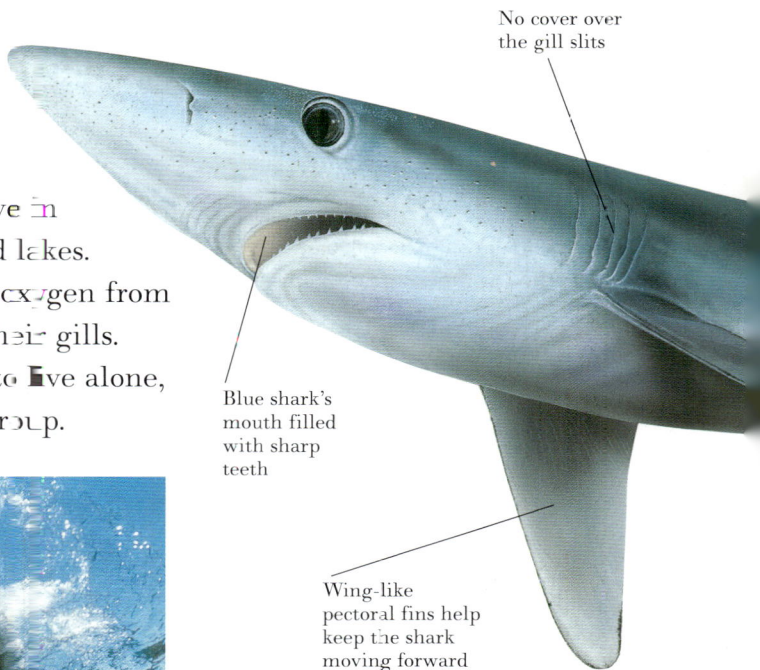

No cover over the gill slits

Blue shark's mouth filled with sharp teeth

Wing-like pectoral fins help keep the shark moving forward

◄ WHITE DEATH
The awesome great white shark (*Carcharodon carcharias*) is the largest hunting fish in the sea. It has an exaggerated reputation as a killer, partly because a killer shark appears in the film, *Jaws*. In reality, great white sharks do often eat large prey, but they attack people only occasionally, in cases of mistaken identity.

► **SHARK SCHOOL**
Some sharks live alone, others live in schools (groups). Every day, schools of female scalloped hammerhead sharks (*Sphyrna lewini*) like these gather off the Mexican coast. At night, the sharks separate and hunt alone.

Triangular dorsal (back) fin for stability

Body packed with muscles for strength

▲ **GENTLE GIANT**
Although the basking shark (*Cetorhinus maximus*) is the second largest fish after the whale shark, it is not a hunter. It funnels water through its huge mouth, using gill rakers (giant combs) to filter out the tiny plankton that it eats.

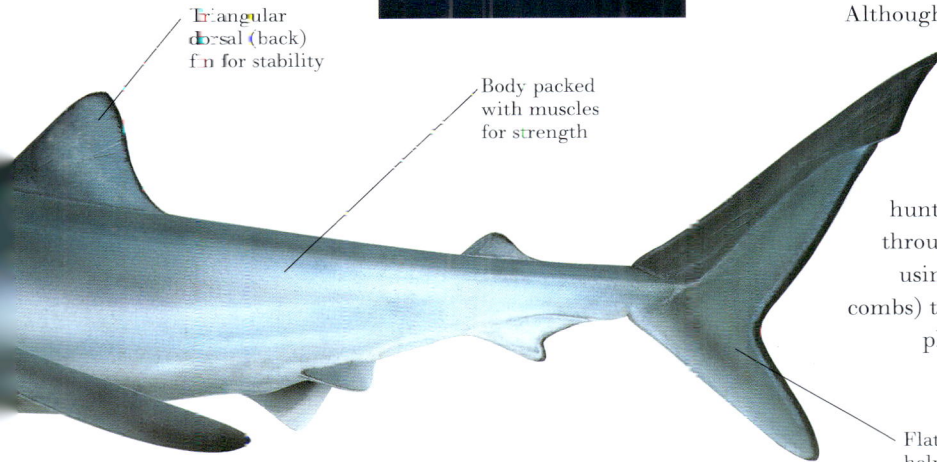

Flattened tail to help propel (push) through water

▲ **REEF HUNTERS**
Whitetip reef sharks (*Triaenodon obesus*) are one of the smaller species (kinds) of shark. They rarely grow over 2m/6½ft long and hunt along tropical coral reefs at night.

Maya Origins
The monkey head from Central America has been decorated with shark teeth. It is thought that the word shark comes from the Maya people of Central America. It may be based on the Maya word xoc (fury). The Maya symbol (word picture) for xoc is a shark-like creature.

393

Shapes and Sizes

Many hunting sharks have long, rounded shapes, like the slim blue shark and the bulkier bull shark. Angel sharks have a flattened shape suited to hiding on the sea floor, while eel-like frilled sharks swim in the deep sea. Horn sharks have spines on their back, and megamouths (big mouths) have big, blubbery lips. As their names suggest, hammerhead sharks have hammer-shaped heads, and sawsharks have elongated, saw-like snouts. Giant sharks, such as the whale shark, are as long as a school bus, and there are midget sharks, such as the Colombian lantern shark, which you could hold in the palm of your hand. Whatever the kind of shark, they are all perfectly adapted for the waters in which they live.

▲ GROTESQUE SHARK
The goblin shark (*Mitsukurina owstoni*) has an unusual, horn-shaped snout. This shark seems to have also lived in the dinosaur age. A fossil of a similar shark has been found in rocks that were created about 150 million years ago. Today, the goblin shark lives in very deep waters found off continental shelves.

▶ DEEP-SEA NIPPER
The pygmy shark is one of the smallest sharks in the world. When fully grown, it is no more than 20cm/8in long, making it smaller than a whale shark embryo (baby). It roams the gloomy waters of the Caribbean Sea, hunting in packs.

Pygmy shark
Europtomicrus bispinatus)

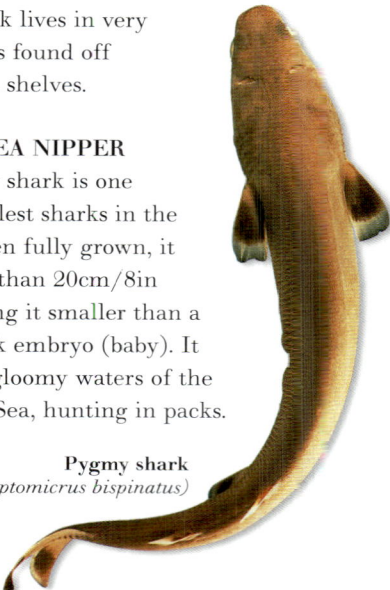

▲ STRANGE HEAD
The amazing heads of the hammerhead, bonnethead and winghead sharks are shaped like the letter T. These sharks use their hammers to detect prey and to aid swimming.

394

Zebra bullhead shark
(*Heterodontus zebra*)

Did you know? The largest shark ever measured was 12.65 m/41½ ft long.

▲ SAFETY SPINES

A striped pattern helps the colourful zebra bullhead shark to camouflage itself (blend in) among corals and seaweed. For further protection, at the front of each dorsal fin is a sharp spine. If swallowed, the shark's spines will stick into the throat of any attacker, forcing it eventually to spit out its prickly meal.

▲ ROCK DISGUISE

Unlike many sharks, the spotted wobbegong shark (*Crectolobus maculatus*) has a flattened shape. It is a carpet shark (a family of camouflaged sharks that lie on the seabed), and disguises itself as part of the coral reef. The tassels under its mouth look like seaweed.

▶ UNDERWATER TIGER

A young tiger shark has pale stripes along its body, which fade as it grows older. The powerful tiger shark (*Galeocerdo cuvier*) has a long, rounded shape, typical of hunting sharks. Some can rival great whites in size.

◀ BIG GULP

The whale shark (*Rhincodon typus*) is aptly named. Bigger than any other shark, it is closer in size to the giant whales. It is the largest fish in the sea, can grow to 12m/39ft in length and weigh up to 12 tonnes/tons. With its giant mouth and large gill slits, the whale shark is a filter feeder.

Light and Strong

Although most fish are bony, the skeleton of a shark is made up almost entirely of cartilage, which is also found in the human nose. It is lighter and more elastic than bone, and it is this that makes the shark skeleton very flexible. This cartilage structure is strong enough to support a shark's huge muscles and bendy enough to allow it to move with ease. Because sharks' skeleton cartilage and soft body parts decay (rot away) so quickly after they die, it is unusual to find complete shark fossils (preserved bodies) in ancient rocks. Only the hard teeth and spines are fossilized.

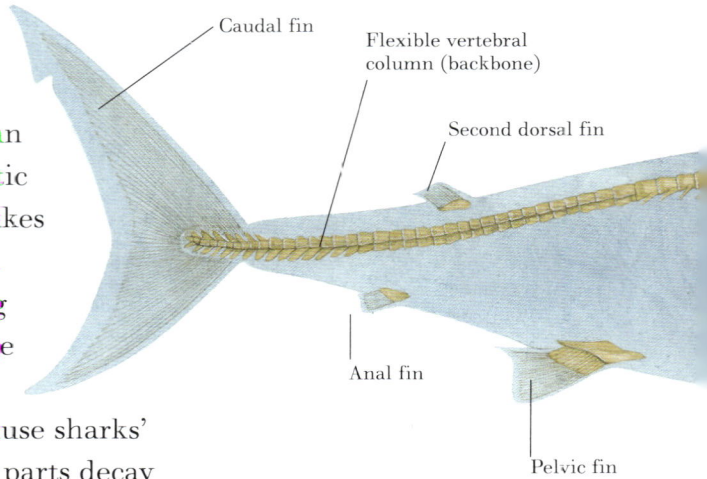

Caudal fin

Flexible vertebral column (backbone)

Second dorsal fin

Anal fin

Pelvic fin

▼ PROTRUDING JAWS
A shark's jaws are attached to the skull by flexible ligaments. These allow some sharks to thrust their jaws forward when taking a bite.

Teeth in upper jaw slice like a knife

▲ DARK TRIANGLE
Like the keel of a yacht, a shark's stiff dorsal fin helps it to balance in the water and stops it from slipping sideways. Most sharks have two dorsal fins. one at the front and one at the back, but some have just one.

▶ AIRCRAFT FINS

A shark's pectoral fins, one on each side, act like the wings of an aircraft. As water passes over them, the fins give lift.

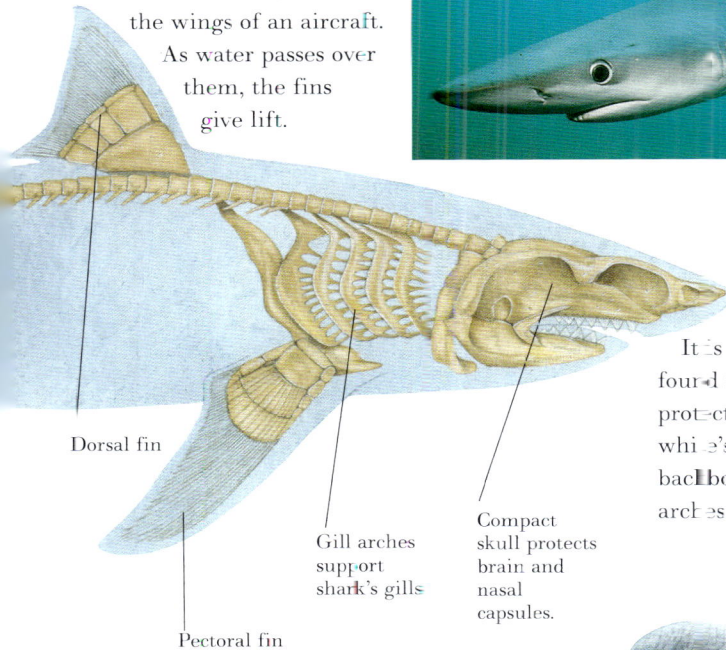

Dorsal fin

Gill arches support shark's gills

Compact skull protects brain and nasal capsules.

Pectoral fin

◀ SHARK SKELETON

The skeleton of a great white shark. It is tough, flexible and typical of that found in most sharks, providing support and protection for the entire body. The great white's muscles are attached to a long backbone, the gills are supported by gill arches and a box-like skull protects the brain.

▲ CARTILAGE SOUP

These fins have been cut from sharks and are drying in the sun. The cartilage in a shark's fin helps to make it stiff. When boiled in water it makes a gluey substance that is used in the Far East to make shark's fin soup.

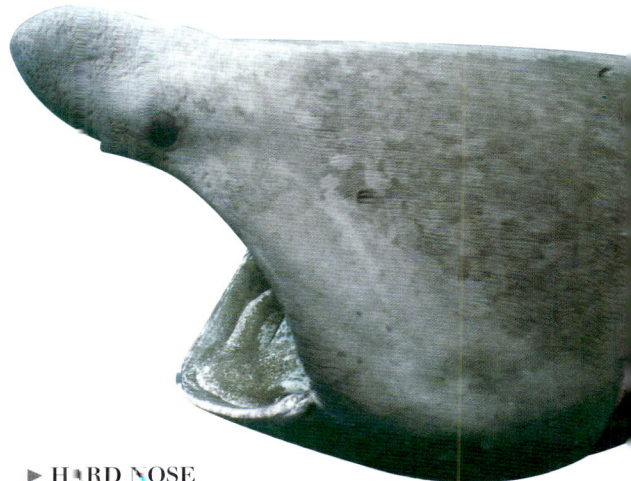

▶ HARD NOSE

The shark pictured above is an adult basking shark. At birth, this shark has a strange, hooked nose, like that of an elephant. When the basking shark starts to grow, the cartilage in its snout gradually straightens.

397

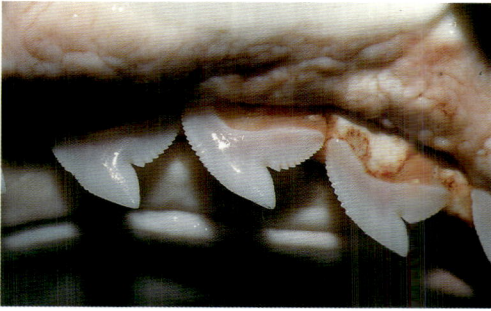

Tough Teeth

A shark species can be identified by the shape of its teeth alone. Each species has its own distinctive shape, designed for the type of food it eats. Some have sharp, spiky teeth that can hold on to slippery fish and squid. Others have broad, grinding teeth that can crack open shellfish. The teeth of some species of shark change as they get older and hunt different prey. Although sharks lose their teeth regularly, the teeth are always replaced. Behind each row of teeth lie more rows. If a front tooth is dislodged, an extra tooth simply moves forward to take its place.

▲ SHARK SAW

The teeth of a tiger shark are shaped like the letter L. They can saw through skin, muscle and bone, and can even crack open the hard shell of a sea turtle. A tiger shark eats its prey by biting hard and shaking its head from side to side, slicing into its food like a chain saw.

▼ AWESOME JAWS

When it is about to grab its prey, a sandtiger shark opens and extends its awesome jaws. The rows of spiky teeth inside are perfect for grabbing and holding slippery fish and squid. Once caught, the prey is swallowed whole.

Sandtiger shark
(Eugomphodus taurus)

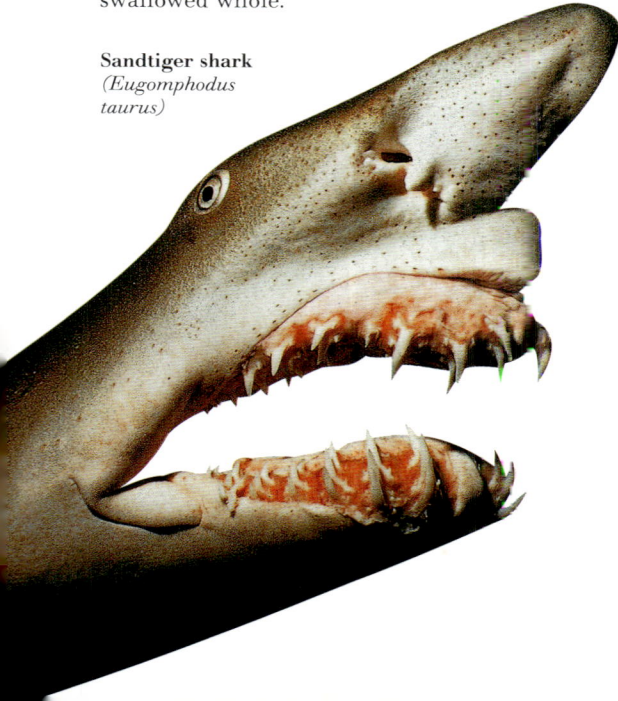

▲ NEEDLE POINT

This 2m/6½ft long leopard shark (*Triakis semifasciata*) has rows of small, needle-sharp teeth. Although it is thought to be harmless, in 1955 a leopard shark sunk its tiny teeth into a skin diver in Trinidad Bay, California. This was an unprovoked attack and the diver escaped.

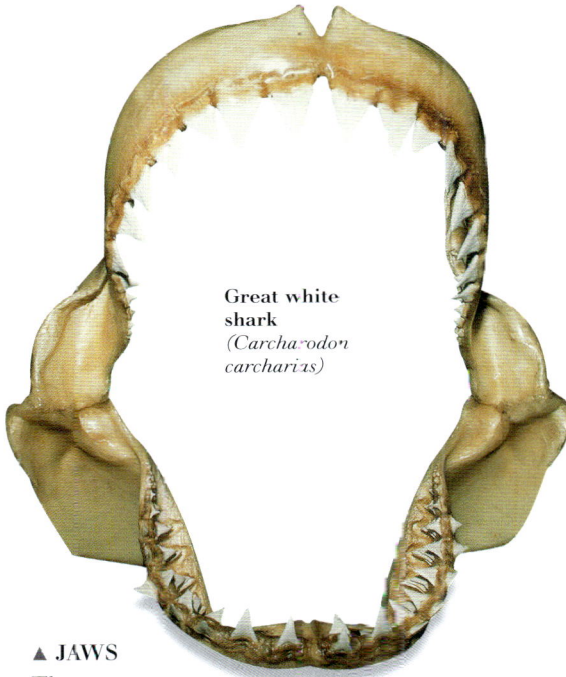

Great white shark
(*Carcharodon carcharias*)

▲ **DUAL SETS OF TEETH**

The Port Jackson shark (*Heterodontus portus jacksoni*) has small, sharp teeth for catching small fish and broad, crushing teeth that can crack open shellfish.

▼ **BIG TEETH**

The cookie-cutter is a small shark, reaching only 40cm/20in long. However, for its body size, it has the biggest teeth of any shark known. It uses them to cut round chunks out of its prey, which includes dolphins, whales and large fish.

▲ **JAWS**

The awesome jaws of a great white shark are filled with two types of teeth. The upper jaw is lined with large, triangular teeth that can slice through flesh. The lower jaw contains long, pointed teeth that are used to hold and slice prey.

Cookie-cutter shark
(*Isistius brasiliensis*)

Shark Man
Ceremonial carvings, such as this one, were used in ritual dances performed in the South Pacific Solomon Islands. These traditional dances were handed down from one dance master to another through many generations. They told of myths in which sharks turned into men and men turned back into sharks again.

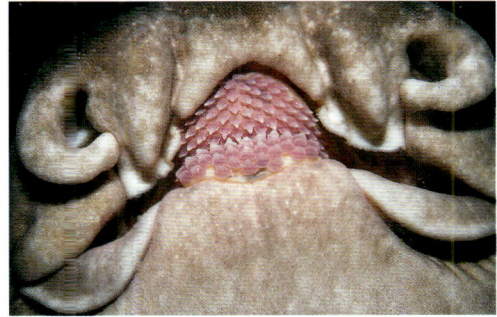

Shark Bodies

Sharks are incredible machines, packed with muscle. Some sharks, such as the great white and mako, can even keep their muscles, gut, brain and eyes warmer than the temperature of the seawater around them. They do this with special blood vessels, which work like a radiator to collect the heat in the blood and send it back into the body. These make muscles more efficient, allowing the sharks to swim faster. They also help these sharks to hunt in seas of different temperatures. Sharks have a huge, oil-filled liver that helps to keep them afloat. However, like an aircraft, they must also move forward in order to stay up. Open ocean sharks must swim all the time, not only to stop them from sinking, but also to breathe. Some sharks can take a rest on the seabed by pumping water over their gills to breathe.

▲ GILL BREATHERS
Like this sixgill shark (*Hexanchus griseus*), most sharks breathe by taking oxygen-rich water into their mouths. The oxygen passes into the blood and the water exits the gill slits.

▲ OCEAN RACER
The shortfin mako shark (*Isurus oxyrinchus*) is the fastest shark. Using special, warm muscles, it can travel at speeds of 35–50kph/22–31mph and catch fast-swimming swordfish.

◀ SUSPENDED ANIMATION
The sandtiger shark (*Eugomphodus taurus*) can hold air in its stomach. The air acts like a life jacket, helping the shark to hover in the water. Sandtiger sharks stay afloat without moving, lurking among rocks and caves.

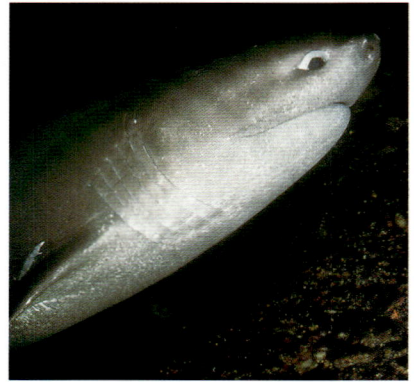

► KEEP MOVING

Like many hunting sharks, the grey reef shark (*Carcharinhus amblyrynchos*) cannot breathe unless it moves forward. The forward motion passes oxygen into its gills. If it stops moving, the shark will drown.

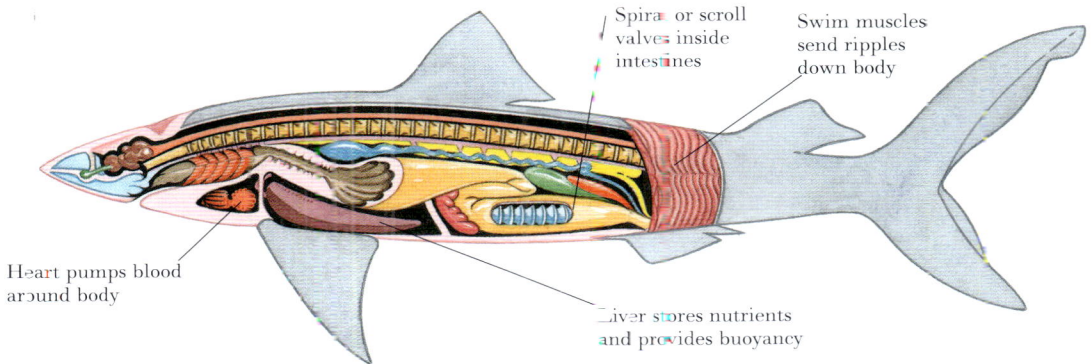

Spiral or scroll valves inside intestines

Swim muscles send ripples down body

Heart pumps blood around body

Liver stores nutrients and provides buoyancy

▲ INSIDE A SHARK

If you could look inside a shark, you would find thick muscles, an enormous liver, an intestine with a special spiral valve and a complicated system of blood vessels that supply the shark's gills.

Did you know? Mako sharks have been seen to leap 6m / 19½ft clear of the water.

◄ ABLE TO REST

The tawny nurse shark (*Nebrius ferrugineus*) pumps water over its gills by lifting the floor of its mouth. This allows it to rest on the seabed, yet still breathe. Whitetip reef sharks, lemon sharks, catsharks and nursehounds also do this.

401

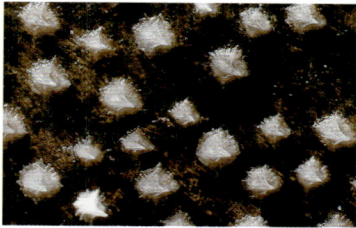
Skin teeth of Greenland shark

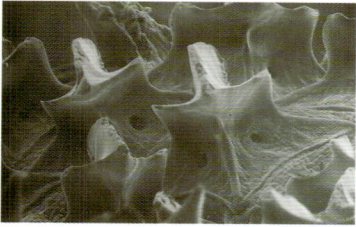
Skin teeth of spiny dogfish

Skin teeth of dusky shark

▲ SKIN TEETH

A shark's skin is covered with tiny skin teeth called dermal denticles. These teeth help to speed the shark through the water by controlling the flow of water over its body.

▶ STREAMLINED SHARK

The upper part of the grey reef shark's tail is slightly larger than the lower. Because of this, the tail's downward movement is so powerful that it balances the lift from the pectoral wings. Scientists believe that this helps the shark to move evenly through the water.

Wings in Water

A shark has two pairs of fins (pectoral and pelvic) that work like a plane's wings, lifting the shark as it moves forward. Its dorsal fins and anal fin stop it from rolling sideways, like the tail fin of an aircraft. A shark moves forward in an S shape by rippling a series of waves down its entire body. These waves increase in size as they reach the shark's tail, helping it to propel the body forward. The shape of the tail can vary from shark to shark, depending on the area of water it inhabits. Sharks that live at the bottom of the sea, such as the nurse shark, tend to have large, flat tails. Sharks that swim in open oceans, such as the tiger shark, usually have slimmer, more curved tails. Both types have a larger upper part to their tail. Sharks that stalk and dash to catch their prey, such as the great white and mako shark, have crescent-shaped tails with top and bottom parts the same size.

▲ SEABED SWIMMERS

Hammerhead sharks have unusually small
pectoral fins, which allow them to swim and
feed close to the seabed. The wings of the
hammer-shaped head give the shark extra lift
in the water and allow it to turn very tightly.
Hammerhead sharks are very adaptable and
skilful hunters.

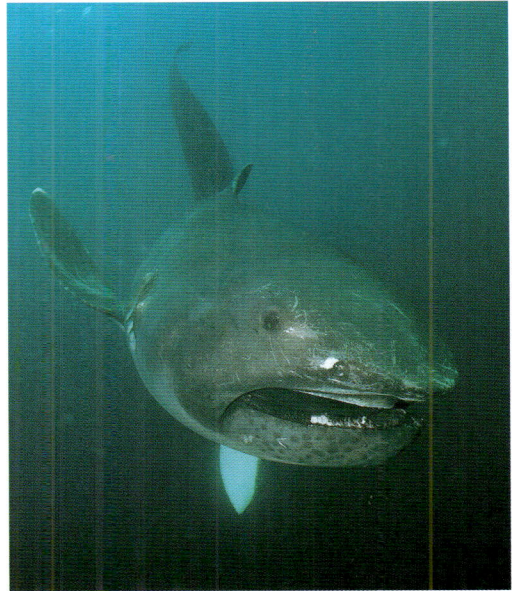

▲ DEEP-SEA GIANT

The megamouth shark (*Megachasma pelagios*)
was only discovered in 1976. It lives in deep
water and swims very slowly. Megamouth does
not chase anything. It eats deep-sea shrimp
filtered through its gills.

▲ OCEAN TRAVELLER

The blue shark (*Prionace glauca*) has long
pectoral fins that help it to sail through the
sea like a glider plane, making long journeys
easy. It swims to the surface, then glides
effortlessly to the depths before swimming
back to the surface again.

▲ OCEAN CRUISER

The oceanic whitetip shark (*Carcharhinus
longimanus*) swims in the open oceans and is
often present at the scene of sea disasters. It is
a very distinctive shark, and can be easily
recognized by its dorsal and pectoral fins,
which are shaped like rounded garden spades.

Brain and Senses

A shark's brain is small for its size, but its senses are highly developed. Sharks see well, and see in colour. They can also recognize shapes. Just as amazing are a different range of senses that allow sharks to pick up sounds and vibrations from kilometres/ miles around. They can detect changes in the ocean currents, recognize smells and follow the trail of an odour right back to its source. Some species have shiny plates at the backs of their eyes that collect light to help them see as they dive to deep, dark water. They also have membranes of dark colour that they draw across the shiny plates to avoid being dazzled by the light when they return to the surface. Sharks even have special nerves in their noses that can detect minute electrical fields, such as those produced by the muscles of their prey.

▲ ELECTRICAL SENSE
Like all sharks, sandtiger sharks have tiny pits in their snouts, known as the ampullae of Lorenzini. Inside these pits are special nerves. These help the shark to find food by detecting minute electrical fields in the muscles of its prey.

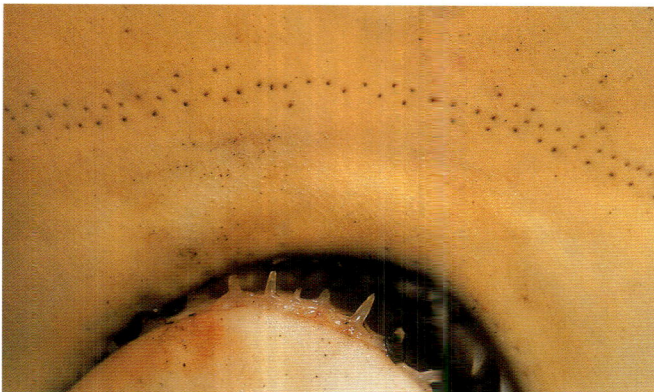

◄ PREY DETECTOR
In a hammerhead shark the special pits that can sense electrical fields in its prey are spread across the hammer of the shark's head, helping it to scan for prey across a wide area. The hammerhead searches for food by sweeping its head from side to side, rather as if using a metal detector. It can find any prey buried in the sand below.

◄ SIGHT, SMELL AND SOUND

The nostrils of the hammerhead shark are positioned wide apart on its head. This gives the shark "stereo smelling" with which it can more easily track odours to their source. But, because its eyes are at the ends of its hammer, it must turn its head from side to side in order to see forward.

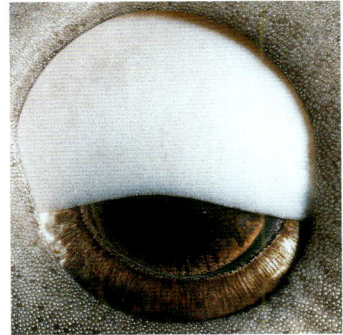

▲ EYE PROTECTION

When a shark bites, its eyes can easily be injured by the victim's teeth, spines or claws. To prevent this, sharks, such as this tiger shark, have a special membrane (sheath) that slides down across the eye during the attack.

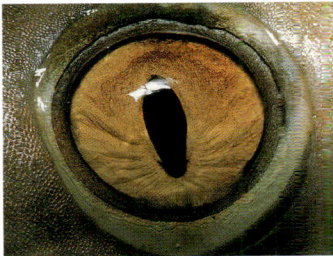

Scalloped
hammerhead shark
(*Sphyrna lewini*)

Eye of blacktip reef shark
(*Carcharhinus melanopterus*)

Eye of bluntnose sixgill shark
(*Hexanchus griseus*)

◄ DEEP AND SHALLOW

The blacktip reef shark has a small eye with a narrow, vertical slit. This type of eye is often found in shallow-water sharks. Sharks that swim in deeper waters, such as the sixgill shark, tend to have large, round pupils.

Did you know?
Sharks find their way through mazes as fast as rabbits.

Shark Callers

On the islands of the South-west Pacific, sharks are the islanders' gods. To test their manhood, young shark callers attract sharks by shaking a coconut rattle under the water. Sensing the vibrations, a shark will swim close to the canoe. It is then wrestled into the boat, and its meat divided among the villagers as a gift from the gods.

Focus on the Blue

The blue shark is an open ocean hunter. Continually looking for food, it can pick up the sounds and vibrations of a struggling fish from over 1km/½ mile away. From 500m/1,640ft, it can smell blood and other body fluids in the water. As it gets closer, the shark can sense changes in the water that help it locate moving prey. Finally, vision takes over. First, only movements are seen, but then the prey itself. As the blue shark closes in for the kill it pulls down its eye protectors and swims blind. Its electrical sensors then lead it to its prey.

2 Smells, sounds, vibrations and water movements attract the blue shark. The movements made by a school of jack mackerel will initially lead the shark to them. It then uses its sight to find an easy target.

1 When hunting, the blue shark uses all its senses constantly to search the ocean ahead for prey. It will also watch the behaviour of other blue sharks in the water, sometimes joining them to hunt in packs.

Shark Hunt

3 Sharp eyesight, quick reactions and an ability to speed through the water all help the blue shark to chase its chosen target. In an attempt to escape, this group of mackerel fish will dart all over the place, then crowd close together to confuse the pursuing shark.

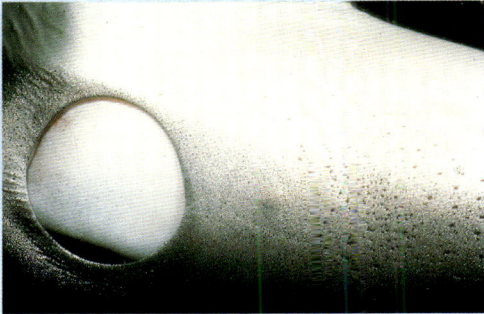

4 As the blue shark closes in to grab its target, a protective membrane covers each eye. At this stage the shark is swimming blind and relies on the electrical sensors in its snout to guide it to its prey. These home in on the electrical field made by the fish's muscles, leading the shark for the last few centimetres.

5 As the shark bites, it extends its jaws and impales its prey on the teeth of the lower jaw. Next, the upper jaw teeth come into action, clamping down on the fish. The shark then removes its lower jaw teeth from the prey and pushes them forward to pull the fish back into its mouth. The prey is then swallowed by the shark.

Feeding

Sharks catch a variety of foods, eating
whatever they can find in their area.
Most sharks eat bony fish and squid, but
they can be cannibalistic (eat each
other). They often feed on other smaller
sharks, sometimes even on their own
species. Some sharks prefer particular
kinds of food. Hammerheads like sting
rays, while tiger sharks will crunch a sea
turtle's shell for the meat inside. Shortfin
mako sharks hunt bluefish and swordfish.
Great white sharks eat fish, but as they
get older will also hunt seals and sea
lions. Sharks will scavenge (feed on dead
animals) whenever they can. The bodies
of dead whales are food for many sharks
that swim in open waters, including
tigers, blues and oceanic whitetips.

▲ **FEEDING FRENZY**
Large quantities of food will excite
grey reef sharks, sending them into a
feeding frenzy. When divers hand out
food, the sharks will circle with interest,
until one darts forward for the first bite.
Other sharks quickly follow, grabbing at
the food until they seem out of control.

▲ **FOREVER EATING**
A large shoal of mating squid will send blue
sharks into a frenzy. The sharks feed until
full, then empty their stomachs to start again.

▲ **FISH BALL**
A group of sharks will often herd shoals of fish
into a tight ball. The sharks will then pick off
fish from the outside of the ball, one by one.

▶ BITE A BROTHER

Sharks do not look after their relatives. Big sharks will often eat smaller sharks, and sharks that swim side-by-side in the same school will often take a nip out of each other. The remains caught on a fishing line of this blacktip shark show that it has been eaten by a large bull shark.

Did you know? The great white shark sometimes eats crabs and lobsters.

◀ PERSONAL TASTE

Tiger sharks are well known as the sharks that will eat not just living things, such as fish, or dead animals floating in the sea. Tiger sharks have been known to eat coal, rubber tyres (tires) and clothes. They are found all over the world and grow to a length of 5.5m/18ft. Not surprisingly, tiger sharks have been known to try eating humans.

▼ BITE-SIZE CHUNKS

The cookie-cutter shark feeds by cutting chunks out of whales and dolphins, such as this spinner dolphin. The shark uses its mouth like a clamp, attaching itself to its victim. It then bites with its razor-sharp teeth and swivels to twist off a circle of flesh.

Spinner dolphin
(*Stenella longirostris*)

▲ OPPORTUNISTS

Sharks will often follow fishing boats, looking for a free meal. This silvertip shark is eating pieces of tuna that have been thrown overboard.

409

Focus on

1 Huge groups of albatrosses nest on the ground close to the shore of Hawaiian islands, including the island of Laysan. The birds in each group breed, nest and hatch their babies at the same time. When it is time, the young birds all take their first flight within days of each other.

Sharks can be found wherever there is food in or near the sea. Tiger sharks are rarely seen around some Hawaiian islands in the Pacific Ocean until the islands' young seabirds start to fly. Then the sharks arrive. Any birds that fall into the sea are quickly eaten. The waters are too shallow for the sharks to attack from behind and below as most sharks do. Instead, the sharks leap clear of the surface, then drag the birds underwater to drown and eat them. Sharks arrive for their island feast at the same time each year. How they remember to do so is yet to be explained.

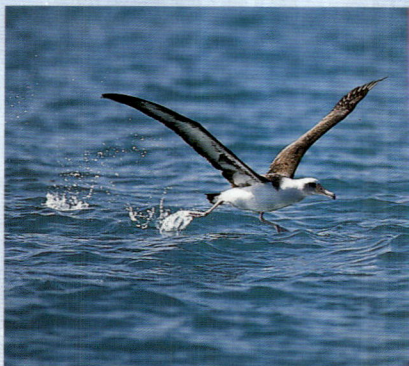

2 When ready to fly, a baby bird practises by flapping its wings in the face of the islands' fierce winds. Eventually, the baby must make its first real flight over the ocean. When it does so, the tiger sharks are waiting in the water below.

3 Tiger sharks patrol the clear, shallow waters close to the albatross nests. Their dark shapes can be seen clearly against the sandy sea floor. Every now and again, a tiger shark's triangular dorsal fin and the tip of its tail can be seen breaking the water's surface.

Tiger Sharks

4 Any baby bird that dips into the sea is prey for the waiting tiger shark. At first, the shark tries its usual attack, from below and behind. However, in the shallow waters the shark cannot make a full attack. Rather than hitting its prey at force, the shark just pushes the bird away on the wave made by its snout.

5 After failing to catch a meal, the shark soon realizes its mistake and tries another approach. Its next style of attack is to shoot across the surface of the water, slamming into its target with its mouth wide open. This technique seems to be more successful and the shark usually catches the bird.

6 The shark then attempts to drag the bird below the surface to crown it. If a bird is pushed ahead on the shark's bow wave, it will bravely peck at its attacker's broad snout and, sometimes, may even escape. Some birds also manage to wriggle free as the shark grapples with them underwater.

7 Many albatross babies do not manage to escape a shark attack. They are grabbed by the sharks and drowned. Inside the tiger shark's jaws are rows of sharp teeth that can slice into a bird's body like a saw. Sometimes the tiger shark tears off the bird's wings and leaves them aside to eat the body whole.

Filter Feeders

Some of the biggest fish in the sea eat some of the smallest living things there. Giant species, such as the whale shark and basking shark, use their gill rakers to comb plankton (tiny animals and plants) from the water. In the same way as hunting sharks, they use their sharp senses to track down huge areas of food. Whale sharks are often seen near coral reefs, where, at certain times of the year, large amounts of animal plankton can be found. Basking sharks often swim in the area between ocean currents, feeding on plankton that gathers on the boundary. Whale and basking sharks swim in the upper layers of the sea. The giant megamouth shark lives deeper down, sieving out the shrimp that live in the middle layers of the ocean.

▲ FOOD CHAIN
Eggs and sperm released on the same night by the corals of the Ningaloo Reef in Australia are eaten by the larvae (young) of crabs and lobsters. The larvae are eaten by fish and krill. The fish and krill, in turn, become food for the hungry whale sharks that swim off the coral reefs.

◄ WHALE OF A FEAST
Exactly two weeks after the coral has spawned at Ningaloo, the whale sharks appear. By this time, each creature, from the smallest larvae to the reef's fish and krill, will have fed upon the coral's rich food. Each night, the whale sharks swim with their huge mouths wide open, scooping up food which they sieve from the sea's surface.

▲ BIG GULP

The basking shark swims slowly, funnelling food-filled water into its great mouth. In one hour, it can filter 7,000 litres/1,850 gallons of seawater. When enough food has been trapped, the shark closes its mouth and swallows with one gulp.

▲ COLD WATER SKIMMERS

The basking shark has gill slits that almost encircle its gigantic body. These are used to filter food, such as shellfish larvae and fish eggs, from the water. The shark passes water through its gill chamber, where enormous gill rakers comb the food from the water.

▲ BIG MOUTH

Patrolling the middle waters of the deep, the megamouth shark scoops up tiny shrimp as they cross its path. Since this shark's discovery in 1976, a further 13 examples have been discovered and some of these have been examined by scientists.

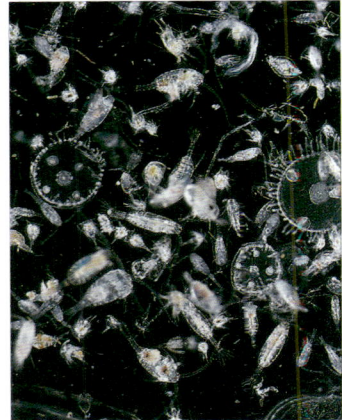

▲ PLANKTON

Plankton is made up of tiny plants and animals that float together in huge clouds on and just below the sea's surface. Both animal and plant plankton are eaten by the basking shark.

413

Keep in Line

No shark is alone for long. Sooner or later, one shark will come across another, including those of its own kind. In order to reduce the risk of fights and injury, sharks talk to each other, not with sound, but with body language. Sharks have a clear pecking order. The bigger the shark, the more important it is. Not surprisingly, small sharks tend to keep out of the way of larger ones. Many species use a sign that tells others to keep their distance. They arch their back, point their pectoral fins down and swim stiffly. If this doesn't work, the offending shark will be put in its place with a swift bite to the sides or head. Bite marks along its gill slits can be a sign that a shark has stepped out of line and been told firmly to watch out.

▲ GREAT WHITE CHUMS
Once great white sharks were thought to travel alone, but it is now known that some journey in pairs or small groups. Some sharks that have been identified by scientists will appear repeatedly at favourite sites, such as California's Farallon Islands, 48km/30 miles off the coast of San Francisco. There they lie in wait for seals.

Did you know? Some great whites return to the same place every year.

◄ BED FELLOWS
Sharks, like these whitetip reef sharks, will snooze alongside each other on the seabed. They search for a safe place to rest below overhanging rocks and coral, where, as fights rarely break out, they seem to tolerate each other. The sharks remain here until dusk, when they separate to hunt.

◄ PECKING ORDER

This grey reef shark has swum too close to another, larger shark and has been bitten on its gill slits as a punishment. The marks on its skin show that its attacker raked the teeth of its lower jaw across the sensitive skin of the grey reef's gill slits. A shark's injuries heal rapidly, so this unfortunate victim will recover quickly from its wounds.

► REEF SHARK GANGS

Sharks have their own personal space. As they patrol the edge of a reef, schools of blacktip reef sharks will tell others that they are too close by moving their jaws or opening their mouths. During feeding, order sometimes breaks down and a shark might be injured in the frenzy.

◄ SHARK SCHOOL

Every day schools of scalloped hammerhead sharks gather close to underwater mountains in the Pacific Ocean. They do not feed, even though they come across shoals of fish that would normally be food. Instead, they swim repeatedly up and down, as though taking a rest.

415

Focus on

By day, scalloped hammerhead sharks swim in large schools around underwater volcanoes in the Pacific, the Gulf of California off Mexico and off the Cocos and Galapagos islands. This species of shark cannot stop swimming or it will drown. Schools are a safe resting place for them. Even sharks have enemies, such as other sharks and killer whales, so there is safety in numbers. In schools, scalloped hammerheads can also find a mate. At night, they separate to hunt. They swim to favourite feeding sites, using their electric sensors to follow magnetic highways made by lava on the seabed.

BAD-TEMPERED SHARKS

The larger a female hammerhead becomes, the less likely she is to get on with her neighbours. Older and larger hammerhead sharks like more space than smaller, younger sharks. In hammerhead schools, the relationship between sharks seems to be controlled by constant displays of threat and small fights.

FEMALES ONLY

The sharks in this huge school of hammerheads are mainly females. Larger sharks swim in the centre and smaller sharks on the outside. Large sharks dominate the group, choosing the best positions in which to swim. Not only is the middle safer, but it is also the place where male sharks look for a mate.

Hammerheads

READY FOR A SCRUB

At some gathering sites, such as Cocos Island in the eastern Pacific, sharks drop out of the school and swoop down to cleaning stations close to the reef. From the reef, butterfly fish dart out to eat the dead skin and irritating parasites that cling to the outside of the shark's body.

BODY LANGUAGE

Larger sharks within a school perform strange movements and dances to keep smaller sharks in their place. At the end of the movement, a large shark may nip a smaller one on the back of the head.

STRANGE HEAD

The scalloped hammerhead is so named because of the groove at the front of its head, which gives it a scalloped (scooped out) appearance. The black tips on the underside of its pectoral fins are another way of identifying this particular shark.

Courtship and Mating

Male sharks find female sharks by their smell. The female gives off odours that drift in the currents of the sea, attracting every male shark within smelling distance. The males follow her closely, until one grabs hold of a pectoral fin with his mouth and hangs on tightly in preparation for mating. Fortunately, the female has thickened skin on her pectoral fins, which prevents her from being hurt. The male has a pair of claspers (sex organs) one of which he places inside the female's sexual opening. During mating, the male shark shakes occasionally, to make sure that the female accepts his presence. Once he is sure of this, the male will complete his mating with her.

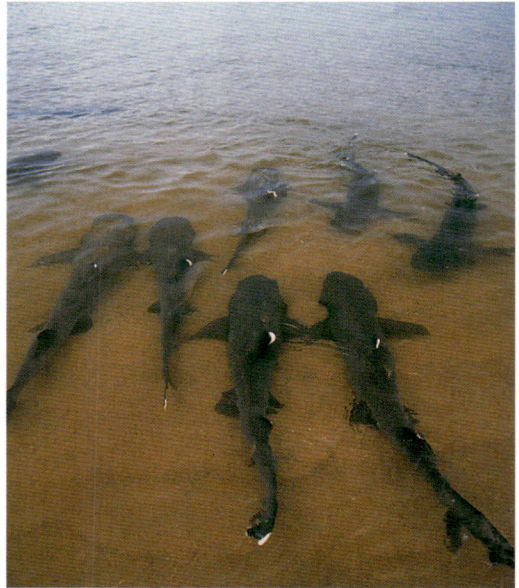

▲ ENGAGEMENT IN THE SHALLOWS
A group of male whitetip sharks will be stimulated by the sexual smell of a female ready to mate. Following her in the shallow waters of a coral reef, the males compete for the female. Eventually, one will win possession by grabbing hold of one of her pectoral fins.

◄ HANGING AROUND
Sandtiger sharks hover in the water at special meeting places, waiting for members of the opposite sex. At these sites, lots of shark teeth are found on the sea floor. It is believed that they fall out during the rough and tumble of courtship and mating.

◄ **THREE IS A CROWD**
Male sharks are usually smaller than females of the same age. Here two males have each seized a female's pectoral fin, but only one male will be able to mate with her.

Did you know?
Only one in ten of nurse shark matings are successful.

► **NURSE SHARK NUPTIALS**
Nurse sharks (*Ginglymostoma cirratum*) travel to traditional mating sites. The male nurse shark grips the female's pectoral fin and arches his body alongside hers. He will then insert his right or left clasper, depending on which pectoral fin he has seized.

▲ **MALE SEX ORGANS**
The claspers (sex organs) of male sharks are pelvic fins that have been adapted for mating. Similar to the penises of mammals, they are used to transfer sperm from the male into the female.

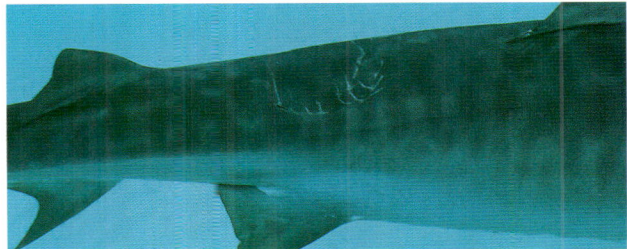

▲ **MATING SCARS**
The courtship and mating of sharks can be a rough affair. Female sharks, like this tiger shark, can be scarred with bite marks made by her mate. However, females have thicker skin than males, which prevents further damage.

Inside and Outside

Sharks bring their young into the world in two ways. Most sharks grow their eggs inside the mother's body and give birth to breathing young called pups. Others lay eggs in which the pup grows outside of the mother's body. Catsharks and nursehound sharks grow their young in cases called mermaid's purses, which they lay outside their bodies. These can sometimes be found washed up on beaches after a storm. Each mating season, catsharks lay up to 20 mermaid's purses. Inside each is one pup. When the case has been laid in the sea, the mother shark does not guard or look after it in any way. Instead, she relies on the tough, leathery case to protect the pup inside.

▲ **EGG WITH A TWIST**
The horn shark (*Heterodontus francisci*) egg case has a spiral-shaped ridge. The mother shark uses her mouth like a screw-driver to twist the case round into the gaps in rocks.

▲ **TIME TO LEAVE**
When it is ready to leave its egg, the baby horn shark uses special scales on its snout and pectoral fins to cut its way out of the tough egg case. On its dorsal fins are tough spines that protect it from the moment it emerges.

Mermaid's Purses
The mermaid is a mythical undersea creature with a woman's body and a fish's tail. In legends, the mermaid lured men to their death with beautiful songs. Catshark and skate cases that are washed up on beaches look like pouches, and are often called mermaid's purses.

50 days   100 days   150 days   200 days

▲ IN THE SAC

In the earliest stages of development, the catshark pup is tiny. It is attached to a huge, yellow yolk sac from which it takes its food. Inside the egg case, the growing catshark pup makes swimming movements, which keep the egg fluids and supply of oxygen fresh. After nine months, the pup emerges, with diagonal stripes that eventually turn into spots as it grows.

▶ SWELL SHARK

The length of time it takes the swell shark (*Cephaloscyllium ventriosum*) pup to grow depends on the temperature of the sea water around it. If warm, it can take just seven months. If cold, it might take ten months. As it emerges, it uses special skin teeth to tear its capsule open.

421

Into the World

Most sharks give birth to fully formed, breathing pups. However, pups grow in many different ways. Baby nurse and whale sharks start their lives in small capsules. The pups then hatch from the capsules inside their mother's body, where they continue to grow before being born. Other shark pups, such as blue sharks, also grow inside their mothers, in a womb. A sandtiger shark might have just two pups, but a blue shark can grow up to 135 at one time. The length of time it takes a pup to grow also varies. Nurse sharks take just five months, but frilled sharks take two years. Some pups feed on unfertilized eggs inside the womb. Baby sandtiger sharks eat each other.

Piked dogfish
(Squalus acanthius)

▲ DOGFISH YOLK SAC

Up to 12 piked dogfish pups can grow inside one mother. At first, all the pups are enclosed in one capsule that breaks after six months. Each pup then feeds off its own yolk sac until it is born three months later.

▶ RESTING

When birth is near, a pregnant whitetip reef shark will rest in a protective area. This pregnant shark is resting on rocks near Cocos Island in the Pacific. Inside her womb, she may develop up to five pups. Each will be fed by a placenta attached to the womb wall. The pups are born after five months.

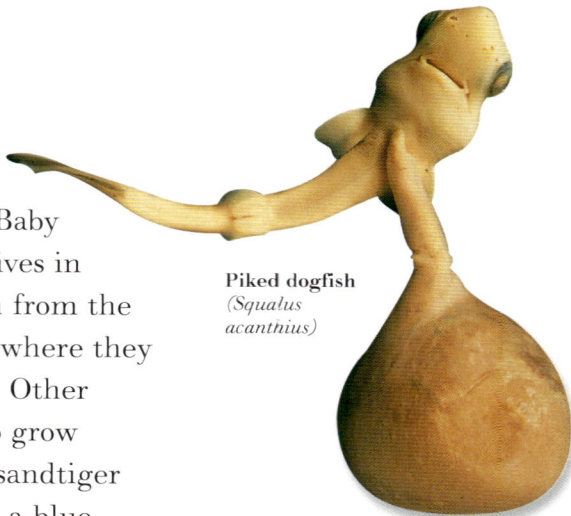

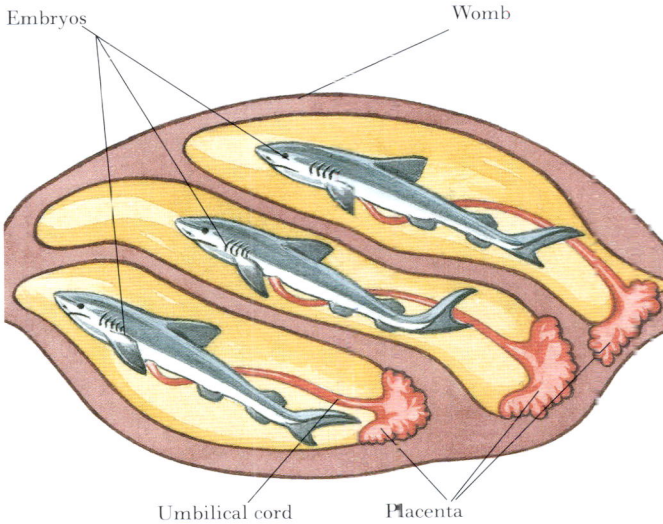

Embryos   Womb

Umbilical cord   Placenta

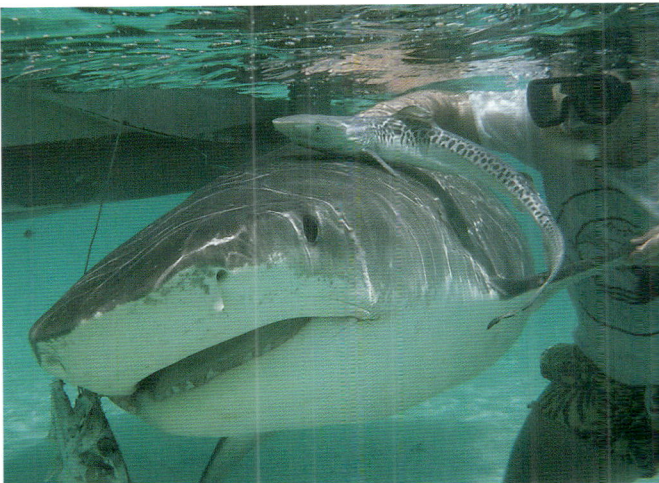

▲ WOMB MATES

In some species of shark, such as the whaler shark, embryos develop inside the pregnant female as they do in mammals. At first, each embryo has its own supply of food in a yolk sac, but when this is used up, its sac turns into a placenta that attaches itself to the wall of the womb. Nutrients and oxygen pass directly from the mother across the placenta and along the umbilical cord to its own body. Waste products go the other way.

▲ BIG BELLIES

Some baby sharks will eat unfertilized eggs in their mothers' wombs. They eat so much so fast their stomachs become swollen. These baby shortfin mako sharks, caught off the coast of South Africa, have gorged themselves on unfertilized eggs, filling their tiny stomachs.

◀ STRIPED SHARK

Safe inside its mother, this baby tiger shark will have fed on both the nutrients from its yolk sac, and on a fluid produced by the wall of the womb. The pattern of blotches on the newborn baby's skin will form stripes, which will gradually fade as it gets older.

423

Focus on Lemon

A year after mating, pregnant lemon sharks arrive at Bimini Island in the Atlantic Ocean. Here, they give birth to their pups in the island's shallow lagoon where males do not enter. An adult male is quite likely to eat a smaller shark, even one of its own kind. In many species of shark, pregnant female sharks leave the males and swim to safer nursery areas to give birth. Some scientists even believe that females lose their appetite at pupping time, to avoid eating their own young. After birth, however, the lemon shark pups live on their own.

1 By pumping sea water over her gills, a pregnant lemon shark (*Negaprion brevirostris*) can breathe and rest on the seabed at Bimini Island. She gives birth on the sandy lagoon floor to the pups that have developed inside her for a year.

2 Baby lemon sharks are born tail first. There might be five to17 pups in a mother's litter (family). Each pup is about 60cm/24in long. After her litter is born, a female lemon shark will not be able to mate again straight away. Instead, she will rest for a year.

Shark Birth

3 A female lemon shark can give birth to her pups as she swims slowly through the shallows. The pups are still attached to the umbilical cord when born, but a sharp tug soon releases them. The small remora fish that follow the shark everywhere will feast on the afterbirth.

4 After birth, a baby lemon shark makes for the safety of the mangroves at the edge of the lagoon. It spends the first few years of its life in a strip of mangrove 40m/131ft wide and 400m/1,312ft long feeding on small fish, worms and shellfish, taking care to avoid larger sharks. Its home overlaps the territory of other young sharks.

5 To avoid being eaten, young lemon sharks gather with others of the same size. Each group patrols its own section of the lagoon at Bimini. This young lemon shark is about one year old. When it is seven or eight, it will leave the safety of the lagoon and head for the open reefs outside.

Look in any Ocean

Sharks live throughout the world's oceans and seas and at all
depths. Some sharks, such as bull sharks, even swim in rivers
and lakes. Whale, reef and nurse sharks are all tropical species
that prefer warm waters. Temperate-water sharks, such as the
mako, horn and basking sharks, live in water that is
10–20°C/50–68°F. Cold-water sharks often live in very
deep water. The Portuguese shark, frilled shark,
and goblin shark are all cold water sharks. A few
species will swim in extremely cold waters,
such as the Greenland shark which
braves the icy water around
the Arctic Circle.

NORTH
AMERICA

ATLANTIC
OCEAN

PACIFIC
OCEAN

SOUTH
AMERICA

▶ SWIMMING POOLS
This map shows the main parts of the world's
oceans in which different kinds of sharks live. The
key beneath the map shows which sharks live where.

▶ OCEAN WANDERER
The oceanic whitetip shark
swims the world's deep, open
oceans, in tropical and sub-
tropical waters. It is also one
of the first sharks to appear
at shipwrecks.

KEY

whale shark
basking shark
bull shark
tiger shark
whitetip shark
Greenland shark
great white shark

◀ ISLAND LIVING
The Galapagos shark
(*Carcharhinus galapagensis*)
swims in the waters of the
Galapagos islands, on the
Equator. It also swims around
tropical islands in the Pacific,
Atlantic and Indian oceans.

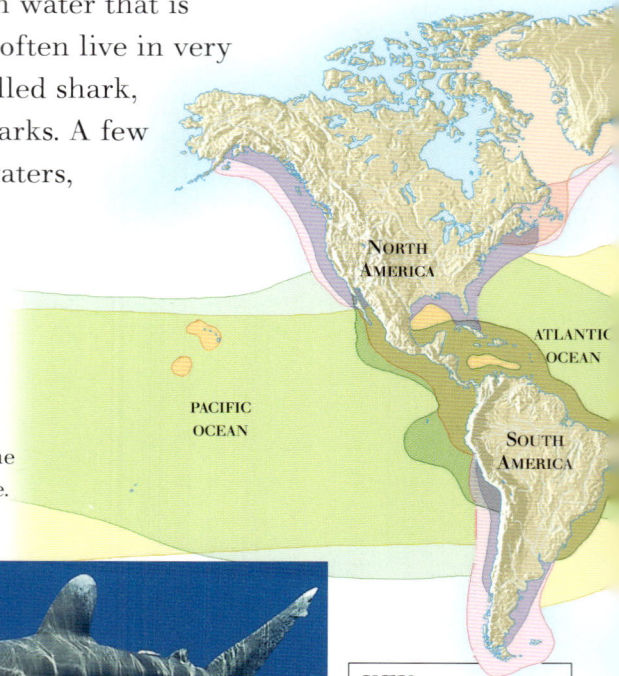

◀ UNDER THE ICE

The Greenland shark (*Somniosus microcephalus*) is the only shark known to survive under polar ice in the North Atlantic seas. It has a luminous parasite attached to each eye that attracts prey to the area around its mouth.

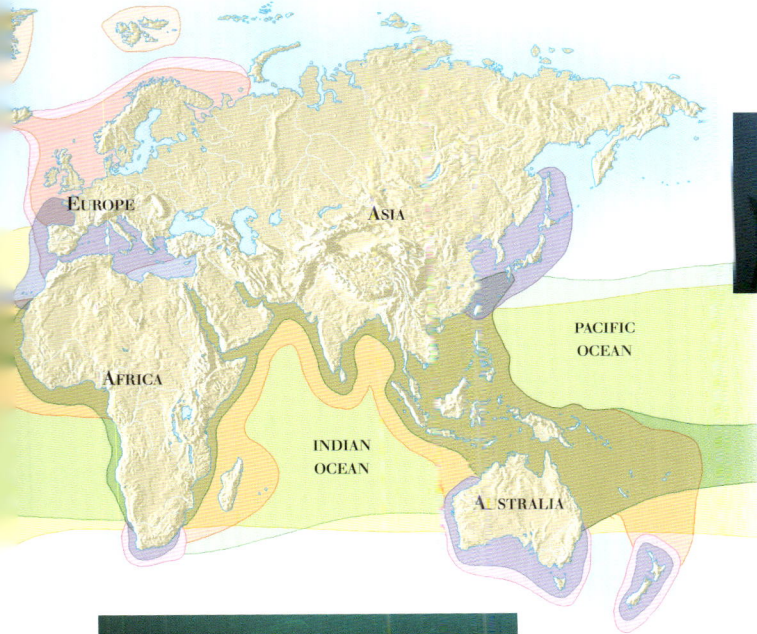

▲ TEMPERATE PREDATOR

The great white shark lives in temperate, sub-tropical and tropical seas, including the Mediterranean. It usually swims in coastal waters rather than the open sea.

▲ TIGER OF THE SEAS

The tiger shark swims in mainly tropical and warm temperate waters, both in open ocean and close to shore. Tiger sharks have been seen off Morocco and the Canary Islands.

◀ REEF SHARK

The blacktip reef shark patrols reefs in the Indian and Pacific oceans. It also lives in the Mediterranean and Red Sea and as far west as the seas off Tunisia, in North Africa.

427

Upwardly Mobile

Not all sharks travel far afield. Some prefer to stay close to home, swimming in only one small area. Others have a daily routine, spending the day in deep waters, but moving closer to shore to feed at night. A few deep sea sharks make a different daily journey, spending the day in the deep and rising to the surface to feed at night. Some sharks travel vast distances, crossing oceans. This has only recently been discovered with the tagging of sharks. Rather than killing sharks when they catch them, scientists and fishermen now give them a special tag. Each tag has its own number, which identifies the shark. So, when the shark is caught again, scientists can see how much it has grown and also how far it has travelled.

Sandbar shark
(Carcharinus plumbeus)

▲ INTO THE GULF

Atlantic sandbar sharks can travel over 3,000km/1,865 miles, from the Atlantic coastline of the United States to the coast of Mexico. These sharks grow incredibly slowly, only about 3cm/1⅛in a year, not reaching adulthood until 30.

◀ GIVEN A NAME

This tiger shark has been tagged (marked) by scientists and is being released back into the sea. Tagging has shown that tiger sharks travel great distances across oceans. Previously, people had believed that they stayed in one place.

◄ **OCEAN MIGRATOR**
Female blue sharks in the North Atlantic go on a very long migration. They circle the Atlantic Ocean, mating off North America and then giving birth near Spain and Portugal at the end of their journey.

► **EPIC JOURNEY**
Female blue sharks travel from North America to Europe where they give birth. Then they turn back towards America. They travel at about 40km/25 miles per day. A shark swimming fast might cover the round trip of 15,000km/9,400 miles in 15 months.

▼ **FOLLOW THE TEMPERATURE**
Shortfin mako sharks travel into the North Atlantic, but rarely swim the whole way across. They like to swim in an exact temperature of 17–22°C/ 63–72°F. They follow thermal water corridors through the ocean to winter in the Sargasso Sea.

Shortfin mako shark
(*Isurus oxyrinchus*)

► **DOUBLE BACK**
Migrating mako sharks travel to the middle of the Atlantic Ocean and then turn back towards America. The sharks do not go further because from the middle of the ocean to Europe the water is not the temperature they prefer to swim in.

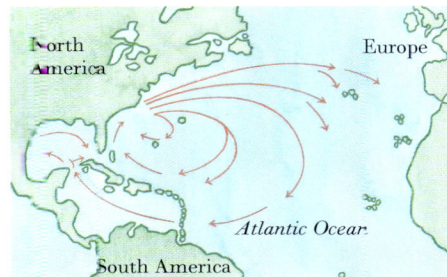

429

Frilled shark
(Chlamydoselachus anguineus)

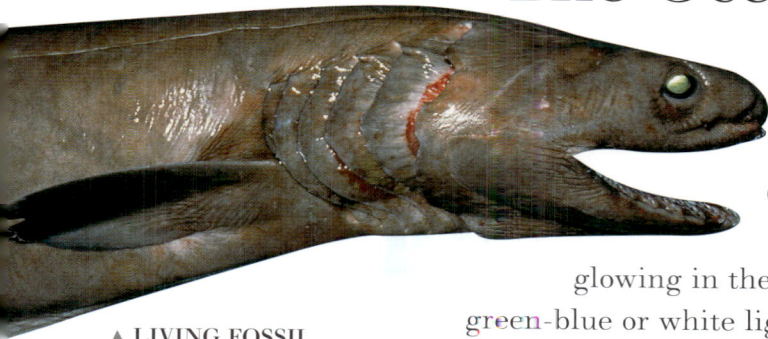

The Ocean Depths

Many sharks are rarely seen because they live in the darkness of the deep. Catsharks and dogfish live in these gloomy waters, glowing in the dark with a luminous green-blue or white light. Some of these species travel and hunt in packs, following their prey to the surface at night, returning into the depths by day. Most of the world's smallest sharks live here. Pygmy and dwarf sharks, no bigger than a cigar, travel up and down the ocean for several kilometres/miles each day. On the deep-sea floor are such enormous sharks as the sixgill, sevengill and sleeper sharks. These eat the remains of food that sinks down from the sea's surface. Many deep-sea sharks look primitive, but strangest of all are the frilled and horned goblin sharks. These look like the fossilized sharks that swam the seas 150 million years ago.

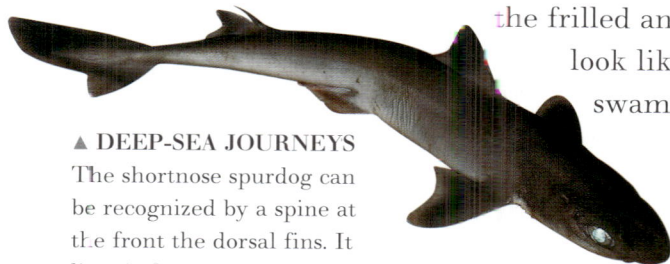

▲ LIVING FOSSIL

The frilled shark is the only shark shaped like an eel. It has six feathery gill slits, 300 tiny, three-pointed teeth and a large pair of eyes. Instead of a backbone, it has a firm, but flexible rod of cartilage. These features tell us that the frilled shark resembles sharks that lived in the oceans millions of years ago.

▲ DEEP-SEA JOURNEYS

The shortnose spurdog can be recognized by a spine at the front the dorsal fins. It lives in large packs made up of thousands of sharks. It swims at depths of 800m/2,625ft in the northern Atlantic and Pacific oceans. Seasonally, the packs make a daily migration, from north to south and from coastal to deeper waters.

Shortnose spurdog
(Squalus megalops)

▼ DEEPEST OF THE DEEP

The Portuguese dogfish holds the record for living in the deepest waters. One was caught 2,718m/8,917ft below the sea's surface. At this depth, the water temperature is no higher than a chilly 5–6°C/41–42.8°F.

Portuguese dogfish
(Centroscymnus coelolepis)

◀ **SIXGILL SLITS**

Most modern sharks have five gill slits, but primitive sharks, such as bluntnose sixgill sharks (*Hexanchus griseus*), have more. These sharks are found at huge depths around the world. They have evolved (developed) slowly, and still have the features of sharks that lived millions of years ago.

▼ **SEVENGILL SLITS**

Broadnose sevengill sharks have seven gill slits. They have primitive, sharp teeth that look like tiny combs. They use these to slice up ratfish, small sharks and mackerel. Because some of their prey live near the surface, sevengill sharks travel to the sea's surface to hunt at night.

Broadnose sevengill shark
(*Notorynchus cepedianus*)

Did you know? Many deep-sea sharks have light-organs on their bodies.

Velvet belly
(*Etmopterus spinax*)

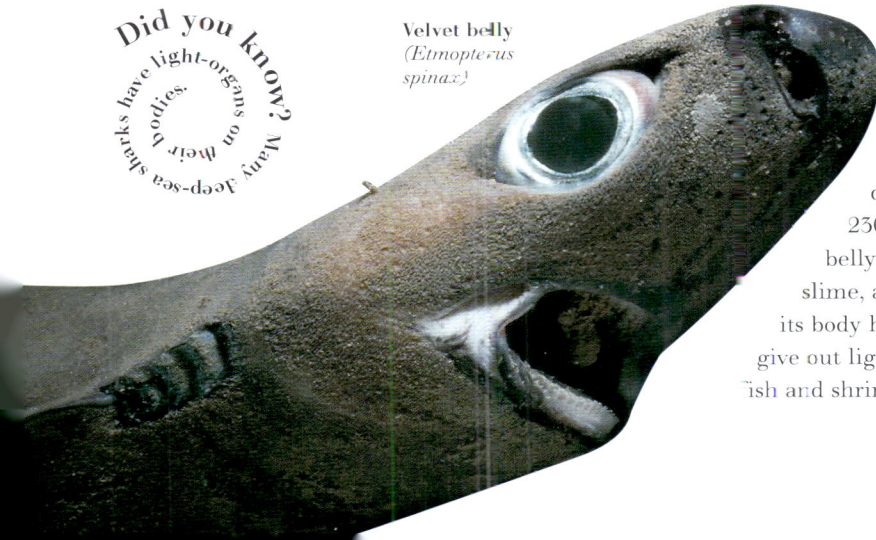

◀ **SLIMY COAT**

The velvet belly is 66cm/26in long. It lives in the Atlantic and Mediterranean, at depths of 70–2,000m/ 230–6,562ft. The velvet belly is covered with luminous slime, and the underside of its body has special organs that give out light. It feeds on deep-sea fish and shrimp.

431

Freshwater Sharks

Although most sharks live in the salt water of the sea, others, such as the bonnethead and sandbar sharks, swim to the mouths of rivers to give birth. There are a few sharks that swim all the way up rivers and some swim into freshwater lakes. Atlantic sharpnose and spadenose sharks, and Ganges and Borneo river sharks swim in fresh water. Bull sharks are the species most often seen in fresh water. How this species' bodies cope with fresh water is not known. A fish that usually swims in salt water needs to find a way of coping with water that is not salt. On entering a river or lake, a fish used to salt water would be expected to absorb water and blow up like a balloon, but bull sharks do not. Somehow, they have found a way to keep the levels of salt in their blood low, so reducing water absorption in fresh water.

▲ HOLY RIVER
Shark attacks on pilgrims bathing in the holy Ganges River in India were once blamed on the Ganges river shark. Instead, they were probably made by the bull shark, which feeds on cremated bodies thrown into the river.

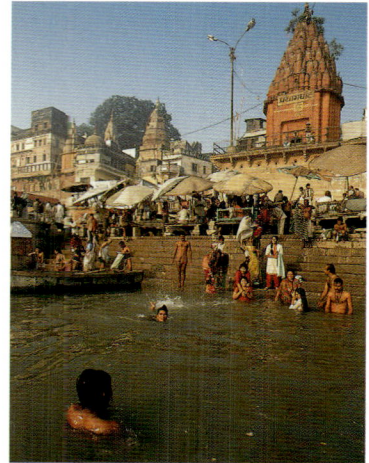

◄ RIVER JOURNEYS
Bull sharks have been seen in the Amazon, Congo and Mississippi rivers and in other tropical rivers and lakes around the world. They gather at the river mouth, where edible rubbish is found during floods. Bull sharks are also sometimes called Zambezi sharks because they make regular journeys up Africa's Zambezi river.

Vishnu

In Hindu religion, the god Vishnu is believed to be the protector of the world. In legendary tales, Vishnu saved the sacred religious texts of India when the whole world was covered in water. This Indian picture shows him emerging from the mouth of a monstrous fish, probably a shark.

▲ KEYS SWIMMER

This bonnethead shark (*Sphyma tiburo*) lives near river mouths in the Florida Keys, in the South-east of the United States.

► BORN-AGAIN SHARK

The Borneo river shark (*Glyphis*) was believed extinct until one was caught in 1997 by a fisherman in Sabah in South-east Asia. Until then, the only known specimen was 100 years old and displayed in an Austrian museum.

Borneo river shark
(*Glyphis*)

◄ LAKE NICARAGUA

Although they do not live all the time in Lake Nicaragua in Central America, bull sharks (*Carcharhinus leucas*) are also called Nicaragua sharks because they travel between the lake and the Caribbean Sea. It is thought that some female bull sharks swim to the lake in order to give birth to their pups.

433

Life on the Seabed

People once thought that all sharks died unless they kept swimming. This is not true. Many sharks that live close to the sea floor do so without moving for long periods of time. Wobbegong and angel sharks have flattened bodies that help them to lie close to the sea floor. Their skin colour also blends in with their background, hiding them from their prey as they lie in wait. These sharks take in water through a special spiracle (hole) behind their eye to stop their gills becoming clogged with sand. Some sharks that live on the sea floor, such as catsharks and carpet sharks, are not flattened. Whatever their shape, most are camouflaged with spots, stripes or a mottled pattern on their backs.

▲ OCEAN CAMOUFLAGE
Sharks that live near the surface can also camouflage themselves. From above, the great white's dark back blends in with the ocean depths.

▼ SPOTTED ZEBRA
The adult zebra shark (*Stegostoma fasciatum*) has spots instead of zebra stripes. It has stripes on its skin as a pup. These break up into spots as the shark grows. It lives in the Indian and Pacific Oceans.

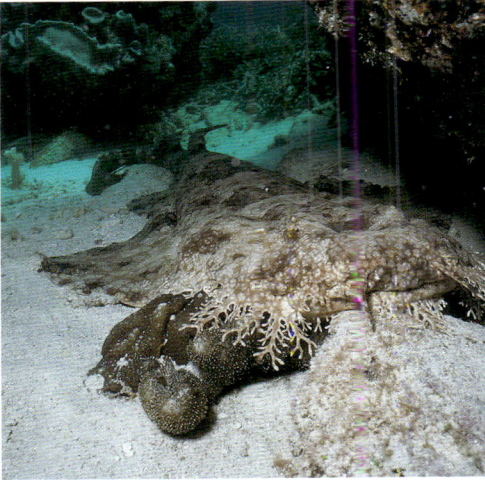

▲ CORAL COPYCAT

This tasselled wobbegong (*Eucrossorhinus dasypogon*) is invisible to its prey. It copies the colour of rock and coral and has a fringe of tassels hanging down below its mouth that looks like seaweed.

▶ SHELLFISH EATER

The leopard shark lives in the shallow waters of the Pacific, along the west coast of the United States. It swims slowly, searching the sea floor for the molluscs that it eats.

▲ AMBUSH EXPERT

The Pacific angel shark (*Squatina californica*) buries itself in the sand and watches for prey. When a fish comes close, the shark rises up and engulfs the fish in its huge mouth. It then sinks back to the seabed, swallowing its food whole.

◀ JAGGED SNOUT

The common sawshark (*Pristiophorus cirratus*) has a long snout with tooth-like barbs along each side. Two sensitive barbels (bristles) hang beneath its snout. It mows through sand and seaweed on the seabed, catching its prey by slashing about with its barbed snout.

The Eight Families

Sharks fall into eight main orders (groups) divided according to different features. The most primitive order, including frilled and sevengill sharks, has more than five gill slits. Dogfish sharks have long, round bodies, and include luminous (glow-in-the-dark) sharks that live in very deep water. The seven or more species of sawshark have a saw-like snout. Angel sharks look like rays and lie hidden on the seabed. Bullhead sharks have spines on both of their dorsal fins, and carpet sharks, such as the wobbegong sharks, have short snouts and bristles on their snouts. Mackerel sharks, with their special, warm muscles, are awesome hunters. These sharks include the great white and mako. The ground sharks include the widest range of all, from catsharks to bull sharks, hammerheads, blue sharks and oceanic whitetips.

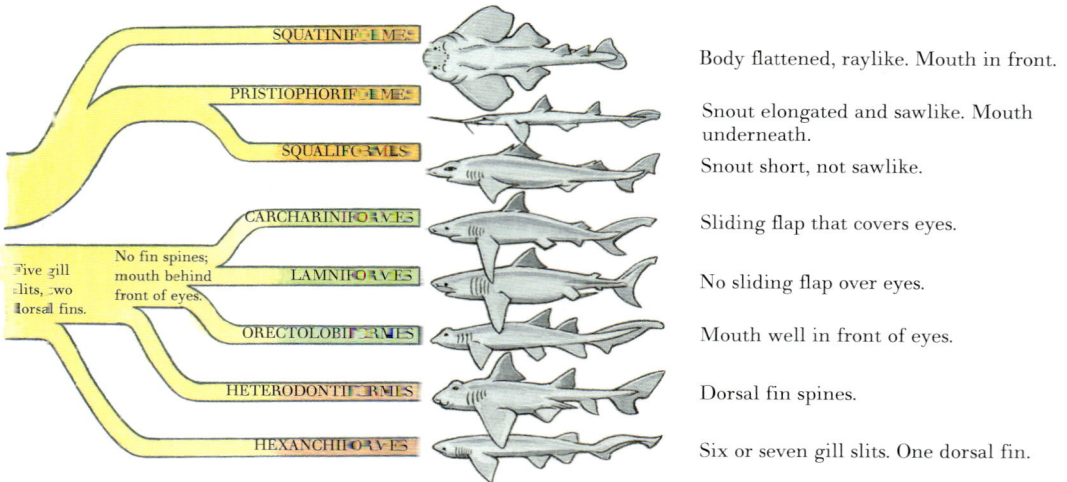

▲ **REEF WALKER**
Two pairs of muscular pectoral fins allow the epaulette shark (*Hemiscyllium ocellatum*) to walk over its tropical reef home. It feeds on the seabed of shallow waters around the Australian reefs.

▼ **TYPES OF SHARKS**
Modern sharks are divided into eight large family groups. These groups are divided into over 30 smaller families, and nearly 400 species. This number will probably rise as more species of shark are discovered.

SQUATINIFORMES		Body flattened, raylike. Mouth in front.
PRISTIOPHORIFORMES		Snout elongated and sawlike. Mouth underneath.
SQUALIFORMES		Snout short, not sawlike.
CARCHARINIFORMES		Sliding flap that covers eyes.
LAMNIFORMES		No sliding flap over eyes.
ORECTOLOBIFORMES		Mouth well in front of eyes.
HETERODONTIFORMES		Dorsal fin spines.
HEXANCHIFORMES		Six or seven gill slits. One dorsal fin.

No fin spines; mouth behind front of eyes.

Five gill slits, two dorsal fins.

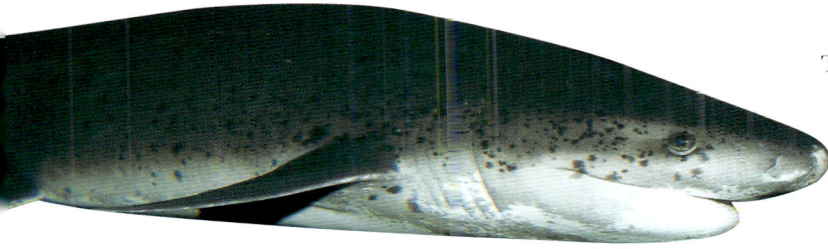

◄ PRIMITIVE SHARK

The broadnose sevengill shark (*Notorynchus cepedianus*) is one of five species of primitive sharks. Each has six or seven gill slits. All swim in deep waters.

▲ GROUND SHARK

The swell shark (*Cephaloscyllium ventriosum*) is a ground shark. It blows up like a balloon by swallowing water and storing it in its stomach. When it is threatened, this amazing shark wedges itself firmly inside the cracks between rocks. It can be very difficult to remove.

Did you know? Pacific Island children ride on nurse sharks' backs.

Food for the sharks

The Carib peoples buried the bodies of their dead relatives by ceremonially putting them into Lake Nicaragua in Central America. Many of the bodies were then eaten by bull sharks in the lake. One chief made a fortune by catching the sharks, slitting them open and removing jewels that had decorated the bodies of the dead. Until he was caught, that is …

► REQUIEM SHARK

The sandbar, or brown, shark (*Carcharhinus plumbeus*) is a requiem shark, meaning "ceremony for the dead". All members of this family are active hunters. They rule tropical seas, hunting fish, squid and sea turtles. They are probably the most modern group of shark.

437

Friends and Enemies

No sharks spend all their time alone. They attract all kinds of hangers-on, including pilot fish, bait fish and a wide range of parasites, both inside their bodies and out. Sandtiger sharks are often seen surrounded by a cloud of baby bait fish. Too small for the shark to eat, the bait fish crowd around it for protection. Basking sharks are sometimes covered with sea lampreys, which clamp on to the shark's skin with their sucker-like mouths. To get rid of these pests, the giant sharks leap clear of the water and crash back down to dislodge them. Smaller parasites live inside each shark. These have adapted so well to life with sharks that they can survive in only one species, some in only one part of the shark's digestive system.

▲ STRIPED PILOTS
Tiny pilot fish often ride the bow wave in front of a shark's snout. Young golden trevally fish swim with whale sharks. When they are older and lose their stripes, they leave the shark and return to their reef homes.

▼ HITCHHIKER
A remora fish stays with a shark for most of its life. Its dorsal fin is designed like a sucker, which the fish uses to attach itself to the shark's belly. The fish then feeds on scraps from the shark's meal.

▶ SCRAPING CURE

Some fish use the shark's rough, sandpaper-like skin to remove their own parasites. Rainbow runner fish will rub against a whitetip reef shark's side. Behind one shark might be an entire group of fish lining up for a scrub.

◀ BARBER SHOP

Many sharks visit what scientists call cleaning stations. Here, small fish and shrimp remove dead skin and parasites from the shark's body, even entering the gills and mouth. This hammerhead shark is gliding past a cleaning station where several king angel fish have darted out to clean it.

▼ UNWELCOME FRIENDS

Strings of parasitic copepod eggs trail behind the dorsal fin of this shortfin mako shark. These parasites will have little effect on the shark's life, but if large numbers of parasites grow inside the shark, it can die.

▶ BLOOD SUCKER

A marine leech feeds by attaching itself to any part of the shark's skin and sucking its blood. Other parasites feed only on certain areas of the shark's body, like the gills, mouth and nasal openings.

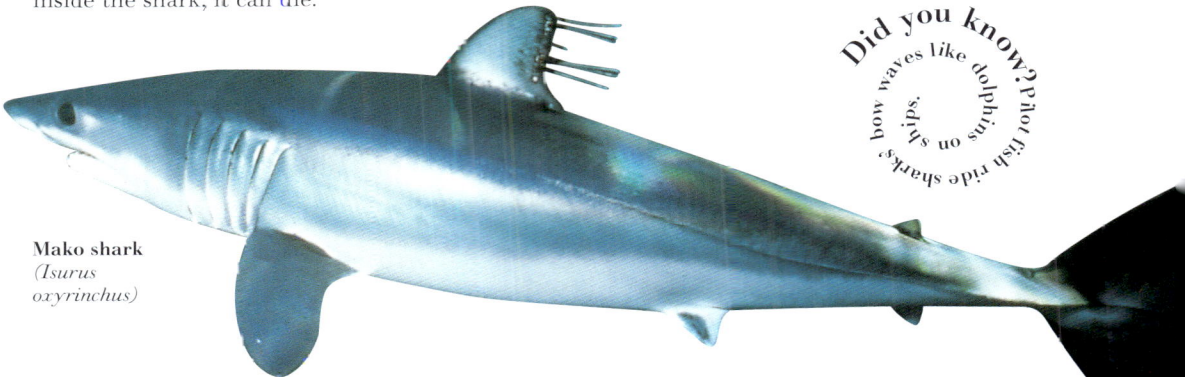

Did you know? Pilot fish ride sharks' bow waves like dolphins on ships.

Mako shark
(Isurus oxyrinchus)

Sharks and People

Sharks are feared because they attack people. However, only a few such attacks take place each year. People are more likely to be killed on the way to the beach than be killed by a shark in the water. Fortunately, attitudes are changing. Today, people have a healthy respect for sharks, rather than a fear of them. As we come to understand sharks, instead of killing them, people want to learn more about them. Diving with sharks, even with such known threats as the great white shark or bull shark, is more accepted. People study sharks either from the safety of a cage or, increasingly, in the open sea without any protection. Such is our fascination with sharks that aquariums are being built all over the world. Here, more people will be able to learn about sharks at first hand, and not even get wet.

Jaws
The book and film Jaws *featured an enormous great white shark that terrorized a coastal town. The film drew great crowds and its story terrified people all over the world. It also harmed the reputation of sharks, encouraging people to see them as monsters, rather than the extraordinarily successful animals that they are.*

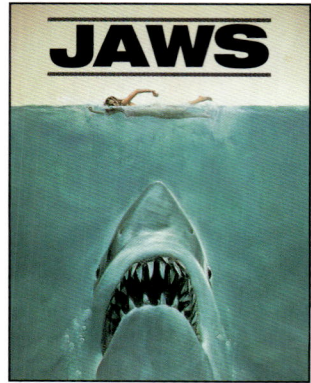

◀ **FEEDING TIME**
At tourist resorts in the tropics, divers can watch sharks being fed by hand. This activity is not always approved of. Sharks come to rely on this free handout, and may become aggressive if it stops. Inexperienced divers may also not know how to behave with sharks, resulting in accidents, although these are rare.

◀ ANTI-SHARK MEASURES

Anti-shark nets protect many popular South African and Australian beaches. Unfortunately, these nets not only catch sharks, like this tiger shark, but also other sea life, including dolphins and turtles. Less destructive ways of reducing people's fear of attack have yet to be invented.

▶ SHARK POD

Although a similar system is not yet available to bathers, one anti-shark invention seems to work for divers and, possibly, surfers, too. A shark pod can produce an electric field that interferes with the electrical sensors of a shark, encouraging the animal to keep its distance.

◀ SHARK ATTACK

Occasionally, sharks do attack. While diving in Australian waters, Rodney Fox was attacked by a great white shark. Rodney was possibly mistaken for a seal. He is probably alive because he did not have enough blubber on him to interest the shark and he was able to get away.

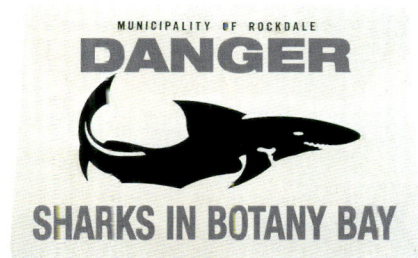

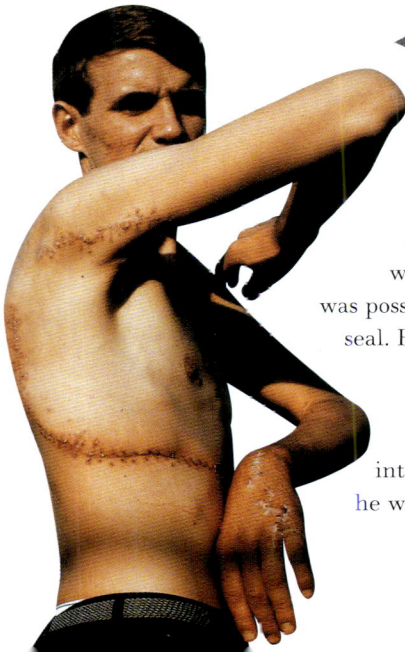

MUNICIPALITY OF ROCKDALE
DANGER
SHARKS IN BOTANY BAY

▲ SHARK WARNING

On many beaches, shark warning signs are used to tell people that sharks might be present. During the day, danger of attack is low, but it increases at night, when the sharks move inshore to feed.

441

Focus on the Great

INTELLIGENT SHARK
The great white shows signs of "intelligent" planning. It stakes out places off the Farallon Islands west of San Francisco, United States, where young elephant seals swim. It can then avoid the large, possibly aggressive, adult bulls that could do it damage.

The great white shark grows to over 6m/20ft long and is the largest hunting fish in the sea. Its powerful jaws can bite a full-grown elephant seal in half. Many people believe that the great white will attack people readily. This is not true. In the whole world, only about ten people a year are bitten by great whites. Great whites are aggressive, powerful fish and will attack people when they mistake them for their natural prey, such as seals. If they realize their mistake, there is a chance that a person can survive – that is, if the blood loss from the first bite can be stopped.

BODY PERFECT
The great white has the torpedo shape typical of a hunting shark. Its crescent-shaped tail, with its equal upper and lower parts, helps the shark to speed through the water. Although it is called the great white, it is not white all over, but grey on top and white underneath.

White Shark

GIANT SHARK ENCOUNTER

A great white shark dwarfs any diver. To a diver in a cage, it can sometimes seem that a shark is trying to attack. In reality, the shark's electrical sensors are probably confused. The diver's metal cage produces an electrical field in seawater — the shark is then likely to react to the cage as if it were prey.

TERRIBLE JAWS

As a great white rises to take bait, its black eyes roll back into their protective sockets. Its jaws thrust forward, filled with rows of triangular teeth ready to take a bite. This incredible action takes place in little more than a second.

SHARP TEETH

The powerful, arrow-shaped teeth in the upper jaw of a great white have a serrated (jagged) edge. These teeth can slice through flesh, blubber and even bone. The shark saws through the tissue of its prey by shaking its head from side to side.

GAME FISH

To fishermen who hunt great whites for sport, the large breeding female sharks are the most attractive. The killing of these sharks has brought them near extinction in some places.

Whales and Dolphins

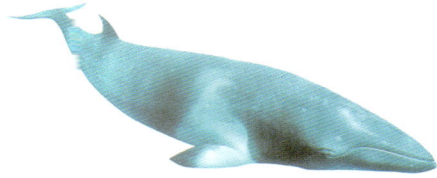

Whales and dolphins are often depicted as kind
and gentle creatures, but in reality they can be
quite violent to one another. Male whales will
fight other males of their own kind for the
right to breed, and resident dolphins will
exclude outsiders or even fight with them
to the death. It's a far cry from the smiling,
playful dolphins we see at marine circuses.

Whale Order

Like fish, whales and dolphins spend all their lives in the sea. But unlike fish, they breathe air, have warm blood and suckle their young. They are more closely related to human beings than fish because they are mammals. Many whales are enormous – some are as big and as heavy as a railway carriage (railroad car) full of passengers. Dolphins are much smaller – most are about the same size as an adult human being Porpoises, which look much like dolphins, are also roughly the same size as humans. Although smaller, dolphins and porpoises are kinds of whales, too. All whales belong to the major group, or order of animals called Cetacea.

▲ HEAVYWEIGHTS
The largest of the whales are the biggest animals ever to have lived. This leaping humpback whale is nearly 15m/49ft long and weighs over 25 tonnes/tons – as much as five fully-grown elephants. Some other whales, such as the fin and blue whales, are very much bigger.

► WHALE ANCESTORS
More than 50 million years ago, creatures like this were swimming in the seas. They seem to have been ancestors of modern cetaceans. This creature, named basilosaurus (meaning king lizard), grew up to over 20m/66ft long. It had a snake-like body with tiny front flippers and traces of a pair of hind limbs.

▼ BALEEN WHALES
These humpback whales are feeding in Alaskan waters. They belong to the group, or suborder of whales known as the baleen whales. These are, in general, very much larger than those in the other main group, the toothed whales.

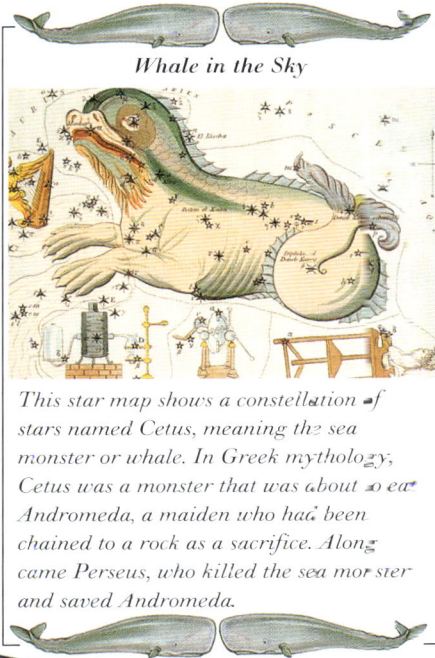

Whale in the Sky

This star map shows a constellation of stars named Cetus, meaning the sea monster or whale. In Greek mythology, Cetus was a monster that was about to eat Andromeda, a maiden who had been chained to a rock as a sacrifice. Along came Perseus, who killed the sea monster and saved Andromeda.

▲ TOOTHED WHALES

A bottlenose dolphin opens its mouth and shows its teeth. It is one of the many species of toothed whales. Toothed whales have much simpler teeth than land mammals and many more of them. The bottlenose dolphin, for example, has up to 50 teeth in both its upper and lower jaws.

◄ BREATHING

Because they are mammals, whales and dolphins breathe air. This common dolphin breathes out through a blowhole on top of its head as it rises to the surface. It can hold its breath for five minutes or more when diving.

Did you know? A blue whale can weigh as much as 25 elephants.

447

Whales Large and Small

Most large whales belong to the major group of cetaceans called the baleen
whales. Instead of teeth, these whales have brush-like plates, called baleen, that
hang from their upper jaw. They use the baleen to filter food from the water.
The sperm whale, on the other hand, belongs to the other major cetacean group,
toothed whales. This group also includes the
dolphins, porpoises, white whales
and beaked whales. These
cetaceans have teeth.

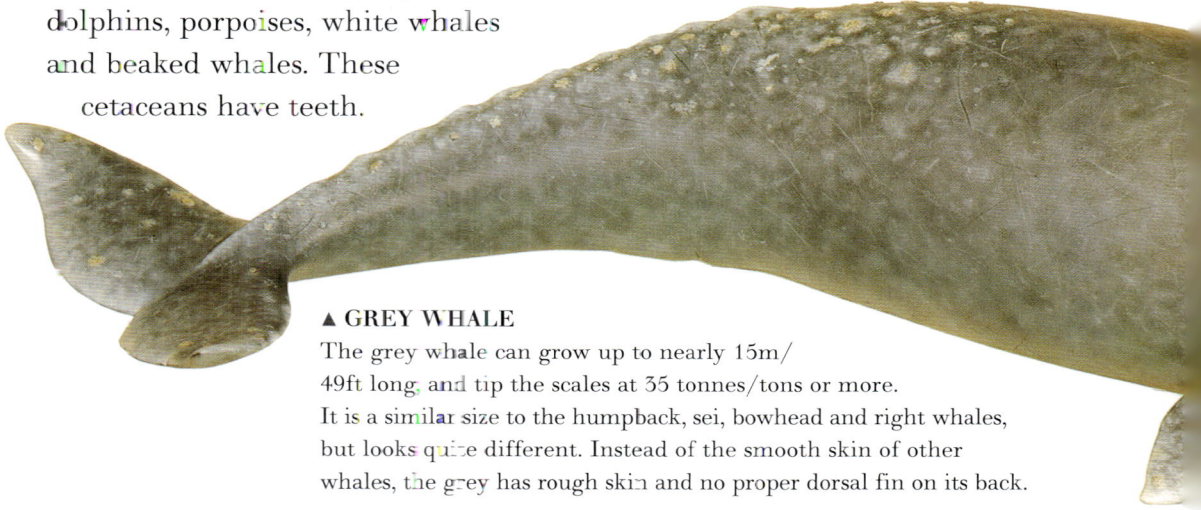

▲ GREY WHALE
The grey whale can grow up to nearly 15m/
49ft long, and tip the scales at 35 tonnes/tons or more.
It is a similar size to the humpback, sei, bowhead and right whales,
but looks quite different. Instead of the smooth skin of other
whales, the grey has rough skin and no proper dorsal fin on its back.

Did you know? Some whales have as many as 3,000 baleen plates in their jaws.

▲ BLACK AND WHITE
The bowhead whale, which has a highly curved jaw, grows to 16m/52½ft. It is closely related to
the right whale. The bowhead is famous for its long baleen plates and thick layer of blubber. The
toothed whales we call belugas *(above left)* grow to about 5m/16½ft at most. The first part of the
word beluga means white in Russian and belugas are also known as white whales.

▶ SEI WHALE

At up to about 16m/52½ft, the sei whale looks much like its bigger relatives, the blue whale and the fin. All members of the group called rorquals, they have deep grooves in their throats. These grooves let the throat expand to take big mouthfuls of water for feeding. Seis have up to 60 grooves in their throat.

Did you know? The blue whale's tongue weighs as much as an African elephant.

▶ RELATIVE SIZES

Whales come in many sizes, from dolphins smaller than a human to the enormous blue whale, which can grow to 30m/98ft or more. In general, the baleen whales are much bigger than the toothed whales. The exception is the sperm whale, which can grow up to 18m/59ft.

Porpoise

Dolphin

Narwhal

Killer whale

Beaked whale

Grey whale

Sperm whale

Right whale

Blue whale

▲ RISSO'S DOLPHIN

The dolphin pictured leaping here is a Risso's dolphin. It has a blunt snout and as few as six teeth. Most of the toothed whales that we call dolphins are on average about 2–3m/6½–10ft long. Risso's dolphins can grow a little bigger — up to nearly 4m/13ft long.

Whale Bones

Like all mammals, whales have a skeleton of bones to give the body its shape and protect vital organs such as the heart. Because a whale's body is supported by water, its bones are not so strong as those of land mammals and are quite soft. The backbone is made up of many vertebrae, with joints in-between to give it flexibility. While providing some body support, the backbone acts mainly as an anchor for the muscles, particularly the strong muscles that drive the tail. Instead of limbs, a whale has a pair of modified fore limbs, called flippers.

► BONE CORSET
This advertisement for a "whalebone" corset dates from 1911, a time when women wore corsets to give them a shapely figure. The corsets were, in fact, made from the baleen plates found in whales' mouths.

► UNDERNEATH THE ARCHES
Arches built from the jaw bones of huge baleen whales can be seen in some ports that were once the home of whaling fleets. This jaw-bone arch can be seen outside Christ Church Cathedral in Port Stanley, Falkland Islands. Nowadays, whales are protected species and building such arches is forbidden.

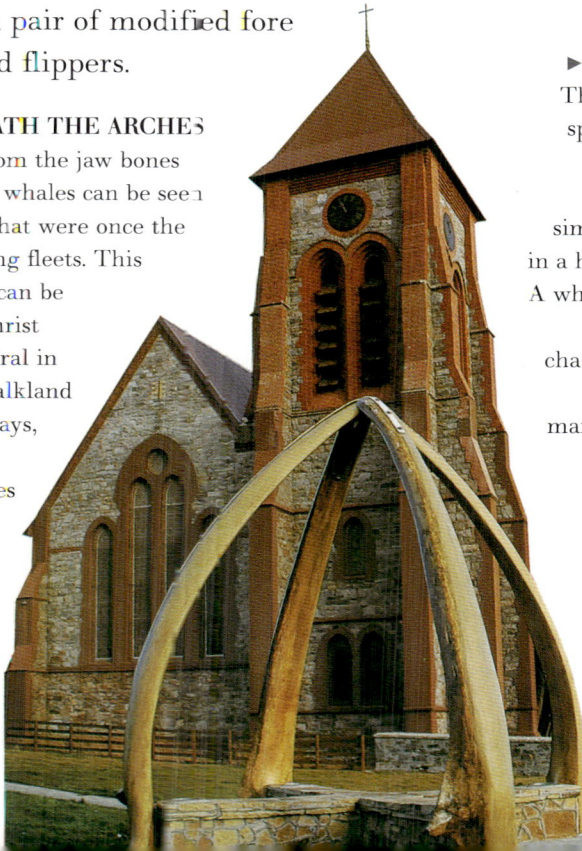

► HANDS UP
The bones in a sperm whale's flipper are remarkably similar to those in a human hand. A whale's flippers are a much changed version of a typical mammal's front limbs. Both hands have wrist bones, finger bones and joints.

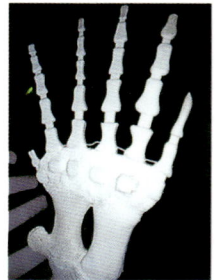

Sperm whale flipper

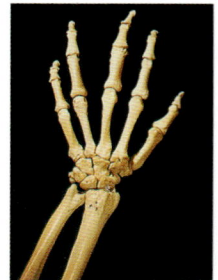

Human hand

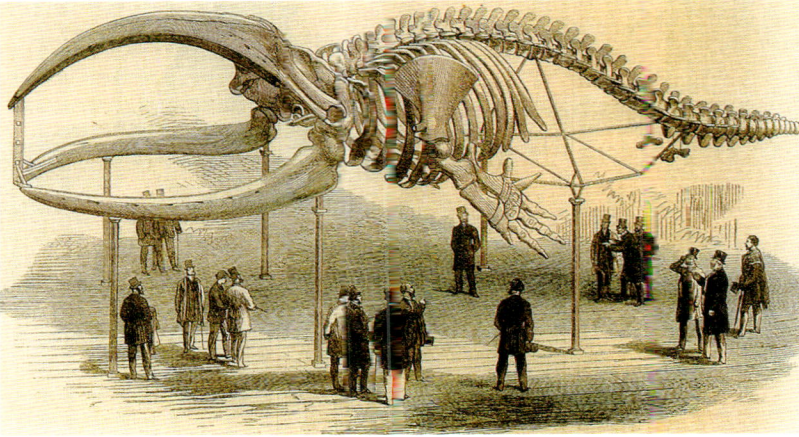

◀ BIG HEAD

This right whale skeleton was displayed in London in 1830. Its large jaw bones tell us that it is a baleen whale, which needs a big mouth for feeding. Like other mammals, it has a large rib cage to protect its body organs. However, it has no hind limbs or pelvic girdle.

Did you know? whales are very oily and very smelly

▼ TOOTHY JAW

This is the skeleton of a false killer whale, one of the toothed whales. The head is much smaller than that of the baleen whales and its jaws are studded with teeth. Its long spine is made up of segments called vertebrae. The vertebrae in the whale's waist region are large, so that they are strong enough to anchor the animal's powerful tail muscles.

▼ KILLER SKULL

Both jaws of this killer whale skull are studded with vicious, curved teeth that are more than 10cm/4in long. The killer whale is a deadly predator, attacking seals, dolphins and sometimes whales that are even bigger than itself.

Whale Bodies

Over many millions of years, whales have developed features that suit them to a life spent mostly underwater. They have long, rounded bodies and smooth, almost hairless skin. Like fish, whales move about using fins. They have the same body organs, such as heart and lungs, as land mammals. In the big whales, however, the body organs are much larger than in land mammals.

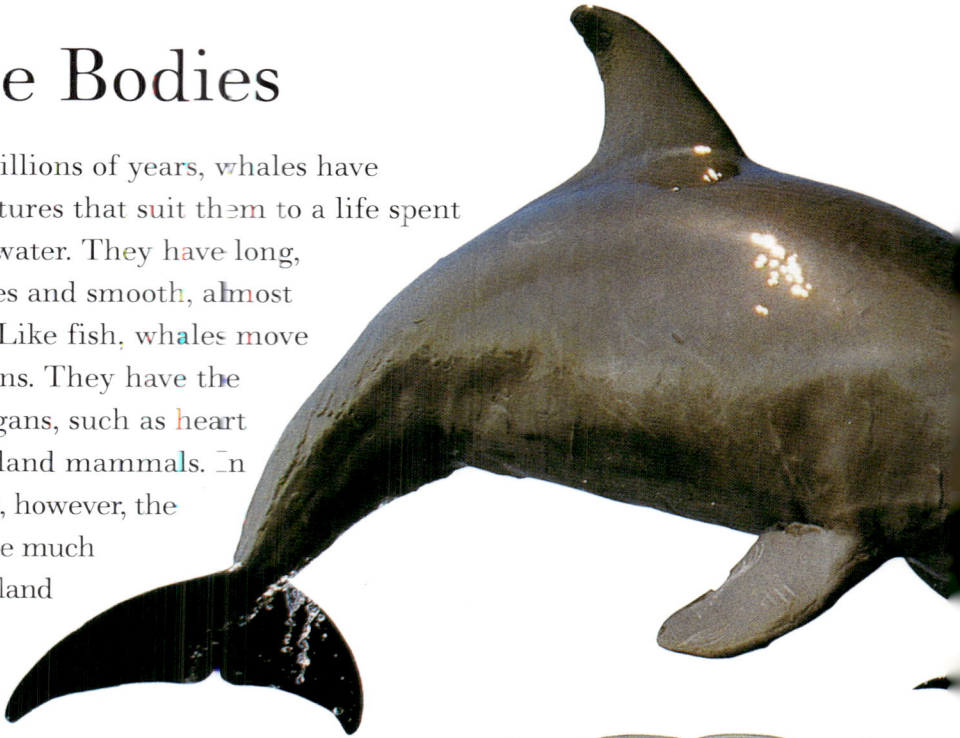

▼ BIG MOUTH

This grey whale is one of the baleen whales, and the baleen can be seen hanging from its upper jaw. Baleen whales need a big mouth so that they can take in large mouthfuls of water when they are feeding. Grey whales usually feed at the bottom of the sea.

Baleen

Jonah and the Whale

This picture from the 17th century tells one of the best known of all Bible stories. The prophet Jonah was thrown overboard by sailors during a terrible storm. To rescue him, God sent a whale, which swallowed him whole. Jonah spent three days in the whale's belly before it coughed him up on to dry land. The picture shows that many people at this time had little idea of what a whale looked like. The artist has given it shark-like teeth and a curly tail.

▼ LEAPING DOLPHINS

A pair of bottlenose dolphins leap effortlessly several metres/feet out of the water. Powerful muscles near the tail provide them with the energy for fast swimming and leaping. They leap for various reasons – to signal to each other, to look for fish or perhaps just for fun.

▲ HANGERS ON

This humpback whale's throat is covered with barnacles, which take hold because the whale moves quite slowly. They cannot easily cling to swifter-moving cetaceans, such as dolphins. A dolphin sloughs rough skin away as it moves through the water. This also makes it harder for a barnacle to take hold.

► LOUSY WHALES

The grey whale's skin is covered with light-coloured patches. These patches are clusters of ten-legged lice, called cyamids, about 2–3cm/¾–1⅛in long. They feed on the whale's skin.

◄ BODY LINES

A pod, or group, of melon-headed whales swims in the Pacific Ocean. This species is one of the smaller whales, at less than 3m/10ft long. It shows the features of a typical cetacean – a well-rounded body with a short neck and a single fin. It has a pair of paddle-like front flippers and a tail with horizontal flukes.

Did you know? Whales have whiskers on their faces.

453

Staying Alive

Whales are warm-blooded creatures. To stay alive, they must keep their bodies at a temperature of about 36–37°C/ 97–99°F. They swim in very cold water that quickly takes heat away from the surface of their bodies. To conserve body heat, whales have a thick layer of fatty blubber just beneath the skin. Whales must also breathe to stay alive. They breathe through a blowhole, situated on top of the head. When a whale breathes out, it sends a column of steamy water vapour high into the air.

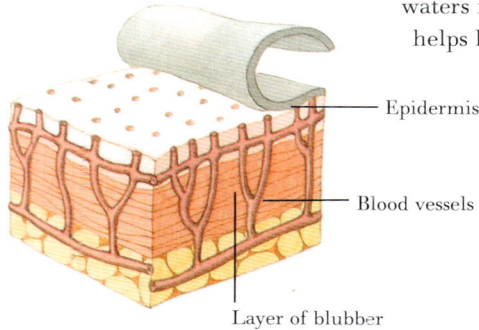

▲ IN THE WARM
Southern right whales feed in icy Antarctic waters in summer. The whales' size helps limit the percentage of body heat they lose to the water.

Epidermis

Blood vessels

Layer of blubber

◄ SKIN DEEP
This is a cross-section of a whale's outer layer. Beneath its skin, a thick layer of blubber insulates it from ice-cold water.

► SMALL BODY
Atlantic spotted dolphins are about the size of a human. Because it is small, its body has a relatively large surface area for its size and so loses heat faster than its big relatives. This is probably why the Atlantic spotted dolphin lives in quite warm waters.

Did you know? *The temperature of a whale is about the same as yours.*

▶ **SKY HIGH**
A humpback whale surfaces and blows a column of warm, moist air. As it rises it cools and the moisture in it condenses into a cloud of tiny water droplets.

▼ **DEEP DIVING**
Whales feed at different depths. Most dolphins feed close to the surface. The sperm whale holds the diving record, being able to descend to about 2,000m/6,562ft and stay under water for 1 hour.

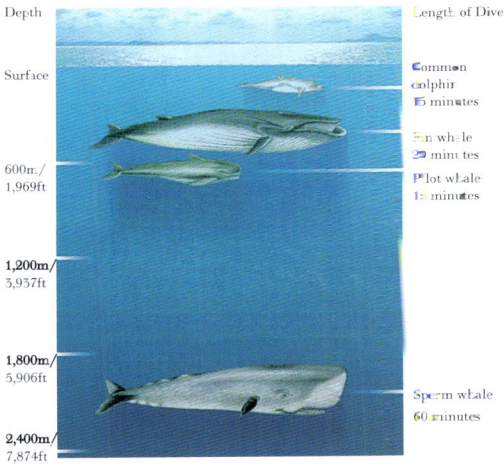

Depth		Length of Dive
Surface		Common dolphin 5 minutes
		Fin whale 20 minutes
600m/ 1,969ft		Pilot whale 15 minutes
1,200m/ 3,937ft		
1,800m/ 5,906ft		
		Sperm whale 60 minutes
2,400m/ 7,874ft		

▼ **ONE BLOWHOLE**
Like all toothed whales, a bottlenose dolphin has only one blowhole. When the dolphin dives, thick lips of elastic tissue close it to stop water entering, no matter how deep the dive.

▲ **TWO BLOWHOLES**
The humpback whale breathes out through a pair of blowholes, located behind a ridge called a splashguard. This helps prevent water entering the blowholes when the whale is blowing.

455

Whale Brain and Senses

A whale controls its body through its nervous system. The brain is the control centre, carrying out functions automatically, but also acting upon information supplied by the senses. The sizes of whale brains vary according to the animal's size. However, dolphins have much bigger brains for their size. Hearing is by far a whale's most important sense. They pick up sounds with tiny ears located just behind the eyes.

▲ EYES
Compared with its large body, a whale's eyes are tiny. It can see quite well when it is on the surface and often lifts its head out of the water to look around.

Did you know? A sperm whale's brain is five times the size of a human's.

◄ CLOSE ENCOUNTERS
A group of Atlantic spotted dolphins swims closely together in the seas around the Bahama Islands. Like most other cetaceans, the dolphins often nudge one another and stroke each other with their flippers and tail. Touch plays a very important part in dolphin society, especially in courtship.

◀ SLAP HAPPY

A humpback whale slapping its tail, or lob-tailing, a favourite pastime for great whales. Lob-tailing creates a noise like a gunshot in the air, but, more importantly, it will make a loud report underwater. All the other whales in the area will be able to hear the noise.

Cupids and Dolphins

In this Roman mosaic, cupids and dolphins gambol together. In Roman mythology, Cupid was the god of love. Roman artists were inspired by the dolphin's intelligence and gentleness. They regarded them as sacred creatures.

◀ BRAINY DOLPHIN?

Some dolphins, such as the bottlenose, have a brain that is much the same size as our own. It is quite a complex brain with many folds. However, the dolphin is not necessarily highly intelligent.

▶ IN TRAINING

A bottlenose dolphin is shown with its trainer. This species has a particularly large brain for its size. It can be easily trained and has a good memory. It can observe other animals and learn to mimic their behaviour in a short space of time. It is also good at solving problems, something we consider a sign of intelligence.

Sounds and Songs

Whales use sounds to communicate with one
another and to find their food. Baleen whales
use low-pitched sounds, which have been
picked up by underwater microphones as
moans, grunts and snores. The toothed whales
make higher-pitched sounds, picked up as
squeaks, creaks or whistles. Whales also use
high-pitched clicks when hunting. They send
out beams of sound, which are reflected by
objects in their path, such as fish. The whale
picks up the reflected sound, or echo, and works
out the object's location. This is
called echo-location.

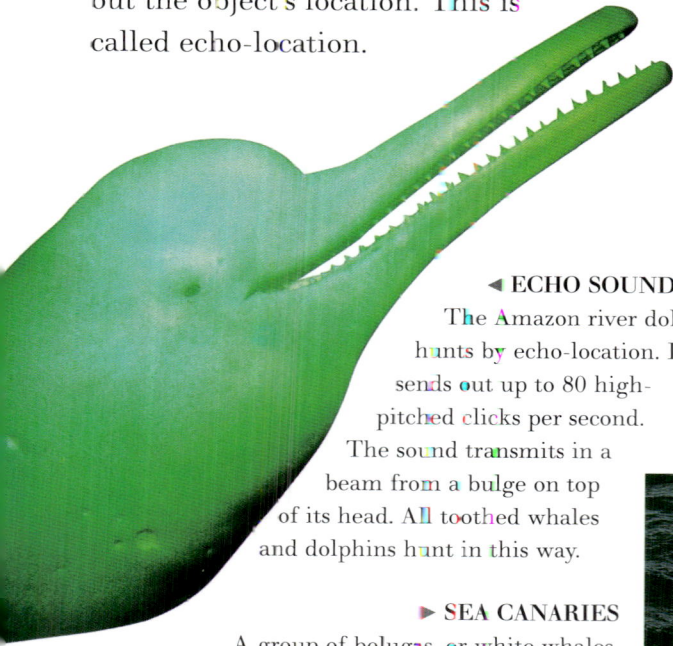

Blowhole

Melon

Skull

Ear

◄ ECHO SOUNDINGS

The Amazon river dolphin
hunts by echo-location. It
sends out up to 80 high-
pitched clicks per second.
The sound transmits in a
beam from a bulge on top
of its head. All toothed whales
and dolphins hunt in this way.

▲ MAKING WAVES

A dolphin vibrates the air in its nasal
passages to make high-pitched sound
waves, which are focused into a beam by
the melon – a bulge on its head. The
sound beam transmits into the water.

► SEA CANARIES

A group of belugas, or white whales,
swims in a bay in Canada. Belugas'
voices can clearly be heard above the
surface. This is why they are known
as sea canaries. They also produce
high-pitched sounds we cannot hear,
which they use for echo-location.

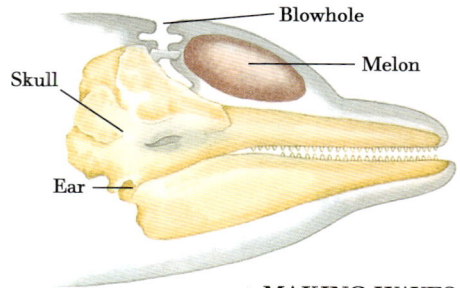

◄ SUPER SONGSTER

This male humpback whale is heading for the breeding grounds where the females are gathering. The male starts singing long and complicated songs. This may be to attract a mate or to warn other males off its patch. The sound can carry for 30km/19 miles.

▼ LONG SONGS

This is a voice print of a humpback whale's song, picked up by an underwater microphone. It shows complex musical phrases and melodies. Humpback whales often continue singing for a day or more, repeating the same song.

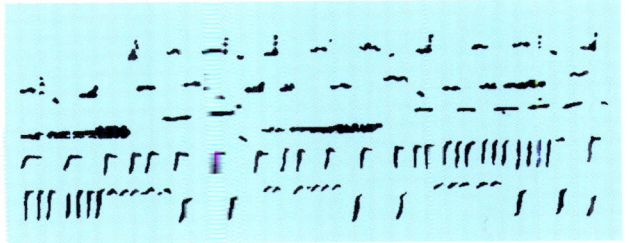

▼ SOUND ECHOES

A sperm whale can locate a giant squid more than 1km/½ mile away by transmitting pulses of sound waves into the water and listening. The echo is picked up by the teeth in its lower jaw and the vibrations are sent along the jaw to the ear.

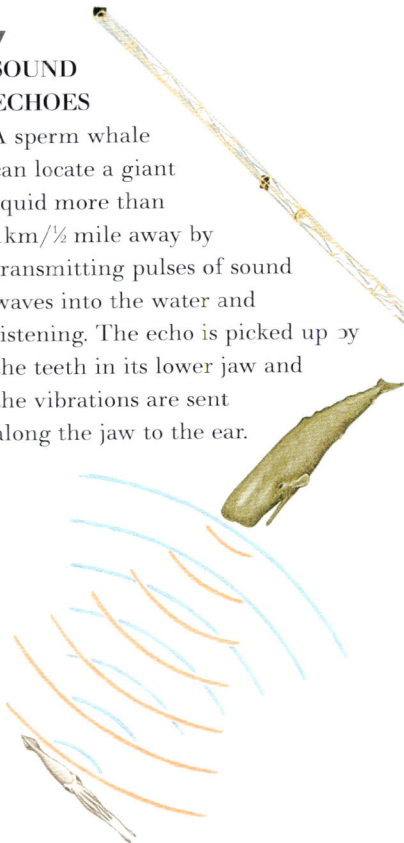

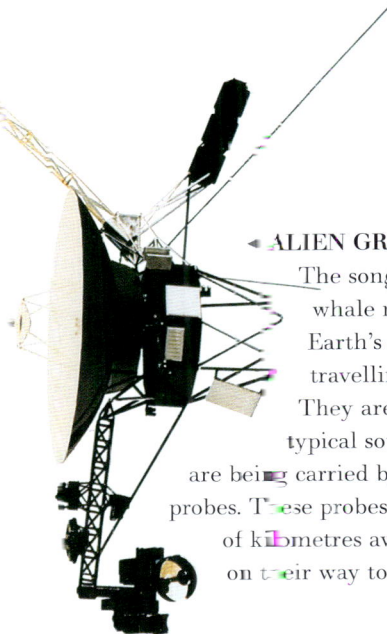

Did you know? A dolphin picks up sounds through its lower jaw.

◄ ALIEN GREETINGS

The songs of the humpback whale not only travel through Earth's oceans, but they are also travelling far out into Space. They are among the recorded typical sounds of our world that are being carried by the two Voyager space probes. These probes are now many millions of kilometres away from Earth and are on their way to the stars.

459

Feeding Habits

Most baleen whales feed by taking mouthfuls of seawater containing fish and tiny shrimp-like creatures, called krill, or plankton, as well as algae, jellyfish, worms and so on. The whale closes its mouth and lifts its tongue, forcing water out through the bristly baleen plates on the upper jaw. The baleen acts like a sieve and holds back the food, which the whale then swallows. Toothed whales feed mainly on fish and squid. They find their prey by echo-location.

▲ CRUNCHY KRILL

These crustaceans, known as krill, form the diet of many baleen whales. Measuring up to 75mm/3in long, they swim in vast shoals, often covering an area of several square kilometres/miles. Most krill are found in Antarctic waters.

◄ PLOUGHING

A grey whale ploughs (plows) into the seabed, stirring up sand. It dislodges tiny crustaceans, called amphipods, and gulps them down. Grey whales feed mostly in summer in the Arctic before they migrate south.

◄ SKIM FEEDING

With its mouth open, a southern right whale filters tiny crustaceans, called copepods, out of the water with its baleen. It eats up to 2 tonnes/tons of these plankton daily. It eats so much because of its huge size – up to 80 tonnes/tons. Usually, right whales feed alone, but if food is plentiful, several will feed cruising side by side.

◄ **SUCCULENT SQUID**

Squid is the sperm whale's favourite food and is eaten by other toothed whales and dolphins as well. Squid are molluscs, in the same animal order as snails and octopuses. Unlike octopuses, they have eight arms and two tentacles, and are called decapods (meaning ten feet). Squid swim together in dense shoals, many thousand strong.

◄ **TOOTHY SMILE**

A Ganges river dolphin has more than 100 teeth. The front ones are very long. Ganges river dolphins eat mainly fish and also take shrimp and crab. They usually feed at night and find their prey by echo-location.

Did you know? A blue whale eats nearly 1,000kg/2,205lb of krill in a single meal.

► **LUNCH**

Belugas feed on squid and small fish, which are in plentiful supply in the icy ocean. Unlike common dolphins, belugas do not have many teeth. They may simply suck prey into their mouths. Many beaked whales, which also feed on squid, have no teeth suitable for clutching prey.

▲ **HUNT THE SQUID**

The sperm whale is the largest toothed whale, notable for its huge head and tiny lower jaw. It hunts the giant squid that live in waters around 2,000m/6,562ft deep in the dark by echo-location.

Focus on

Among the toothed whales, the killer whale, or orca, is the master predator. It feeds on a wider variety of prey than any other whale. It bites and tears its prey to pieces with its fearsome teeth and may also batter them with its powerful tail. It is the only whale to take warm-blooded prey. Fortunately, there is no record of a killer whale ever attacking human beings. As well as fish and squid, a killer whale will hunt seals, penguins, dolphins and porpoises. It may even attack large baleen whales many times its size. Killer whales live in family groups, or pods. They often go hunting together, which greatly improves the chance of success.

1 A killer whale will go hunting by itself if it chances upon a likely victim, such as this lone sea lion. This hungry whale has spotted the sea lion splashing in the surf at the water's edge. With powerful strokes of its tail, it surges towards its intended prey. The whale's tall dorsal fin shows that it is a fully grown male.

2 The sea lion seems totally unaware of what is happening but, in any case, it is nearly helpless in the shallow water. The killer whale is scraping the shore as it homes in for the kill.

Killer Whales

3 Suddenly the killer's head bursts out of the water, and its jaws gape open. Its vicious teeth, curving inwards and backwards, are exposed. It is ready to sink them into its sea lion prey. The killer whale may have fewer teeth than most toothed whales, but they are large and very strong.

4 Now the killer snaps its jaws shut, clamping the sea lion in a vice-like grip. With its prey struggling helplessly, it slides back into deep water to eat its fill. Killer whales sometimes almost beach themselves when they lunge after prey but, helped by the surf, they usually manage to wriggle their way back into the sea.

Focus on

The humpback whale usually scoops up water as it lunges forward and upward to feed. Grooves in its throat let the mouth expand to take in tonnes/tons of water containing food, which it filters through its baleen plates. This way of lunge-feeding is typical of the baleen whales known as the rorquals, which also include the blue, fin, sei and minke whales. Before lunge-feeding, humpbacks may blow a circle of bubbles around the fish. The bubbles act like a net to stop the fish escaping.

ON THE LOOK-OUT

A humpback whale spy-hops in the feeding grounds of Alaska. It is looking for signs of shoals of fish, such as cod. In the Northern Hemisphere, humpbacks feed mainly on fish. The Southern Hemisphere humpbacks feed mainly on plankton, such as krill.

FORWARD LUNGE

Once in the middle of a shoal, the humpback opens its mouth and lunges forwards. The throat grooves expand as water rushes in. It uses its tongue and cheek muscles to force the water through its baleen plates, leaving the fish behind in its mouth.

Lunging for Lunch

UPWARD LUNGE

Here, the humpback is using a different technique. It sinks below the surface and then flicks its tail to help it to shoot upwards again. With mouth gaping open, it lunges at the fish from below.

RING OF BUBBLES

The surface of the sea is boiling with a ring of frothy bubbles. Unseen, beneath the water, one or more humpback whales swim in circles, letting out air as they do so.

BUBBLE NETTING

The circle of bubbles rises to the surface from the whales circling under the water. It forms a kind of net around a shoal of fish. The whales then swim up to the surface, mouths gaping, to engulf the netted prey.

Swimming

All whales are superb swimmers. All parts of the whale's body help it move through the water. The driving force comes from the tail fin, or flukes. Using very powerful muscles in the rear third of its body, the whale beats its tail up and down and the whole body bends. It uses its pectoral fins, or flippers, near the front of the body, to steer with. The body itself is streamlined and smooth to help it slip through the water easily. The body can change shape slightly to keep the water flowing smoothly around it. Little ridges under the skin help as well.

▲ STEERING

Among whales, the humpback has by far the longest front flippers. As well as for steering, it uses its flippers for slapping the water. Flipper-slapping seems to be a form of communication.

◀ TAIL POWER

The tail flukes of a grey whale rise into the air before it dives. Whales move their broad tails up and down to drive themselves through the water.

▼ MASSIVE FIN

The dorsal fin of a killer whale projects high into the air. The animal is a swift swimmer and the fin helps keep its body well balanced. The killer whale has such a large dorsal fin that some experts believe it may help to regulate its body temperature or even be used in courtship. Most whales and dolphins have a dorsal fin, although some have only a raised hump.

Did you know? A killer whale can swim up to 65kph/40mph.

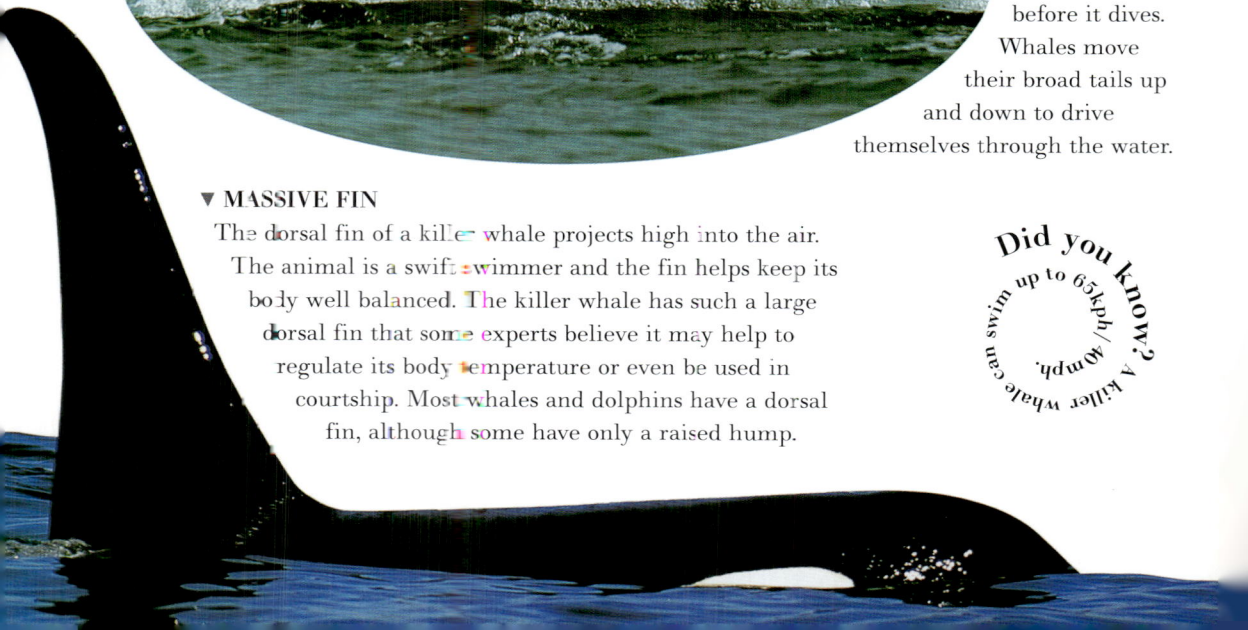

◄ STREAMLINING
Atlantic spotted
dolphins' bodies are
beautifully
streamlined
(shaped) so that they
slip easily through
the water when they
move. The dolphin's
body is long and
rounded, broad in
front and becoming
narrower towards
the tail. Apart
from the dorsal fin
and flippers, nothing
projects from its
body. It has no
external ears or
rear limbs.

▼ HOW A DOLPHIN SWIMS
Dolphins beat their tail flukes up and down by means
of the powerful muscles near the tail. The flukes force
the water backward at each stroke. As the water is
forced back, the dolphin's body is forced
forward. Its other fins help guide it
through the water. They do not
provide propulsion.

◄ SMOOTH-SKINNED
This bottlenose dolphin is
tailwalking – supporting
itself by powerful thrusts of its
tail. Unlike most mammals, it
has no covering of hair or hair
follicles (the dimples in the
skin from which the hair
grows). Its smooth skin
helps the dolphin's
body slip through
the water.

▼ HOW A FISH SWIMS
It is mainly the tail that provides the
power for a fish to swim. The tail has
vertical fins, unlike the horizontal fins
of the dolphin. It swims by beating its
tail and body from side to side.

467

Focus on

Most whales feed beneath the surface, some often diving deep to reach their food. We can usually identify the species of whale from the way it prepares to dive, or sound. The sperm whale, for example, is one of the species that lifts its tail high into the air before it descends into the ocean. It is the deepest diver of all the whales, sometimes descending to more than 1.6km/1 mile in search of squid. It can stay underwater for an hour or more before it has to come up for air. As in other whales, its lungs collapse when it dives. It is thought that the great mass of oil in its head helps the whale when diving and surfacing.

1 Two sperm whales swim at the surface. The one on the right is preparing to dive. Its head is in the air and it fills its lungs with air in a series of blows. The sperm whale's blow projects forward, as in no other whale.

2 The diving whale lashes its tail and accelerates through the water, creating a foaming wake. Now the whale starts the dive, thrusting its bulbous head down and arching its back steeply. The rounded hump on its back rises high into the air. The lumpy knuckles behind the hump become visible as the body arches over.

Diving

3 As the whale's head goes under, the oil in its head freezes and becomes heavier on the way down, then melts and becomes lighter again on the way up. If it is going to make a deep dive, the whale may not take another breath for more than an hour.

4 Soon the body disappears with just the tail flukes poking out of the water. The body is now in a vertical position, and that is how it remains as the whale dives swiftly into the deep. Descending at speeds of more than 149m/490ft per minute, it is soon in darkness, scanning its surroundings by beams of sound for the squid on which it feeds.

Social Life

Every day we meet, work, play and communicate with other people. We are sociable animals. Some whales are also sociable and live together. Sperm whales live in groups of up to about 50. A group may be a breeding school of females and young or a bachelor school of young males. Older male sperm whales live alone, except in the breeding season. Beluga whales often live in groups of several hundred. Baleen whales are not so sociable. They move singly or in small groups, probably because of their huge appetite – they could not find enough food if they lived close together.

▲ HERD INSTINCT

Beluga whales gather together in very large groups, or herds, and they mostly stay in these herds for life. Many of the animals in this group, pictured in the Canadian Arctic, have calves. These can be recognized, not only by their smaller size, but also by their darker skin colour.

Did you know? Dolphins will nudge a sick member of the group up to the surface, so it does not drown.

▼ NOSY ORCAS

Two killer whales, or orcas, spy-hop in Antarctic waters. They rise out of the water together, as if on a signal. They are members of the same pod, who stay together all their lives. The bonds between the animals are very strong. This helps them coordinate their activities, especially when hunting for food.

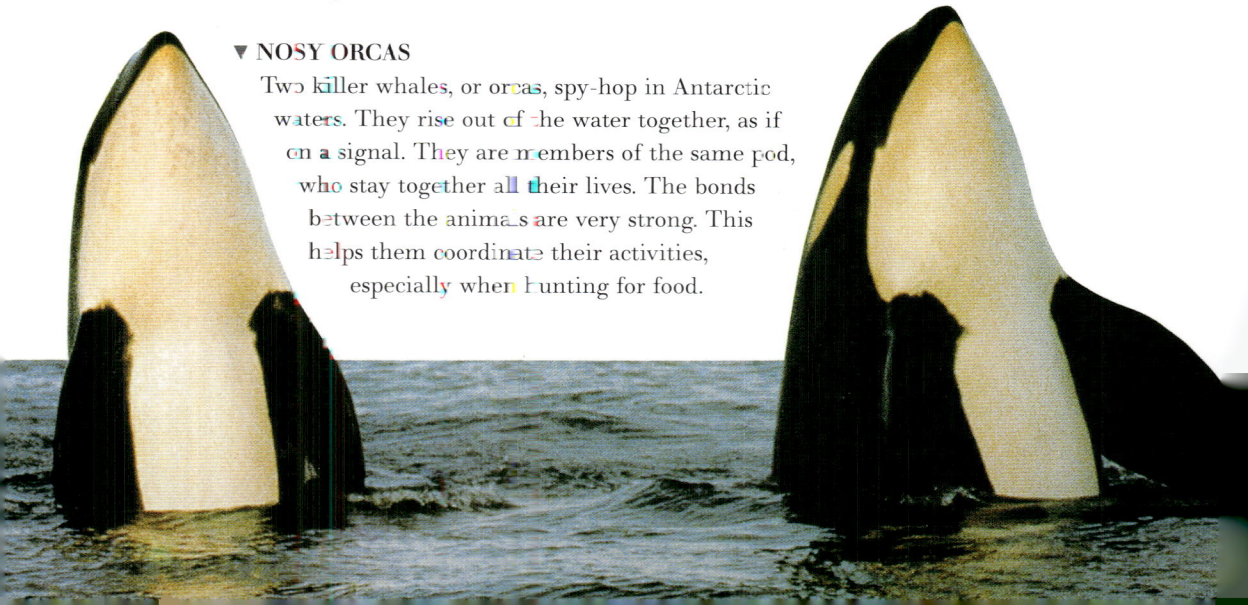

Did you know? Male whales often try to help injured females. Females rarely try to help injured males.

◀ **STAYING CLOSE**

Two Atlantic spotted dolphins swim with their young. The young's spots will not start to appear until the animals are about a year old. As with many other species, the young stay very close to their parents most of the time.

▼ **HUMAN CONTACT**

A bottlenose dolphin swims alongside a boy. These dolphins live in social groups, but lone outcasts or animals that have become separated from their group often approach humans.

▲ **SOLITARY SWIMMER**

An Amazon river dolphin rests on the river bed. It spends most of its life alone or with just one other. This solitary behaviour is typical of river dolphins, but atypical of most whales and ocean dolphins.

▶ **PILOT ERROR**

These long-finned pilot whales are stranded on a beach. Pilot whales usually live in large groups with strong bonds between group members. One whale may accidentally strand itself on a beach. The others may try to help it but get stranded also.

471

The Mating Game

Whales mate at certain times of year. Baleen whales mate during the late autumn (fall) after the whales have migrated to their warm-water breeding grounds. One whale will mate a number of times with different partners. Several males may attempt to manoeuvre a female into a mating position. Often the males fight each other for the chance to mate. Male narwhals even fence with their long tusks. But mating behaviour can also be gentle, with the males and females caressing one another with their flippers.

▲ **WHITE WEDDING**
A pair of belugas show interest in each other. Males and females spend the year in separate groups, only mixing in the mating season. They mate and calve in bays in the far north.

◄ **LOVE SONG**
Whales attract mates by body language and sound. This humpback can pinpoint another's position, and perhaps exchange messages over great distances.

◄ **MATING TIFFS**
Two grey whales court in the winter breeding grounds off Baja California, Mexico. Usually, a group of males fights for the right to mate with a female, causing commotion in the water. The female might mate many times with them.

◄ ROLLOVER

Courtship for these southern right whales is nearly over. The male *(top)* has succeeded in getting the female to roll over on her back and is moving into the mating position.

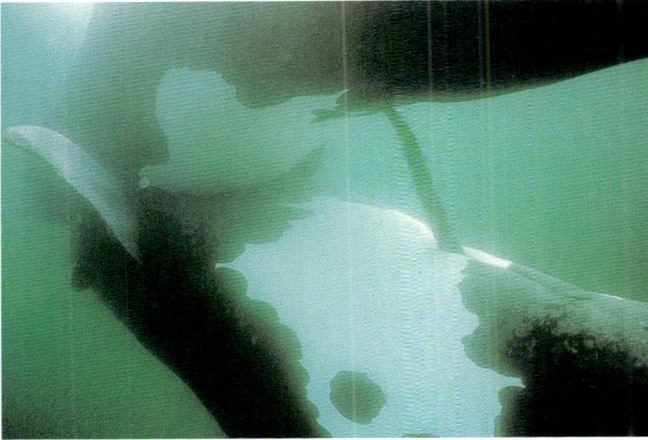

The Fabulous Unicorn

In the breeding season, male narwhals fight each other using their long tusks, which often break. Long ago, when these small whales were little known, people found the tusks and wondered what kind of creature they came from. This may have led to the idea of the unicorn, a horse-like beast with a long spiral horn (like the narwhal's) on its forehead.

◄ BELLY TO BELLY

A pair of southern right whales mate, belly to belly. The male has inserted his long penis into the female to inject his sperm. Usually, the male's penis stays hidden in the body behind a genital slit. It will be nine months or more before the female gives birth to a single calf.

▼ BIG BABY

A sperm whale calf snuggles up to its mother. A calf might measure up to 4.5m/14¾ft long when born, nearly 15 months after mating took place. The mother feeds it for a year or more, leaving it only to dive for food.

Did you know? Female sperm whales can mate at the age of 8. Males cannot mate until they are nearly 20.

473

Focus on

BIRTHDAY
A bottlenose dolphin gives birth. The baby is born tail-first. This birth is taking place near the bottom of an aquarium. In the wild, birth takes place close to the surface so the baby can surface quickly and start breathing.

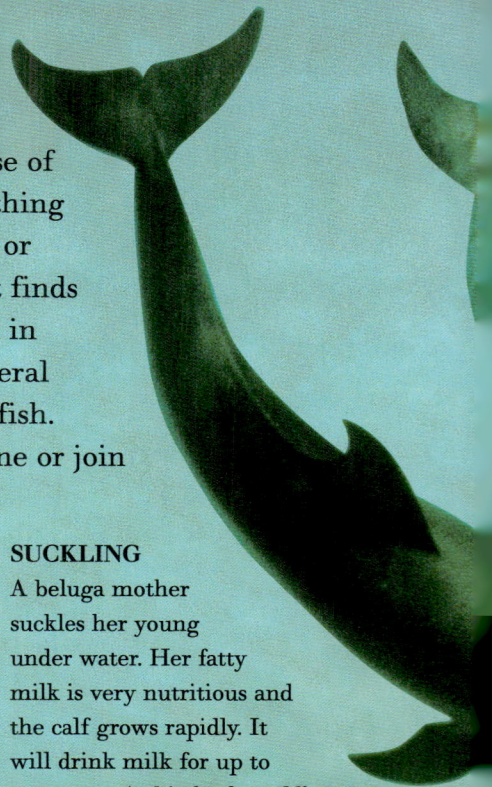

After mating, the female whale becomes pregnant and a baby whale starts to grow inside her body. After about a year, the calf is ready to be born. By now it can weigh, in the case of the blue whale, up to 2.5 tonnes/tons. The first thing the calf must do is take a breath and the mother or another whale may help it to the surface. Soon it finds one of the mother's nipples to suck the rich milk in her mammary glands (breasts). It suckles for several months until it learns to take solid food, such as fish. Mother and calf may spend most of the time alone or join nursery schools with other mothers and calves.

SUCKLING
A beluga mother suckles her young under water. Her fatty milk is very nutritious and the calf grows rapidly. It will drink milk for up to two years. At birth, the calf's body is dark grey, but it slowly lightens as the calf matures.

Bringing Up Baby

Did you know? The calves of baleen whales stop breastfeeding after about 9 months — much sooner than toothed whale calves.

AT PLAY

A young Atlantic spotted dolphin and its mother play together, twisting, turning, rolling and touching each other with their flippers. During play, the young dolphin learns the skills it will need later in life when it has to fend for itself. The youngster is darker than its mother and has no spots. These do not start to appear until it is about a year old.

TOGETHERNESS

A humpback whale calf sticks closely to its mother as she swims slowly in Hawaiian waters. The slipstream, or water flow, created by the mother's motion helps pull it along. For the first few months of its life, the calf will not stray far from its mother's side.

Having Fun

Dolphins have long delighted people with their acrobatic antics. They somersault, ride the bow waves of boats and go surfing. Dusky and spinner dolphins are particularly lively. Some antics have a purpose, such as sending signals to other dolphins, but often the animals seem to perform just for fun. In most animal species only the young play. In whale and dolphin society, adults play too. Southern right whales play a sailing game. They hang in the water with their heads down and tails in the air. The tails act like sails and catch the wind, and they are blown along.

▲ **PLAYFUL PAIR**
Two Atlantic spotted dolphins jostle as they play with a sea fan. Dolphins spend much of their time playing, especially the younger ones. They make up games, using anything they can find. Their games can last for hours.

▼ **JUMPING FOR JOY**
A pair of bottlenose dolphins leaps high, leaving the water together, as if they have rehearsed the act. They seem to jump for joy, but their behaviour may have a social function within their family group.

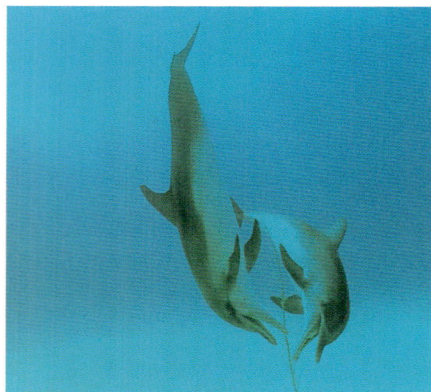

▶ **PORPOISING ON PURPOSE**

A group of long-snouted spinner dolphins go porpoising, taking long, low leaps as they swim. They churn the water behind them into a foam Many dolphins practise porpoising. in order to travel fast on the surface.

Did you know? Killer whales like brushing against each other as they swim at high speed.

◀ **RIDING THE WAKE**

A Pacific white-sided dolphin surfs the waves. This is one of the most acrobatic of the dolphins. It is often seen bow-riding in front of boats. Other species of dolphins also like to ride in the waves left in the wake of passing boats.

Did you know? The rough skin on a porpoise's back may be for giving calves piggy-back rides.

▶ **AQUATIC ACROBAT**

This dusky dolphin is throwing itself high into the air. It twists and turns, spins and performs somersaults. This behaviour is like a roll call – to check that every dolphin in the group is present and ready to go hunting. The behaviour is repeated after hunting to gather the group together once more.

Did you know? A dolphin may play cat and mouse with its prey before eating it.

Focus on

A whale leaps from the sea and crashes back to the surface in a shower of spray. This activity, called breaching, is common among humpbacks. Some may breach up to 200 times in succession. When one animal starts breaching, others follow suit. Whales put on other displays as well, including slapping their flippers and tail on the surface. These activities could, like breaching, be some form of signalling. Spy-hopping is another activity, often done to look for signs of fish to eat.

BREACHING

Propelled by powerful thrusts of its tail. the humpback launches its vast bulk into the air, twisting as it does so. For a creature weighing up to 30 tonnes/ 29½ tons, this is no mean feat. As breaching ends, it crashes back to the surface with a splash. This time it lands on its back, with one of its flippers in the air.

FLIPPER-FLOPPING

The humpback swims on the surface, raising one flipper in the air. It rolls over and slaps the flipper on the water several times, perhaps to warn off rivals. Its flipper-flopping is noisy because its flippers are so large.

Whales on Display

WHAT A FLUKE!

The humpback raises its tail in the air during the display known as lob-tailing or tail-slapping. The tail is also exposed when the whale is about to dive — behaviour called fluking. It is easy to tell if a humpback is lob-tailing or fluking. In fluking, the tail disappears below the surface quietly.

LOB-TAILING

In lob-tailing, the tail slaps on the water with a noise like a gunshot. The only other time a humpback shows its flukes is when it is about to go on a deep dive.

SPY-HOPPING

The humpback on the right of the picture is spy-hopping. It positions itself vertically in the water and pokes out its head until its eyes are showing. Then it has a good look round. The other humpback here is doing the opposite, poking out its tail, ready to lob-tail.

Where Whales are Found

Whales are found in all the world's oceans. Some range widely, while others are found only in a certain area. They may stay in the same place all year long or migrate from one area to another with the seasons. Some whales stick to shallow coastal areas, others prefer deep waters. Some live in the cool northern or southern parts of the world. Others are more at home in tropical regions near the Equator. Some species even live in rivers.

▼ **OCEAN WANDERER**
A humpback whale surfaces to blow while swimming at Cape Cod off the North-east coast of North America. In winter, the humpback feeds in high latitudes. It migrates to low latitudes to breed during the summer.

▲ **MUDDY WATERS**
The mud-laden waters of the River Amazon in South America are the habitat of the Amazon river dolphin. Here, one shows off its teeth. This species ranges along the Amazon and its tributaries.

Did you know? Some dolphins come and go between salt water and fresh water.

◄ **WORLDWIDE KILLER**
Among ice-floes in the Arctic Ocean, a killer whale hunts for prey. Killer whales are found in all the oceans. They live in coastal areas, but may venture out to the open ocean. They also swim inshore among the surf, and may beach to snatch their prey.

▶ **SNOW WHITE**
These belugas, or white whales, are in Hudson Bay, Canada. These cold-water animals live around coasts in the far North of North America, Europe and Asia. They venture into estuaries and even up rivers. In winter, they hunt in the pack ice in the Arctic.

◀ **TROPICAL MELONS**
A pod of melon-headed whales is shown swimming in the Pacific Ocean. These creatures prefer warm waters and are found in sub-tropical and tropical regions in both the Northern and Southern Hemispheres. They generally stay in deep water, keeping well away from land.

▶ **WIDE RANGER**
A bottlenose dolphin lunges through the surf in the sunny Bahamas. This animal is one of the most wide-ranging of the dolphins, being found in temperate to tropical waters in both the Northern and Southern Hemispheres. It is also found in enclosed seas, such as the Mediterranean and Red Sea. Mostly it stays in coastal waters. When bottlenose dolphins migrate to warmer areas, they lose weight. When they return to colder climes, their blubber increases again.

High and Dry

Dead whales are often found washed up, or stranded, on the seashore. Live whales are sometimes found too, particularly open ocean species, such as sperm whales. Some live whales probably strand when they become ill. Others strand when they lose their sense of direction. Whales are thought to find their way using the Earth's magnetism as a kind of map. Any change in the magnetism may cause them to turn the wrong way and head for the shore. Mass strandings also take place, with scores of whales left helpless. This happens particularly among sociable species, such as the pilot whales.

▲ BEACHED DOLPHIN
This Atlantic white-sided dolphin is stranded on a beach in the Orkney Islands. The dolphins usually travel in big groups, so mass strandings occur too.

▲ WAITING FOR THE TIDE
People come to the aid of stranded long-finned pilot whales in New Zealand. They cover the whales to prevent sunburn and throw water over them to keep their skin moist.

Did you know? When people help stranded whales, the whales often swim back and get stranded again.

◄ RARE STRANDING

Marine biologists examine a stranded Stejneger's beaked whale. Beaked whales are among the least known of all the cetaceans. Most of our knowledge about them comes from occasional strandings. Several beaked whales, such as this one, have a large tooth protruding from the jaws.

Did you know? Whales stranded in Britain belong to the monarch.

► IN THE SHALLOWS

Three belugas became stranded in shallow water as the tide went out. Polar bears may attack when they are beached. Belugas rarely become stranded and usually survive until the tide comes in again.

▼ BIG FIN

A huge fin whale has become beached on a mudflat. This animal is dead, but even if it were alive, it would be impossible to return to the water. When a whale of this size is not supported by water, its internal organs collapse. Scientists examine stranded bodies to learn about whales.

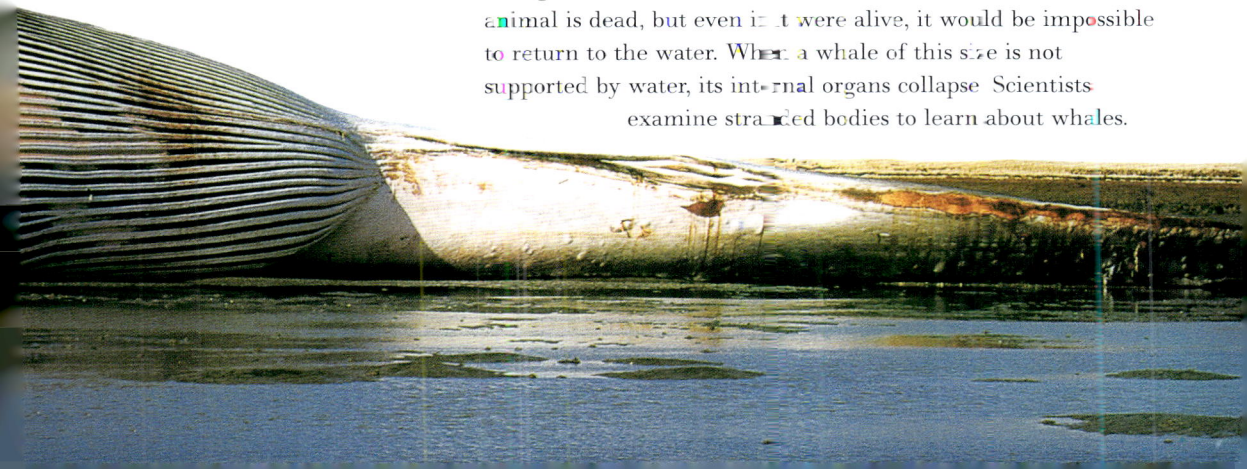

Grey and Right Whales

Grey whales and the three species of right whale, including the bowhead, are all filter-feeders with baleen plates in their upper jaws. The bowhead has the longest baleen of all, while the grey whale has short baleen. Unlike most baleen whales, the grey whale feeds mainly on the seabed. It is found only in the Northern Hemisphere, but there are right whales in both hemispheres. Right whales were named by whalers because they were the right whales to catch for their high yields of oil and baleen. They swam slowly, they could be approached easily and floated when dead.

▲ **MOTTLED MAMMAL**

The long, narrow head of a grey whale breaks the surface. Its closed blowholes are in the middle of the picture. The head is covered here and there with clusters of barnacles and lice. This, together with lighter body patches, gives the animal a mottled appearance.

◄ **LIVELY LOB**

Near the coast of Argentina in South America, a southern right whale is lob-tailing. In seconds, its tail will crash down on the surface with a smack that will echo off the cliffs on the shore. The noise will be heard by other whales, many kilometres/miles away. Right whales often lob-tail and also do headstands, waving their tails in the air.

▲ **WHITE CHIN**

A bowhead whale thrusts its head out of the water, exposing its unique white chin, covered with black patches. The skin is smooth, with no growths like those on the skin of the northern and southern right whales.

Did you know? We know a lot about grey whales because they stay in shallow waters near the coast.

◀ **BEARDED**

A southern right whale cruises in the South Atlantic. One distinctive feature of this whale is the deeply curved jawline. Another is its beard and bonnet. These are large growths on the whale's chin and nose, which become infested with barnacles.

◀ **HAIRY MONSTER**

The northern right whale lives in the North Atlantic. Whalers used to call the crusty hard skin on its head a bonnet or rock garden. Lice and barnacles live on the skin, which can grow enormous. Right whales are the hairiest of all whales, keeping more hair after birth than other cetaceans. It even grows facial hair.

Did you know?

you can tell a grey whale by its unique long, very narrow head

▶ **BRISTLY JAWS**

A grey whale opens its mouth, showing the baleen plates on its upper jaw. The baleen is quite short, stiff and coarse. The whale uses it to filter out the tiny creatures it digs out of the seabed when feeding. Grey whales are not shy and sometimes swim up to the boats of whale-watchers.

Rorquals

The rorquals are a
family of baleen
whales that includes the
largest creature ever to live, the
blue whale. They are named
after the grooves on their throat — the
word rorqual means a furrow. All rorquals,
except the humpback, have a long streamlined body with a sharp nose and a
dorsal fin set well back. They can swim at up to 30kph/19mph. The humpback
is a slower swimmer with a chunkier body. It has knobbly flippers and a hump
in front of the dorsal fin. It is famous for the songs it sings. The minke whale is
the smallest rorqual. Bryde's whale lives mainly in tropical and sub-tropical
waters, while the other rorquals often venture into colder waters as well, often
venturing into polar waters in the summer.

▼ TINY MINKE
The minke whale grows to only about one-third
of the size of the blue whale and never exceeds
10 tonnes/tons in weight. It has a slim snout and
a curved dorsal fin. Its flippers are short and
can be marked with a
broad white band.

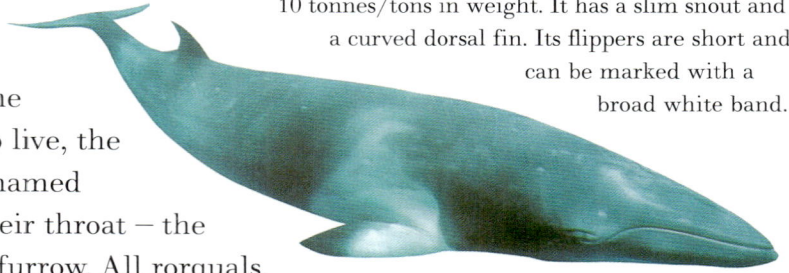

▲ WHALE WITH A HUMP
This picture of a humpback whale shows the feature that
gives it its name very well. Its small dorsal
fin sits on top of a pronounced hump on
its back. This profile view of the animal
also shows the prominent splash guard
on its head in front of the blowholes.

Did you know? Humpback whales can live to age 95.

▼ KNOBBLY FLIPPER
A humpback whale swims
on the surface, with one of
its flippers up in the air
like a boat sail. The flippers
of the humpback are by far
the most distinctive of all
the whales. They are sturdy
and very
long —
up to a
third of the
length of the
whale's body. The
flippers have knobs
along their front edge.

Flipper

◀ **BIG GULP**

A blue whale feeds in Californian waters. It has taken in a mouthful of water containing thousands of the tiny shrimp-like krill it feeds on. The grooves on its throat that allow its mouth to expand can be clearly seen. A blue whale typically has between 60 and 90 of these grooves.

▶ **DRIPPING FLUKES**

A blue whale fluking, with its tail flukes rising out of the water before the animal dives. Among rorquals, only blue and humpback whales expose their flukes before diving. The humpback's tail flukes are quite different. They are knobbly at the rear edges and have white markings on the underside.

Did you know? A blue whale's heart is about the size of a small car.

◀ **SEI WHALE**

The sei whale can be found in most of the oceans. It feeds in the cool Arctic or Antarctic waters during the summer and migrates to warmer waters in the winter to breed. With a length of up to about 18m/59ft, it is slightly larger than the similar Bryde's whale.

487

Sperm and White Whales

The sperm and the white whales are two families of toothed whales. The sperm whale and dwarf and pygmy sperm whales have an organ in their head called the spermaceti organ, which is filled with wax. The wax may help the animals when they dive and may play a part in focusing the sound waves they use for echo-location. The sperm whale and the two white whales (the beluga and the narwhal) have no dorsal fin. The sperm whale has teeth only on its lower jaw. The beluga has up to 20 teeth in each of its jaws, but the narwhal has only two. In the male narwhal, one tooth grows into a spiral tusk, up to 3m/10ft long.

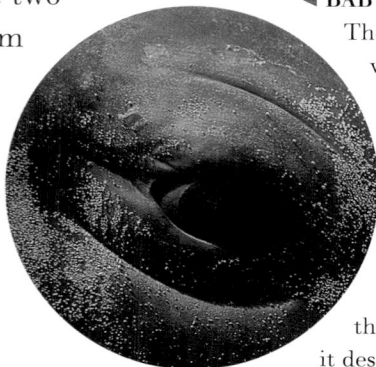

◄ BABY EYES

The eye of a sperm whale calf. Like all whales, the sperm whale has tiny eyes compared with those of most other mammals. But this does not matter because when the whale dives to feed, it descends deep into the ocean where light never reaches. It depends on its superb echo-location system to find its prey.

Did you know? Perfume is made from foul-smelling wax made in sperm whales' guts.

Did you know? A sperm whale can dive as deep as 3,000m/9,843ft in search of squid.

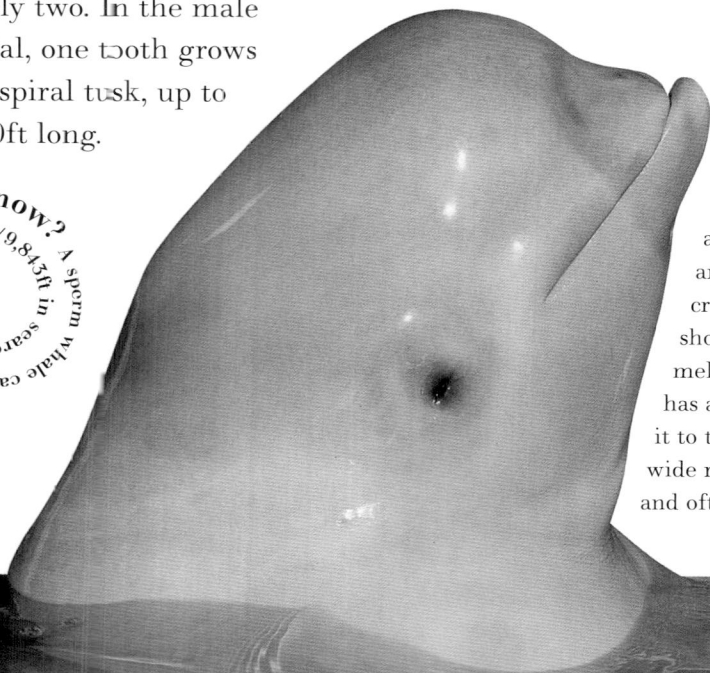

◄ LOOKING AROUND

A beluga raises its head above the water to look around — they are inquisitive creatures. Belugas have quite short heads with a rounded melon. Unusually for whales, it has a noticeable neck, allowing it to turn its head. It also has a wide range of facial expressions and often appears to be smiling.

◄ COW AND CALF

A sperm whale cow swims with her calf. Cows suckle their young for at least two years in a nursery group with other cows and calves. This picture shows the sperm whale's unique body shape, with its huge blunt snout. The sperm whale does not have a dorsal fin, just a triangular lump on its back.

► HIGH SOCIETY

This pod of belugas is swimming in Arctic waters off the coast of Canada. Belugas are usually found in such pods because they are very social animals. Note the typical body characteristics, including broad stubby flippers and the lack of a dorsal fin.

▼ LONG IN THE TOOTH

In freezing Arctic waters a male narwhal comes to the surface to blow, its long tusk raised. The tusk has a spiral shape and can be up to 3m/10ft long. It is one of the animal's two teeth. A few males produce twin tusks.

Tusk

▲ COLOUR, SHAPE AND WEIGHT

The narwhal's stocky body is much like that of the beluga. Both grow up to about 5m/16¼ft long and weigh up to 1,500kg/3,307lb. The main difference is in the colour. The beluga is white, but the narwhal is mostly a mottled grey.

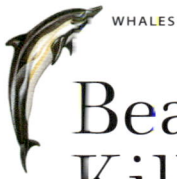

Beaked, Pilot and Killer Whales

Beaked whales are named after their beak, which is rather like that of many kinds of dolphin. Unlike dolphins, they have hardly any teeth — most have just two. Beaked whales live mainly in the deep ocean and little is known about them. Pilot and killer whales are better known. They are part of the dolphin family and, like many dolphins, tend to live in quite large groups. Because pilot whales and killer whales are mostly black, they are often called blackfish. The killer whale is the largest and best known of the family and is a fierce predator.

▲ A TELLING TAIL
A killer whale lob-tails. Its tail is black on top but mainly white underneath, with a distinct notch in the middle. Note also the pointed tips of the flukes.

◄ KILLER LEAP
A killer whale leaps high into the air while breaching in Alaskan waters. The whale may twist and turn before it falls back to the surface with a resounding splash. Look at this killer whale's broad paddle-shaped flippers. The size and shape of the flippers and the dorsal fin mark this specimen as a male.

Did you know? Killer whales have never been known to attack humans in the wild.

◄ **CRUISING PILOT**
The short-finned pilot whale has a broad, bulbous head and, for this reason, is sometimes called the pothead whale. It has sickle-shaped flippers and a curved dorsal fin. This pilot whale prefers tropical and sub-tropical regions. The long-finned pilot whale is similar, but with slightly longer flippers, and lives in the Southern Hemisphere in cool and warm waters.

► **WHITE LIPS**
A pod of melon-headed whales swims close together. One of them is spy-hopping and shows its melon-shaped head. Note its white lips.

◄ **SLEEK LINES**
Note the streamlined body of the killer whale as it comes out of the water while performing at Sea World in California. The picture shows its white patches behind the eye and at the side, and the white chin. There is a greyish saddle patch behind the dorsal fin.

▼ **FALSE TEETH**
A false killer whale spy-hops. False killer whales have as many as 20 teeth in each jaw. It does not look much like the killer whale and is much smaller. It has no white patches and its head is more slender.

► **LONER**
A beaked whale swims alone. Most spend a lot of time alone or with one or two others. They prefer deep waters and some species dive very deep indeed.

Oceanic Dolphins

Dolphins are the most common of all cetaceans. They are swift swimmers and have sleek, streamlined bodies with, usually, a prominent dorsal fin. They have dark grey backs and white or pale grey bellies. Many dolphins have contrasting stripes along the sides. About half the dolphin species have a long beak and as many as 250 teeth The rest have short beaks and fewer teeth. Dolphins can be found in most oceans, but not usually in the cold waters of far northern or far southern regions. Most are highly sociable, some travelling together in groups of hundreds.

◄ STRIKING STRIPES

Distinctive black and white striped bodies tell us that these two animals are southern right whale-dolphins. The back is jet black, while the beak, forehead, belly and flippers are white.

▼ PORPOISING DOLPHINS

A group of common dolphins is porpoising – taking long, low leaps. They have long beaks and yellow markings on their sides. The dark skin on the upper back looks rather like a saddle. This is why it is also called the saddleback dolphin.

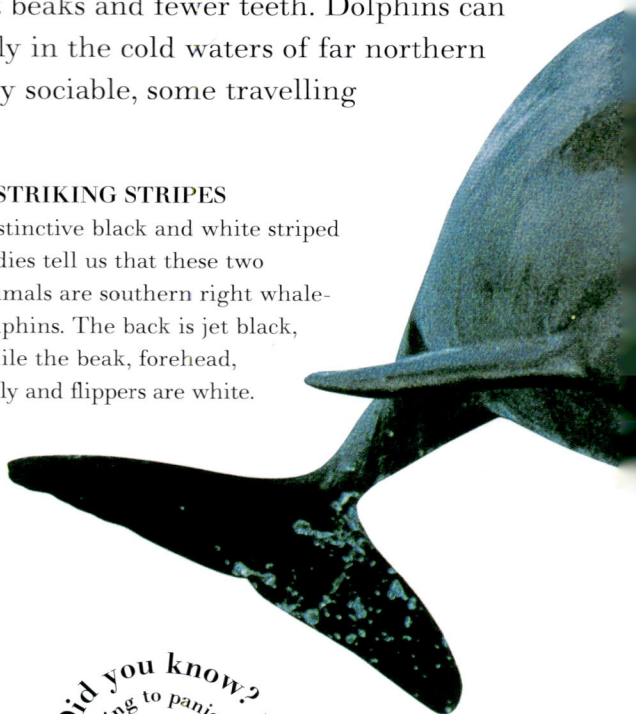

Did you know? Dolphins make loud noises when hunting to panic fish into bunching together.

◄ GREAT LEAPERS

Two bottlenose dolphins launch themselves with great energy several metres into the air. Their bodies are mainly grey in colour. The head of the bottlenose dolphin is more rounded than that of most other beaked dolphins.

► BLUNT HEADS

A group of Risso's dolphins is easy to recognize by their blunt heads and tall dorsal fins. Their bodies are mainly grey on the back and sides. The colour becomes paler with age and some old adults are nearly all white.

▼ PALE FACE

The odd-looking Irrawaddy dolphin has a rounded head and a distinct neck, rather like the beluga. Its flippers are large and curved. It is found in rivers and estuaries, as well as coastal waters from south of India as far as northern Australia.

Dolphin Rescue

An old Greek tale tells of a famed poet and musician named Arion. After a concert tour, sailors on the ship that was taking him home set out to kill him for his money. They granted his request to sing a final song. Then he jumped overboard. He did not drown because a dolphin, attracted by his beautiful song, carried him to the shore.

Porpoises and River Dolphins

Porpoises look rather like dolphins, yet they form a separate cetacean family. They are smaller than most dolphins and do not have a typical dolphin beak. Their teeth are different, being spade-like instead of cone-shaped. Most porpoises are shy. The rare river dolphins form a separate family. They have long slender beaks and rounded foreheads. Their flexible necks allow their heads to turn, unlike oceanic dolphins. In the muddy waters where they mostly live, they use echo-location rather than their poor eyesight to find the fish and other creatures they feed on.

▲ BEAKED BOTO

The Amazon river dolphin, or boto, has the typical long beak of the river dolphins. Its colour varies from pale bluish-grey to pink. It has no dorsal fin, just a fleshy ridge on its back.

◄ RESTING PORPOISE

A Dall's porpoise displays the body features of its species. It has a stocky black body, with a large white patch on the sides and belly. Its dorsal fin and tail flukes have flashes of white as well. Unlike most porpoises, which are shy, the Dall's porpoise loves to bow-ride fast boats.

▼ RARE SNEEZER

Like all river dolphins, the Yangtze river dolphin, or baiji, has poor sight. Its blowhole is circular and its blow sounds like a sneeze. This dolphin is one of the rarest of all cetaceans, numbering maybe only 150 individuals.

Did you know? The harbour porpoise is rarely seen in harbours.

► FAST AND FURIOUS

Dall's porpoises are the most energetic of all the porpoises. Their swimming is fast and furious. They kick up great fountains of spray as they thrust themselves through the surface of the water.

► NOISY SNORTER

The harbour porpoise seldom comes near boats. It has a noisy, snorting blow. The general body colour is dark grey on the back with paler patches on the flanks. Its belly is white, and it has black flippers and lips.

Did you know? Dall's porpoises are one of the fastest marine mammals – travelling at 65kph/40mph

◄ DOLPHIN OR PORPOISE?

Porpoises are close relatives of dolphins, but they belong to a different family with different body features. Scientists can take advantage of strandings such as this one to study these very shy creatures.

495

Fellow Travellers

Whales are not the only aquatic mammals. Other examples include otters and seals. Seals are well adapted to life in the water, with a sleek, streamlined body and flippers. They have some fur, but it is the thick layer of fatty blubber under the skin that keeps them warm in the water. It also insulates against the cold air when seals are on land. The dugong and the manatee are also at home in the water. Often called sea cows, these creatures have a bulky seal-like body. They live in rivers and coastal waters in tropical and sub-tropical regions.

▲ **BEAR AT SEA**

The polar bear drifts on pack ice in the Arctic Ocean, often taking to the water to hunt seals. In addition to a thick layer of blubber, a polar bear has a thick furry coat to protect it from the Arctic climate.

◄ **FIN-FOOTED**

The Californian sea lion swims using powerful strokes of its front flippers. Its body is much more adapted to the water than an otter's, with its paddle-like flippers. Its body is partly hairy, partly smooth.

Did you know? Whales are probably descended from a 4-legged land mammal called a mesonychid.

► **FURRY SWIMMER**

The otter is at home on land or in water. Its four-legged, furry body is adapted for life in the water. Its legs are short and its toes are webbed making efficient paddles. Its fur is waterproof.

▲ WHALE-LIKE

The whale shark is not a whale, but the biggest fish of all – a harmless member of the shark family. The whale shark is more than 15m/49ft long. It feeds on plankton, which it takes in through its gaping mouth. It sieves out the plankton from the water through a special gill structure.

Did you know? The largest whale shark ever caught weighed 15 tonnes. tons.

◄ SEA COW

A dugong swims in the Pacific Ocean, just off Australia. Unlike the seals, which leave the water to breed on land, dugongs spend all their time in the sea. They have no hind limbs, but a tail, similar to that of a whale. The alternative name for the creature – sea cow – is a good one because the animal feeds on sea grasses.

► EXCAVATOR

The walrus is a mammal of the seal family. Like the true seals, it has no external ears and it swims by means of its rear flippers. It feeds mainly on the seabed, using its whiskers to locate buried clams and its armoured snout to grub them out. The walrus excavates clams by squirting a high pressure jet of water from its mouth into the clam's burrow.

Whale Slaughter

The baleen whales and sperm whale are so big that they have no natural predators. Until a few hundred years ago, the oceans teemed with them. In the 15th and 16th centuries, whaling grew into a huge industry. Whales were killed for blubber, which could be rendered down into oils for candles and lamps. The industry expanded following the invention of an explosive harpoon gun in the 1860s and, by the 1930s, nearly 50,000 whales a year were taken in Antarctica. In 1988, commercial whaling was banned.

▲ **WHALE SOAP**
The sperm whale was once a prime target for whalers. They were after the waxy spermaceti from the organ in the whale's forehead. This was used to make soap.

▶ **DEADLY STRUGGLE**
Whalers row out from a big ship to harpoon a whale in the early 1800s. It was a dangerous occupation in those days because the dying whales could easily smash the small boats to pieces.

Did you know? Whale blubber was made into lipstick and other sorts of make-up.

▼ **FIN WHALING**
A modern whaler finishes cutting up a fin whale. A few whales are still caught legally for scientific purposes, but their meat ends up on the table in some countries. The fin whale used to be a favourite target for whalers because of its huge size.

◄ PILOT MASSACRE
Every year, in the Faroe Islands of the North Atlantic pods of pilot whales are killed, a traditional practice that has not been stopped. The blood of the dying whales turns the sea red.

Did you know? Early whalers killed their prey by throwing harpoons from rowing boats.

► KILLER NET
This striped dolphin died when it was caught in a drift net. It became entangled and was unable to rise to the surface to breathe. Tens of thousands of dolphins drown each year because of nets cast into the oceans.

Did you know? In the 1800s baleen was used to make umbrellas.

Whale Tale
Moby Dick *was written by Herman Melville in 1851. The one-legged Captain Ahab searches for a great white whale (a sperm whale) called Moby Dick. Eventually he harpoons Moby Dick, but he and all but one of his crew die.*

Glossary

abdomen
The rear part of a spider's body.

adapt
When an animal or group of animals changes – physically or in behaviour – in order to survive in new conditions.

aestivation
A period of rest during heat and drought, similar to hibernation.

algae
A group of very simple plants, some of which are only the size of a single cell. Others are much larger. Most types of algae live in water, but they also grow on damp soil and tree trunks.

alpha pair
The top male and female in a wolf pack. Only this strong, healthy pair of animals breeds.

ambush
When an animal hides, waiting for prey to walk past, then pounces on it in a surprise attack.

anaconda
A type of boa.

Antarctic
The region around the South Pole and Southern Ocean, including the continent of Antarctica.

antennae
A pair of feelers on an insect's head, used mainly for smelling, but also for feeling things.

arachnid
One of a group of small meat-eating animals with eight legs, such as spiders, mites, ticks and scorpions.

araneidae
The family of spiders that usually build orb webs.

artery
A blood vessel that carries blood away from the heart.

arthropod
An animal without a backbone that has many jointed legs and an exoskeleton on the outside of its body. Arthropods include spiders, insects, crabs and woodlice.

baleen
A tough and flexible material, which forms comb-like plates in the upper jaw of baleen whales.

baleen whale
A whale that has baleen plates in its mouth instead of teeth.

binocular vision
The ability to see things with both eyes at the same time, which helps animals to judge distances well and pounce on prey.

bioluminescence
The production of light by living organisms.

bladder
Where urine is stored in the body before being expelled.

blow
The cloud of moist air that is blown from a whale's blowhole when it breathes out.

blowhole
The nostril of a whale. Baleen whales have two blowholes, toothed whales have one.

blubber

boas
A group of snakes that live mainly in North and South America. They kill by constriction and give birth to live young.

breed
An animal that belongs to one species, but has definite characteristics, such as colouring, body shape and coat markings.

broadwing
A term used in falconry for birds with broad wings, such as buzzards.

bull
A male whale or crocodilian.

calf
A baby whale.

camouflage
The colours and patterns on an animal's body that help it to blend in with its surroundings so it can hide from enemies or sneak up on prey.

canid
A member of the dog family. Wolves, jackals, coyotes and foxes are all canids.

canine
A sharp, pointed tooth next to the incisors that grips and pierces the skin of prey.

cannibalism
Animals eating others of their own kind.

carapace
The shell-like covering over the front part of a spider's body, the cephalothorax.

carcass
The dead body of an animal.

carnassials
The strong, shearing teeth at the back of a carnivore's mouth.

carnivore
An animal that feeds mainly on the flesh of other animals.

carrion
The bodies of dead animals.

cartilage
The strong but flexible material from which the skeletons of sharks and rays are made, rather than the bone that is found in most other animals with backbones.

catshark
The common name given to a group of sharks that are known in the British Isles as dogfish.

cetacean
A whale, dolphin or porpoise, all of which belong to the animal order Cetacea.

cephalothorax
The front part of a spider's body, to which the legs are attached.

chelicerae
The jaws of a spider. Each jaw has two parts — a large basal segment and a fang.

cobras
Poisonous snakes in the elapid family, with short, fixed fangs at the front of the mouth.

cocoon
A silky covering or egg case made to protect a spider's eggs.

cold-blooded
An animal whose body temperature varies with that of its surroundings.

colubrids
Mostly harmless snakes. These snakes make up the biggest group — nearly three-quarters of the world's snakes.

conservation
Protecting living things and helping them to survive in the future.

constrictor
A snake that kills by coiling its body tightly around its prey to suffocate it.

cow
A female whale.

crab spiders
Ambushing spiders in the family Thomisidae that do not usually build webs and are often shaped rather like crabs.

crocodilian
A member of the group of animals that includes crocodiles, alligators, caimans and gharials.

crustacean
A creature with a hard body that lives in the sea. Shrimp and krill are crustaceans.

cub
A young wolf, dog, bear or big cat.

cultivation
The preparation and use of the ground in order to grow crops.

den
The home of an animal such as a wolf or fox. A den may be an underground burrow or a cave, or simply a nest in the long grass.

dew claw
The toe found high on a big cat's and wolf's foreleg, which does not touch the ground. It is used by big cats to knock down prey. On a wolf it has no obvious use.

diaphragm
A sheet of muscle separating the chest cavity from the abdominal cavity, the movement of which helps with breathing.

diet
The usual types of food eaten by an animal.

digestion
The process by which food is broken down so it can be absorbed into the body.

diurnal
Active by day.

dolphin
A small, toothed whale that has cone-shaped teeth.

domestic cat
A species of cat whose wild ancestors were tamed by people and bred in captivity.

domesticated
Describes animals that have been tamed by people. Cows, sheep and horses are all domesticated.

dominant animal
An animal that takes first place in a group.

dorsal fin
The tall triangular fin on a shark's back. Some sharks have two dorsal fins, the front fin larger than the back one. Also, the usually triangular fin on the back of a whale's body.

down
Fine, hairy feathers for warmth not flight. Young chicks have only down and no flight feathers.

dragline
The line of silk on which a spider drops down, often to escape danger, and then climbs back up.

echo-location
The method toothed whales use to find their prey. They send out pulses of high-pitched sounds and listen for the echoes produced when the pulses are reflected by objects in their path.

ectotherm
A cold-blooded animal.

elapids
A group of poisonous snakes that includes the cobras, mambas and the coral snakes. Elapids live in hot countries.

embryo
The early stage of an animal before birth.

environment
The surroundings in which an animal or plant lives. It includes both living things (other animals and plants) and non-living things (such as stones, the air, temperature and sunlight).

epidermis
Outer layer of the skin.

evolve
When a species of animals or plants changes gradually over time, to become better suited to the conditions in which it lives.

exoskeleton
The hard outer skin or shell that covers a spider's body.

extinct
When a whole species or larger group of animals or plants has disappeared, dying out completely.

facial disc
A circle of tiny feathers around the face of an owl.

falconry
Flying falcons or hawks as a sport. Also called hawking.

fang
A long, pointed tooth that may be used to deliver venom.

fertilization
The joining together of a male sperm and a female egg to start a new life.

filter-feeder
Animals that sieve water through giant combs called gill rakers, for very small particles of food.

fish ball
The ball that schools of fish make when attacked.

fledging
The time when a bird starts to fly. A fledgling is a bird that is just beginning to fly.

flipper
A whale's paddle-like forelimbs.

flukes
The tail of a whale.

fluking
Raising the flukes into the air before diving.

fossil
The remains of a once-living plant or animal that have turned to stone over thousands or millions of years.

gastroliths
Hard objects, such as stones, swallowed by crocodilians, that stay in the stomach to help crush food.

genetic
Relating to the genes, inside the cells. Genes control the characteristics passed on from parents to their offspring.

genus
A grouping of living things, smaller than a family, but larger than a species. The genus is the first word of the Latin name, e.g. in the King vulture's latin name *Sarcoramphus papa*, the genus is *Sarcoramphus*.

gestation
The period of time between conception and the birth of an animal.

gills
The organ used by aquatic animals, such as sharks, for breathing.

gizzard
A muscular chamber in an animal's gut that grinds large lumps of food into small pieces or particles.

gland
An organ in the body that produces chemicals for a particular use.

grizzly bear
Another name for the brown bear. It is particularly used to mean North American brown bears.

gut
The long tube in which food is digested and absorbed, running a winding path through an animal's body.

habitat
A place that has certain kinds of animals and plants living there, such as tropical rainforest or semi-desert.

herbivore
An animal that eats plants.

hibernation
A period of sleep during the winter when body processes slow down. Animals hibernate mainly because food is scarce and they might starve otherwise.

hierarchy
A strict social order within a group of animals.

hybrid
The offspring of two animals from different species or sub-species.

incisor
Front tooth used for biting off chunks and cutting up meat.

incubate
To sit on eggs to keep them warm so that the baby animals will develop inside.

incubation
Keeping eggs warm so that development can take place.

infrasounds
Very low sounds which are too low for people to hear.

insect
A small animal with a body that is divided into three parts, with six legs and usually one or two pairs of wings

insulation
A covering, such as a layer of thick fat beneath a polar bear's skin, that prevents heat leaving a warm body to the cold outside.

intestine
Part of an animal's gut where food is broken down and absorbed into the body.

invertebrate
An animal that does not have a backbone.

jawless fish
Primitive fish with sucker-like mouths. They had their origins 500 million years ago and living descendants include lampreys and hagfish.

jumping spiders
Spiders in the family Salticidae that are daytime hunters with two stout front pairs of legs.

jungle
The dense undergrowth found in a rainforest.

juvenile
A young animal before it grows and develops into a mature adult.

kidney
An organ of the body that filters blood to remove waste products, called urine.

krill
Small shrimp-like creatures that swim in huge shoals. Krill form part of the diet of filter feeders such as whale sharks.

ligament
A band of white, fibrous tissue that cannot stretch. It connects bones in a joint and strengthens them.

light organs
Special structures in a fish's skin that produce "cold" light. They work by mixing particular chemicals together

litter
A group of young animals born to a mother at one time.

liver
An organ that processes food from the digestive system (gut). One of the liver's main tasks is to remove any poisons from the blood.

lob-tailing
Raising the tail into the air and then slapping it down on the surface of the water.

lungs
An organ of the body that takes in oxygen from the air.

lure
An imitation bird swung on a line to act as a target when training a falcon.

lynx spiders
Spiders in the family Oxopidae that hunt on plants.

mammal
A warm-blooded animal with a bony skeleton and hair on its body. Female mammals produce milk from mammary glands (equivalent to human breasts) to feed their young.

manning
Making a hawk tame by getting it used to people.

mantling
Standing over a kill with wings spread to hide it.

mating
The pairing up of a male and female to produce young. During mating, the fertilization (joining together) of a male sperm and a female egg takes place, which starts a new life.

mature
Developed enough to be capable of reproduction.

maxillae
A pair of small jaws on a spider that are used to break up food.

melon
The rounded forehead of a toothed whale. It is thought to help direct the sounds the animal uses for echo-location.

migration
A regular journey some animals make from one place to another, because of changes in the weather or their food supply, or to breed. Many birds of prey fly to warmer climates for the winter.

mimicry
When a spider copies the shape of another animal or an object such as a bird dropping or stick. Spiders use mimicry to hide from enemies and prey.

mobbing
When prey birds gang up against their predators and try to drive them away.

molar
A broad, ridged tooth in the back of a mammal's jaw, used for grinding up food. In crocodilians, the molar is used for crushing.

moulting
The process by which an animal sheds its skin.

muzzle
The jaws and nose of an animal such as a wolf.

mygalomorph
A more primitive spider with jaws that strike downward. Mygalomorphs have two pairs of book lungs and no tracheae (breathing tubes). Most species are large, hairy and live in burrows, such as trapdoor spiders and tarantulas.

nerves
Fibres that carry electrical impulses to and from the brain.

nestling
Young bird before it leaves the nest.

nipple
A teat through which young suck milk from the mammary glands.

nocturnal
An animal that rests by day and is active during the night.

nursery-web spiders
Females in the family Pisauridae that carry their egg cases around with them in their jaws and make a silk tent when the eggs are ready to hatch.

nutrients
Chemicals in food that, when digested, build blood, bone and tissue. This tissue maintains growth and strength in the body.

oesophagus
Part of the gut of an animal, usually long and tube-shaped. It transports swallowed food from the mouth to the stomach.

order
A major grouping of animals, larger than a family. E.g. owls belong to the order Strigiformes.

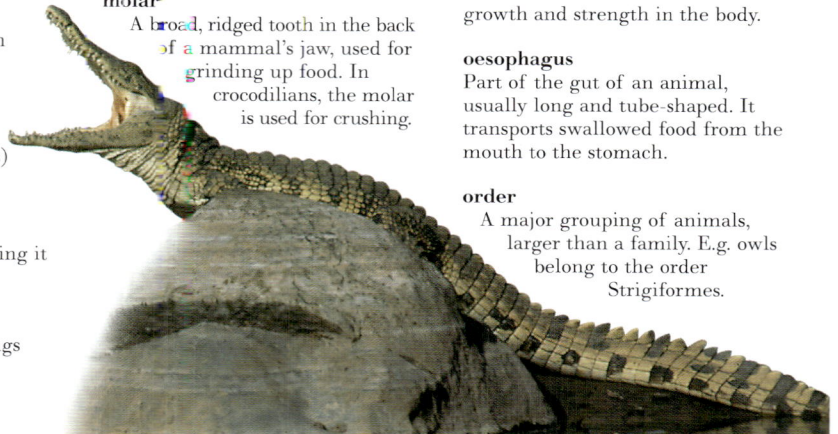

pack
The name given to a group of wolves or wild dogs that lives and hunts together.

palate
The roof of the mouth. An extra or secondary bony palate separates the mouth from the breathing passages.

palp (pedipalp)
Short, leg-like feeler either side of the mouthparts of spiders. In the adult male, the end segment is modified for putting sperm into the female.

paralyse
To make an animal powerless and unable to move, although it is still alive.

pectoral fins
The pair of large wing-like fins on either side of a shark's body.

pectorals
The powerful breast muscles of a bird, used in flight.

pellet
A ball of indigestible matter coughed up by birds of prey.

pelvic fins
The pair of small fins on the underside of a shark's body behind the pectoral fins.

pheromone
A chemical scent produced by spiders to attract members of the opposite sex and, in some cases, to attract prey.

pigment
Colouring

piracy
When one bird harries another to make it let go of prey it has caught.

pits
Heat sensors located on either side of a snake's head.

placenta
A disc-shaped organ that is attached to the lining of the womb during pregnancy. It is through this that the embryo receives oxygen and nutrients.

plankton
Tiny sea creatures and plants. They form the basic foodstuff for all life in the oceans.

playfight
Early preparation for learning how to fight when cubs are older. Playing helps to build up muscles, improve co-ordination and develop good reflexes.

poaching
Capturing and/or killing animals illegally and selling them for commercial gain.

pod
A group of whales. Also a group of young crocodilians just out of their eggs.

polar region
The area around the North or South Pole, where it is very cold.

porpoise
A small toothed whale with spade-shaped teeth.

porpoising
Leaping in and out of the water while swimming fast

predator
A living thing that catches and kills other living things for food.

Pregnant
When a female animal has a baby developing in her womb.

prehensile tail
A tail that is capable of grasping and holding on to objects such as branches.

prehistoric
Dating from the time long ago, before people wrote down historical records.

prey
An animal that is hunted by animals or by people for food.

primitive
Keeping physical characteristics that may have origins millions of years ago.

pup
A young shark, particularly when it has just been born.

pupil
In animals with backbones, the dark, circular opening in the middle of the eye that allows light to enter.

python
A group of snakes that lives mainly in Australia, Africa and Asia. Pythons kill their prey by constriction. They lay eggs.

range
The maximum area in which an animal roams.

raptor
Any bird of prey. From the Latin *rapere* meaning to seize, grasp or take by force.

rattlesnakes
Snakes that live mainly in the south-west United States and Mexico. They have a warning rattle made of empty tail sections at the end of the tail.

receptor
A cell or part of a cell that is designed to respond to a particular stimulus such as light, heat or smell.

regurgitate
When an animal brings up half-digested food to feed its young.

reptile
A scaly, cold-blooded animal with a backbone, including tortoises, turtles, snakes, lizards and crocodilians.

rodent
An animal with chisel-shaped incisors (front teeth), used for gnawing. Rats, mice, beavers and porcupines are all types of rodent.

rorqual
A whale that belongs to the family of baleen whales.

saliva
A colourless liquid produced by glands in the mouth. Saliva helps to slide food from the mouth to the throat. In some snakes, saliva also aids digestion.

scavenge
Feed on the remains of a kill left behind by another animal or on naturally dead animals or rubbish.

scavenger
An animal that feeds mainly on the remains left behind from another animal's meal.

school
Another name for a group of whales.

scrape
A patch of ground cleared by a bird to lay its eggs on.

sensory system
The collection of organs and cells by which an animal is able to receive messages from its surroundings.

social animal
An animal that lives in a group, usually with others of its own kind. Social animals co-operate with other group members.

spawn
Produce eggs in large numbers to be fertilized.

species
All living things are grouped into species. Animals of the same species are similar to each other and can breed with each other. They produce young that in turn can breed together.

spiderling
A young spider that looks more or less like the fully-grown adult, but is smaller.

spinneret
An opening at the end of a spider's abdomen through which silk is pulled out.

spiral valve
A complicated folding of the tissues in the intestine of sharks that aids efficient digestion of nutrients.

spitting spiders
Spiders in the family Scytodidae with a domed carapace and large venom glands that produce glue as well as venom.

stalk
When a hunting animal follows its prey cautiously to avoid being seen until close enough to pounce.

stooping
When a falcon dives on its prey from on high at great speed, with wings nearly closed.

streamline
The rounded, tapering shape that allows water (or air) to flow smoothly around an object

streamlined
Shaped to slip through air or water easily without much resistance.

submissive
When a junior animal gives way to a more powerful animal.

subspecies
A species is sometimes divided into even smaller groups called subspecies, which are sufficiently distinct to have their own group.

sweat glands
Small organs beneath an animal's skin that produce sweat. Sweat helps to keep the body cool.

tail fin
Another name for a whale's flukes.

tarantula
One of the giant, hairy spiders belonging to the family Theraphosidae.

taste buds
Tiny bumps on an animal's tongue, which have nerve endings that pick up taste signals.

temperate
Mild regions of the Earth that do not experience extreme heat or cold, wet or dry.

territory
An area in which an animal or group of animals live. The borders of territories are marked, so that others of the same species know to keep out.

thermal
A rising current of warm air, on which vultures and other birds of prey soar.

threat display
The aggressive behaviour shown by some species of sharks when confronted by other sharks or sea creatures.

toothed whale
A whale that has teeth and not baleen plates in its mouth. Toothed whales include sperm whales, dolphins and porpoises.

trachea
The windpipe running from the nose and mouth used to transport air to the lungs.

venom
Poisonous fluid produced in the glands of some snakes and by nearly all spiders that is used to kill their prey.

vertical migration
The daily movement that sharks make downward into the deep sea by day and upward to the surface waters at night.

vipers
A group of very poisonous snakes with fangs that fold. Some vipers have heat pits on their faces. Most vipers give birth to live young.

warm-blooded
An animal (such as a mouse or a human being) that is able to maintain its body at roughly the same temperature all the time.

warning colours
Bright colours that show others that an animal is poisonous. Bright colours also warn predators to keep away.

whale
A cetacean. Commonly the term is applied to the large whales, such as the baleen and sperm whales.

whalebone
A popular name for baleen, but baleen is not bone.

whaling
Hunting whales for their meat and blubber.

windpipe
The tube leading from the mouth to the lungs through which an animal takes in fresh air (containing oxygen) and gives out used air (containing carbon dioxide).

wingspan
The distance across the wings, from one wing-tip to the other.

womb
An organ in the body of female mammals in which young grow and are nourished until birth.

yolk
Food material that is rich in protein and fats. It nourishes a developing embryo inside an egg.

yolk sac
An outgrowth of the embryo's gut containing food that sustains the shark embryo before it is born. As the yolk is used up the sac is withdrawn into the embryo's body.

Index

Picture Credits

b=bottom, t=top, c=centre, l=left, r=right

Spiders

AKG: 26bl, 42br. Heather Angel: 31bl. Bridgeman Art Library: 21b. BBC Natural History Unit: G Doré: 53b/Premaphotos: 55b/ Doug Wechsler: 22bl. Bruce Coleman Ltd: Jane Burton: 27tr,35t/John Cancalosi: 19c/Gerald Cubitt: 24t/Adrian Davies: 58br/A. Dean: 61b/ Jeremy Grayson: 53t, 61t/Carol Hughes: 64t/Janos Jurka: 20br/George McCarthy: 57t, 58bl/Dieter & Mary Plage: 65tr/andrew Purcell: 62b/ John Shaw: 16t/Alan Stillwell: 25c, 26t, 58t, 60, 61c/ an Taylor: 40t, 47tr/Kim Taylor: 25b, 56b, 58bl/John Visser: 27tl, 45/Fred Williams: 17tr. Mary Evans Picture Library: 15c, 51cr. Michael and Patricia Fogden: 18bl, 42bl, 46t&b, 47t, 57b. FLPA: 27br, 65br/Chris Mattison: 50c/L. Lee Rue: 45br/Roger Tidman: 64b/Larry West: 41t, 5t, 65c/Tony Wharton: 65bc. Microscopix Photolibrary: 23t, 24b/A. Syred: 28c. Natural Science Photos: 52b, 57b. Nature Photographers Ltd: 22br, 50tl, 57c, 57cr, 65bl. NHPA: 41tr, 52b. Oxford Scientific Films: 55t, 56b, 47t1, 55c. Papilio Photographic: 21t, 30br, 56t, 55t-, 5°t, 65-l.Planet Earth Pictures: D. Maitland: 20t,41tl/BrianKenney: 60br/Ken Preston-Mafham: Premaphotos Wildlife: 16bl, 17b, 18br, 25tl&tr, 51cl, 55cl 54b, 55c, 58t&br, 59b, 40b, 44l&r, 45bl&r, 48&br, 49tr&b, 50t&b, 51t&c, 52, 54t, bl&br, 56t, 57cl, 59b, 62t, 65b. Dr Rod Preston-Mafham: Premaphotos Wildlife: 16br, 26br, 27bl, 52t, 55cr, 42t, 48bl. Warren Photographic: Jane Burton: 20bl, 29t, 51b, 56bl/Jan Taylor: 15tl, 25tl, 49t&b/Kim Taylor: 15tr&b, 17-, 22t, 25tr, 50t, 51t, 59t, 45tl&t, 55tl&br, 29c.

Snakes

Jane Burton/Warren Photographic: 95c, 104–105, 112r. Bruce Coleman Ltd: 70bl, 72bl, 78br, 79r, 80tl, 81tl, 82tl, 83-a, 84cl,tr&br, 85cr&bl, 86br, 91br, 92t, 95b, 94br, 95t, 97cr&br, 98-1, 100c, 101bl, 105br, 108cl&br, 110bl&br, 112tr,cr&b, 114cr&b, 117tr 118bl. Ecoscene: 81cr. Mary Evans Picture Library: 109tr, 117br. FLPA: 25cr&cl, 80c, 82bl, 87tl&tr, 90tl&c, 95cr, 96–97, 99tr&bl, 102cr, 105t&bl, 104–105, 1C7tr, 109cl&br, 112cl, 115bl, 114–115, 116b&r, 119tl. Holt Studios International: 86tl, 110trl. Nature Photographers: 9-b-. NHPA: 71bl, 7-tl, 75tr&bl, 75tl, 78tl, 82br, 85tl&br, 86bl, 87bl&b- 85cl, 100–101, 101tr&cr, 102bl, 106cl, 111tl,cl&bl, 115cl&r, -14tl, 115c, 117c. Oxford Scientific Films: 70tc, 76–77, 88–89, 106t, 107b. Planet Earth Pictures: 9-b, 96cl, br&tr, 102tr, 106br, 107c, 118b&br, 119cc. Visual Arts Library: 69br, 75b, 91bl. Zefa Pictures: 115br.

Crocodiles

ABPL: 155t/C. Haagner: 123c, 140b/C. Hughes: 146c/M. Harvey: 125tl, 156bl/ R. de la Harper: 154b, 155t/S. Adev: 161b. Ancient Art & Architecture Collection: 160br. BBC Natural Histo-y Unit: A. Shah: 145c/J. Rotman: 128bl/M. Barton: 126bl/P. Oxford: 167tr/T Pooley: 155c. Biofotos: B. Rogers: 161t. Adam Britton: 151br, 157bl 141cl, 144cr, 145cl, 147cr, 155br, 166tr. Bruce Coleman: Animal Ark: 165tl/C.B. & J.W. Frith: 169br/E. & P. Bauer: 170b/ G. Cozzi: 156b- J. McDonald: 165c/L.C. Marigo: 157bl, 159br, 164t, 167r/R. Williams: 129br. C.M. Dixon: 126br. art archive: 144bl. FLPA: G. Lacz: 140tl/W. Wisniewski: 154b. Heather Angel: 157cr. M. & P Fogden: 152t, 159bl, 164t, 165cl, 165b, 172t. Mary Evans Picture Library: 122bl, 158br, 156bl. Nature Photographers Ltd: E.A. James: 128br/ R. Tidman: 127b/S-S. Bissenois: 144br. NHPA: 156t/D. Heuchlin: 128c, 141t, 152t, 155c, 165b&h), 172b, 175tr&b/E. Soder: 169bl/H. & V. Ingen: 125bl/ J. Shaw: 167t/S. Schafer: 145c/M. Harvey: 158bl/M. Wendler: 125t, 156c, 171cr/N. Wu: 145b/N.J. Dennis: 157cl/O. Rogge: 154tl/P. Scott: 172c/S. Robinson: 155br. Oxford Scientific Films: A. Bee: 169br/B. Wright: 129tr/Breck P. Kent: 173c-l/E. Robinson: 122tr, 148b/ E.R. Degginer: 125cr/F. Ehrenstrom: 124tr/F. Schneidermeyer: 155cl/F. Whitehead: 158t/J Macdonald: 125c/J. McCammon: 170t/ J. Robinson: 158tl/M. Deeble & Stone: 155tl, 157cl, 144t, 147t&b, 151b, 154t, 157cr/M. Fogden: 155tl/M. Pitts: 166b/M.

Birds of Prey

Heather Angel: 181bl, 195bl, 220br, 225bl, 227tl. Ardea: 24 Watson: 204bl. BBC Natural History Unit: Bernard Castelein: 188tl, 225tl/ Nick Garbutt: 184tr/Tony Heald: 191tr, 206bl/Klaus Nigge: 194tr, 201tr/Dietmar Nill: 179tr, 200bl/Pete Oxford: 201cr/Chris Packham: 197m/Rico & Rui ... 206bl,213tl/ Artur Tabor: 218bl/Richard du Toit: 185m, 189br/Tom Vezo: 197tl/Tom Walmsley: 195m. Bruce Coleman: Jane Burton: 214tl/John Cancalosi: 224tl/ Robert C- Carr: 189tr/Jose Luis Gonzalez Grande: 185tl, 218tl/Peter A. Hinchliffe: 181br/

Big Cats

ABPL: 287tl, 295cebl&cbr, 305c/Daryl Balfour: 523t/Peter Chadwick: 299t/Nigel Dennis: 286b, 298t, 500t, 555t/Clem Haagner: 274–285c, 290t, 506t, 52 t 551cr, 552b/Dave Hamman: 505tr, 551t/Roger de la Harper: 297cl/Lex Hes: 508t&b/Gerald Hinde: 292b, 509t, 515tl/ Luk Hunter: 512–515c, 519t1, 525b/Beverly Joubert: 504c, 518t, 521c/ Pete- Lillie: 501t, 504b/Anup Shah: 500c, 520b, 521b. BBC Natural History Unit/Keith Scholey: 501b/Lynn Stone: 286c/Tom Vezo: 295tl. Bridgeman Art Library: 504t, 511tr, 555br. Bruce Coleman Ltd/Erwin & Peggy Bauer: 299b, 506bl, 507b, 517c, 526b/Alain Compost: 297t, 527t&cl/Pete- Evans: 515b/Christer Fredriksson: 505b; Paul van Gaaen: 295tr-EPH Photography: 289bl/Leonard Lee Rue: 295t, 507-/Joe McConald: 507t, 511br, 514b, 551b/Antonio Manzanares: 505tl/Rita Mexer: 295b/Dieter & Mary Plage: 517b, 525c/Hans Reinhard: 295c-524b/Anup Shaw: 285b, 510b/Kim Taylor: 287t, 555c/Gunter Ziesler: 506br, 524t. C.M. Dixon: 554t, 555t. Mary Evans Picture Librarye 551cl, 554b. FLPA: 525cl/Leonard Lee Rue: 550b/ Mark Newman: 520t/Philip Perry: 294t, 505tr, 515t, 552t, 555bl/Fritz Polking: 298t, 500b, 501c/Terry Whittaker: 285tl, 291t, 295b, 297b, 502b, 516t, 522b&b/E. Woods: 517bl. Grant Museum/A. Lister: 289br. Michael Holfert: 290t. Natural Science Photos/D. Allen Photography: 288t, 502b, 546c, 522t, 525cr, 550t/Ken Cole: 287c, 288b, 528t/Carlo Dani & Ingrid Jeske: 287b, 517t/Lex Hes: 297b, 510–511t/C Jones: 514t/David Lawson: 510c/M.W. Powles: 511bl/Keren Su: 528br/John Warden: 516t, 522b, 525t. NHPA/Martin Harvey: 555br/Yves Lanceau: 292t/Andy Rouse: 526t. Papilio Photographic: 284t, 287tr, 295c, 296t, 29--ctr, 505tl, 527bl, 528bl. Planet Earth Pictures: 515c, 519b, 527br/ Anup Shah: 1 6tr/Manoj Shah: 518bl&br. Tony Stone: 284b/Geoff Johnson: 294t/Nicholas Parfitt: 512b/Bryan Parsley: 529c/Mark Petersen: 504t/Manoj Shah: 512t. Visual Arts Library: 285tr. Werner Forman Archive: 555bl. Photo of Jim Corbett p535 by permission of th- British Library (neg B19186).

Wolves

Bryan and Cherry Alexander Photography: 557tr, 506br, 561tl, 562t, 571br, 577c. Ardea London: John Daniels: 544b, 545tl/Chris Martin Bahr: 545cl/Jean Paul Ferrero: 552b, 567t, 587c/Liz Bonford: 560bl/ Stefan Meyers: 578b/Francois Gohier: 580t/M. Krishnan: 581tl. BBC Natural History Unit: Françoise Savigny: 558tr/Simon King: 570t, 571bl, 580br/C. Hamilton James: 540b, 575br/Pete Oxford: 554bl, 581tr/Tom Vezo: 558l, 555br/Louis Gagnon: 559cr/Jeff Foott: 540tr/ Pete Oxford: 541cr/Tony Heald: 545c/R. Couper Johnston: 545b/Keith Scholes: 547br/Richard Tu Tout: 555tr/Lockwood and Dattatri: 559tl, 567br/Richard Du Toit: 559b/Andrew Harrington: 563tl/Christopher Becker: 565tr/Vadim Sidorovich: 564t/Lynn M. Stone: 575b/Ron O'Connor: 587br. The Bridgeman Art Library: 548bl. Bruce Coleman Collection: Gunter Ziesler: 555b/Hans Reinhard: 559br, 549br/ Rod Williams: 555tl, 575cl/Bruce Davidson: 568t&b, 569cl/ Erwin & Peggy Bauer: 574t, 575b/Staffan Widstrand: 576b/Rita Meyer: 580bl/Jeff Foot: 587t. Mary Evans Picture Library: 575cr, 588bl&br. Gettyone Stone Images: Art Wolf: 561tr/Rosemary Calvert: 555c/ Kathy Bushue: 575tl, 576cr. NHPA: Gerard Lacz: 555c/Andy Rouse: 560t, 575tl/Martin Harvey: 541tr/Jany Sauvanet 551c, 579cl, 585tr&b/ T. Kitchin & V. Hurst: 551br, 567br, 585c&b/Rich Kirchner: 559c, 570b/K. Ghani: 565c/Mirko Stelzner: 579t. Oxford Scientific Films: Daniel J. Cox: 547cr, 550tl&bl, 554tl, 557bl, 561b, 571cr, 572t, 585cl/ Victoria McCormick: 554br/Nick Gordon 542t/Charles Palek: 559cl/ Stan Osolinski: 549tr/Steve Turner: 552t/Lon E. Lauber: 556t, 557cr, 567bl, 585tr/Konrad Wothe: 556b, 571t/Alan and Sandy Carey: 559tl/ Krupaker Senani: 565c/Peter Weiman: 5659b/Richard Day: 564b/ Michael Leach: 565cl/Anthony Bannister: 565cr/Michael Sewell: 565b/David Cayless: 569t,cr&b/M. & C. Tibbles: 572b/Matthews-Purdy: 573bl/Richard Packwood: 574b/Colin Willcock: 577tl/Tom Ulrich: 577tr/Mike Hill: 578t/Vivek Sinha:579cr/Villarosa/Overseas: 579b/Joe McDonald: 581bl/Bob Bennett: 581b/Rafi Ben-Shahar: 586t/Joel Bennett: 586b/Steve Turner: 587bl/Anna Walsh: 589bl/ Claude Steelman: 589t/Owen Newman: 589cr. Papilio Photographic: 582t. Peter Newark's Pictures: 547bl. Planet Earth Pictures: Ken Lucas: 549tl. Still Pictures: John Newby: 584t/Klein/Hubert: 541cl, 584bl&br. Warren Photographic: Jane Burton: 551tl.

Sharks

BBC Natural History Unit: A James, 415t/J. Hall: 429cl/J. Rotman: 597br, 599tl, 405tl&tr, 409tl, 411tl/M. Dohrn: 452tl/T. Krull: 452br. Bridgeman Art Library: 420br, 455tl. British Museum: 595br. FLPA: DP Wilson: 415br, 421tr/L.S. Sorisio: 417bl. Gallo Images: G. Cliff: 425tr/J. Rotman: 597bl, 598bl. Heather Angel: 459cr. Innerspace Visions: A. Nachoum: 596bl/B. Cranston: 595tl, 405b, 406bl, 407bl, 416tl, 417br, 441bl/D. Fleetham: 409cp/B. Rasner: 405tr/D. Fleetham: 400tr, 428tl, 442tl/D. Perrine: 400bl, 401bl, 402cl, 405tl&bl, 404bl, 405cl&bl, 415c, 419bl, 425tl, 426b, 427bl, 428tr, 455tr, 458t/D. Shen: 594tl/F. Schulke: 414br/H. Hall: 400cr, 4201&bl/J. Campbell: 445b/ J. Jaskolski: 459cl/J. Knowlton: 418bl/J. Morrissey: 425bl, 450br/J. Rotman: 419br, 451bl, 445tl/J.C. Carrie: 419cl/J.D. Watt: 592bl, 414tr, 427br/M. Conlin: 419tl, 421br, 451cr, 457cl, 459tr/M. Strevens: 598br, 407tl&cl, 408br/M.P. O'Neill: 422bl/M.S. Nolan: 409tl&l, 410tl/N. Wu: 422tl/P. Humann: 416bl/R. Cranston: 599bl/R. Herrmann: 406tr/ R. Kuiter: 594br, 450tl/S. Drogin: 408tl/S. Gonor: 451tl, 442bl/T. Haight: 415bl/W. Schubert: 402tl. Mary Evans Picture Library: 457cr. N. Calogianis: 427tl. NHPA: 595cr&bl, 412tl&bl/K. Schafer: 410bl/N. Wu: 411all, 415bl, 429tl, 445cl. Oxford Scientific Films: D. Fleetham: 405br, 426cl, 441cr/G. Soury: 409br, 414bl/H. Hall: 595tr, 422bl/ N. Wu: 445tl, 455tl/K. Gowlett: 599tr/M. Deeble & V. Stone: 424, 425bl/M. Gibson: 440bl/N. Wu: 596bl/R. Herrmann: 408bl, 457tl/R. Kuiter: 450c-l/W. Wu: 455tr, 459b. Papilio Photographic: 404tl, 457bl. Planet Earth: D. Perrine: 424br, 425br/G. Bell: 595, 598tl/G. Douma: 410br/J. Seagrim: 421tl/J. & A. Moran: 445cr/K. Amsler: 458b/K. Lucas: 455cl, 445tl/L. Snyderman: 595bl, 597tr, 417tl, 455c/N. Wu: 595tr, 599br/P. Atkinson: 401tr. Scott Mycock & Rachel Cavanagh: 455cr. Seitre Bios: 596br. South American Pictures: R. Francis: 455bl. Universal Pictures: 440tr. Zefa: M. Jozon: 415tl.

Whales and Dolphins

Animals Animals: 455tr, 480tc, 485c, 495t. Bruce Coleman: 446b, 451b, 455tr&br, 457cl, 461tl, 462t, 465t, 464t, 469b, 481t, 482b, 485c, 485t, 486t, 488b, 494b, 499b. Bridgeman Art Library: 475cr, 499b. Ecoscene: 450cl&bl, 451c. Mary Evans Picture Library: 451tl. FLPA: 449tr&bl, 452tl&bl, 454b, 456t, 461cl&cr, 465t, 466c, 472c, 474–475, 474t&b, 476b, 477t, 478–479, 478l, 482t, 490t&bl, 492–495, 492el, 492b, 495bl, 494c, 495b, 496l, 499b. NASA: 459br. Natural History Museum: 446–447c, 448c, 489cl. Natural Science Photos: 460c, 468b. Nature Photographers: 455c, 498t. NHPA: 454tr, 457b, 466tl&b, 471t&b, 476t, 477b, 479t&b, 480bl, 496c, 497c&b, 498c. Oxford Scientific Films: 447bl, 448b, 450cr, 455bl, 458bl&br, 460tl, 462b, 465b, 464c&b, 467b, 469t, 470t&b, 471cl&cr, 472tl, 475t&cl, 475c, 477b, 478b, 480cr, 481b, 482c, 485t, 484c, 489cr&b, 498c, 496b, 499t. Planet Earth Pictures: 446tr, 455bl, 456b, 458t, 460b, 461b, 465c, 467t, 468t, 475b, 481c, 484t&b, 485b, 486c&b, 489t&b, 488t, 489t, 490c, 491cr,bl&br, 494c, 499c, 499tc. Spacecharts: 447t, 459b. Visual Arts Library: 452cr, 457c, 495br. Zefa Pictures: 447tr, 491t. Sewell: 126t/O. Newman: 159tr/R. Davies: 161b/S. Leszczynski: 135cr, 171t/S. Osolinski: 124bl, 150tr, 148t, 145cl, 161c/S. Turner: 167bl/W. Shattil: 159t. Planet Earth: A. & M. Shah: 145c/B. Kenney: 152b/C. Farneti: 150b/D. Kjaer: 157tl/D. Maitland: 158br/D.A. Ponton: 157b/G. Bell: 141c/J. Lythgoe: 150t/J. Scott: 155tr, 142b-, 145b, 149bl/J.A. Provenza: 158tr/K. Lucas: 122–125, 129bl, 152t, 171cl/M. & C. Denis-Huot: 152cl/N. Greaves: 142tl/R. de la Harper: 151tl, 160t, 164b. Survival Anglia: F. Koster: 162b/ M. Linley: 168t/M. Price: 160bl/V. Sinha: 127t, 151cr. Twentieth Century Fox: 168b. G. Webb: 129tl, 155c, 159c, 171b.